THE EMERGENCE OF
LIBERAL CATHOLICISM
IN AMERICA

THE EMERGENCE OF
LIBERAL CATHOLICISM
IN AMERICA

Robert D. Cross

HARVARD UNIVERSITY PRESS

Cambridge, Massachusetts

1 9 6 7

*Publication of this book has been aided by a grant
from the Ford Foundation*

LIBRARY OF CONGRESS CATALOG CARD NUMBER 58–5593

PRINTED IN THE UNITED STATES OF AMERICA

FOR BARBARA

PREFACE

My purpose in this book is to examine a major attempt to improve the often unhappy relations between Catholics and American culture. By concentrating on the activities over a limited number of years of a specific group of Catholics, I have tried to avoid that recurrence to deductive logic which has, in my opinion, too often marred the studies of more enterprising authors. I have also tried to avoid the several pitfalls of my own approach. My criteria for "liberal Catholicism" are not simply attitudes and actions which I happen to like or dislike, and so, by diligent seeking, manage to discover in the late nineteenth century. A wide variety of observers were fully aware in those years that a coherent challenge was being made to traditional Catholic folkways by a group of clergy and laity anxious to promote a friendly interaction between their religion and American life. The Catholics active in this effort did not compose an organized faction. The distinctly liberal John Lancaster Spalding occasionally spoke out against Catholic innovations, and the congenitally conservative Bernard McQuaid backed some liberal enterprises, but I do not think that statistical arrays are necessary to substantiate the evidence presented that in the late nineteenth century the American Church was divided on certain major questions of policy as distinctly as was, say, the Supreme Court between 1932 and 1937. I have tried to avoid minimizing the great extent of belief and practice shared by all American Catholics. Just as such contrasting justices as Brandeis and Sutherland readily joined in holding the National Recovery Act unconstitutional, so American Catholic leaders stood united against not only the crude onslaughts of the American Protective Association, but also the subtler attacks of modernism on the importance and uniqueness of the Church. The extent of this consensus was sometimes forgotten by contemporaries, who, noting the vigor of the controversies among Catholics, and assuming that a hierarchical, orthodox Church requires absolute uniformity of its members, concluded that the American Church was about to break up. It is true that in the late nineteenth century a schism of Polish-Americans did develop, and that some individuals left the Church for Protestantism and free thought, but I can find little reason to attribute much of these losses to the debates brought on by the liberal Catholic proposals. If the existence of contending parties lessened the ability of Catholics to point to their Church as a refuge from the dissidence of dissent, and if the conflict between parties was at times so uncharitably bitter as to preclude effective Catholic action even on programs all Catholics approved, in the long run the spirited debate probably facilitated the orderly adaptation of the Church to a swiftly changing American society. And this adaptation, rather than a domination-or-schism policy, was surely the purpose of the American liberals; except in moments of excited rhetoric, they were willing to admit that even their most uncompromisingly conservative critics were playing a vital role in the historical evolution of the Church.

In the final chapter I have ranged rather freely over twentieth-century American Catholic history, but I have not done so in the illusion that I am writing more than a tentative survey of that remarkably complex history. And I am aware that the Church's present problems and interests can not be adequately summed up in the categories which seemed relevant to the Church's experience sixty years ago. I do find, however, in the contemporary confrontation between a changed Church and a changed culture some significant continuities of the spirit that the great liberals infused into their apologetics in the 1890's.

I am happy to acknowledge my obligation to Professor Perry Miller of Harvard University for insights into American religious history I would not have received elsewhere. The editors and readers of Harvard University Press provided me with extremely useful criticism of both the general form and specific detail of this essay. I am particularly indebted to Professor Oscar Handlin of Harvard for his stimulating courses on American social history and for his counsel while this essay was being written. Amazingly generous with suggestions, liberal with exhortations to labor, profligate with blue-penciling, he has helped me most by the personal example he has set of the possibilities of academic life.

No one can work in this field without drawing heavily upon the able research being done by a distinguished group of Catholic scholars: Monsignor John T. Ellis, Father Thomas T. McAvoy, Father Henry J. Browne, Professor Aaron I. Abell, their associates and students. I wish to record my particular gratitude to two of these scholars, who, when my research was at an early stage, offered access to a considerable body of documentary material to me, a stranger and a non-Catholic. In a decade when many polemicists are ransacking Church history to find justifications for preconceived attacks, these courteous offers were manifestations of a truly catholic spirit. I wish to thank Professor J. E. Roohan of Yale University for permitting me to read his thesis on "American Catholics and the Social Question" before it was available to the public. Neither teachers nor acquaintances, of course, should be held responsible for errors of fact or interpretation that may be detected in this essay.

While I have used some of the correspondence Catholic scholars have uncovered to illustrate attitudes towards secular culture, my primary interest has been in the public record of interaction. Books, speeches, interviews, and especially the articles in leading periodicals like the *Catholic World* and the *North American Review* have been my major recourse. The libraries of Harvard, Pennsylvania, Villanova, and Yale Universities, Swarthmore and Bryn Mawr Colleges, Crozer Theological Seminary, and the cities of Boston and Philadelphia provided invaluable aid. And I am indebted to the many libraries which cooperated with the Inter-Library Loan Service, and to the staff members in charge of that service at Harvard and Swarthmore.

Robert D. Cross

Swarthmore College
March, 1957

Note to the Second Printing

In this second printing I have corrected several factual and typographical errors, and I am particularly indebted to Monsignor John Tracy Ellis for calling many of these to my attention. I have refrained, however, from modifying the text to make it reflect certain changes in my view of a time which, I agree with Professor Thomas T. McAvoy of Notre Dame, was a "critical period in American Catholicism." Nor have I attempted to reply to reviewers; but I shall allow myself one Parthian shot. In the 1950's, I did not know Italian, nor was I able to forecast that Cardinal Roncalli would become Pope. If I were to write this book today, I would not use the term "liberal Catholicism," but rather *aggiornamento* — which, if not without its own ambiguities, is not generally regarded as logically contrary to the meaning or future of Catholicism in America.

Robert D. Cross

New York City
May 1967

CONTENTS

THE EMERGENCE OF
LIBERAL CATHOLICISM
IN AMERICA

CHAPTER I

CATHOLICISM AND CULTURE
IN NINETEENTH-CENTURY EUROPE

Western Christianity, because of its ambition to become a truly catholic church, had to evolve strategies by which to deal with the institutions and beliefs — that is, the "culture" — of those as yet outside the Church.[1] While all spokesmen for the Roman Catholic Church have been firmly convinced that the Church is protected by Christ from final failure in its task, some have approached culture with great caution; others have ventured forth on the mission with sublime confidence. The confident ask the Church to stress apologetics in order to hasten the conversion of a culture, which with all its faults is nevertheless surely redeemable. They recall the success of teachers like Paul, who reconciled Roman citizenship and Greek modes of thought with the gospel of Christ; they point to the triumphs of the gentle Philip Neri, who "preferred to yield to the stream and direct the current . . . of science, literature, art, and fashion, and to sweeten and sanctify what God had made very good and man had spoilt."[2] The cautious emphasize the need for maintaining the doctrinal and disciplinary ramparts of the Church against an age always essentially hostile. They glorify the martyrs who chose to die rather than compromise an iota of belief; they praise the firmness of Boniface VIII, who replied to an aggressive culture with heightened rather than retrenched claims of ecclesiastical authority.[3]

In almost every era, therefore, the Church is forced either to tolerate markedly different policies, or else to require one group of the faithful not to speak or act according to its deeply felt convictions. The problem is most severe in periods of rapid cultural change like the nineteenth century when traditional policies are satisfactory to neither the cautious nor the confident. Through the preceding century, the rationalism of the Enlightenment had been reconciled, to the satisfaction of most Catholics, with the trusting faith demanded by Christian orthodoxy.[4] But the problems presented to the Church by Newton, Locke, and Voltaire were trivial compared to the challenges of scientists like Lyell, Darwin, and Virchow, of philosophers like Bentham and Spencer, of historians like Strauss and Renan. The collapse of the old regimes during and after the French Revolution also drastically affected the Church. Catholic leaders, accustomed to dealing with anointed monarchs, were confronted with governments conceived in revolution, and dedicated to the rights of man and the sovereignty of the people. Social relationships were also in flux. Moral theologians, therefore, had to turn to such novel problems as the ethical responsibilities of factory owners and industrial laborers. Parish priests had to learn how to care for a flock not scattered over a countryside, but jammed into urban tenements. And the immense migrations from country to city, from nation to nation, even from continent to continent, taxed the ingenuity of bishops to build diverse classes and nationalities into a united Church.

In the face of these confusing developments, the prevailing confidence of eighteenth-century Catholicism gave way to fear and suspicion. Catholics began to demand greater vigilance in distinguishing and defending the City of God from the City of Man.[5]

I

It was the deep conviction of many Catholics that the disturbing changes agitating their era were all parts of the most dangerous conspiracy ever mounted by Satan against the Church.[6] The chief instruments of evil were the freemasons. Condemned by the papacy early in the eighteenth century, masonry had continued its activities with such success that Friedrich Schlegel found modern history hopelessly confusing unless one recognized that "there was a deliberate, though secret, preparation of events" by the masons.[7] Years later in the century, a French bishop admitted that "people never dreamt the night before" that such events as the Revolution of 1848 and the Paris Commune were about to occur. But the masonic lodges, "laboratories of revolution and of new ideas," had been able to convulse society at any time they chose.[8] Disasters in the past were the work of secret masons like Melanchthon and Coligny; the steady rise of modern Italy was due to the collusion of the masonic Carbonari, masons among the House of Savoy, and Lord Palmerston, the Orient of Orients and secret head of world masonry. Masons were to be found even among the Catholic clergy; their false counsel had lulled all too many of the faithful into accepting the false doctrines and practices of the age.[9] Even where masonic intervention could not be detected, it was enough for Catholics to know that the evils of the modern era were "legion," and "legion is nowhere and everywhere. It is in the air. It speaks in all languages. All the echoes in the world respond to its voice. . . . Legion is the *Spirit* which blows today over all the world" against the Church.[10]

And, bad as the present age was, many Catholics believed that the future had worse in store. Count Joseph De Maistre, the pessimistic French diplomat, insisted that "the attacks against the Catholic edifice *always* grow stronger; one is *always* mistaken when one says that things can get no worse."[11] The age, a Spanish Catholic thought, was in all likelihood headed for "the greatest catastrophe in history."[12] Nothing man could do would halt the destructive progress of the age.[13]

With the world bent on subverting rather than accepting the ministrations of the Church, it was the responsibility of Catholics, the Abbé Jules Morel wrote, to cloister themselves from the world, and to strengthen the Church against the world's aggressions.[14] The Society of Jesus, which in the eighteenth century had supplied many spokesmen for the Catholic rapprochement with modern tendencies, now took the lead in combating the age, reminding themselves that one of Loyola's prayers had been that his order should always be an object of the world's hatred.[15] To a famous Catholic liberal, such conservatives seemed to have renounced "worldwide" ambitions, and to have set about narrowing "the lines of communion, . . . using the language of dismay and despair . . . instead of . . . going out conquering and to conquer."[16]

Catholic doctrine should be taught in its full stringency, allowing no concessions to the predilections of the age for "liberty of conscience." Teachers should not hesitate to defend, as admirably Catholic, the very events which the tolerant, humanitarian, modern mind stigmatized, such as the Spanish Inquisition, the Revocation of the Edict of Nantes, and the Duke of Alva's rule in the Netherlands.[17] This Catholic group so distrusted the age as to glory in antagonizing it. A French layman, in angry protest, declared that this perverse spirit

searches out the boldest paradoxes, the most contestable theses, provided only they irritate the modern mind. It presents the truth to men not in a way that attracts them, but rather in one that repels them. It seeks not to win back unbelievers, but to excite the passions of believers.[18]

Many who preached in this way were avowed traditionalists, who refused to acknowledge that they advocated the slightest modification of historical Catholicism to fit the new circumstances of the age. "We had always believed," Morel remarked sarcastically, "that the Church was a supernatural power, . . . with which one could not compromise, which taught with authority, and which one listened to with the docility owed to the Word of God." Catholicism had no "human" or changeable side, he argued.[19] A growing number of conservatives, however, agreeing with Morel that it was presumptuous to ask the Church to fit its presentation to the whim of the age, nevertheless vigorously supported the development of those principles already implicit in Church teaching and those contemporary practices that would, they fervently hoped, strengthen it for its death struggle with the age. By 1860, these more activist conservatives had almost unanimously subscribed to two such developments: the increased centralization of the Church under a papacy of unlimited power; and an intensified devotionalism.[20]

For de Maistre, the revolutionary chaos of Europe from 1789 to 1814 was proof that no stability would be achieved until the world recognized an absolute authority, "which governs and is not governed, which judges and is not judged." As long as a secular state claimed independence of spiritual control, citizens were left dangerously free to choose between two masters.[21] Even if a state acknowledged the control of the Church, de Maistre argued that confusion would still prevail unless all churchmen accepted, without qualification, the authority of the Pope. Sovereignty must be unitary, he maintained; "to divide it is to destroy it." It must be continuous, since a 'sovereignty that is periodic or intermittent is a contradiction in terms; for sovereignty must always live, must always be on the alert, must always act. For sovereignty, there is no difference between sleep and death." An active, infallible pope was obviously the only alternative to chaos. Popes would usually act wisely, de Maistre believed, but in most cases it was less important that political and social questions be settled with absolute justice than that they be settled "without delay and without appeal." [22]

In the fifty years after de Maistre wrote, the nations of Europe showed no disposition whatever to refer crucial decisions to the popes. In 1870, in fact, Italy completed its unification at the expense of the Roman territories Pius IX had declared were essential to his political role. For many Catholics, however, it had always seemed more important that the Pope rescue them from the anarchy of personal decision in matters of religious and intellectual concern than on merely political problems. One of the most outspoken of these Catholics was William George Ward, an associate of Newman. Just before Ward converted to Catholicism, he had declared that the chief attraction of the Church was its closed system of truth, together with an authority willing and able to expound that truth. Depressed by the skepticism of his time, he wanted "a watertight compartment for faith, sealed by authority, in which all religious beliefs should be safely locked up." [23] As an editor and professor of theology, he regularly petitioned the Pope for more definitive teaching. Denouncing those theologians who distinguished between the degrees of assent demanded by the several types of papal pronouncement, Ward went so far at one time as to declare that every doctrinal teaching was binding on every Catholic conscience under penalty of mortal sin. [24] Like de Maistre, he was less concerned with the final truth of papal decisions than with their constant availability. With characteristic gusto, he announced that he would like to have a papal bull every morning before breakfast. [25]

The popes and the Roman Congregations began to respond to demands for increased direction, multiplying the number of encyclicals and allocutions until, as John Newman protested, Catholic intellectual life consisted mostly of analyzing papal teaching.[26] The process was self-accelerating: the more decisions Rome made, the greater the temptation to appeal every question to Rome; the more appeals, the more pronouncements had to be made.[27]

The life of the Church increasingly centered in Rome. The major religious orders, like the Jesuits and Redemptorists, whose generals were resident in Rome, gained prestige and power at the expense of the national hierarchies tied to distant dioceses. Both the English and American hierarchies, as well as many individual bishops, established "agents" in Rome to look out for their interests.[28] In the national churches, the "Roman" cleric was increasingly influential. Archbishop Manning, on his return from Rome, systematically fought "English" traditions; to be "English" or "acclimatized to English society" was to be less than fully Catholic.[29] When Paul Cullen became Archbishop of Dublin, he set out to eliminate "low views" on papal power, virtually eliminating the old clergy in the process.[30] The desire to be Roman was one reason so much of Europe in the middle years of the century adopted the Roman liturgy, replacing the local service with its vernacular hymns and prayers, its local customs and dress. Ultramontanists like Nicholas Wiseman in England and Dom Guéranger of Solesmes in France were enthusiastic sponsors of the Roman liturgy for this reason.[31]

While strengthening the authority of the Church against all challengers, the conservatives were also anxious to give rebuffs to the modern rationalistic temper. Derogating men's ability to learn or to understand the really vital truths in life, men like Chateaubriand argued the value of the nonrational aspects of Christianity.[32] De Maistre, calling for the faithful to accept the new Latin liturgy, flatly asserted that "if they do not understand the words, so much the better. Respect increases. . . . He who understands nothing understands better than he who understands badly." The Latin liturgy was an excellent means for humbling the pretensions of "science," the idol of the age, de Maistre argued; "let the Church say to her in Latin the only thing she needs to say: That there is no salvation for pride."[33] To the English architect, Augustus Welby Pugin, the elaborate perfection of religious ritual was surer to preserve the faith of believers, and even to bring in converts, than the most logical apologetic.[34]

The devotional spirit was sedulously cultivated. In relatively new devotions like the Forty Hours, and the Perpetual Adoration, the believer was asked to affirm his religion through extraordinary acts of self-sacrifice.[35] Abbé Jean Gaume wrote a treatise to show that a wider use of holy water would eradicate most of the ills of the century.[36] Sophisticated English converts tried to emulate the religious services of primitive Italian villages.[37] Devout Catholic authors produced a flood of devotional histories and biographies of saints, so replete with supernatural occurrences as to require of the reader an almost continuous act of faith.[38]

Although Saint Joseph was exalted as never before, the Virgin Mary was the primary object of the new devout spirit. Pius IX was more disposed than some of his predecessors to credit new supernatural phenomena, and the Church supported reports that Mary had appeared at La Salette and at Lourdes, and that the Holy House had been transported to Loretto. Pilgrimages to these shrines became an increasingly important part of Catholic life.[39]

The climax to this heightened devotion was the promulgation by Pius IX in 1854 of the dogma of the Immaculate Conception of the Virgin. Sixteen years later, many prelates at the Vatican Council asked that the Virgin's bodily assumption also be proclaimed.[40] Her intercessory power and her rights as "the Mother of God" were believed by many Catholics to be almost unlimited.[41]

Both the authoritarian and devotional drives heightened the antagonism between the Church and the modern age. The defense of order and authority won the conservatives the support of the upper classes, especially those in France whom de Maistre had reminded in 1819 that "the alliance between the priest and the noble is natural, essential, necessary, French."[42] But the middle classes, whether intellectuals, libertarian republicans, or simply those individuals more interested in doing business with the world than in condemning its errors, were largely alienated. The chief reason that Catholicism did not shrivel into a sect was the support the conservative program enlisted among the lower classes.[43]

The masses of Irish immigrants swarming into English manufacturing cities in the nineteenth century had traditionally regarded the parish priest as virtually infallible on every important question, and had never felt a desire to reconcile the mysteries of Catholic devotion with modern rationalism. The Catholicism of the uprooted German peasants and of the French farmers impoverished but clinging to the land was similarly uncomplex. Though the industrial proletariat was eventually alienated from the Church in many countries of Europe, most of the rest of the lower class rendered to the Church the total loyalty that the ultramontanists so earnestly desired.

By the 1850's, conservatives were gratefully acknowledging the sound judgment of classes whose opinions previously had been generally ignored, if not positively distrusted. "Less to blame than the others," Gaume wrote, "the popular classes, who, despite their disorders and indifference, have maintained the principles of faith, will turn to the Church and beg her to save them. This will be the dawn of the new world." [44] In England, Manning and Wiseman agreed that the Church would prosper more by guarding the true faith of the Irish peasant immigrants, than by catering to Catholic intellectuals and social thinkers.[45] The latent ultramontanism of the masses was most brilliantly exploited by Louis Veuillot, a French convert for whom, it could be said, that "all human, social, and political struggles were determined . . . exclusively by their relations to the Church." [46] His journal, *Univers*, was the first of many successful Catholic periodicals to find a responsive audience among the peasants in the provinces for proposals to strengthen papal power, to sponsor new devotions, and to censure all less stringent souls as traitors to the needs of the Church. Despite the protests of liberal Catholics, Veuillot succeeded in bringing the opinion of his readers to bear on Church issues by encouraging them to present huge petitions to prelates and councils for the ultramontane program.[47] Bolstered by this popular support, the conservatives were resolved to make no compromises, but to fight off the depredations of the age, through intensifying the defensive armor of the Church.

II

Meanwhile, another group of Catholics, more liberal in their estimate of the century, more confident in expecting its conversion, firmly resisted the new conservative program. Far different from the *salon abbés* and the culture-Catholics so prominent in the eighteenth century, these men were intensely loyal Catholics who found much that was objectionable in the present era, and were as outspoken as the conservatives in their condemnations. Félicité de Lamennais, who before leaving the Church articulated most of the liberal principles that were advanced during the century, had written fiery denunciations of religious "indifference," and of irresponsible libertarianism.[48] Bishop Félix Dupanloup of Orléans and Count Charles de Montalembert were severe critics of many political legacies of the Revolution as well as of modern revolutionaries like Garibaldi and Cavour. Bishop Wilhelm von Ketteler of Mainz and Professor Frédéric Ozanam of the Sorbonne flatly rejected the popular social panaceas of Lassalle and Saint-Simon. And John Henry Newman considered the rationale of his life to lie in his sustained attack on doctrinaire "liberalism." [49]

But, despite their refusal to idolize the age, these Catholics were distinctly eager to find in the world not the cunning malevolence of Antichrist, but partial virtues suggesting the possibility of general redemption. The true policy for Catholics, Ozanam wrote, was

to search out in the human heart all the secret cords which can lead it back to Christianity, to reawaken in it the love of the true, the good, and the beautiful, and finally to show in revealed faith the ideal of these three things to which every soul aspires; to regain, in short, the strayed spirits, and to increase the number of Christians.[50]

When Dupanloup was called upon to eulogize his Voltairean predecessor in the French Academy, the bishop stressed his preference for seeking out not "that which separates, but that which brings us together; not dissension but agreement; a common ground to start from; after that I like to go on to find a more complete and perfect agreement in infallible truth." [51] Montalembert admitted that the world was indeed divided into the followers of Christ and the followers of Satan, but only Christ had the vision to discern who was on the Lord's side, and the prerogative to proclaim that "he who is not with me is against me." Humans should admit the fallibility of their judgment, Montalembert argued. He himself was confident that "we have more allies than we think," and he enjoined his audiences to believe that "he who is not against us is with us." [52]

While conservatives were maintaining that never before had the Church been subjected to such a concerted assault, the liberals interpreted history more optimistically. Montalembert and Dupanloup agreed that the Revolution was a *felix culpa,* which, in spite of itself, gave the Church "everything." [53] Most liberals could endorse Montalembert's declaration that "except for some rare and fleeting moments, the world has never been worth very much more than today." [54] There was, therefore, no need either to hate or to fear the present age. "I would like to pass on to the souls of all of you," Montalembert told a Catholic congress at Brussels, "the confidence which fills me; confidence which does not spring from the enthusiasm of youth, but calm, cool confidence, based on my experience of the men and events, the ideas and revolutions of the nineteenth century; confidence matured by time and adversity." [55] If loyal Catholics would only regain confidence, they could do much to improve the age. "I do not believe," Montalembert wrote on another occasion, "that one can cite a single misfortune of these last years which could not have been averted by its victims, if they had had more courage, good faith, and sound sense. . . . What modern society lacks above all is the energy to improve its condition." [56] Ozanam reminded his students at the Sorbonne "that God has made the nations healable." [57] And modern men and modern institutions, when approached in a liberal spirit, were certain to welcome Catholic ministrations. "We must open our arms to the century," Dupanloup wrote his clergy; "and we must above all open our hearts. It will listen to us when we know how to speak to it." [58]

At one time or another, these liberals turned their attention to virtually every area of interaction between Catholicism and nineteenth-century culture. Both the most persistent and the most troubling questions involved relations between church and state, the economic and social welfare of the people, and the reconciliation of faith and reason.

One of the most striking political results of the French Revolution was the conception of a secular state which renounced all subordination to the Church, denied it financial assistance, and proclaimed complete freedom of conscience. Rome, by condemning Lamennais' attempt to "baptize the Revolution," made clear that Catholics should not hail the new political arrangements as ideal; but the liberals refused to consider them unmitigated calamities. Renouncing as "abstract" and "academic" any discussion of the Catholic "thesis," they continued to defend as "hypotheses" various compromises with the revolutionary ideal. They felt free, one conservative complained, "to take up on the ground of facts . . . the campaign they were prevented from pursuing on the ground of principles." [59] "I do not promulgate any doctrine," Montalembert declared; "I state only facts, and I draw from them purely practical consequences." [60]

One group of "facts" regularly stated were the concrete disadvantages of the old regime. Antonio Rosmini-Serbati, an Italian priest and philosopher, published *Five Wounds of Holy Church*, attacking the "feudal" arrangements for imposing heavy temporal responsibilities, while diminishing the real liberty of the Church.[61] Montalembert emphasized that wherever liberty of conscience was denied, "Catholicism marched from defeat to defeat." Those "paradises of religious absolutism," which produced a small number of *zelanti* and a huge mass of virtual infidels, nominally Catholic, but indifferent to the Church's welfare, "have become the scandal and despair of every Catholic heart." [62]

The liberals were certain that there was nothing to fear from freedom. The recent successes of the Church in Belgium for example were due, Montalembert told Catholics there, to "liberty, nothing but liberty, and the struggle made possible by liberty. . . . Yes, political liberty has been the safeguard and the instrument of the Catholic revival in Europe." [63] As liberty was benefited by religion's restraint upon unwise enthusiasms, so liberty prevented religion from becoming a mere hothouse plant, subject to the ruthless whim of the political despot.

Montalembert summed up his convictions in the phrase "a free church in a free state." Not that he in any way approved the harassment and spoliation of the Church which Cavour justified under the same slogan; to Montalembert, the new Italy was better described as "a despoiled church in a despoiling state." [64] Instead he envisaged a church and a state really equal in power and really respectful of each other's privileges. In such a case, religious and political leaders could in good conscience compromise with each other whenever desirable. Montalembert, supported by Dupanloup, helped negotiate a compromise school law with the Second Republic, a law which Louis Veuillot, speaking for the conservatives, denounced as "a bargain with evil, a monstrous alliance between the ministers of

Satan and those of Jesus Christ." Montalembert retorted that while the Church would have liked greater freedom, it has "always preferred a real and present good, however incomplete, to the indefinite postponement and impracticable demands that result from absolutist logic." [65]

Montalembert, like many nineteenth-century liberals, showed little interest in the social problems of his times. Most of his sympathies were reserved for the bourgeoisie, the epitome of the modern spirit he so much admired. In his Brussels speech, he expressed regret that "imprudent Catholics," acting either from aristocratic haughtiness or from plebeian jealousy, had unrepentantly alienated the middle classes from the Church. The peasants he ignored, and the urban working class he regarded chiefly as a threat to social order and as a potentially tyrannical ruler.[66] But some of the liberal Catholics were less selective in their sympathies. Appalled by the living and working conditions imposed upon the lower classes by the nascent industrial revolution, and unwilling to emulate the conservatives by offering only the traditional supernatural consolations of the Church to the oppressed, they set out to enlist Catholics in the movements for social and economic reform.

Frédéric Ozanam, as a student in Paris, recognized that working class Catholics were being seduced from their faith by secular reformers who offered "social" programs for social needs. Aroused when a Saint-Simonian challenged the Church to demonstrate by works as well as words her concern for the people, Ozanam and other laymen organized in 1833 the St. Vincent de Paul Society to help the Paris poor. Physical aid was accompanied by spiritual consolation and advice, as well as by personal solicitude.[67] Ozanam was anxious for the clergy to play its part as well. He believed that just as the Church in the fifth century had triumphed through shaking off its dependence on the Roman Empire and extending its work to the barbarian tribes, the modern clergy should leave the courts of monarchs and dedicate their lives to the people; and not just the desperately needy, but also "those other poor who do not beg, who live by their labor, and to whom the right of labor . . . will never be secured in such a manner as to guarantee them from the want of help, of advice, of consolation." [68]

In Germany, Bishop von Ketteler laid the basis for a genuine "social Catholicism" in his book *The Labour Question and Christianity*, which demanded that the Church support a system of coöperatives to alleviate the evils of the wage system. If the Church played its proper part, von Ketteler was confident that the working class would forego atheistic socialism and cleave to the Church.[69] Both Ozanam and von Ketteler were ahead of their times, but the movements of social Catholicism in the late years of the century, and the social teachings of Pope Leo XIII owed a great deal to their pioneering efforts.

Though disagreeing on the social responsibilities of the Church, the liberals were unanimously anxious for a rapprochement with the leaders of the intellectual world. This indispensable class, they believed, could be won for the Church, if Catholic scholars showed that the results of the most dispassionate scholarship did not contradict the central conclusions of religious faith. Historical arguments against the continuity of the Church should be met, not with dogma, but with more comprehensive history; the apparently destructive conclusions of Biblical criticism with a more acute philology; scientific assaults on Genesis with a more perceptive science and with a clearer understanding of just what beliefs were central to the faith. The sedulous pursuit of truth wherever it was to be found was the best apologetic to the intellectual world.

One of Ozanam's major enterprises was the refutation of Gibbon's sneers, and the historical writings of Montalembert and Dupanloup won them membership in the Academy, the highest recognition secular France could pay to the quality of this form of apologetic.[70] But the greatest liberal Catholic spokesman to modern culture was John Henry Newman, who as a convert passed from the leadership of an influential segment of English intellectual life to membership in a Church as yet inconsequential in the thought of his country. Unlike William George Ward, Newman dedicated his life to justifying the claims of Catholicism to the natural sympathies of all Englishmen. Though his central books, *The Development of Doctrine* and *The Grammar of Assent*, struck many Catholics as unsound because of Newman's emphasis on the changes in the Church's explicit teaching and the long difficult process that intelligent assent often required, they fronted the problems central for non-Catholic inquirers.[71]

In order to promote a wider understanding of the true relation of Catholicism to culture, Newman agreed to become the first rector of the Catholic University of Ireland. In his famous inaugural lectures, he condemned training which was narrowly "religious." A university is not a seminary, he argued; its purpose is to train "good members of society. Its art is the art of social life, and its end is fitness for the world." Liberal education should give men an understanding charity towards the world that a strictly religious indoctrination ignored.[72]

In his lectures, Newman also gave the definitive liberal answer to the curious campaign initiated by Abbé Jean Gaume a few years earlier to restrict very severely the reading of all "pagan classics." Though all literature could be misused, Newman argued that only by knowing it well could Catholics understand the men with whom they lived; such knowledge was essential to those who wished to influence their age to higher ends.[73]

In all their liberal enterprises, these Catholics proved willing to find fault with the Church, not in its dogmatic decisions, but in continuing many practices and principles acquired in past eras; and they urged Catholics in and out of authority to hold fast only to that which was best. Appeals to prelates to abandon their unrelenting hostility to the state, to the clergy to seek out new opportunities to help the oppressed, to lay scholars to compete with the new learning on its own ground — all these were common liberal themes. Such calls for reform naturally annoyed conservative leaders bent on maintaining a Church united in the defense of the glorious legacy of the past.

Both groups looked to the papacy for encouragement and justification, the conservatives hoping for infallible teaching to bolster conformity, the liberals for reproofs to the Gallican and national churches rooted in a stultifying traditionalism. During the rule of Gregory XVI, the liberals received little but censure from Rome. But they did not lose hope that future popes would prove more tolerant of their programs for promoting beneficial commerce between the Church and secular culture.

III

When the popular cardinal-bishop of Imola, Giovanni Mastai-

Ferretti, became pope in 1846 as Pius IX, the liberals were jubilantly expectant. Rosmini called to his attention the "five wounds" of the Church, confident that Pius would revive Catholic interest in education, develop a modern apologetic, and recognize the benefits the Church would derive from abandoning temporal power and responsibilities. While Pius never evinced great interest in meeting the needs of modern intellectuals, he did grant a constitution to the papal states, and seemed willing to coöperate with the nationalistic ambitions of Piedmont.[74]

But however liberal were Pius' intentions, he was not strong enough or radical enough to shift the Church as rapidly from its alliances with Austria and the petty Italian states and from its own claims of special privilege, as republicans and nationalists desired. The assassination of the Pope's constitutional minister, and Mazzini's abortive Roman Republic ended for at least a century the dream of a liberalized Italian Catholicism. When the Pope returned from exile on the strength of foreign bayonets, he took drastic steps against both Mazzinian and Catholic liberalism. Rosmini's book was placed on the Index; and the Jesuits established a periodical, *Civiltà Cattolica*, to emphasize the contrast between Christian ideals and the misshapen tendencies of the age.[75]

In 1854, Pius promulgated the doctrine of the Immaculate Conception, and in the next decade issued a series of admonitions to Montalembert and to Catholic scholars, warning against forwardness in advocating new departures in politics and science.[76] But his most important action was to publish in December, 1864 a "Syllabus," in which he grouped "the principal errors of our time," as they had previously been stigmatized in his various pronouncements and letters. Covering a vast range of subjects — from pantheism to the relations between secular and spiritual power — the Syllabus of Errors delighted the conservatives who had been anxious for a general condemnation of the liberal Catholics' attempts at mediation.[77]

Besides denying that in the present day a separation of secular and spiritual power was desirable, and denying that "the morals and minds of the people" profited by the greatest amount of civil liberty, the Syllabus also reproved modern scholars for their heedlessness of traditional Church teaching, and even ventured to declare

authoritatively that certain statements of historical fact were erroneous. The final decree, however, seemed the most destructive of
liberal Catholic hopes; it was false, the Syllabus concluded, that "the
Roman Pontiff can and ought to reconcile himself to, and agree
with, progress, liberalism, and modern civilization."

The unusual form of this papal teaching — drawn up by an unknown hand, and couched in statements which it was an error to
maintain — promoted widely different interpretations. An Austrian
Jesuit transposed all the errors into positive affirmations; number
eighty, properly understood, taught that the Pope could not reconcile
himself with modern civilization. This interpretation was supported
by the *Civiltà*. Louis Veuillot insisted further that the consciences
of all Catholics were completely bound by these teachings. Non-
Catholics had reason to be alarmed that the Pope was preaching a
crusade against the first premises of modern culture.[78]

Liberal Catholics, such as Dupanloup and Newman, maintained
that the republication of a papal reproach to a German historian, for
example, did not give it a wider applicability than before. Furthermore, the proper interpretation of the last proposition was that the
Pope was not bound to reconcile the Church with every aspect of
modern civilization. Dupanloup restated the liberals' belief that
the separation of church and state was condemned only as a thesis,
not as a hypothesis tolerable in certain circumstances. And Newman
argued that the type of papal teaching in the Syllabus deserved
respect and obedience, but not the full interior assent that the infallible voice of the Church demanded.[79]

Though Pius thanked both groups for their commentaries, neither
side was completely vindicated. If the conservative version violated
logic as well as the theological tradition, Dupanloup's reading left
the Pope no reason for having issued the Syllabus. In all probability,
Pius was attempting a kind of middle discourse between the traditional restraint of papal teaching, and the strong, explicit, avowedly
infallible teaching desired by the ultramontanists. There was no
question that Pius agreed with the conservatives on the necessity of
mobilizing the Church against modern errors, even at the cost of
further isolating her from the age.

By this time, the liberals were unmistakably disillusioned with the
actions of Pius IX. As early as 1852, Montalembert, while agreeing

that the conception of papal "monarchy" was the "one true theory" of papal power, insisted that the Pope was a constitutional monarch; every one of his subjects, bishop, cleric, and layman, had his "own traditional, imprescriptible right." [80] Newman bitterly resented the increasing centralization of the Church, which prevented true freedom of inquiry by juxtaposing "the Pope and the individual Catholic . . . face to face, without media, in collision." [81]

But the liberals were unable to halt the sweep of ultramontanism. Five years after issuing the Syllabus, Pius convened the Vatican Council, with the purpose, his conservative supporters asserted, of enforcing upon the whole Church a spirit of hostility towards the secular world. Not only would the Council establish as infallible those beliefs most under debate, but by declaring the Pope infallible, it would obviate the need for further councils, and make possible the flow of authoritative pronouncements that men like Ward and Veuillot so ardently desired.[82]

Both prospects distressed the liberals, who did not believe that conditions were dangerous enough to warrant the heroic ministrations of a council, and who feared that, by premature definition, the Church might block the discussions and tentative compromises which were necessary preliminaries to a wise rapprochement between Church and culture. Montalembert, Dupanloup, von Ketteler, and Newman all attempted to rally lay and clerical support against the calling of a council, or, failing in this, against discussing any but noncontroversial topics.[83] But the conservatives, who had learned to interpret opposition to Church centralization as simple disloyalty, readily dismissed every protest; indeed, the more protests that were made, the more necessary a council seemed.

During the seven months of the Council, the prelates ratified two dogmatic constitutions, both deeply conservative in tenor.[84] The first, *Dei Filius*, on the Faith, cited the many perversions of Truth which had been advanced in the modern era, and defined Catholic belief on "God," "Revelation," "Faith," and "Faith and Reason." Highly traditional in spirit, the new teaching later proved of great importance in the war against modernism. While few of the liberals at the Council were even remotely modernistic, many of them regretted the hasty definition of questions still being warmly debated by established Catholic theologians.

They disliked still more the hatred and contempt the conservatives expressed for the opinions of Protestant thinkers. On March 22, 1870, the liberal Croatian Bishop Joseph Strossmayer vigorously protested against attributing all errors to the influence of Protestantism. The Church could not afford, he argued, to overlook the plain facts that the center of rationalism had been Catholic France, and that the materialism against which *Dei Filius* inveighed had been a menace to the Church a thousand years before the Reformation. Furthermore, he said, many Protestants had been sincere friends of the Church; many in Germany, England, and America were especially devout Christians, erring, but erring in good faith. The conservative majority at the Council was so noisy in its disapproval that the presiding officers warned Strossmayer not to enrage the fathers by praising Protestants. When the bishop defended the right of the minority to be heard, pandemonium broke out, and the meeting was hastily adjourned, with the ultramontanists shouting, "He is another Luther, throw him out; he is Lucifer, anathema, anathema." [85]

The protracted debates over the constitution, *De Ecclesia*, generated similar antagonisms. The only chapter finally ratified declared that the pope was infallible when teaching the Universal Church, *ex cathedra*, on matters of faith and morals; the chapter explicitly overruled the fourth Gallican Article of 1682 which had given ecumenical councils the right to reverse a papal decision. A further conservative purpose was realized in the provision that the pope possessed ordinary jurisdiction within every diocese, thus placing every Catholic directly under the pope even on matters not fitting for infallible, universal decrees. Ten to 20 percent of the prelates opposed these provisions, but a closure on debate was voted, and the chapter was passed and accepted by Pius IX just before the Council was prorogued for the summer. Many of the liberals left Rome rather than vote for the constitution, and in Germany the Old Catholic Schism was formed by men who refused to accept the Council's decrees.[86]

While the vast majority of the liberals loyally accepted the decisions of the Council, they did not abandon their conviction that the best course for the Church was not to issue anathemas against the age, but to coöperate with its better tendencies. If the battle in Europe seemed to have been lost, at least for the time being, many of these Catholics eagerly looked for vindication to the experience of the rapidly growing Church in America.

IV

Throughout the nineteenth century, European Catholics had been of two minds about America and the American Church.[87] To de Maistre and his spiritual descendants, the country was the epitome of the radical nationalism and libertarianism of '89. Prophesying at first that no nation so conceived could long endure, they never ceased to deplore its continued existence as a denial of the best aspects of Christian civilization.[88] They were depressed at seeing masses of Catholic immigrants disappearing into an anti-Catholic state, and they were enraged by the flagrantly Protestant spirit which led to persecution of Catholics in America and the organization of mission societies to spread gospel news in Italy and France.[89] They were convinced that America was steeped in materialism and "go-aheadism," and that its leaders had, in Pius IX's words, "not much asceticism, and but little interest in things spiritual." [90] America could be rescued from its growing paganism only if Catholic leaders there set their faces sternly against any compromise of Church doctrine.[91]

The ultramontanists were pleased to note that such influential American churchmen as Archbishop Francis Kenrick of Baltimore and Father Franz Weninger, a distinguished missionary, had been early advocates of papal infallibility.[92] And Paul Cardinal Cullen of Dublin was undoubtedly delighted to hear from Martin Spalding, who succeeded Kenrick as Archbishop of Baltimore and who would lead the American delegation to the Vatican Council, that the American Church "thank God . . . was Roman to the core." [93]

Liberal Catholics in Europe entertained a far different conception of America and of the role and character of the American Church. Lamennais had been an outspoken admirer of America's political settlement, and de Tocqueville's conclusion, that the Church was thriving and felt no need to war on American culture, influenced European opinion throughout the century.[94] Montalembert frequently praised America, and, but for illness, would have visited there. His friend, Guillaume de Chabrol, did make the journey, and his glowing report of the harmonious relations between Catholicism and secular society awakened wide interest in both France and Germany.[95] Convinced by such reports and by interviews with American Churchmen in Europe that all parties were content with church-culture relations in the United States, many of the European liberals confidently expected the Americans to be strong allies in the testing of strength at the Vatican Council. The prominent German scholar, Ignaz von Döllinger, wrote every American bishop in the hope of strengthening the putative alliance.[96]

In fact, neither the liberals nor the conservatives were wholly satisfied with the performance of the American representatives at the Council. This was partly because many of the Americans came to the Council not fully aware of the real issues under debate. Dr. James Corcoran, sent to Rome in advance by Spalding to help prepare the agenda, had been amazed to find that the "Romans," whose ideals the Americans thought they shared, were determined to condemn "hundreds of opinions hitherto held or tolerated in Catholic schools," including many dealing with the thorny questions of church and state.[97] Distressed at this prospect, Spalding disappointed European conservatives by helping form a "third force" at the Council. This group proposed that papal infallibility be defined only implicitly, thus satisfying the huge majority of Catholics who already believed in it, without antagonizing a critical age. Eventually, Spalding and his associates recognized that the Council was determined to make explicit and necessary what had previously been a matter of free opinion; only then did Spalding join the majority, or conservative, bloc.[98]

Other Americans swiftly joined the liberals. A group of prelates, led by Archbishop Peter Kenrick of St. Louis, spoke several times in opposition to both the constitutions presented to the Council.[99] The influential Paulist Father Isaac Thomas Hecker, who had been a close friend of Montalembert, rapidly became an active coordinator of the international "minority." [100] These American liberals outdid even their European allies in professions of respect for the good faith of men outside the Church.[101]

Many of the Americans left Rome rather than accede to the final definition of papal infallibility, and Bishop Edward Fitzgerald of Little Rock cast one of the two dissenting votes at the final polling. But no American Catholics left the Church because of the decisions of the Council. Indeed, within a generation, a distinguished foreign observer was to comment on how completely and whole-heartedly papal infallibility had been accepted in America.[102] But this was a testimony not that the American Church had become wholly ultramontanist, but that many Americans did not believe that the definition of papal infallibility in any way ruled out the liberal approach to secular culture. Very shortly after the Vatican Council, Hecker began to argue that the main effect of the definition was to conclude the unhappily militant Reformation era. Henceforth, he thought, just because the Church's base of operations was perfectly safeguarded against internal dissension, Catholics need be less circumspect in their methods of meeting the world.[103]

In the 1890's, European conservatives were to complain that American acceptance of Hecker's rationalization proved that the liberal Catholicism of mid-nineteenth century Europe had not been killed at the Vatican Council, but had simply emigrated to the United States.[104] This view suited men suspicious of inter-national Masonic conspiracy better than it did the facts. Liberal Catholicism was not brought to America by exiled European lib-erals, by secret society courier, or by prelates whose eyes had been opened by the events of the Vatican Council. The liberal Catholicism which developed in America after the Civil War was, fundamentally, the response of an increasing number of Catholics to a secular culture that seemed far less hostile to the Church than European ultramontanists could believe was possible in modern times.

CHAPTER II

LIBERALS AND CONSERVATIVES
IN THE AMERICAN CHURCH

In 1889, when the American Church celebrated its hundredth anniversary, it could look back on a century of sensational progress. From the handful of priests and laymen Bishop John Carroll had led, the Church had grown till it numbered nearly nine million members.[1] Except for the French in Louisiana and the Spanish in the Southwest, most of these Catholics were clustered in the northern states, especially in the great cities. A smaller contingent, mostly German, had settled in the smaller cities and on the farms of the Middle West.[2] While Rome treated America' as a missionary country until 1908, every decade of the nineteenth century had seen vicars-apostolic with titular sees converted into bishops with established dioceses and an increasing complement of churches, schools, seminaries, and other special institutions.[3] The leadership of the Church, largely French in the early years, had gradually been assumed by priests and prelates of Irish birth and descent; in the ecclesiastical provinces of Cincinnati and Milwaukee, however, the Germans predominated.[4]

Growth alone could not conclusively prove that Catholicism was triumphant, nor did it, in fact, convince all the faithful that America was an ideal matrix for Catholic civilization; many believed that the progress of the Church would have been far greater had the European immigrants come to a land less deeply anti-Catholic. Such convictions were not wholly perverse. The mass of Catholic immigrants arriving in the years before the Civil War had not found Americans especially sympathetic hosts.[5] In the North, the newcomers were often regarded as less desirable than the freed Negro; in the South, they were considered more expendable than the slave and were thus assigned to the more dangerous work.[6] Immigrants could frequently find jobs only through a political boss or *padrone*, who could bridge the deep abyss between the "Americans" and themselves; they were warned off from many of the better jobs by the notice, "No Irish need apply." Mine and mill workers found themselves relegated, on the basis of their religion or national origin, to the lowest class of jobs.[7] Catholics taken into Protestant homes often felt pressed to abandon their religion.[8] The "opportunity" for which America was famed, Catholics might well conclude, was either to renounce their religion as the price of acceptance, or else to accept a status of apparently permanent inferiority.

Their alienation was enforced on them by their living apart from "Americans." Partly because certain quarters of large cities were most readily adaptable to housing large numbers of indigent immigrants, partly out of fellow feeling and the need to live near people of their own language and customs, Irish and German and, somewhat later, Italian quarters developed, ghettoes in fact, if not in name, with a deep sense of solidarity against the society outside. Some Church leaders like Bishop Fenwick of Boston attempted to alleviate the hardships of urban life by settling agricultural colonies in the hinterland, but these ventures seldom succeeded; even where one prospered, it did not alter the basic pattern of separation between immigrant and native.[9]

Just before the Civil War, social tensions had merged with religious prejudices and political differences to produce the noisily anti-Catholic Know-Nothing episodes. A block of marble which the Pope, following the example of other European rulers, had sent to be placed in the Washington Monument was indignantly dumped into the Potomac by a liberty-loving group. The Pope's special envoy was frequently in physical danger from mobs of republican sympathizers. Catholic buildings were destroyed, and Catholic lives were taken in city riots. Some states passed discriminatory laws against Catholic convents and churches.[10]

Catholic prelates, appealing to European aid societies, stressed the hostility of the American scene to everything Catholic, and the Redemptorist Father Rumpler, welcoming a Catholic sister to the missions in America, warned her to "remain with God, the holy and just. You are here in Sodom and Gomorrah."[11] Archbishop Martin Spalding, who, as a member of an old American family, had suffered none of the immigrants' trials, and who was certainly no alarmist, nevertheless expected that America would do its worst when the Syllabus was promulgated. Even if its harshest provisions were explained away, he wrote his nephew gloomily, Americans would seize the opportunity to attack the Church on one pretext or another.[12]

Not surprisingly, therefore, many Catholics developed a comprehensive hostility to America and Americans. The attacks made on the true faith by both sincere Protestants and professional anti-Catholics reinforced the immigrants' traditional antipathy to all religions but their own. They found it hard to believe that converts were sincere in their new professions, or that the Church should devote much money and manpower, desperately needed for churches, schools, and charitable institutions, to the vain hope of making Americans into Catholics. The state, "heathen *ex professo*," in reality was the tool of an aggressive Protestantism.[13] The public asylums and penitentiaries were open to visits by Protestant proselytizers, but frequently closed to Catholic priests.[14] So far as the public school provided any religious education at all, it was usually tailored to Protestant desires.[15] In practice, Catholics were barred from holding high political office. The Republican party, only thinly disguising its anti-Catholicism, made several attempts after the Civil War to prevent any division of government from appropriating funds to "sectarian" undertakings; and the Democratic party had betrayed its many Catholic followers on several occasions.[16] Many Catholics disliked the persistent attempts to legislate reforms, such as temperance, compulsory education, and women's rights, which threatened traditional patterns of life. It was hard to have faith in a political process which required them to combine and compromise with their unreliable and unfriendly neighbors.

Their alienation from society reinforced their innate conservatism. They did not understand Americans' contempt for the warnings of the past. They suspected that the future would be as bad as the present, if not worse. They doubted that human reason could discover important truths any more than it could discern better patterns of social life. They feared that men who were given unprecedented liberty and encouraged to unprecedented activity would do both society and themselves far more harm than good. They refused to believe that contemporary America was exempted by nature or by God from the evils which other nations had suffered throughout history. If anything, America was already in worse condition than most lands; it seemed plausible that the reason the Free Masons were less anticlerical in America was that they had already done most of their deviltry long since.[17]

Hostile to the Protestant majority, suspicious of governmental enterprise, and averse to the active, melioristic spirit of the times, these Catholics met secular culture so far as possible only on their own terms. Their Catholicism was the symbol as well as the seal of their separation from that culture. Like their ultramontane counterparts in Europe, they opposed all innovations except those that would obviously strengthen the defensive armor of the Church against the age.[18]

Catholics of this conviction did not issue many manifestoes, nor did they require many spokesmen. Protected by the many autonomies, legal and practical, existing in a not fully established church structure, they were able to resist, simply by procrastination and noncoöperation, the occasional attempts of liberals to commit the Church to profitable encounters with the age. Only when necessary would spokesmen for these conservatives come forward; and on such occasions, their declarations usually reflected their passionate aversion to change more accurately than any deep comprehension of their adversaries' arguments. Almost invariably, their indignant outcries were more appreciated in Europe than in America.

In the last decades of the nineteenth century, the Germans, of all the older nationality groups in the American Church, were the most tenaciously devoted to their own language and culture. With several national organizations, an active press, and many able priests and bishops, they regularly supplied the most voluble spokesmen for the mass of Catholic immigrants.[19] Convinced that the Irish-American hierarchy was acclimatizing the Church to the American scene at a reckless rate, German leaders strongly denied that the Church was prospering. Unhindered by reliable statistics, they regularly asserted that as much as two-thirds of the potential Catholic population of America had been lost.[20]

In an influential pamphlet published in 1889, Father Anton Walburg of Cincinnati attributed most losses to the radical anti-Catholicism of American culture. The language itself was so pervaded with Protestantism that an English-speaking Catholicism could never flourish, he thought. Though the strength of the old sects was probably waning, the culture which remained was a "hotbed of fanaticism, intolerance, and radical ultra views on matters of politics and religion. All the vagaries of spiritualism, Mormonism, free-loveism, prohibition, infidelity, and materialism, generally breed in the American nationality. Here also we find dissimulation and hypocrisy." To Walburg, the right course for the Church to follow was obvious; instead of encouraging the denationalization of the immigrants, thus jeopardizing their religious loyalty, it should concentrate on fanning "the embers of faith" still smoldering in them. Until the immigrants' religious loyalty had been safeguarded, churchmen should not look around for other responsibilities.[21]

While it was of course necessary for a non-German prelate like Michael Corrigan, Archbishop of New York, to reject Walburg's indictment of all English-speaking Catholics, he was a staunch ally of the Germans in their immigrant ultramontanism. A cautious, even timid man, Corrigan had been sheltered by his affluent family from acquiring the intimate experience with American life that might have altered his stereotyped rejection of its basic characteristics.[22] Provided with a thorough, if parochial education, he went to the American College in Rome, from which he emerged, in 1864, a thoroughly "Roman" cleric. Rising rapidly in the Church, he became Archbishop of New York in 1885, thus acquiring the see most inundated with newly arrived immigrants. Even had his personal disposition been more liberal, Corrigan would necessarily have had to shape policy to accord with the traditionalism and conservatism of these immigrant charges. At the same time, he was so readily deferred to by the New York Tammany machine that he felt no need to seek working alliances with non-Catholic elements. While courteous and charitable towards those outside the Church, he did not wish his priests to expend a large share of their energies in seeking converts, and he forthrightly opposed all suggestions that the Church should modify its teachings or behavior for that purpose.

Corrigan enjoyed throughout his life the tireless support of his truculent diocesan and former teacher, Bernard McQuaid, Bishop of Rochester.[23] One of his ablest lieutenants was his vicar-general, Thomas Preston, a convert from Episcopalianism who brought to the Church not the charity of a Newman but the fiery zeal of the younger Manning. Described as "uncompromising in enforcing ecclesiastical discipline and extremely conservative" in religious and secular affairs alike, Preston found in Pius IX's Syllabus of Errors the best formula for judging "American Catholicity." Its most crucial failing, he thought, was the unwillingness to acknowledge that America was no ideal environment for the Church. Heady institutional growth and the absence of the overt anticlericalism of a Renan or Jules Ferry did not justify Catholics in overlooking the many sins of the society in which they were living.[24] Other clerical leaders, such as Bishop Richard Gilmour of Cleveland and Bishop Francis Chatard of Indianapolis, were regular allies of Corrigan and the Germans; Archbishops William Elder of Cincinnati and Patrick Ryan of Philadelphia joined with the conservatives on some issues.[25]

As in Europe, the Jesuits were steadfast opponents of all liberal innovations. Some like Salvatore Brandi lived in America only a short time, but remained influential authorities on the failings of the American Church the rest of their lives. Others, like Augustine Thébaud, persisted in their critical attitudes through a half century or more of intimate experience. Viewing all Catholic affairs in relation to the welfare of the Pope, and approving the immigrant Catholics' alienation from American culture, the Jesuits provided formidable theological critiques of every peculiarly American institution, secular or religious.[26]

Most of the conservatives' spokesmen were priests, but a few lay editors of Catholic periodicals like Arthur Preuss of the St. Louis *Review* and Condé Pallen of the St. Louis *Church Progress* were outspoken critics of all liberal innovations. The strength of their antagonism was clearly revealed in 1899 when Preuss seconded the malicious attacks of ultraconservative European Catholics on American liberal leaders, and Pallen adapted, without moderating, a Spanish cleric's attack on Liberalism, "the evil of all evils." [27] In this intemperate book, Pallen warned American Catholics that the culture in which they found themselves "exhales an atmosphere filled with germs poisonous and fatal to Catholic life." The policy the Church should follow was therefore obvious. "Amidst a host of swarming foes our armor should be without flaw from greave to helmet, our weapons well-tempered, keen and burnished, not only to ward off the hostile blow, but ready to deal a telling stroke home whenever the enemy's weakness exposes him." [28]

To all these conservatives, the crowning misfortune was that many Church leaders seemed largely oblivious to such warnings. In Europe, the Jesuits and the principles they stood for had long been in the ascendancy, but in America, Thébaud and Brandi, like Walburg, Preston, Preuss, and Pallen, wrote as if they felt themselves a beleaguered minority within the Church as well as within the world. Whether they spoke for a majority or minority of Catholics, they were right in detecting within that very American culture they so profoundly feared a strong flowering of the same kind of "liberalism" that Montalembert and Newman had struggled to cultivate.[29]

II

Although the Church continued to glory in being the "Church of the immigrants," leaders had to speak for an increasing number of Irish, English, French, and even German Catholics who no longer thought of themselves as immigrants, but as Americans, — if not by birth, then by the wholehearted acceptance of American ideals and practices.

So far as this American spirit existed at all in the first two-thirds of the century, it was supplied by those descendants of the handful of Catholics in America at the time of the Revolution.

Of unimpeachable family, the Carrolls and the Spaldings had been spared the trial of winning acceptance for themselves, or of demonstrating the compatibility of their faith with American institutions. Most of them were as little interested as were their Catholic contemporaries in England in making converts to a faith they tended to regard as a family treasure.[30]

The identification of Catholicism and Americanism was, to a limited extent, promoted by the conversion of such noted citizens as Augustine Hewit, Francis Baker, James Deshon, and James Roosevelt Bayley, the last of whom succeeded Martin Spalding as Archbishop of Baltimore, and proved to be the last non-Irish cleric to hold that post.[31] But there were not many converts in the early years, and many of those who did come renounced, like Preston, not only Protestantism but all deep sympathies with American life as well. Orestes Brownson, the greatest intellectual convert, denounced all non-Catholics and all non-Catholic ideas as often as he enjoined his new associates not to neglect the scattered virtues of American life.[32] The major sources of a significant American spirit had, therefore, to be the very immigrant stock which had produced the harsh anti-Americanism of Father Walburg.

The immigrant invasion had never been one homogeneous mass of uncultured, indigent, famine-driven peasants. Some had emigrated well fortified by intellectual training or experience in urban, industrial life against the insecurity of American experience. They were able to adapt themselves to free competition in religion as well as economics, and to recognize that all non-Catholics did not act like anti-Catholics. Others brought to America the professional status, manual skill, or financial resources which enabled them to win economic and social independence relatively simply and rapidly. Because they were not so readily coerced by American society, they were less likely to resist it as strenuously, and more free to adopt its patterns and principles. They were more apt to recognize the great opportunities America offered to the enterprising individual. They were, in short, more readily acculturated.[33]

What these immigrants rapidly achieved, others attained more gradually. Some who had been brought to America as children, and a very large proportion of the second generation, managed, often at the cost of a violent rift with parents and neighbors, to adapt to the American scene, to move out of the ghetto, in fact and in spirit, and to look at America through the lace curtains of economic and social success.[34] Inevitably much of their parents' pessimism about a man's ability to improve his worldly condition by his own efforts, much of the distrust of innovation, much of the suspicion of strangers, weakened under the impact of an experience which belied these premises. The heady confidence of a booming America was contagious for those who were beginning to prosper. The ambition fostered by a mobile society became an integral part of the psychology of men who had left the ghetto behind them. Faith in work came readily to men enjoying the rewards of strenuous activity.

The Civil War accelerated the changes taking place in immigrant attitudes. The willingness of immigrants to answer the urgent calls for manpower won them a degree of acceptance undreamed of in the previous decade when Know-Nothings were impugning the patriotism of all Catholics, and especially the foreign-born.[35] Forty-five years after the war was over, a Baptist minister affectionately addressed John Ireland as "my archbishop," remembering his services as a gallant chaplain of an Illinois regiment.[36] At the same time, the immigrants, by participating in the crucial test of America's nationality, increased their own attachment to that nationality. Like other Americans in the years after the war, they pointed to their heroic services as proof of their patriotism; they offered their membership in veterans' organizations as certificates of their full-hearted love for America.

New feelings about America did not necessarily lead to new conceptions of the relation of the Church to the surrounding culture. But it was possible for those who had successfully made the transition from one culture to another, as it was not for men who clung to their old ways with desperate intensity, to believe that the Church in America might well comport itself differently from the Church in Ireland and in Hesse. Instead of defending passionately and uncritically everything done in the past in the name of the Church, they might attempt to discriminate between the transient — what had been merely the accretions of an old secular culture upon the faith — and what was permanent and truly Catholic. Instead of attributing all difficulties to the aggressions of a hostile age, they might entertain the hypothesis that Catholics were themselves sometimes to blame. In fact, some individuals developed great ingenuity in detecting the motes in the eyes of fellow Catholics rather than complaining of the beams in the eyes of non-Catholics.[37] The conservative James Loughlin of Philadelphia was certain that Catholic confessions of error "invariably" led to "deplorable mischief," by annoying the faithful and catering to the vulgar misapprehensions of the secularists and Protestants.[38] But to the liberals, or "Americanists" as they were aptly called, admissions of failure were prerequisite to necessary reforms. And "there is nothing," one Catholic editor wrote, "short of what is necessary to salvation, which every Christian should not be willing to do . . . to render the Church . . . more attractive to the eyes of those who sincerely seek after the truth, . . . or are anxious to find it in a more perfect form." [39]

Even when the Church seemed unjustly persecuted, the liberals were willing to suggest that trials might well serve "as a wholesome medicine and stimulant to counteract inward diseases and increase all the vital forces of the Catholic Church." [40] But the liberals did not expect that the Church would suffer many afflictions in America. Quite on the contrary, they dared to believe that just as the Church could save American culture, so might that culture have much to teach individual Catholics about the "human" side of their religion. At the very least, they could testify that American culture was not such an ineradicably hostile environment to Catholicism as men like Walburg had insisted. In the late nineteenth century, they happily pointed to several developments in American life which promised to make the environment even more congenial to Catholicism.

No one claimed that all hostility had miraculously disappeared. While the widespread antagonisms of the Know-Nothing era had waned, America continued to produce men like Father Chiniquy, Tom Watson, and the more flamboyant spokesmen of the American Protective Association, who gave substance to the conservatives' contention that the country was as unsympathetic in the 1890's as it had been forty years earlier.[41] The competent historian, John Gilmary Shea, compiled enough evidence of overt hostility to conclude that "the public opinion of this country is overwhelmingly against" the Church, and that it could be arrayed in active opposition at the whim of "any fanatic." [42]

Yet a growing number of Protestant leaders were publicly acknowledging that coexistence with a prosperous Catholic Church had proved less horrific than anticipated. Protestants were not being terrorized; indeed, many ministers and laymen were acquiring "growing personal acquaintance and friendship" with Catholic neighbors. So thought Leonard Bacon, a Congregational minister whose father had for years been a member of the stridently anti-Catholic Evangelical Alliance, but who himself acknowledged his pleasure in welcoming in 1893 the arrival of a papal delegate to the United States. Though not all of his colleagues were so hospitable, Bacon could justifiably note the profound improvement in interfaith relations since the unhappy visit of a papal representative in 1853.[43] Religious tolerance was generally regarded as a sign of maturity. A group of Minnesota Protestants, hailing the appointment of an old friend as coadjutor archbishop of the see of St. Paul, proudly asserted that "the days of bitter animosities for differences of opinion upon religious maters have passed," yielding to "the more genial spirit of this progressive age." [44]

Profound changes in Protestantism furthered this growing tolerance. Many churchmen, abandoning a loyal Biblicism for the less stringent imperatives of liberal Christianity, or even "progressive orthodoxy," had lost their taste for theological combat. T. T. Munger treated differences fought over by churchmen of the past as insignificant variations which an evolutionary process would soon eliminate. Charles Briggs was convinced that Catholic and Protestant theology was 90 per cent identical; the few disagreements were both trifling and compromisable.[45] The Reverend Thomas Dixon shrugged off an individual's religious affiliation as a mere accident of birth; the differences between various churches were mostly matters of "ecclesiastical machinery." [46]

Some Protestants were anxious to convert the widespread church reunion movement into a force that would include Roman Catholics. "God has great surprises in store," one leader prophesied. "Free America, where all the churches are commingling and rivalling with each other, may become the chief theater of . . . a reunion of Christendom." [47] Though a stalwart anti-Catholic like the Reverend Daniel Dorchester violently disapproved of such a hope, Leonard Bacon insisted that "the idea that has so long prevailed . . . that the only Christian union to be hoped for in America must be a union to the exclusion of the Roman Catholic Church and in antagonism to it, ought to be reckoned an idea obsolete and antiquated." [48] Most of the proponents of church union expressed such a strong opposition to ecclesiasticism and dogma that their proposals were hardly tempting to Catholics; yet to be declared eligible to join the fraternity of the future was a flattering and friendly gesture. [49] And a few ministers were so forthright in their praise for particular Catholic doctrines that a Philadelphia paper could ask "Are Protestants Racing for Catholic Shrines?" and declare that all the leading clergymen of the area were "more or less affected in the tendency toward a return to Catholic unity." [50]

Protestantism, especially in the larger cities, was increasingly interested in good works. "Creeds are falling away," the editor of the *Arena* exulted, "and deeds are taking their place. The religion of the morrow will emphasize life rather than dogma." [51] One of the distinguishing marks of American Christianity, Dorchester believed, was concern for "practical spirituality." [52] And in efforts to meet the obvious maladjustments of modern civilization, Catholic assistance was often necessary. At an Evangelical Conference in 1888, Professor Simeon Baldwin of Yale was criticized for praising the Catholic Church; he replied spiritedly:

I have found in my own state . . . no truer friends in many of these questions . . . than gentlemen of the Roman Catholic Church. . . . It guards the family; it looks at the children, it looks at the home from the standpoint of a Christian organization; and we ought to make friends with that Church, we ought to bring them in with us in all these causes of Christian and social reform. [53]

At a testimonal dinner in 1887, the Presbyterian minister Theodore Cuyler asserted that Father Sylvester Malone, a Brooklyn priest, was "as much honored among us Protestants as he is among his own people. . . . In the mighty conflict with infidelity, Sabbath desecration, atheism, drunkenness, and socialism we find the assistance of such men . . . to be of no small importance." [54]

The good works Cuyler hoped for were clearly not all strictly religious, and secular appreciation for secular services was perhaps the strongest element in the developing friendliness to the Church. For whatever ambitions some Protestants cherished of bringing all Americans into their churches, and however diligently a handful labored to make church services available to lower class immigrants, American Protestantism was fast becoming, in the cities at least, the religion of the middle class.[55] The empty pews of downtown churches contrasted painfully with the several crowded masses at Catholic churches, and the trickle of converts to Protestantism blinded only a few observers to the virtual monopoly the Church was establishing over those members of the lower classes who maintained any interest in Christianity.[56]

To men who believed Protestant Christianity the only true path to salvation, this was a sombre conclusion. To the practical men of affairs who thought of religion as an effective means of social control, the natural reaction was to look upon the welfare of the Church with increased solicitude. Even men who regarded Catholicism as a "dangerous tendency in American life" had to admit that it had "a hold upon classes among us which no other religious body seems able to reach."[57] Fearful of the masses of unassimilated foreigners, Thomas Dixon thought that New York "could not be held from the devil for twenty-four hours if it were not for the power of the Catholic priesthood," while Bishop William Doane of the Episcopal diocese of Albany believed that "brute force" was the only alternative Protestants had to giving the Church "every opportunity" to maintain her hold over "the most turbulent element in our citizenship."[58]

The business tycoons, the real spokesmen for America in this era, saw the problem with cold realism. "Look at the millions of foreigners pouring into this country," the Canadian-born James J. Hill said, "to whom the Roman Catholic Church is the only authority they either fear or respect. What will be their social view, their political action, their moral status if that single controlling force should be removed?" His biographer completed Hill's thought by arguing that businessmen should support "the anointed agents of the only authority" that many immigrant workers would obey. "This is as much a matter of good business as is the improvement

of farm stock or the construction of a faultless railroad bed." [59]
This way of thought was, perhaps wryly, summarized by the
Catholic World:

Practical, hard-headed business men are beginning to realize that for
the money invested the output of religion as a manufactured article is
of higher quality and better grade and more of it to the yard from the
Catholic loom than from any other source. This is the secret of many
of the generous donations made by non-Catholics to Catholic religious
effort.[60]

Political leaders were also grateful. Mark Hanna was supposed
to have said that the only two safeguards against anarchy in the
United States were the Supreme Court and the Roman Catholic
Church. William Howard Taft, under attack for allegedly dis-
criminating in favor of the Church, sturdily retorted that he considered Catholicism "one of the bulwarks against socialism and
anarchy in this country, and I welcome its presence here." [61] Either
from gratitude for Catholic principles or from fear of the increasing Catholic voting power, politicians began to extend governmental
aid to the Church. Many cities and states voted subsidies to Catholic charitable institutions. Church properties were frequently exempted from taxation because "they served as moral agencies and
diminished the expense of police administration." [62] The insulting
nunneries-inspection laws of the 1850's were now inconceivable.
The federal government instructed its foreign service to defend
American citizens who were engaged in subverting British rule
in Ireland for the honor of freedom and Catholicism.[63] And, in
1884, at the request of Archbishop Corrigan, Secretary of State
Frelinghuysen intervened — without much legal justification — to
protect the American College in Rome from being confiscated by the
Italian government.[64]

Both major political parties gave Catholics greater recognition
than ever before. In 1892, both had Catholics as national campaign
chairmen.[65] President Cleveland named the first Catholic to the
Supreme Court since Roger Taney, and McKinley made Joseph Mc-
Kenna the first Catholic cabinet officer since the Civil War; later
McKenna was named to the Supreme Court.[66]

While Catholics could not always approve of the motives of their new admirers among the clergy, the business class, and political leadership, evidence of respect for their Church could hardly be anything but gratifying.[67] If Americans as yet saw only as through a glass darkly the saving innovations the Church could make in American life, it was plain to most Catholics relatively liberated from their immigrant heritage that the Church need no longer remain on the defensive.

III

Though it was Catholic laymen who were most in contact with this promising America, the responsibility for reformulating the Church's role was left to the clergy almost exclusively. A consciously "American" Church would develop only after leaders appeared who would hold fast to all that was best of the old-country traditions at the same time that they welcomed much that was new. It was the good fortune of both the Church and American society that in the late nineteenth century there emerged a remarkable group of priests and bishops anxious to undertake this onerous and occasionally thankless task of mediation.

The career of James Gibbons, named archbishop of Baltimore in 1877, and cardinal of the Church in 1886, illustrated the growing recognition by both Catholics and non-Catholics that the Church in America was ready to "come out of the catacombs." [68] Born in this country of Irish parents in 1834, the young Gibbons was spared the anguished poverty that beset many immigrants. When his father's health failed, the family had the resources to avoid the hospital and asylum to which so many defeated immigrants had to retreat, and returned to Ireland. He received all his clerical training in America, however, and in 1868 was appointed vicar-apostolic of North Carolina. His experience at this post may have been the most important factor in shaping his future, for he was, almost from the start, most cordially welcomed by non-Catholics; he was invited to preach mission sermons in courthouses, in Protestant churches, even occasionally in Masonic lodges; he drew many Protestants to his meetings, and converted a number of them. Gibbons' first recorded act as a priest was, symbolically, the reception of a convert.[69] To improve the Church's appeal to American non-Catholics, he wrote a clear exposition of Catholic dogma and discipline, devoid of recrimination and hard sayings. *The Faith of Our Fathers* sought to answer objections by finding analogies to American ideals; papal infallibility was compared to the power of the Supreme Court, the adoration of the Virgin to Americans' traditional respect for womanhood. Over and over, Gibbons denied that any grounds existed for doubting Catholics' reverence and loyalty to American political and social institutions. He was a master apologist, and his book became one of the bestsellers of American religious history.[70] A later book, *Our Christian Heritage*, was similarly successful; the *Edinburgh Review* praised its spirit of "perfect brotherhood. . . . From cover to cover it does not contain six pages which would not be endorsed by any Protestant divine, from the right reverend bench in the House of Lords to the pastors of the Reformed Church in France." An Ohio pastor made it the subject of a sermon, in which he endorsed all Gibbons' works.[71]

As Archbishop of Baltimore, Gibbons continued for more than forty years his mediatorial services between Church and country, his character and judgment winning him influential friends in government and private life. He was a frequent public speaker, was consulted by presidents, and, as he grew to great age, became the acknowledged elder statesman of church—state relations. A wholehearted believer in religious tolerance, he was as ready to speak out for Protestant and Jewish as he was for Catholic causes. At the jubilee of his priesthood in 1911, citizens of all faiths gathered to honor him; President Taft, ex-President Roosevelt, Elihu Root, and James Bryce were among the speakers.

Anxious as he was to promote the rapprochement of his Church with American society, Gibbons was prevented both by his temperament and by his position from becoming the crusading leader of a determined faction of liberals. He was a mild, gentle man, and his charity extended to the conservatives within the Church as well as to the non-Catholics without. As the unofficial primate of the American Church, he was necessarily responsive to the large immigrant membership who distrusted all novel apologetic measures, and he never underestimated the conservatism of the universal Church. His characteristic injunction to all parties was "be prudent."

More dynamic liberal leadership came from bishops and priests with less extensive responsibilities. Catholics who settled in the West or South had already broken away from the immigrant pattern, as had those who finally settled in the more prosperous sections of the large eastern cities. Their leaders were free to undertake "missions" to American culture which, in more conservative areas, would have been considered radical innovations. In more frequent, more amiable contact with Americans of all sorts, they were less likely to desire to recreate a traditional European culture. Quite on the contrary, many suspected that their acceptance by America would not be complete until they had demonstrated, by word and deed, the perfect compatibility of American and Catholic ideals.

Undoubtedly the most celebrated, and to some conservatives the most notorious, spokesman for these liberals was John Ireland, Archbishop of St. Paul since 1888.[72] A man of vigor and decision, frequently compared to the great business tycoons of the era, he was referred to on occasion as the consecrated blizzard of the Northwest.[73] A profound admirer of Gibbons, he steadily urged the cardinal to take bolder action. When Gibbons was discouraged by conservative opposition to the establishment of a Catholic University, and proposed to abandon the work of several years, Ireland denounced "so cowardly a surrender," and carried the battle through to victory.[74]

This remarkable man had been brought to America as a small boy, and had moved with his family several times until finally settling in St. Paul. Educated in France, where many of his professors were liberal Catholics, and where he came to venerate Bishop Dupanloup, Ireland returned to America in time to serve as a chaplain in the Civil War, where he acquired an unequaled sense of patriotic nationalism.[75] He rose rapidly in the Church, and for the last twenty-five years of his life expected, and, characteristically, strenuously worked for, a cardinalate.[76] He took the lead in promoting, though without much success, the colonization of Catholics in the West, for he deeply believed in the superior virtues of a life outside the ghetto. The colonies he established were not limited to Catholics, but were intended as communities in which men of all faiths could intermingle to their mutual benefit.[77] He became an enthusiastic temperance advocate, totally abstaining himself, and working for severer regulation of the liquor trade.[78]

Ireland took a prominent part in American politics. As the most celebrated Catholic Republican, he spoke at the convention in 1896, and exerted, one anti-Catholic noted bitterly, "a soporific influence over Republican financiers and politicians."[79] He gave press interviews on every mooted secular and religious question so that an Ohio district attorney was able to declare to the State Supreme Court that "the most illustrious divine in that Church today in this country is Archbishop Ireland."[80] Personal success corroborated what a man of Ireland's confident disposition felt instinctively — that America was uniquely suited to Catholicism, that it welcomed the Church's efforts, that if the Church acted boldly, it might win back America to the true faith. A Catholic Americanism and an American Catholicism were his most cherished goals.

The Catholic Lay Congress of 1889, the Church's counterpart to the long series of centennial celebrations held since 1876 to commemorate America's unique virtues, was an appropriate time for Ireland's most eloquent testimony. His sermon, "The Mission of Catholics in America," started from the premise of a hundred years of increasing Catholic success. A reticent, defensive spirit was no longer a fit attitude. Instead, he challenged his hearers to dedicate themselves to two great tasks: "to make America Catholic, and to solve for the Church Universal the all-absorbing problems with which religion is confronted."[81] Both tasks were simple if Catholics acted energetically, confidently, and in harmony with the deepest spirit of America and the Church.

Because of his energy, because his personal ambitions in the Church and in society became inextricably mixed with the fortunes of the liberal enterprise, John Ireland was the real protagonist of the liberals throughout the 1890's. This was not altogether fortunate; ambition, enthusiasm, and a distinct penchant for devious, intra-Church politics were dangerous qualities for a man engaged in delicate church—state negotiations, and in the reforming of long-cherished Catholic folkways. He engendered such extreme antagonism among German conservatives as to be dubbed, on one occasion, the "Antichrist of the North." The resentments of McQuaid, and of Corrigan, whom he once privately characterized as "all that is vile and damnable," were nearly as bitter.[82] By 1897, one liberal prelate felt that "Archbishop Ireland is a hoodo — whatever he touches seems to go wrong." [83] Furthermore, broad as Ireland's interests were, he had little understanding of the intellectual problems which the liberal approach to secular culture posed for Catholic theology. Other men were needed to do for America what Cardinal Newman had done in England.

One such man was John Lancaster Spalding, nephew of Archbishop Martin Spalding, and, since 1877, bishop of Peoria.[84] Excellently educated in Europe, with a keen mind and great oratorical abilities, Spalding in his early years as a priest had disavowed all compromises with secular culture.[85] But as he grew older, rage for doctrinal orthodoxy yielded to an appreciation of the deep symbolism of Catholic dogma. While Spalding stopped short of the modernists' attempts to reformulate dogma, he shared their desire to destroy the sharp separation between secular and spiritual, and to make every action religiously meaningful.

It was depressing for Spalding to observe how sharply the deep piety, intellectual torpor, and economic failure of the Catholic immigrant contrasted with the economic and intellectual vitality and howling religious error of the American non-Catholic. Like Ireland he concluded that Catholics had a mission not only to spread the faith, but also to demonstrate that true religion was a liberating, not an enervating force. *The Religious Mission of the Irish People*, which he wrote primarily to encourage emigration from the cities to the West, was a passionate exhortation to embrace life fully as the surest way to embrace it religiously.[86]

Throughout his career, he continued to believe in the "promise" of American life. In a long series of books on "opportunity" and "education," he reveled in the challenges that life offered.[87] Anxious to distinguish his message from that of Carnegie and Conwell, he regularly emphasized that religious truth was incommensurately more valuable than culture, and culture more valuable than material success. But his explicit acknowledgement of diverse values ensured that he, like Newman, would sometimes be censured for an insufficient devotion to religion.

Spalding's greatest contribution to liberal Catholicism was his eloquent defense of the importance of formal education in helping Catholics perceive and live a full life.[88] Like other churchmen, he established parochial, primary schools to teach children that re-ligion was fundamental to all knowledge. But he wanted more, and he firmly believed that only in a great university where all secular learning was cherished could young men and women be properly stimulated to the "higher life." The great moment of Spalding's career was the establishment in 1889 of the Catholic University of America; though it did not immediately realize all his hopes, it promised to further the sympathetic approach to secular culture that Spalding most deeply believed in.

Spalding was so greatly influenced by German philosophy, both in the original texts and in Emerson's expropriations, that he was occasionally accused of ontologism. His orations and essays, fur-thermore, were so untraditional in content and so orphic in ex-pression that they commonly distressed Catholic audiences.[89] But Spalding, confident of his orthodoxy and proud of his family back-ground, felt little interest in leading a popular crusade. Though his fine perceptions helped him avoid the vulgarity into which Ireland occasionally stumbled, his intellectualism disabled him, especially in his later years, from exerting on his fellow Catholics the influence that his talents and his sympathies might have won him.

IV

While prelates like Ireland and Spalding had the most splendid opportunities to proclaim their affection for the non-Catholic world, much of the hard work needed to realize good relations between Church and culture devolved upon the clergy. The religious orders contributed little to this mission. Belonging to dominantly Euro-pean organizations, serving under European superiors, bound by constitutions and vows which reflected another age and place, the "religious," whatever their personal dispositions, were more apt to be missionaries of European ultramontanism than heralds of harmony between Catholicism and America.

Among the "secular" priests, those gathered into the Society of Saint Sulpice and the Congregation of Saint Paul were undoubted-ly the most active. Many Sulpicians had come to America as part of the clerical exodus from France at the time of the Revolution, and had devoted themselves to the education of the American clergy. Though centered abroad, they never developed very great sympathy with the ultramontanist trend in the nineteenth century, preserving much of the liberal, somewhat eclectic spirit characteristic of French Catholicism in the era of the Enlightenment. Requiring no such vow as bound the strictly religious, and dedicated to serve in "direct dependence on the bishops," they were ready to coöperate in any new enterprise.[90] They staffed the seminary at Baltimore throughout the century, and for a while maintained the important seminaries in Boston and New York; in 1918, Gibbons was to declare with great feeling that God never did more for the American Church than when He sent the Sulpicians.[91] The Society's American superior during the last quarter of the century was Alphonse Magnien, a close friend and advisor of the cardinal. Another leading Sulpician was John Hogan, whose influential essays on clerical education were as broadly liberal as Spalding's.[92] Bishop McQuaid was convinced that the Sulpicians were the most devoted liberals in America.[93]

Even more American, and perhaps more liberal, were the Paulists. Isaac Hecker, the founder of the congregation, had been the early herald of the liberal spirit. A convert who was expelled from the Redemptorist order because he was too wedded to American principles, he had established the Congregation of St. Paul in 1858 to convert America through a generous recognition of her noble qualities.[94] Though Hecker himself fell ill in 1872, and remained partly incapacitated until his death in 1888, his apologetic was carried on through the *Catholic World*, and the Catholic Publication Society, which he had founded as harbingers of truth to Protestant America. The congregation always remained small, but included a number of born activists and reformers who exhorted Catholics to break down the barriers of mistrust separating them from the world, and invited Protestants to inspect the virtues of the True Church. Alfred Young vindicated the role of Catholicism in the progress of civilization, Augustine Hewit showed the harmony of Catholic theology and American ideals, Alexander Doyle took a leading part in the Total Abstinence movement, and Walter Elliott, a lawyer converted to the clergy by a Hecker lecture, became a leading missionary to Protestant communities.[95]

Both Sulpicians and Paulists were anxious to draw the diocesan clergy into the liberal enterprises, knowing them to be "more numerous, more widely distributed, more permanent in residence, better known to the non-Catholic people . . . than are the members of the religious orders." [96] But priests with dominantly immigrant parishes were in no position to join the crusade. And, while priests with liberal superiors sometimes gave loyal service, the liberal clergy who acquired most prominence were those in the archdioceses of New York and Milwaukee who combined apologetics to non-Catholics with notorious warfare against conservative ecclesiastical authorities. Louis Lambert of Waterloo, New York was sometimes called "the American Newman" because of his devastating attacks on "the tactics of infidels" like Robert Ingersoll, but was nearly equally famous for his appeals to Rome against the harassments of Bishop McQuaid.[97] Edward McGlynn won a wide personal following through his crusade for Henry George's land theories, but disobeyed Archbishop Corrigan so incontinently that he was excommunicated temporarily.[98] Perhaps the most successful liberal priest was Father Sylvester Malone of Brooklyn, who, because he was less dogmatic theologically than Lambert, and less radical economically than McGlynn, escaped the punishment, if not the hostility, of the New York hierarchy.

Born in Ireland and trained in Trinity College, he brought to America the memory of unusually genial personal relations between Protestants and Catholics which his experience in America only fortified. From the outset, he adopted social and political views at variance with those of the immigrants of New York City. He was a mild abolitionist before the Civil War, and a friend of the Negroes during and after it. He supported Lincoln, flew a Union flag from his church, and encouraged his parishioners to enlist in the righteous war.[99] Malone was free to express these views because his parish was made up of relatively prosperous Catholics, most of whom had probably broken their geographical and spiritual ties with the immigrant community. Malone enjoyed excellent relations with his Protestant neighbors, and, late in life, was honored by election to the State Board of Regents. Malone's fiftieth jubilee as a priest was attended by Archbishop Ireland, by Bishop John J. Keane, the liberal rector of the Catholic University of America, and by several Paulists, though, conspicuously, not by Archbishop

Corrigan.[100] Keane spoke of society's need for both brakemen and engineers; Malone, he said, was definitely an engineer, for he used "energy and push," in his anxiety that no one should manage to "get ahead of Jesus Christ." He was, the bishop concluded, an apostle of the "true liberalism." [101]

Laymen were strenuously urged to take part in the liberal enterprises, and a few, like John Boyle O'Reilly of Boston, William Onahan of Chicago, and Henry Spaunhorst of St. Louis did perform useful service on occasion. But without question the liberal movement in the American Church was dominated by the clergy.[102]

There was no official roster of liberal Catholics; there was no formal organization; and no detailed platform could have been drawn up to which any sizable number would have totally assented. Spalding disliked the drive to "Americanize" the Germans, Ireland professed total ignorance of the nature or purpose of a graduate university, and Father Malone desired greater independence for the priests than any of the bishops would have approved. On the other hand, the conservative McQuaid was as nationalistic as Malone and Ireland, and probably more concerned than most liberals for educational reforms in the seminaries. The German Catholics were almost certainly in the lead in seeking social reforms, at least after 1900.[103] Yet friends, enemies, and neutrals recognized the existence of a coherent group of liberal Catholics. McQuaid and the Germans spoke darkly of a malevolent cabal. President William Hyde of Bowdoin distinguished within the Catholic Church a "Romanist element . . . which is the bigoted, implacable foe of everything free, everything progressive, everything American," and a "catholic element . . . which is as broad and tolerant and truth-loving and patriotic as any that can be found" in any religion in America.[104] When in 1896 the unexpected removal of Bishop Keane from the rectorship of the Catholic University startled the public, secular newspapers flatly asserted that the American Church was polarized into the conservatives, and the Gibbons-Ireland-Keane group, which was variously described as "liberal," "Americanist," "modern," and "progressive." [105] All the adjectives pointed to a common rationale — the desire to foster a more harmonious relationship between Catholicism and secular culture.

V

The strength of the liberal party was always debatable. In most controversies of the late nineteenth century, the liberals could count on at least a majority of the archbishops — Gibbons of Baltimore, Ireland of St. Paul, Kenrick (later Kain) of St. Louis, Feehan of Chicago, Gross of Oregon City, and Riordan of San Francisco. In all likelihood, on the other hand, a majority of the laymen, of the lower clergy, and of the bishops preferred tradition to innovation, polemics to apologetics. Despite the manifest popularity of the liberals with the non-Catholic world, therefore, they would have been overborne in most trials of strength had they not received surprisingly strong backing from Rome.

In 1878, Pius IX had finally died. Even with the new powers he had won for the papacy, and the intenser devotion he had promoted among some Catholics, the Church did not seem to be prospering. Victor Emmanuel's Italy was firmly entrenched in Rome, Bismarck was mounting a formidable assault on German Catholicism, and France was governed by the very secular ministries of the Third Republic. Many Catholic intellectuals were extremely anxious to respond to the new rationalisms with something more effective than the anathemas of the Vatican Council. Other Catholic leaders thought they could forestall the rising tide of socialism if the Church would squarely endorse programs for Christianizing the social order. Interests and events of this type could of course be proudly ignored by the most fervent ultramontanists, but many of the cardinals, especially those from outside Italy, were hopeful of electing a pope who, without detracting from the new devotion and centralization of the Church, would evolve more subtle strategies than those Pius IX had fallen back upon in 1848. With the more intransigent cardinals disagreeing among themselves, this group quickly elected Cardinal Pecci of Perugia, who took office as Leo XIII.[106]

A member of the minor Italian nobility, he had attended the Academy for Ecclesiastical Nobles, where he was prepared for a career as a diplomat of the Church. As nuncio to Belgium, he distinguished himself for his facility and charm in dealing with a country experimenting with "liberal" church-state relations. Later, as Cardinal-bishop of Perugia, he encouraged his seminarians to become familiar with the most advanced secular studies, not just for apologetic purposes, but to train their own minds. No churchman, he believed, should, from an excess of piety, cut himself off from "all that is beautiful and useful in today's progress"; clearly the cardinal had little sympathy with the extremist interpretations of the Syllabus of Errors. Because he recognized the need for reform in the administration of the Papal States, he was critical of Pius IX's defense of the status quo. When the papal territories were finally overrun by Piedmont, he insisted on "the duties of urbanity" in treating with the new national government.[107]

These same characteristics were obvious in the Pope. He established diplomatic relations with every country that would receive a mission, and negotiated from explicit ententes, rather than from an avowed moral leadership, which, too often in the past, had been rudely ignored. He proved remarkably willing to sacrifice the absolutist demands of Catholic minorities in many countries in order to promote friendly relations between Rome and non-Catholic rulers. The Center Party in Germany was ordered to moderate its opposition to Bismarck's armament program; Polish Catholics were required to compromise their demands in return for tsarist approval of a papal mission at St. Petersburg; and the Irish were told to forego the stringent Plan of Campaign, at least in part because of the request of Lord Errington, British representative at the Vatican.[108] Leo's success in gaining the trust of the secular governments of Europe was pronounced, even though he received little assistance in his quest for the restoration of the Temporal Power; before the end of his papacy, he had been asked to settle at least five international controversies.[109]

Though Leo was both more diplomatic and more successful than his predecessor in dealings with the states of Europe, he shared Pius IX's antipathy to Revolutionary Liberalism. And his violent aversion to the secret societies was paralleled by his inability to understand the constructive role ordinary citizens could play in shaping public opinion and in controlling democratic government by legal means. Willing on occasion to approve republican governments, he persisted in visualizing the democratic process as a technique for registering the consent of the "ruled" to the decisions of the "rulers." On relations between the secular and the spiritual authorities, however, he was far less traditional; instead of pronouncing anathemas on every advance in governmental power, he attempted to define, in a series of lucid encyclicals, the just prerogatives of state as well as Church, and the principles by which "concord" could be maintained between them.[110]

This judicious spirit informed his unprecedented attempt to arouse both state and Church to the urgency of the "social problem." He regularly warned the faithful that doctrinaire socialism would result in economic injustice and political tyranny. But in 1891 he also gave impetus to the mission begun by Ozanam and von Ketteler by promulgating the encyclical "On the Condition of Labor," in which he asserted that the Church "is not so preoccupied with the spiritual concerns of her children as to neglect their earthly, temporal interests." Sanctioning state intervention to meet certain economic problems, and recommending independent workers' organizations, he enjoined every priest to labor for social betterment, throwing "into the conflict all the energy of his mind, and all the strength of his endurance." [111]

Leo also called for a revival of scholastic philosophy. Explicitly warning Catholic thinkers against uncritical adoption of every conclusion cherished by the thirteenth century, he nevertheless maintained that Thomism provided the soundest basis for securing Catholic thought against the pervasive contemporary neo-Kantianism. It was Leo's fond hope that, with the age's intellectual doubts removed, Catholicism and culture might develop as profitable an interaction as had marked the century of Albertus Magnus and Thomas Aquinas.

Never before had a pope issued such a volume of teaching, but it is by no means certain, or even likely, that Leo intended all of it to be regarded as infallible pronouncement. As a cardinal, he had emphasized the desirability of leaving as much freedom as possible to intellectuals and men of affairs. "Practice is a necessary coefficient," he had written, "born of the exact knowledge of real needs. . . . Certain questions should, therefore, be solved in the domain of facts, case by case, by those who are chiefly concerned." Much should be left to "time and experience." [112] Conservatives could rejoice in the volume of authoritative teaching that emanated from Rome; liberals could consider the encyclicals more as general guides and incitations to further study than as strict demands upon the assent of all believers. In part the beneficiary, in part the cause of the increased respect in which the Church was held in America, Leo enjoyed among all classes there a popularity unrivaled by that of any previous pope.[113] Protestant leaders were gratified by the charity which led Leo to refer to Protestants as "our brothers separated from us," and by his restraint in dogmatic pronouncements.[114] Conservatives, who "a quarter of a century ago," Father Henry Brann recalled, "looked upon the Pope as a spook with which to scare children and Puritans, now consider him the champion of the rights of property." [115] Some of the more liberal pointed to his espousal of the interests of the working class as evidence that he understood the age, and was moving the Church to coöperate with it. Henry George, who had clashed with the Pope over the definition of private property, admitted in 1893 that his admiration had "reached the highest point." [116] An Ohio lawyer declared in court that he wished to cite Leo "as an authority" on public school questions; "I say we have in the present Pope a great, enlightened, and liberal mind," he declared.[117] Leo became an "idol" with the American press, who, recognizing his popularity, provided many stories on his personality, tastes, and responsibilities. Even his Latin verse was regularly printed in metropolitan papers. At his death, the Associated Press ordered its staff members to omit nothing which would do him honor.[118]

This popularity of the Pope was of course gratifying to American Catholics, but they were also deeply concerned with the congruence of his policies with their own needs. The conservatives, who had gloried in the ultramontanist program of Pius IX, asserted that a change of popes would not affect the Church's policy towards the age; and they pointed happily to many conservative statements in Leo's teachings as proof.[119] Privately, the irreconcilable James McMaster freely expressed his dislike for Leo's "worldly" interests and principles.[120]

To the liberals, such reservations were the voices of the past, the work of men, Archbishop Ireland proclaimed, "whose sickly nerves suffer from the vibrations of the ship moving under his hand with accelerated velocity; reactionaries, who think that all the wisdom and all the providential guidance of . . . the Church are with the past." [121] For it rapidly became a tenet of the liberal faith that just as God had rendered the American scene increasingly favorable to the spread of Catholicism, so He had given the Church a Pope who would work determinedly to realize that growth. Isaac Hecker maintained that Pius IX had been forced to use strongly authoritarian measures to save the Church and Christian society from the abyss; Leo XIII, on the other hand, had been given "the more consoling mission of pointing out to the world the good tendencies of the age, interpreting its truths and virtues in that light which will make the way clear to society of a loftier and better future." [122]

Bishop Keane prepared a lecture on "The Providential Mission of Leo XIII," which he delivered to many American audiences, and which was reprinted by the Propaganda in Rome. [123] Keane hailed the movement Leo was leading towards rapprochement with the people and conciliation with the secular states. And, while other popes had thought of America as a refuge from worse injustice elsewhere, Keane asserted that Leo "recognizes in our country the furthest advance yet attained by the true spirit of our era." [124] The liberals were proud that the Pope had commended the example of their Church to Catholics of France and Brazil. [125] It seemed to them that the Pope would be a sure ally against those at home or abroad who denigrated the main developments of American life, or the establishment of good relations with American culture. In a letter to Cardinal Gibbons from Rome in June, 1892, Archbishop Ireland gloried in this assumed alliance: "the Pope has decided that bishops must be in touch with their country. There is, he said to me, otherwise no hope for the Church. He is determined to put down 'intransigents,' reactionaries, and men of backward movements. To his mind, Corrigan is a prince of such men." [126]

At times, the liberals had to admit that Leo was not singleminded in his "Americanism," but their devotion to him never significantly lessened. Hecker, in 1888, noted that Leo's encyclical on liberty seemed to some Americans excessively concerned with refuting claims of unqualified individual liberty. Critics should remember, Hecker insisted, that the Pope was writing primarily for people of an "eastern" mentality, whether in Europe or America, and certainly intended no strictures on truly American ideas of liberty. [127] And when, in 1896, Leo removed Bishop Keane from the Catholic University, the liberals preserved their putative alliance with the Pope by arguing that he had been the victim of malicious advice.[128] Though still convinced that Leo represented the "better element" in Rome, they were less sure in the late nineties that the unreconstructed conservatives would not return to power after his death. "He has still a great work to consummate," the *Catholic World* announced in 1897. "A few more years will round out his providential mission. May God grant them to him!" "May Leo's spirit long dominate in the Vatican!" said Archbishop Ireland. "All will then be well." [129]

However deep and persistent Leo's allegiance to the Americanists was in fact, the widespread conviction that they had a powerful ally in the Pope served as a profound dynamic to bold and forthright action. Gibbons and Ireland regularly took their troubling problems to Rome with as much confidence as Veuillot or Ward would have appealed to Pius IX. But the Americans did not go as ultramontanes; their loyalty was to Leo and to Leo's policies, and they did not idealize the centralized authoritarian decision as an escape from personal or national choice. They were unenthusiastic at the prospect of having a papal delegate in America, and received him well only while he supported their own policies. Their gloom at the imminence of Leo's death revealed how little they were true ultramontanes.

But in 1890, such reservations were not prominent in their minds. Conscious that the majority of Catholics in America were indifferent if not actively hostile to their program, the liberals rejoiced in the existence of a pope who would endorse their efforts. It was with enthusiastic confidence that they set out on their twin tasks: "making America Catholic," and solving the political, social, and economic problems of the age for the benefit of the world and the glory of the Church.

CHAPTER III

THE CHURCH AND AMERICAN
PROTESTANTISM

On no point were the liberal and conservative factions within American Catholicism more at odds than on the proper policy for the Church to adopt towards Protestantism. To the European ultramontane, Protestants unquestionably were leagued with Masons, Jews, and infidels in a war to the death against the Church. At the Vatican Council, Bishop Strossmayer had been denounced as a Luther or a Lucifer for insisting on the good faith and good character of many non-Catholics.[1]

Conservative Catholics in America for years had entertained similar suspicions. Immigrants rationalized lack of worldly success and inability to revenge social and economic slights with the cheerful knowledge that the prosperous Protestants were doomed to an eternity of hellfire.[2] Theologians found Protestantism permeated with damnable errors. John Fitzpatrick, Bishop of Boston from 1846 to 1866, was so sure that Isaac Hecker could not possibly have shed all the errors of his religiously radical past that the young man had to go to a New York bishop to be admitted into the Church.[3] Churchmen who enjoyed good relations with Protestant neighbors were suspected of unsound views, or at best a misguided charity; "Protestant priests," John Hughes, the uncompromising archbishop of New York called them.[4]

If in the last decades of the century American Protestantism was really changing, it was only descending from faulty Christianity to pagan naturalism. Bishop McQuaid noted bitterly that Gardiner Spring, a New York Presbyterian, had said years earlier that he preferred the infidelity of Voltaire to the corruptions of Catholicism; "his co-religionists," the bishop wrote in 1883, "are heirs of his preference with a vengeance." [5] Nor were the conservatives deluded by protestations of friendship. Father Augustine Thébaud, a French Jesuit missionary to America since 1838, admitted that in 1880 "a far greater number of liberal Protestants . . . profess to be friendly to Catholics, hold intercourse with them and with their priests, and seem to be ready to render any service in their power." But Thébaud was convinced that Protestants were in fact "as prejudiced against us as their Puritan ancestors. . . . There is always among them a lurking fear of Catholics. . . . Exceptions . . . are so few and insignificant that they do not deserve to be mentioned." [6] Thomas Preston suspected that even the sincerely well-meaning Protestants were "often the dupes of the one great enemy of religion and society. The adversary of man, who is wiser than those whom he deceives, binds them in various ways" to work against the Church.[7]

On the other hand, Patrick Corrigan, a liberal priest from Hoboken, New Jersey, asserted that the blind prejudice of the past no longer existed, and that "the very sects that thirty years ago were most bitterly opposed to [the Church], and that laughed at and despised her so-called pretensions, are today loud in their praises of her." [8] The liberals happily compared American Protestants with the "nominal Catholics" and irreverent atheists of Europe, and attributed much of the anti-Catholicism that still flourished in America to recent immigrants.[9] To conservatives who pointed to the appearance in the 1890's of the American Protective Association as proof of Protestant hostility, Archbishop Ireland retorted that "you are making too much about that opposition. I know the American people from the Atlantic to the Pacific, and I trust them. Religious feeling is a foreign importation, and must soon die. It cannot live here." [10] By 1895, the Paulist Father Walter Elliott was jubilantly arguing that the A.P.A. had actually helped the Church. "For if they have turned the stupid for a moment against us," he wrote, "they have helped the intelligent to understand us, and have already caused many conversions to the Catholic faith. Would that it were as easy to pray for all our enemies as for the A.P.A.'s!"[11]

So far as antagonisms were not attributable to foreign influence, Cardinal Gibbons was inclined to dismiss them as wholly "traditional," the unfortunate legacy of centuries of false rumors and misunderstandings.[12] At the Catholic Congress of 1893, Archbishop Patrick Ryan of Philadelphia asserted that if the sins attributed to the Church really existed, Catholics would revile them as strenuously as any Protestant. "Many that are called bigots hate the Church simply because they hate tyranny, because they hate hypocrisy, because they hate a number of things which they imagine are in the Catholic Church." Until Protestants learned the truth about the Church Ryan thought that they were morally right in remaining outside.[13] Bishop Spalding publicly stated that he did not doubt the good intentions of the noisily anticlerical Robert Ingersoll.[14]

The liberals were glad to testify to the positive virtues of their Protestant neighbors. Gibbons denied the canard that Americans cared for nothing but money by pointing to the immense amounts Protestants contributed to church work.[15] For Catholics to consider themselves *"the only honest people* is to be guilty of the most contemptible kind of pharisaism," one liberal argued; and Father Elliott lost patience with "immigrant Catholics" who distorted the virtues and questioned the motives of the "native people."

Their American neighbors are temperate? It is from fanaticism. Are they anxious for a day of quiet and religion? It is because they are bigoted. Are they thrifty, neat, and respectable? It is mere stinginess. Are they self-poised, independent? They are revolutionists and anarchists. Are they determined to enforce the law against beer-gardens and rioters? They are tyrants![16]

Archbishop Ireland steadily maintained that the Protestants had "splendid natural virtues," and, in 1913, gave as his "verdict" after "fifty years of public and private commingling," that there were no people on earth more imbued with civic justice and brotherly tolerance than the American people.[17]

The liberals were anxious to show that the great American heroes were close in spirit to Catholicism. A reviewer noted that Franklin, "like many infidels who have been brought up Protestants," was "good-natured, tolerant, and mannerly." Unbenefited by religious instruction, Franklin and Lincoln were led by "the vigorous action of their minds" to virtual paganism, yet in maturity acquired by themselves many vital religious truths.[18] At the death of Frances Willard, the *Catholic World* paid tribute to her as "a woman without a particle of narrow-mindedness in her intellectual make-up, and with a soul which elevated her to very high plane of womanly virtue. [Had she been a Catholic], she would have ranked along with some of the great women to whose name we prefix Saint."[19] While conservative Catholics were enjoining the faithful to beware of even those Protestants most friendly to the Church, Bishop Spalding used the same generous phrase as had Montalembert: "the vast multitude of those outside the Church here are not against us, and are therefore for us."[20]

II

American Protestants might be admirable fellow citizens, but they espoused false religious beliefs. Yet even as the liberals insisted that full truth could be found only in the Catholic Church, they were also proclaiming that most non-Catholics consciously or unconsciously possessed partial truths that might well prove the basis for complete enlightenment. The layman Richard Clarke concluded from his study of history that the sects cherished "some particulars of true religion, [and] have proved themselves nurseries and promoters of some beautiful features of Christian truth." He praised the Episcopalians for their love of antiquity, the Presbyterians for their respect for ecclesiastical authority, and the Methodists for their emphasis on the personality of God and of the Savior; the Puritans rightly hated Erastianism and idolatry, and the Evangelicals rejected false formalism.[21] Father McGlynn testified that Henry Ward Beecher had taught him a deeper understanding of the fatherhood of God and the brotherhood of man.[22] The Sulpician Father John Hogan wanted all priests to know that "no writer has felt more deeply or expressed more happily the transcendent human beauty of our Lord than the great Unitarian, Dr. Channing."[23]

The liberals expected most conversions from those Protestants already in revolt against some of the false ideals of the sects. Himself once a "seeker," Hecker was convinced that masses of non-Catholics were following the road he had traveled to a state of purely natural religion. Unlike the conservatives, who saw this process as a gradual abandonment of what little religious principle Protestants had ever had, Hecker hailed it as an excellent preparation for the acceptance of full Catholicism.[24]

The liberals were especially pleased when characteristic Reformation doctrines were rejected outright. At last, Hecker thought, Americans had realized that doctrines of human inability were incompatible with the political principles and with daily experience in this sunny land, and so were abandoning a theology which posited a "slave will." The liberals were indignant with any Protestant or Catholic who impeded this happy process. The Paulist Father Henry Wyman denounced Augustus Strong of Rochester Theological Seminary for subordinating God's love to His absolute sovereignty. "Happily," Wyman noted, "the present trend of evangelical theory is in an opposite direction." In what was probably a jibe at Bishop McQuaid as well as at Strong, Wyman concluded, "Enough of this Rochester pessimism." [25]

Hewit was anxious to discredit those Thomists who confused the nature of freedom by distinguishing between men irrevocably predestined to eternal glory, and those merely granted the freedom either to be saved or to be damned. Unlike the genuine Thomism, which, Hewit argued, emphasized the "great doctrines of the universal love of God to his creatures," this perverted view tended to preserve the ancient errors of Calvinistic determinism.[26]

As Protestants continued to shed their errors, and began to call, however uncertainly, for a "coming catholicism," the liberals found it impossible to deny that many non-Catholics deserved to win salvation. Whoever made such an admission was immediately obliged to show how it could be reconciled with the central dogma that out of the Church there was no salvation.

European ultramontanes, suspecting that all who were not in the Church were deeply hostile to it, had sought, unsuccessfully, to have the Vatican Council establish a most rigorous interpretation of the formula.[27] American intransigents like Brownson and Preston regularly argued that to teach any modification was to offer false security to Protestants, and, more important, to shake Catholic loyalty by suggesting that the Church was not the unique road to salvation.[28] In this spirit Peter Manns, a Jesuit parish priest, declared that he would "die . . . before he would qualify or modify" the commonsense implication of the dogma.[29]

The bulk of immigrant Catholics did not desire their clergy to make nice distinctions; as one Paulist remarked, the general attitude seemed to be that "Protestantism, as a system, deserves all the knocks it gets, and if Protestants do not like the blows, they had better get out of the system." [30] A voluble spokesman for this point of view was the Redemptorist Father Michael Mueller, who published in 1886 *The Catholic Dogma: Out of the Church there is no Salvation*. His purpose was to refute "those soft, weak, timid, liberalizing Catholics, who labor to explain away all the points of Catholic faith offensive to non-Catholics, and to make it appear there is no question of life and death, of heaven and hell, involved in the difference between us and Protestants." [31]

The liberals had, as Mueller charged, always handled this doctrine with great restraint. The layman John Reily of West Virginia was pleased that many priests taught the dogma in such a qualified form as "to mean anything else but what the words literally imply." [32] Those Paulists who were converts and felt the continuity of their religious aspirations resented any implication that in their Protestant days they had been beyond the pale of salvation. When Hecker became a Catholic, he said to himself, "Look here, Hecker, if anyone says he is an older Catholic than you, just knock him down. Why I had been a Catholic in heart all my life, and didn't know it!" [33] The Paulists thought that Mueller's essay wrongly gave a "very sombre aspect" to Catholicism, and felt it might alienate prospective converts by its lack of charity.[34]

Catholic theologians had long taught that an individual might belong to the "soul" of the Church without becoming a visible member. But conservatives maintained that to expect that this would apply to many men was to indulge in "Quakerism, transcendentalism, sentimentalism." [35] Even if the conservatives were wrong, the liberals had to show why men who missed daily opportunities to join the true Church deserved to belong to the "soul." Their answer was the doctrine of invincible, and therefore inculpable, ignorance. As Father Elliott stated the principle, in the course of a scathing review of Mueller's book: it is possible for Catholics to believe that "anyone, assisted by divine grace . . . in inculpable ignorance [of the claims of the Catholic Church], 'who fears God and lives up to his conscience,' as Father Mueller says, is now . . . in a state of grace." [36] Of course, if an individual, from sloth or from the fear that knowledge might lead to inconvenient obligations, willfully rejected any opportunity of dispelling his ignorance, he became culpable.[37] But incidents that were subjectively compelling for one man might not start another out of his ignorance. One Paulist testified that as a Protestant he had read much Catholic controversial literature, and had attended Catholic services, without either gaining the incentive to join the Church, or, in his judgment, becoming culpable.[38] In Mueller's opinion, a Protestant who overlooked such opportunities was willfully obstinate and deserved damnation.[39]

Mueller also attempted to rob invincible ignorance of its importance for those who, by some fortune, had maintained it. A few such men might by honesty and diligence live up to their consciences, and those God would reward by sending an angel to "instruct them in the Catholic faith, rather than let them perish through inculpable ignorance." Without such supernatural aid, men would eventually sin, and so be lost. By worshipping in false churches they are "wounded by sacrilege, a most grievous sin; are destitute of charity, which cannot be kept *out of the unity of the Church*, and without which they are nothing." They make a "liar" out of Christ by disobeying His "laws" on divorce and maintaining a married clergy. They sin against His charity in their cruel treatment of Catholics in Europe and America.[40]

The Paulists made short work of Mueller's cavils. Elliott maintained that the whole meaning of invincible ignorance was that men who in good faith failed to join the Church could not be guilty of the formal sins of heresy, schism, and sacrilege; they could not be charged to perform acts only possible in the Church; they could not be held guilty of mortal sin except for personal sins which they did not repent. Mueller had argued that even if Protestants had received grace at baptism and had repented all personal sins, "something more" was still needed for salvation. "What is that 'something more,' " Elliott asked, "which is necessary to put a person who *was once* in a state of grace and is excused from sin into a state of grace *now*? The answer is, nothing whatsoever." [41] As long as a man's faith involved, in the Paulist Father Alfred Young's words, a "spiritual sacrifice of self-authority" to a higher power, "that man is a Catholic in the sight of God, and of. . . the Church, no matter what he calls himself, and though such a one die piously as an Episcopalian, Methodist, Baptist, or whatnot, St. Peter will let him into heaven as a Catholic." [42]

The controversy between Mueller and the Paulists was bound to end inconclusively, as the participants were less interested in clarifying a theological tradition than in expounding their radically contrasting estimates of the religious character of non-Catholics. Mueller wanted to strip all Protestants "of all Christian pretensions, to deprive them of their prestige and the power of seduction . . . by showing them up in their utter nakedness as downright infidels." [43] Young thought many of them "quite indistinguishable (spiritually) from ourselves, so far as to deserve the name of 'true Catholics.' " [44] The liberals had no intention of encouraging Protestant complacency. But they feared that many potential converts would be lost to the Church if asked to believe that all their Protestant relatives and friends were consigned, regardless of knowledge or intention, to everlasting damnation.

III

Neither liberals nor conservatives could be sure how many converts were entering the Church at this time. Accounts of mass confirmations were proudly published, and the *Catholic World* assured its readers that these "stand for a much larger class whose admission to the Church has not been made public." [45] Cardinal Gibbons estimated that the Church was making at least 30,000 converts a year. Denigrators maintained with equal assurance that the vaunted flow was only a trickle.[46] All American Catholics, however, agreed that there had been and would be no mass conversions of a whole sect or a whole nation such as had occurred as late as the sixteenth century. The liberals had some sympathy with Anglican proposals for corporate reunion, and they hoped for the best from the drive for church unity among American Protestants. "Our faith compels us to be more deeply interested . . . than non-Catholics can imagine," Father Wyman wrote. "When we see the great unity movement in which so many non-Catholics are engaged, the way seems to us to be opening up for the truth to win a great victory." [47] But true unity would be achieved only in Roman Catholicism, and even the most friendly Paulist insisted that it was the responsibility of each individual to make the transition himself; to come in any other way would not be worthy of a free, intelligent American.[48]

To Catholics, conversion means the profession of faith, by a former nonbeliever, in the supernatural authority of the Church as the authorized representative of God in all matters concerning salvation. Because conservatives were convinced that the average non-Catholic possessed little religious truth, did not respect the supernatural, and was determined to attack the Church rather than obey it, they visualized conversion as a dramatic, intense remaking of a man's whole life, a spiritual death and transfiguration. When a man finally became aware of his desperate need of the Church, he would expect and desire truths in sharp contrast with everything he had believed before. A man would enter the Church because it offered unity instead of pluralism, absolute dogma instead of an unqualified liberty of opinion, a deep devotionalism instead of an arid rationalism. Only a feckless "mamby-pambyism" led Catholics to offer the potential convert truths analogous to what he was discontented with.[49]

In fact, conservatives did not believe that human efforts were often very effectual in bringing about a conversion. John Gilmary Shea, the able historian of the unhappy early years of the American Church, had little faith that the non-Catholic soul could ever be reached by written or spoken argument.[50] Father Thébaud concluded that even when the mind of converts "began to be convinced, their heart remained as firm as ever in its opposition"; when conversion finally came, "they could not explain [it] except as a free gift from Heaven of which secondary causes had been only blind instruments." [51] The best way for Catholics to discharge their obligations towards the benighted was to seek God's mercy through prayer. Father F. G. Lentz of Bement, Illinois organized an apostolate of prayer, sending prayer cards to Catholics with a promise to say twenty-four masses a year for all those who said a daily prayer for the conversion of America. "Let us reckon with ourselves," Lentz wrote, "and with the strength of giants, because of our belief, besiege the throne of grace, storm heaven with our humble petitions

. . . until we have won for our separated brethren . . . the inestimable favor of Divine Faith." [52] Most conservatives believed that little else could or should be done. They asked the laity to remember that "it is by turning our energies inward, and perfecting ourselves as a body, that we shall actually and most effectively exercise our apostolate to the world at large." The safety of the believers came first, and the clergy's first responsibility was to the flock within the fold rather than to the wolves without.[53] Unquestionably, these policies were deeply satisfying to immigrant groups anxious to preserve their spiritual monopoly. Men, furthermore, who were Catholics because all their ancestors and all their neighbors had been, could not help being skeptical about the sincerity of a convert. One newcomer reported that the general Catholic response to his application for admission was the question, "I wonder what he is up to." [54]

The liberals anxiously sought converts to vindicate their estimate of the redeemability of American culture as a whole, to strengthen the Church, and, most of all of course, to improve men's chances of saving their souls. Because liberal leaders were convinced of the worth of non-Catholic churches, they did not regard their work as a crusade against infidels or satanists, but rather as the natural corollary of America's religious pluralism. A Church which believed itself the surest road to heaven, let alone the only divinely commissioned one, could hardly do otherwise.

A Protestant did not need to go through a tumultuous religious experience to become a Catholic, the liberals thought. Converts, invited to relate their experiences in the *Catholic World*, frequently emphasized that they had been able to retain all their deepest preconvictions. Conversion had meant simply making "integral and complete" truths previously held; it was like the addition of hoops to the barrel staves one already possessed.[55] One would-be convert was assured by Bishop Spalding that no "spiritual convulsions" were "required to fit me to become a Catholic." [56] Father Young testified from his own experience that "to the carnal eye" the barrier between Protestants and the Catholic Church "appears as an impenetrable wall of granite." But to the "spiritual eye" it revealed itself as nothing more than "a sheet of painted paper." He was sure that a Protestant, encouraged by members of the Church and fortified by God's grace, would pass through quickly and "without a scratch" to indicate that the transit had cost "perceptible effort" or involved even the "consciousness . . . of the existence of an obstacle overcome." No "blind, unreasoning plunge," no dying to one's past was necessary.[57]

The liberals were sure that most converts were not anxious their whole previous life be repudiated. No man, Bishop Keane insisted, is likely to take even the shortest step in your direction "if you begin by asserting there is no common standing-ground between you. To tell him he is simply an outside barbarian, is to tell him to give up all hope of understanding your language or accepting your position."[58] The *Catholic World* disliked the proneness of William George Ward to "silence and confound" his opponents, rather than to "persuade and attract" them. Not finding him "a very attractive personality," the journal added that "we do not remember to have heard that he made any converts to the faith."[59] The absolutist psychology, Father Elliott wrote, was close to the Calvinist principle of telling the unbeliever he was totally depraved; the most this would produce, he thought, was pride in the speaker, and hatred in the listener. It was only elementary good sense to begin by treating the non-Catholic with the respect to which his partial knowledge entitled him.[60]

The liberals were confident that human actions could hasten this straightforward conversion process. "It is the day of the convert," a writer in the *Catholic World* proclaimed. "How to make one, how to develop him when made, then how to make more converts — these, it would seem, will presently be the questions most discussed in the Catholic press."[61] Such men did not consider their responsibilities terminated once they had joined in the apostolates of prayer.[62] "Prayer is necessary to get conversions," Major Henry Brownson, a prominent Detroit layman, told the Catholic Congress of 1889, "but its effect is to gain assistance in our efforts, not to render effort unnecessary. . . . The world has never yet been converted by prayer alone, and it is not likely that it ever will be."[63] Archbishop Ireland was even more energetic; "let there be no room among us," he thundered, "for the lackadaisical piety which lazily awaits a zephyr from the sky, the bearer of efficacious grace, while God's grace is at hand entreating to be made efficacious by our own cooperation."

He called on every American Catholic to work hard to promote conversions, and he warned of certain failure "if we are on our knees when we should be fleet of foot, if we are in the sanctuary when we should be in the highways and the market places." [64] Two years later, he told Catholics to "blame yourselves" if converts did not swarm into the Church.[65] To the age-old charge that such activism implied an excessive faith in the works of both converters and converted, Spalding, in a sermon before the Third Plenary Council of Baltimore, responded that "in our day it is easier to go astray in the direction of self-annihilation than in that of self-assertion." [66]

The liberals urged all Catholics to join in the work. To hold back from fear of contaminating the Church by contact with an alien age was to luxuriate in one's faith, as if it were "exclusive property," and to perpetuate, without reason, the "spirit of defense," and the "sensation of exile." Walter Elliott insisted that such an attitude "decatholicized" men. "A Catholic without a mission to his non-Catholic fellow-citizens in these times . . . is only a half-Catholic." He is "a clod; he is unworthy of the name of man." [67] Father Lentz, who in 1893 had wished to concentrate on prayer alone, by 1896 was eager to promote more active missions. Charity demanded them. Furthermore, they would invigorate the Church. "It was not reticence and reserve that revivified the fibre of the Church in the sixteenth century," he wrote, "but the spirit of missionary activity." [68]

It was extremely important, the liberals believed, that potential converts be confronted with Catholic doctrines and practices only in purest form, stripped of the personal, local, and racial accretions which too often were mistaken by Protestant and Catholic alike for the essence of the faith. "It is astonishing," Father Elliott wrote, "how much more liberal the Catholic Church is than Catholic people. . . . The highest encomium that can be passed on a man is to say that he is as broad as the doctrines the Catholic Church teaches." [69] While the Church benignly condoned the extravagant devotional spirit and the elaborate protestations of unqualified obedience which played a great part in the religious life of some of the "immigrant" faithful, no Protestant should be required to accept these "luxuries" as proof of his full Catholicism.[70] Hecker believed that a false emphasis on the authoritarian nature of the Church was more responsible for Protestant opposition than all its other characteristics, real or alleged.[71]

An argument that carried conviction for one convert might well estrange another. The traditional argument from history and reason for the claims of the Church of Rome aroused in many Americans, the liberals believed, an instinctive resistance because of its implied attack on the claims of all other churches. Furthermore, many were neither willing nor able to follow the process of rational dialectic.[72] It had been a disaster for the American Church, Hecker argued, when Brownson had been persuaded to draw his apologetic technique "not from his own life's experience, nor from his own knowledge, intricate and perfect, of his fellow-countrymen, but from books, and from schools, and from human and passing controversial tradition," all of which enjoined on him the historico-logical method.[73]

Objections against rational dialectic were elaborated in the later years of the century in Europe, with some liberal Catholics calling for a "new apologetic," which depended heavily on Kantian philosophy, and virtually denied that the demonstration of the Church's uniqueness could claim objective certainty.[74] American liberals did not go so far; Hecker denounced subjectivism as the root of modern philosophic error, and he accepted the sufficiency of the traditional argument when, but only when, the mind was prepared for its conclusions.[75] He himself had first been disposed to accept the claims of the Church by learning of its moral services to mankind; then "I was ripe for the historical argument . . . [and] it poured its evidence into my mind without the least resistance."[76] The liberals were not prepared to demand that conviction come completely at any given time; Elliott cautioned apologists not to grow disgusted with "half-converts."[77] The sympathetic Catholic should be willing to demonstrate the virtues and claims of the Church over an extended period, and in any of several different ways.

IV

The liberals did not, overnight, convert their fellows to the task of converting non-Catholics by direct missions. The Paulists considered employing laymen as religious lecturers, and they urged newspapermen to lose no opportunity to enlighten their readers about the Church. But even in the most sanguine moments, the *Catholic World* recognized that the laity could not be expected to assume primary responsibility for the apostolate.[78] The secular clergymen were most familiar with non-Catholics, but so urgent was the demand for parish services that most priests spared little time for missions to the gentiles, and not until 1894 was a single priest assigned to full-time home missionary work.[79] In 1904, the Paulists helped establish a house at the Catholic University to give special training to priests for tours of such duty.[80]

Meanwhile, the Paulists continued with their own extraordinary labors. Father Elliott began a series of mission tours through Middle Western small towns. Convinced that few Protestants would attend formal Catholic services, and fearing that those who did would simply be confused by the liturgy, he held a series of meetings in public halls on questions of general interest, such as temperance, and the obligations of citizenship, as well as on the teachings of the Church. Leaflets were widely distributed promising "NO CONTROVERSY! NO ABUSE! ADMISSION FREE." When Elliott was to speak on religious questions, the service began with hymns, frequently Protestant favorites like "Rock of Ages," and "Jesus, Lover of My Soul," but no liturgy was employed, and Elliott did not wear religious dress. He usually concluded his talks by answering every question asked in good faith.[81] In missions of this type, Elliott obviously hoped to reach audiences previously monopolized by lyceum lecturers and Protestant evangelists.

The Paulists also wished to bring knowledge of the Catholic Church to "the street population" which could be taught only through the kind of street preaching that previously had been the unchallenged prerogative of sectaries and the Salvation Army. Despite considerable Catholic criticism, the Paulists encouraged the few priests willing to do such work, and undertook some of it themselves, believing, as Father Alfred Young argued, that no great conversion had ever been accomplished by ministers unwilling to speak out of doors.[82]

Liberal Catholics were quick to accept invitations to speak at Protestant colleges or churches, even when the occasion required them to conduct quasi-religious exercises. Father Young explained that the Church's prohibition on participating "with heretics" in religious matters applied principally to services conducted by Protestant ministers. Bishops, he added, were allowed great discretion in deciding where to speak. Few prelates of the 1890's would go so far as had Bishop Cheverus of Boston when he conducted a whole service in an Episcopalian church, using the Book of Common Prayer; but many had told Young that "they would be only too happy (as who would not be?)" to preach in Protestant churches, and to authorize their priests to, always provided sensitive Catholics were not scandalized. Young himself had twice preached to groups in Protestant churches.[83]

A classic example of this kind of mission occurred when, on October 23, 1890, Bishop Keane came to the chapel of Harvard University at the invitation of President Charles W. Eliot to deliver one of the Dudleian lectures. As the Boston *Pilot* happily pointed out, no event could better symbolize the change in New Englanders' attitude towards the Church, "from distrust, to open-minded, if critical investigation." [84] One of Dudley's purposes for the lectures was

the detecting and convicting and exposing the idolatry of the Roman Church, their tyranny, usurpations, damnable heresies, fatal errors, abominable superstitions, and other crying wickednesses in their high places; and finally, [to show] that the Church of Rome is that mystical Babylon, that woman of sin, that apostate Church spoken of in the New Testament.[85]

Now a bishop of that very Church was invited to deliver a Dudleian lecture (though not the one dedicated to the genealogy and morals of Catholicism).

Before a large audience of professors, students, ministers, and Catholic priests, Keane read from the Bible, announced the singing of "Nearer My God to Thee" and "Rock of Ages," and delivered a lecture on "Revealed Religion." In what he both said and left unsaid, Keane was conspicuously irenic. His theme was the familiar liberal argument that since peoples throughout history had eagerly sought for religious understanding, "symmetry" argued that there was a true religion to correspond to these desires. Of all religious systems, Christianity was at once the most complete and the most consistent. Keane then turned aside from his main theme to consider contemporary threats to Christianity, but his words were extremely general, and he hastened to point out that in the United States the attempts to end the study of Christ in the schools came "not through enmity to Him, but through a mistaken theory as to the best system of education." To close his lecture, Keane had planned to detail the differences between Catholicism and "every other form of Christian belief." "May we not recognize," the conclusion was to have run, "that God did not intend mankind to be enlightened by one or another partial subdivision of Christian truth, but by the fullness of its light, as comprised in the fullness of Catholic doctrines?" Whether for brevity, or because he felt that even such a moderate statement would do more harm than good, Keane did not speak these words.[86] In fact, at no time in the whole lecture, did Keane mention Protestantism or Catholicism, or refer to the True Church.

The lecture was well received, and Harvard, in gratitude for Keane's visit and for his services as rector of the Catholic University, made him a Doctor of Laws at its commencement three years later. The liberal Father Thomas Jefferson Jenkins happily compared Keane's appearance before "the Areopagus of Harvard" with the missions of St. Paul; and the convert Father Fidelis followed Keane's example by preaching at Harvard in 1897.[87] But many conservatives were shocked at the respect for Protestantism such ventures necessarily implied. Bishop McQuaid indignantly refused to give permission to Keane to preach at Cornell University, which lay within his diocese.[88] Thomas Conaty, Keane's successor at the Catholic University, was so impressed by the strength of such sentiments that he refused an invitation to preach at Harvard.[89]

Conservative animus, however, was unable to prevent the liberals from exploiting a unique opportunity in 1893. A Parliament of Religions was summoned to meet in Chicago by a number of Protestants who, seeing the success of secular groups in holding conferences at the World's Fair, agreed that religion might be benefited by a similar assembly. Disavowing any intention of fostering religious relativism, or of striving to achieve "any formal and outward unity," the sponsors, led by J. H. Barrows, a Presbyterian minister from Chicago, sought to show "in the most impressive way, what and how many important truths the various religions hold and teach in common," and "what light each Religion has afforded, or may afford, to the other Religions of the world." [90]

Some Presbyterian groups excused themselves, and the Archbishop of Canterbury declared roundly that Christianity had nothing to learn from paganism. Gibbons, Ireland, and Keane, who had been approached as the Catholics most likely to be favorable, referred the decision to the council of American archbishops. Keane afterwards reported that while none of the prelates would ever have proposed such a parliament, and while some never warmed to the idea, the majority felt that the risk of seeming to waive Catholic claims to uniqueness was outweighed by the signal opportunity such an occasion afforded of presenting Catholic truth to genuinely concerned outsiders.[91]

At the Parliament, each religious group was given a day in which to present its teachings in any way it desired. At the Catholic meeting, presided over by Bishop Keane, liberal speakers deplored Protestant misapprehensions that a meddling, authoritarian clergy stood between a Catholic and his God. The Jesuit Father Thomas Sherman of St. Louis insisted that Catholicism enjoined every man to follow his own conscience, even in the rare cases that it directly contradicted the instructions of the Pope.[92] After the speeches, the clergy answered questions, and were gratified to find there, as in all the meetings of the Parliament, a wide and intelligent interest in the Church.[93]

The great feature of the Parliament was the series of sessions in which all the delegates gathered to hear addresses on a wide variety of theological principles and social applications. In order to avoid controversy, no public discussion interrupted the flow of prepared papers.[94] From the opening meeting, in which Cardinal Gibbons led the delegates in the Protestant version of the Lord's Prayer, through the final meeting, good will prevailed.[95] (The only untoward incident occurred when Mohammed Webb's discussion of the glories of the Moslem heaven offended the moral sensibilities of many of his listeners.) [96]

No safeguards could make the Parliament an easy forum for Catholic speakers. Although granted a very full hearing, they necessarily shared the platform with what the acidulous Bishop

McQuaid called "every pretense of religious denomination from Mohammedanism and Buddhism down to the lowest form of evangelicalism and infidelity." [97] Simply the "appearance of fellowship" between Catholic priests and such men had always seemed to the conservatives a dangerous first step towards religious liberalism.[98] But Keane, Gibbons, and the other Catholic participants believed that the friendly association so often a necessary prelude to successful apologetics could be maintained without compromising the uniqueness of Catholic truth. If their papers frequently started from a recognition of widespread human needs, they usually insisted on the uniqueness of the Church's solutions. Francis Redwood, born in Maryland, but then an archbishop from Australia, seemed to go farther in saying, "I do not pretend as a Catholic to have the whole truth. . . . I can appreciate, love, and esteem any element of truth found outside that body of truth," — words certainly ambiguous in a liberalistic assembly.[99] Gibbons, on the other hand, prefaced his remarks by asserting that, unlike the Parliament, he was not searching for religious truth, "for, by the grace of God, I am conscious that I have found it." [100] And Keane made much clearer than he had at Harvard that the true religion was fully realized only in the Catholic Church.[101]

Most of the liberals enthusiastically defended the work of the Parliament. "Nearly every sentence during those seventeen days," Bishop Keane said later, "tended to show that positive doctrinal differences which had held Christians apart during three centuries are fast being obliterated. The Parliament has been a long stride towards the much desired reunion of Christendom." [102] The *Catholic World* called the Parliament "a great love-feast of the brotherhood of man," and thought it was a clear sign of the coming golden age. Only the willfully myopic would detect an agnostic or indifferentist air, the magazine wrote. "St. Peter in the streets of Jerusalem on the day of Pentecost did not have a firmer conviction of the truths he taught, and the falsity of the religious beliefs of his hearers, than did Cardinal Gibbons when he made his presentation of the belief of the Catholic Church." [103]

As a gesture of confidence, the liberals presented Leo XIII with an extensive edition of the Parliament's proceedings.[104] Privately, they braced themselves for conservative censure. Keane wrote Denis

O'Connell, the rector of the North American College at Rome, that "all the ultra-conservatives" disliked the Parliament. "I take it for granted that I shall be denounced for it." Ireland wrote to O'Connell that he was encountering such severe criticism that he had difficulty believing "the game worth the arrogance we have to suffer." [105] But neither the Archbishop of St. Paul nor any of his liberal allies were willing to abandon their apologetic efforts.

V

The liberals were too much the children of their age to believe that the American people could be converted by even the most persistent, skillful, and generous oratorical demonstrations. "Are you going to convert the world by argument?" Ireland asked Catholics at the Columbian Congress. "By no means. Argument convinces the mind; it does not move the soul. The age, moreover, is tired of argument. The age has told us the evidence it demands, and I admire the good sense of the age. . . . We judge the tree by its fruits." [106] Conservatives had steadily called on the faithful to perfect themselves as the best means of promoting conversions. But Ireland and his allies were quick to emphasize that the virtues they wished to instill in Catholics were not those known only to one's conscience or to one's immediate community. Acts of specifically "Catholic" devotion would little affect the outside world. "How much can Protestants understand of the supernatural virtues — of the faith of Catholics . . . of their divine charity?" Walter Elliott asked his fellow priests. His answer was a challenge: "just as much as you or your people will show forth by the practice of the natural virtues"; these alone were effective "missionary virtues" in America.[107]

From the questions asked him on his missionary tours Elliott was well aware the demands American people most urgently made of the Church. Catholics would have to recognize that while they played an unsavory role in city politics, while they clogged the jails for intemperance, "Chrysostom and Bossuet, aye a Paul and Patrick could not convert men to such a Catholicity." [108] Ireland told the readers of *Ave Maria* that "by your example you preach to the country a hundred times better than we can from the altar." If non-Catholics find "in you the humble man, the true citizen, the devoted patriot, they will say that the Catholic Church brings into being an elevated good," and will have taken the first and most difficult step towards conversion.[109]

The liberal program thus came to place extraordinary responsibility upon every Catholic, lay and cleric, to present himself, and so his Church, faultless before secular society. Liberal leaders would need to be zealous in condemning not only the clear violations of the law, but also such folkways as visits to beer gardens on Sunday afternoon, and bloc voting in the cities. They would have to decide how far Catholics, in order to make their reforms both effective and visible, might share in non-Catholic unions, charitable groups, and reform organizations. They would have to provide schools that would give Catholics as good an education as any other American. There was virtually no limit to their responsibilities, so that it was no accident that the Paulists, dedicated to the religious conversion of America, became leaders of projects for Catholic reform and advocates of dynamic Catholic participation in many areas of national life, even to the point of being called by conservative critics an "order of Hustlers." [110]

CHAPTER IV

CATHOLICISM AND
A NON-CATHOLIC STATE

In theory, the appearance of the modern state required no alteration in the traditional Catholic argument that all authority flowed from God, was subject to His laws, and therefore required the superintendence or instruction of the Church.[1] It had always been necessary for the Church to decide what authority could be delegated to the secular power, what methods of control to employ, and what role the individual Catholic should play in supporting and perfecting the state. But as the state changed from being a bare preponderance of force, remote from the lives of most people, and became a monopoly of force which daily affected the lives of everyone, and as it assumed forms and adopted techniques unknown to theologians of the past, Catholics found that questions of "Church and State" constituted some of the most perplexing problems in the relationship of Christianity and culture.

Traditionalists, looking longingly back to the states of the past whose kings considered themselves the particular defenders of Catholicism, found it hard to believe that the newly declared sovereign people would respect the Church's teachings as conscientiously as would a prince religiously trained and especially consecrated.[2] Conservative suspicions deepened as nineteenth-century radicals, identifying republicanism with the drastic curtailment of the Church's influence, found an ideal of statesmanship in Cavour's attempt to construct a free state wholly separate from the Church. Like Cavour, they were willing to despoil the Church of much of its property and privilege. In bitter condemnation, Father Thébaud admitted that the modern state was not yet completely the "incarnation of Antichrist," but it was in such "a great degree ruled over by really anti-Christian ideas" that the Church and the state "are evidently now arrayed against each other and engaged in a deadly conflict." [3] The Syllabus vigorously denounced all attempts to limit the Church's control over the state.

America, as one of the first republics of the age, had always been an object of admiration for European radicals; and non-Catholic Americans proclaimed to all who would listen that the states, both federal and local, were completely separated from the control of any church. To many Catholics, the states seemed to behave that way. Immigrant groups did not need theological demonstrations to conclude that the state was no helpmate, at least to the True Church. Through favoritism to Protestant clergymen, by the enforcement of Protestant ideals of public morals, by legal restrictions on the Church's property-holding powers, by the support of "godless" public schools, it seemed as much the enemy of the Church as the governments of Francesco Crispi and Jules Ferry. "The truth is," the conservative *Church Progress* of St. Louis complained, "that in the whole world there is not a Catholic country with a non-Catholic population of any importance which does not show more respect for the conscience of the non-Catholic minority than the United States manifests for the conscience of Catholics there." [4] To American Catholics of these convictions, the censures of the Syllabus were badly needed condemnations of the political system under which they lived.

The liberal Catholics resented the innuendo that the American polity was as deeply undesirable as the laicizing states of Europe. Usually taking care not to contradict explicitly the traditional Catholic teaching, they proudly declared, nevertheless, their deepfelt satisfaction with the relations between the Church and the American "state." In their testimonials they seldom bothered to distinguish between the federal government — prohibited by the Bill of Rights from directly supporting any church — and the state governments, still theoretically free to create a full-fledged Establishment. It was in this genial spirit that Cardinal Gibbons declared "'America, with all thy faults I love thee still.'"[5] Like the other liberals he never doubted that the "state" in all its divisions was every year growing more responsive to Catholic rights and interests.

The state's unwillingness to provide direct financial aid was, the liberals devoutly believed, a blessing. The laity had responded with a generous enthusiasm that contrasted strikingly with the sullenness and outright disinterest that characterized lay activities in many "Catholic" countries. "Liberty has, indeed, its inconveniences, its dangers even," Bishop Spalding said, "but the atmosphere it creates is the native air of generous, fair, and noble souls; and where it is not, man's proper good and honor are not found."[6] All the liberals asked was a fair field and no favor. "We are content," Father Hewit wrote, "with the total separation of Church and state . . . leaving us at liberty to propagate our religion. . . . We are content that all Christian sects, Jews, and in general all associations which do not conspire against the laws, should enjoy equal liberty."[7] "None love more ardently" than do Catholics, Bishop Stephen Ryan insisted, "the freedom they enjoy; none have profited more by the liberty of conscience and equality of rights guaranteed to all."[8]

Conversely, the liberals were sure that a closer connection between church and state than existed in America inevitably harmed religion by committing its interests to the whim of political officials.[9] The filiations with the state during the Middle Ages were only "accident," Spalding wrote, not the Catholic ideal; and they had cost the Church the liberty to appoint whom it wished, at the same time that they allowed the clergy and laity to grow lax and indifferent. "The outward honor shown to the Church has generally been at the expense of her inward force," the bishop concluded.[10] Dependence on the state made the Middle Ages "a nightmare" for the Church, Father Joseph Tracy of Boston maintained; dependence today would surely have the same sad result.[11] Father McGlynn announced that he was "willing to go in for perfect, absolute union of Church and State in the Kingdom of Heaven beyond the grave, or in the communities of angelic men," but

nowhere else.[12] And Professor Thomas O'Gorman, in his history
of the American Church, noted that "if the close union of church
and state in the early Christianity of California was of some advantage to the church . . . it was also productive of some disadvantages. *It cannot be* otherwise . . . so long as human nature is what
it is."[13] The liberals rejoiced that the American Church was "free
and unshackled by concordats," which necessarily limited her "action," and cramped her "energy."[14]

In a dominantly Protestant America, it was relatively easy for
the liberal Catholics to accept the "separation of church and state." It
was a bolder step to assert, as unambiguously as they did, that closer
relations had always been harmful. Yet some of the liberals went
even further and happily forecast that when Catholics predominated
in America, the separation would be maintained. Such avowals were
highly reassuring to the many Protestants who suspected that the
Church was libertarian only when Catholics were in a minority.
Bishop Keane promised that, however much of America was
converted, so long as real disagreement on questions of social and
political morality existed, the Church was too tolerant to impose
its beliefs by coercive laws. Keane cited the Church's approval
of the charter of liberties granted in the Catholic France of Louis
XVIII, and in Catholic Belgium. And he repeated Cardinal Manning's assurances to Gladstone that, should Catholics gain controlling
political power, there would be no laws of constraint or privation
enacted against dissenters.[15] The Paulist Father Edward Brady
amplified Keane's reply. Should virtually all Americans become
Catholic, divorce would be abolished, and the Church would insist on a Christian education for Catholic children, — "(she would
not impose it upon others)." She would try to provide an honest
ballot and an upright administration of justice. But "she would
not touch a single stone in the noble fabric of our constitution —
nay, she would safeguard to the utmost of her power our free
institutions, and teach her children to be willing at any moment to
die in their defense."[16]

The liberals claimed that American Catholics had demonstrated
fine tolerance even when local conditions made it possible for them
to have acted otherwise. Richard Clarke testified that the several
Protestant boys cared for in the Catholic Protectory he managed

were respectfully escorted to a Protestant church every Sunday.[17] Cardinal Gibbons used his personal influence to prevent the city of Baltimore from suppressing an atheistical "Sunday School." And the cardinal liked to praise Lord Baltimore for voluntarily establishing religious freedom in his personal colony. His "noble stature" would "reflect unfading glory" on himself, on his state, and on his Church.[18]

The liberals regularly asserted that the Spanish Inquisition had been primarily a political institution, and that American Catholics wished one no more than did American politicians. One Catholic writer maintained that an inquisition would never reappear, because "all history is a record of progress from ignorance to knowledge, from weakness to strength, from bondage to freedom." [19] Cardinal Gibbons, claiming the backing of "every Catholic Priest and layman in the land," emphatically renounced "every species of violence" in religious affairs, and asserted that in the future, doctrinal orthodoxy would be preserved, not by physically coercive means, but by the sword of the spirit, and the fire of the love of Christ.[20]

Even such traditional methods of control as the *imprimatur* and the Index might well, the liberals suggested, be dispensed with. The *Catholic World* cited with approval an English Jesuit's opinion that, in the ideal state of the future, censorship of opinion might well be less necessary and less desirable. "The *imprimatur* might be either . . . obligatory or merely a matter of counsel to obtain it. We are not to adopt promiscuously all the praiseworthy customs of our forefathers." [21] When conservatives in Europe and America demanded that Henry George's *Progress and Poverty* be placed on the Index, the liberals were able to block the move, and their protests implied grave doubts whether such censorship was any longer a useful practice.[22] Canon William Barry, an English ally, stated flatly that the Index was an anachronism.[23]

The liberals made their professions of perpetual loyalty to the American system, serene in the conviction that America had long enjoyed far better relations between churches and the state than either Catholic ultramontanes or American secularists would acknowledge. To the saturnine John Gilmary Shea, many of the founding fathers seemed no better than "base drivelling slaves of the old anti-Catholic bigotry and fanaticism, shutting their eyes to the light and full of fiendish hatred." Even Hecker was, on occasion, less than flattering in his estimate of the religious instincts of the founding fathers.[24] But McGlynn declared firmly that it was a "calumny" to assert that the founders were "irreligious men," and Richard Clarke concluded that Washington's "relations with Catholics were friendly and intimate . . . , always just and sympathetic, characterized by . . . a particular leaning towards them." [25] Bishop Stephen Ryan wrote his clergy on the hundredth anniversary of Washington's inauguration that "when we contrast a Washington, and the illustrious founders of our great Republic — men of deep religious convictions, men of broad, liberal minds, of genuine Christian instincts . . . with the pigmy statesmen, pretended liberals, and radical revolutionaries of other lands," it became obvious why the revolution they led and the government they established were more acceptable to Catholics than anything in Europe.[26] In fact, one layman insisted, the Revolution did not seek to destroy religion, but only to eliminate religious bigotry.[27] The revolt was so certainly "providential," that Gibbons rejoiced in the mistaken notion that no Catholics served with the Tories.[28]

The "governmental spirit of the United States" from the first was not, of course, Christian in the traditional mode, and so the French Canadian Jules Tardivel intransigently concluded that it had always been "by every necessity" dominated by an "anti-Christian spirit." [29] This kind of logic disgusted the *Catholic World*. Relations between church and state were established in America by righteous men dealing wisely with existing conditions, "not by a frantic advocacy of antique methods, or of a state of things which ought to be in the abstract, or of what emotional or traditional temperaments might desire — all legitimate enough, but barred out of here by the sovereign rule" of what the *World* was frank to call "providential conditions." A great deal of "unmistakably Christian sentiment" was "infused into our institutions," the journal continued, as would be obvious to anyone who dispassionately considered the actual operations of the state today.[30]

In salient contrast to conditions in France and Italy, the Church in America could hold all the property it wished.[31] Conservatives remained indignant that civil law regulated the transfer of property titles, as if the Church could be rightfully treated as the creature or subject of the state.[32] But liberals like John Ireland concentrated on the fact that most states had dropped requirements common in mid-century that laymen of the vicinity share in Church property holding. Most bishops were now permitted to designate themselves corporations sole, and where this privilege was not available, Ireland blamed Catholics for not having made clear to the state their desire for it.[33]

Though states did not directly finance the work of the Church, some granted aid to Catholic hospitals and asylums, ostensibly on the grounds of material interest, but often in the desire to help churches in any way constitutional.[34] It was true that some Americans noisily denounced such subsidies, but a proposed amendment to the Federal Constitution "to perfect the cleavage between church and state" never mustered much popular support.[35] Protests made against tax exemption of church property were similarly ineffectual.[36]

The state deferred to the Church by recognizing her clergy as civil officials for such functions as marriage. It appointed and paid chaplains to the armed services; during the Civil War, enough Catholic chaplains had been selected to weaken the old tradition that the faith was discriminated against. The custom of asking clergymen, including Catholics on occasion, to offer prayers at important public meetings had virtually acquired the sanction of law. Most officials took a solemn oath upon the Bible before assuming office. And the proclamation of a day of thanksgiving to God impressed both Americans and foreigners; "what difference is there," a visiting French cleric asked, after reading Cleveland's declaration of Thanksgiving Day, "between this beautiful proclamation of a state leader and the decree of a Catholic bishop?" [37]

Despite these quasi-religious activities, none of the states could be deemed "Catholic," since none explicitly acknowledged the authority of the Church or carried out all its recommendations. One conservative protested that even the Christianity implicit in the common law had been eroded away by the courts; in its place, the legislatures, oblivious of their obligations to enforce the natural law, were "attempting to fabricate a crude religious and moral code, without the guidance of inspiration and influenced solely by temporary prejudice or a mistaken view of public policy." [38]

Hecker, on the other hand, was sure that the courts would continue to punish not only violations of the natural law, but also clear transgressions of revealed religious duty as crimes "against good government." [39] Cardinal Gibbons declared that statute laws were almost invariably so "intimately interwoven with the Christian religion," that the faith had nothing to fear from their application. He was confident that the common law still virtually guaranteed the Christianity of the states." [40]

By appealing to practices rather than to principles, the American liberals tried hard to mediate between the demands of a traditionalist Catholicism and those of contemporary culture. When a popular movement developed to put "God in the Constitution," Gibbons pleased ardent defenders of the separation of church and state by declaring his opposition; at the same time, he placated Catholics by stating that he was not agitated over constitutional phrases so long as the government continued to be guided in so much of its work by a manifestly Christian spirit.[41] A Paulist advised fellow Catholics to work not for union, but rather a more perfect *"entente cordiale"* between church and state.[42]

II

One of the prime justifications for the traditional church-state union was that the individual, a citizen and a Christian at the same time, would never be forced to choose between his religious duty and his patriotism. It was the responsibility of the liberal Catholics to show that at least in happy America there need be no conflicting loyalties. A Catholic could, in Archbishop Ireland's words, "go forward, in one hand bearing the book of Christian truth, and in the other the Constitution of the United States." [43]

The conservatives were apprehensive. The secular state would certainly claim the right to decide the proper limits of the Church's jurisdiction.[44] How much independent authority would be left the Church, the conservatives wondered, if the state followed the prescription of the strongly anti-Catholic lawyer, James King, who defined as "political" everything "that is not evidently and axiomatically religious and altruistic in its purpose," — that is, everything which does not pertain to an individual's "personal character and his personal relations to Christ." [45] How much would be left if every judge emulated the California Supreme Court which characterized a contention that religious obligation transcended state law as an attempt "to exalt the inferior at the expense of the superior, the protected against its protector." [46] The prospect was appalling; to the Jesuit Father Thomas Hughes, the only way for American Catholics to prevent the disastrous fruition of such ideas was to renounce as "un-Catholic" the doctrinaire belief in separation of church and state, and then acknowledge that the Church's primacy is like that of the soul to the body.[47] With that understood, the Church would be able to adjudicate conflicts on the basis of the "public ecclesiastical law," so parlously ignored by Americans in and out of the Church.[48]

According to canon law, the Church, and ultimately the Pope, exercised final authority over Catholics in all religious matters. The Church also possessed an "indirect" power over the faithful in all secular matters when they affected spiritual interests.[49] Leo XIII himself did not use this term; he was not disposed to intervene on every occasion in which temporal activities had spiritual implications; and even when intervention was necessary, he was more inclined to suggest than to command. But in *Immortale Dei*, he had reasserted the Church's unalterable right to judge when affairs of the secular order must yield to ecclesiastical superintendence.[50]

Claims to this "indirect" power invariably annoyed many non-Catholics, including Protestants who assumed much the same right for their own churches, but boggled at the idea of foreign authority.[51] William C. Doane, Episcopal Bishop of Albany, interpreted the Pope to be claiming "an absolute and infallible authority over everybody everywhere." [52] But Sebastian Messmer, a conservative professor of canon law at the Catholic University, doggedly insisted that every Catholic theologian was bound to claim for the Church "the indirect right to concern herself not only with ordinary temporal matters, but even with . . . politics . . . if her end and mission render it necessary." Because there was neither a Catholic prince nor a Catholic party to heed such interventions, Messmer admitted that the indirect power would have to be used "indirectly," — that is, through clerical instruction of individual Catholics.[53]

In fact, bishops and priests had spoken out often enough to arouse deep resentment among non-Catholics, even though no Pope had ever given advice to American voters.[54] The real danger from Catholicism, the Reverend Brooke Herford declared in 1895, was not that the Church was a disguised Babylon, but rather a disguised Tammany.[55] Bishop Doane was convinced that the Church was committed to "perpetual political interference."[56] And Senator Henry Blair of New Hampshire paid the clergy of the late nineteenth century a dubious compliment when he asserted that "priests are not, many of them, inclined to assert the political influence they once did."[57]

The gravamen of these critics' complaints was that the Catholic layman was not left as free to decide political questions as American democracy presumably required. Many believed that the Church threatened to excommunicate every layman or priest who did not follow a superior's orders. The Michigan legislature ordained that any priest who should even "advise" a layman, "under pain of religious disapproval, for the purpose of influencing" him at an election was guilty of a misdemeanor.[58] Some Massachusetts citizens attempted to block priests from using religious censures to dissuade Catholics from sending their children to public schools.[59]

The liberal Catholics, anxious to allay this antagonism to the exercise of ecclesiastical power, stressed that the direct power was actually very circumscribed. They indignantly denounced as un-Catholic the contention of the ultramontanist *Osservatore Romano* that "as the Pope is the sovereign of the Church . . . he is also the sovereign of every other society and of every other kingdom."[60] Over and over they asserted that the Pope had no authority over "purely temporal" affairs. Gibbons assured readers of the *North American Review* that the Pope would be transgressing the laws he was bound to defend, if he interfered in "purely civil matters." Catholics were bound in conscience to resist any such interference.[61]

Under the liberal rhetoric lay the assumption that temporal and religious affairs were intrinsically discrete, — that there were "two spheres" marked out by Christ when He enjoined men to "render unto Caesar the things that are Caesar's, and unto the Lord the things that are the Lord's." They rejoiced that Leo XIII frequently used this conception in his encyclicals, and they were far from sharing the Jesuit Father Hughes' suspicion that few Catholics insisted upon "two spheres" unless they were contemplating disloyalty to the Church.[62] Archbishop Ireland was confident that it was necessary to put neither "Church before Country, nor Country before Church. Church and Country work in altogether different spheres. . . . The Church is supreme in one order of things; the State is supreme in another order." [63] Similar logic enabled Spalding to declare that a Catholic's allegiance "is doubled and not divided." [64] Probably the conception of "two spheres" placated some of those non-Catholics who naively believed that a total separation of church and state existed in America, and were certain that the Catholic Church could be patriotic only if she fully accepted that separation. "It is thought," William Howard Taft wrote, that Archbishop Ireland "has solved the difficulty which sometimes presents itself to the non-Catholic mind, of complete loyalty both to the Church and to the country." [65] But the liberals, in stressing the distinctness of the "two spheres," never explicitly denied that there could be unusual circumstances that would justify the Church in exercising its indirect power over secular questions. It went almost without saying that Catholic authorities could not ignore aggressive war, a "policy of repudiation," treaty violations, or an "immoral law of contract." [66] Because America was basically moral, the liberals did not expect that Church action would be necessary on many occasions; presumably, this was their justification for not claiming the indirect power as forthrightly as did conservatives like Messmer.[67]

Whatever rhetorical advantages lay in stressing the "two spheres," the liberal Catholics could not escape the responsibility of adjudicating between the conflicting claims of churchmen and statesmen; this was no "easy task," Ireland admitted, since all too often men were too "inflamed with passion" to acknowledge that any sphere existed except one's own.[68] The *Catholic World* commended Ireland for offering wise counsel in his volume, *The Church and Modern Society*, but it ruefully admitted that "the prelate who dares to lead men upon the doubtful ground jointly occupied by church and state, is followed only by the more adventurous spirits among Catholics, the rest looking on with bated breath, some with even suspicion and worse than suspicion." [69]

III

One of the most ticklish questions facing Ireland and the other liberals was to determine how vigorously American Catholics should work for the restoration of the "Temporal Power," that is, papal sovereignty over Rome and the adjacent territory. The Vatican Council had been asked to decree that all Catholics must acknowledge the virtues of the temporal power as it had existed before the national unification of Italy had begun. The Council broke up before this proposal was acted upon, and, symbolically, a major reason it never reconvened was the seizure in September, 1870, of Rome by the Italian army.[70] Immuring himself in the Vatican, Pius IX ordered that all masses sung in the old papal states should conclude with special prayers for the conversion of the enemies of the temporal power, and, in 1884, Leo XIII extended this requirement to the world church.[71] In his encyclical *Immortale Dei*, Leo declared that the temporal power was the "surest safeguard" of the Church's vital independence.[72]

Neither Pius nor Leo ever publicly declared that the conflicting claims of church and state might be compromised. But both sides released at various times trial ballons proposing to give the Pope a limited territory, or an international guarantee of political and financial independence. Father Passaglia in 1860 and Father Curci in the 1870's had implied that such a compromise might be a blessing in disguise; the trusted Abbot Tosti of the Vatican Library several times offered to act as an intermediary. Unfortunately, these proposals nearly invariably aroused the wrath of ultramontane Catholics and of the equally intransigent Italian Freemasons, so that the Church or the state was forced to disclaim all interest and to criticize the forwardness of its spokesmen. Church-state relations in Italy were apparently as unsatisfactory in the 1890's as at any time in the past.[73] To the conservative Catholic, a vigorous and unqualified support of the temporal power was held to be an essential criterion of the true faith.[74]

Non-Catholic Americans, respecting the nationalist ambitions of Italy, and favoring the separation of church and state, had been pleased when Rome was added to the Italian state.[75] Even when Leo XIII's life was made miserable by insults from Roman mobs, few Americans outside the Church thought the return of the temporal power would be a satisfactory remedy. Many American Catholics shared these convictions. Archbishop Peter Kenrick, considering the temporal power as a corollary to the papal infallibility he had fought so vigorously, refused to send condolences to Pius IX on the loss of Rome, or, seventeen years later, to express a desire for its return to Leo XIII.[76] Some Irish-Americans, incensed at the Pope's condemnation of the boycott and his criticism of Parnell, professed to see no difference between the right of the Pope to Rome and the right of the Irish to Ireland.[77] Many considered the whole question to be an Italian problem, and one which could not be too serious, since the Church was obviously thriving and Leo XIII notably influential. But the most profound reason for American Catholic disinterest was pointed out, regretfully, by the *Ecclesiastical Review*: "The very name is naturally uncongenial to us, who consider that religion and civil rule have their several fields of actions, almost incompatible with the other." [78]

These attitudes dismayed American conservative leaders. Devoted to increasing papal power and more bravely scornful of non-Catholic opinion than the liberals, they wished to commit American Catholics to strong, public support of the temporal power.[79] Since popes had taught that the temporal power was absolutely desirable, no Catholic had the right to form his own judgment of its worth. Monsignor Joseph Schroeder, a deeply conservative professor of theology at the Catholic University, treated this desirability as a "dogmatic fact," demanding unreserved assent.[80] "If the temporal power is wrong," some Jesuits argued, "the Church, too, is wrong in a way which our faith prohibits us to admit that she can be wrong." [81] Catholics should be scrupulous to avoid the narrowly pragmatic attitude that, because there was no prospect that the temporal power would be immediately restored, they did not need to concern themselves with the question.[82]

While the liberal clergy was indignant at Protestants' callousness towards the sufferings of Leo, they believed too strongly that the Church prospered when "separated" from the state to be anything but reluctant in demanding a restoration of the temporal power in its traditional form.[83] Father Edward McSweeny, a professor of

theology at Mount Saint Mary's College at Emmitsburg, Maryland, argued that the papal states had made the Pope "practically
independent of the faithful, and, not needing their money, [he]
naturally concerned himself less . . . whether they received their
due share" of the world's goods. Now that the Pope had been provi-
dentially forced into the same position as the American Church
in financial matters, McSweeny expected to see develop between
papacy and people "a clearer union and greater interdependence,"
to the certain advantage of the Church.[84] Though the liberals disliked the anticlerical government of Italy, they stubbornly resisted
praying for "disaster to the nation and people."[85] Instead they
shared the hopes of European liberals for a compromise to end
the warfare between Italy and the Vatican.[86]

This intermediate position was not simple to maintain. In the
fall of 1888, the American hierarchy learned that it was expected
by Rome to make a strong public protest against the recent spoliation of certain papal property. Even the conservatives were horri-
fied; American public opinion was certain to regard any united
protest an unwarrantable intervention in the affairs of a foreign
people. After consulting with the archbishops, Gibbons concluded
that only the most generalized statement should be sent. Bishop
Keane, greatly relieved, suggested to Gibbons that the letter need
not be released to the press; if, however, publicity was essential to
the Pope's purpose, Keane recommended that the letter tactfully
stress the Church's need for "independence and freedom of action
without mentioning the *temporal power* at all."[87] In the memorial
which was finally sent, Gibbons appealed to American sympathies
by insisting that Rome had been seized by a "foreign" people,
and by deploring interference with the Pope's spiritual ministrations.
He promised renewed prayers and protests as well, but when the
Pope, in thanking the American prelates, suggested direct representations to the American government, the hierarchy chose to remain silent. Gibbons also refused to take special action when the
Pope protested the unveiling of a statue to Giordano Bruno in
Rome.[88]

The next year the issue of the temporal power arose again.
The first act of the Central Verein on being organized in 1864 to promote the religious and cultural interests of German Catholics in

America had been to extend sympathy to the beleaguered Pius IX, and the Pope's reply made clear his expectation that professions of support for the temporal power would be a primary function of any Catholic Congress. When the first Catholic Congress to which laymen of all nationalities were invited assembled in Baltimore in November, 1889, the precedent for speaking unequivocally on the temporal power was well established by twenty-five years of conformity by German-American Catholics, as well as by congresses of Catholics in many European countries.[89] William Onahan, a Chicago politician and a close friend of Archbishop Ireland, was, accordingly, asked by Gibbons to speak on the nature and history of the temporal power, but he declined, no doubt fearing self-incrimination in the eyes of the American voters. Thomas O'Gorman, at that time rector of Ireland's seminary in St. Paul, agreed to write a paper, and it was approved by a committee of bishops, but when the Congress met, the task of reading it was assigned to Charles Bonaparte, an aristocratic Catholic layman from Baltimore, who had less to lose.[90]

The O'Gorman-Bonaparte paper proved to be more of an erudite history of the temporal power than a passionate protest against present conditions. Bonaparte excused himself, as a layman, from presuming to suggest to the Pope how his independence should be recovered, but he clearly implied that reconfiscation of the old papal states was not the only way. His conclusion was less than resounding. "In failing to say that the Holy Father has been and is gravely wronged and in failing to protest so long as it remains unrighted, Catholics do less than their duty," he said.[91] The *Catholic Mirror* of Baltimore, which was believed to reflect Cardinal Gibbons' opinions on many subjects, endorsed Bonaparte's speech with alarming forthrightness. "We think we voice the intelligent sentiments of American Catholics at least," the paper wrote, "when we say that . . . the kingly prerogatives that formerly inhered in the pontificate [are] neither essential nor indispensable to the spiritual authority or spiritual dominion of the Pope." The Pontiff had "no absolute need for extensive territory," the paper concluded. This was more than even Bonaparte had said, and Gibbons hastened to rebuke the editor "for his indiscretion, not to use a stronger phrase." [92] The moderately conservative John

Mooney reminded Bonaparte that Leo XIII did not wish advice on how to abandon his rightful claims. Mooney insinuated that Bonaparte's purpose had been to minimize the obligations of Catholicism; this might suit "certain minds delicately constituted; but clear minds, conservative minds, direct minds, prefer frank, moderate, and unambiguous words, where great principles are involved." [93]

In the face of such criticism, and of the widespread feeling that the Congress had "incurred the lasting displeasure of the Holy See," Augustine Hewit, editor of the *Catholic World*, declared that the men at Baltimore had expressed themselves "in a sufficiently intelligible manner to be understood by all." Despite his efforts to find a middle ground, Hewit could not keep from his articles the basic liberal conviction that the near future would end the Pope's need to concern himself with the powers of a temporal sovereign.[94] In 1895, the *Catholic World* published a tirade against the "satanic" forces of nationalist Italy; the tenor was most unusual for the Paulist magazine, and Hewit added an explanatory footnote, which made crystal clear how bitterly American Catholics were divided over their obligations to the temporal power. "I have nothing to add," he wrote, "to the foregoing article, written by my request, in accordance with the desire of the Most Reverend Archbishop [Corrigan], except to give it my endorsement." He denied that the Paulists had ever yielded anything but "docility and obedience" to the wishes of the Pope, or desired anything but the speedy restoration of the temporal power.[95]

The difficulty in satisfying the conservatives' demands for enthusiastic support of the temporal power typified the practical problems which resulted from the attempt to maintain an understanding attitude towards the American state, which, if not secular, was surely not as Catholic as the France of Louis IX. If few conservatives objected when Clarke lauded the religious spirit of George Washington, the liberals' praise for the American separation of church and state apparently controverted a generation of papal teaching. And avowals that loyalty to Rome did not imply foreign surveillance of political behavior were threatened by Roman demands that Catholics oppose the policy of the Italian government. On such matters, the liberals were more successful in pleasing non-

Catholic Americans than in convincing conservative Catholics of the orthodoxy of their efforts.

But non-Catholics demanded not only loyalty to the state's sovereignty; they also insisted that Catholics wholeheartedly accept the will of the majority as the best means for deciding most political questions. The democracy of the American state was as great a challenge as its secularism.

CHAPTER V

THE EXPECTATIONS OF
AMERICAN DEMOCRACY

Few immigrants came to America prepared to take part in political life. But as liberal Catholics quickly recognized, more was expected of residents in America than passive obedience to the laws. Partisans of democracy were demanding of all newcomers professions of patriotism unqualified by devotion to fatherlands; they would tolerate no challenge to the government's competence to do all that any state could do; and they expected each citizen to share in the responsibility of governing. The reluctance of many Catholics to meet these demands, the liberals knew, was seriously jeopardizing the Church's apologetic mission to American culture.

The persistence of immigrant loyalties to other lands disturbed the liberals on several counts. Apologists feared that the Church would be less able to attract converts by its unity if, like some of the Presbyterian and Reformed churches in America, it was, in effect, divided along national lines. Some suspected that French and German parishes maintained old national attachments for no better reason than to assert their independence of the liberal leaders who were more fully Americanized. But the prime objection was that so long as there was reason to doubt the loyalty of a single Catholic immigrant, many patriots would challenge the right of the Church to bid for American acceptance. Walter Elliott speaking on citizenship to Middle Western Protestant audiences, Keane and Ireland pleading with Leo XIII not to encourage diverse nationalisms in the American Church, Cardinal Gibbons commending the example of Ruth to German Catholics in Milwaukee, — all were seeking to show that, regardless of immigrant backgrounds, American Catholics were wholly patriotic.[1]

To an increasing number of Americans in the late nineteenth century, to be recognizably foreign was to be unfit for citizenship.[2] A. Lawrence Lowell, criticizing Irish nationalist activity, argued that the crucial step in the Americanization process was the liberation of the individual from his past. "The country is not safe," he wrote, "until all groups of foreigners have become so merged in the American people that they cannot be distinguished as a class, by opinion or sentiment on any subject, from the mass of the population."[3] This merging should not be long drawn out; an era that found the melting pot a suitable metaphor of the process of acculturation did not think it should take several generations to produce an acceptably American individual.

Most of the liberal Catholics echoed these convictions.[4] The *Catholic World* believed that unassimilated populations were "like undigested food in the human stomach, painful and weakening to the body politic," and argued that the Church's duty was to "smooth and hasten the process of Americanizing."[5] Archbishop Ireland thought that no nationality unwilling to be immediately assimilated deserved admission into the country; and any immigrant who did not rejoice in the American way of life "should in simple consistency betake his foreign soul to foreign shores, and crouch in misery and subjection beneath tyranny's sceptre."[6] Speaking in Dubuque, Ireland acknowledged that "the work of transition for our Catholic emigrants must necessarily take time, and I will certainly allow the time, but I demand in the name of religion that it be not retarded."[7] Both Ireland and the *Catholic World* assumed that while each immigrant contributed unique elements to the American type, the final amalgam would be a virtual continuation of the dominantly English culture. They thus met the argument, frequently advanced by German Catholics, that immigrants need not hurry to conform to the merely transitional present type. This argument also helped remove doubt that the liberals themselves were fully Americanized; they were deeply affronted when German Catholics divided the whole hierarchy into national groups, — English, Irish, French, Belgian, and German. "There is not an American among us," Archbishop Gross complained to Cardinal Gibbons.[8]

All foreign loyalties were condemnable. Gibbons and Ireland reproved the more hardy manifestations of Irish nationalism, and both wanted the Irish Catholic Benevolent Union to drop the name "Irish" from its title, to purge itself of the taint of "foreignism."[9] But in the 1890's, it was the German-speaking group which caused by far the greatest tumult. The liberals' offensive against the Germans stemmed in part from nothing more exalted than the desire to eliminate the only significant resistance to the Irish-American domination of the hierarchy; but in an era when pan-Germanism was alarming a good deal of the world, the persistence of a group of the faithful in proclaiming that their Catholicism and their Germanism were closely linked gave the liberals a more exalted justification for their crusade.[10]

Most of the conservatives flatly disagreed with the premises of "Americanization." Archbishop Corrigan told a German convention that patriotism and good citizenship could be "taken for granted. An honest man does not . . . feel bound to prove the legitimate marriage of his parents" at every turn. "Enough for us that we have been born here, or that we have voluntarily made it our home, that our patriotism should not be challenged without good reason."[11] The German spokesmen were even less conciliatory to American expectations. Father Walburg blandly asserted that, without question, Germany stood "foremost in the ranks of civilized nations." He advised Americans not to waste time worrying over war with Germany, since America was patently too weak to defeat Ecuador, let alone a European power.[12] A Middle Western editor noted with satisfaction that America had always belonged to Germany because of the papal grant to Charles V.[13] Hardly concealed by the bombast was the genuine fear that the certain consequences of a forced-draft Americanization, in which language and customs were sacrificed, would be extensive defections from Catholicism.[14]

Liberals could scoff that to suppose souls were most surely saved in America by retarding Americanization was "a suitable theme for comic opera." [15] Such comments only convinced the Germans the more completely that they alone were truly anxious to preserve their countrymen's faith. The *Herald des Glaubens* was sure that there were many "American priests in this country who would rather see several million Germans go to hell than forego the opportunity to convert a few hundred Yankees." [16] Comparing the services of Patrick Ryan and Henry Muehlsiepen, the vicars-general of the Archdiocese of St. Louis, a German historian decided that while

the wonderful eloquence of Father Patrick J. Ryan has done very much to make the Church esteemed and honored by our non-Catholic brethren, the humble, quiet, unselfish, and persevering work of the Vicar-General [Muehlsiepen] . . . has done far more towards consolidating and perpetuating the Church in Missouri.[17]

The Germans believed that only a clergy proud of its German origins would be able to hold adult German Catholics in the faith, and that only parochial schools in which German was the dominant language would save the children from demoralization and de-Catholicization. They therefore indignantly objected when prelates attempted to install Irish or English priests in German parishes, and they fought all state legislation establishing a wider use of English in the schools. The Central Verein formed by German Catholic societies was dedicated, through yearly meetings, to "champion Catholic interests according to the mind of the Catholic Church," to provide mutual insurance benefits, to aid German immigrants, and to maintain close ties with the homeland.[18] Inspired by the stout resistance offered by the Center party to Bismarck's attack on the Church, and sensing growing American dislike of Germanism, the Verein's leaders set out in the 1880's to win their own *Kulturkampf*. An American German Catholic General Assembly was formed to "attain *the same ends* by *the same means* in this country" as the *Katholikentage* organization in Germany.[19] The Assembly stalled off proposals by non-German bishops that it unite with Catholic groups regardless of national origin, and it ignored the claim made by the lay congress of Baltimore that America had no room for foreign-oriented associations.[20] It sent representatives to assemblies in Germany, and leaders of the Center party frequently spoke in America. In Pittsburgh, in 1890, Ernst Lieber warned against too rapid Americanization. "Remain united as Catholics and as Germans," he said. "The world knows that you attack no one when you assert your right to remain American citizens and Germans. . . . Suffer no injustice in the consciousness of your rights."[21]

Remarks so inconsiderate of American patriotic zeal would have provoked antagonism even had the speaker not been a leading political figure of a foreign country. Archbishop Ireland did not hesitate to alert the Associated Press to the responsibility for covering all meetings of the German Assembly in order to keep watch on its "general un-American character."[22] He had good reason to fear for the reputation of the whole American Church. The *New York Times,* alarmed at the intransigence displayed by a later *Katholikentag* toward the public schools and toward the Pope's loss of temporal power, professed itself unable to "recall any other body of American residents . . . so completely out of touch with American institutions. . . . They have kept themselves as clear of any taint of Americanism during their sojourn in this country as if they were Chinese laundrymen." The editorial concluded on an ominous note; "it is not too much to say that, if the spirit of the Roman Catholic Church were expressed in the proceeding of the Newark conference, that Church would be a public enemy."[23]

During the 1880's and the 1890's, the German Catholics made strenuous efforts to persuade Rome to choose more German prelates for the American Church. Besides reflecting on the devotion of the "Americanized" bishops, these attempts to make foreign origin a primary criterion for American churchmen threatened to belie liberal boasts of the Church's patriotism. Even Archbishop Corrigan was outraged, and one of his most doughtily conservative priests wrote a blistering attack which the *Catholic World* was undoubtedly happy to publish.[24] The liberals were especially critical when the proposals came not from Middle Western German clerics, but from a group of European laymen led by Peter Cahensly. A German merchant who had dedicated most of his life to the protection of the religious and social interests of German emigrants,

Cahensly was alarmed at the rapid alienation from faith and father-land of many who settled in America. A congress at Lucerne brought together prominent laymen from several European coun-tries, and a memorial was forwarded to Rome asking, among other things, that more foreign language-speaking prelates be in-stalled in America.

Archbishop Ireland immediately called in newspaper reporters, and predicted to them that neither the Pope nor the American hierarchy would sanction the suggestions. He went on to denounce the "impudence of foreigners" in meddling in American Catholic affairs. This "unpardonable" attempt would be resented by all the faithful, who, he assured the public, acknowledged no foreign loyalties. American Catholics accepted "the Pope of Rome as our chieftain in spiritual matters and we are glad to receive directions from him," he said, "but men in Germany or Switzerland or Ireland must mind their own business and be still as to ours." [25] Through the efforts of Ireland's close friend Denis O'Connell, who was rector of the American College in Rome, press reports from Europe in-sinuated that "Cahenslyism" was a plot hatched by the Prussian government.[26] This theme was repeated by Father John Conway, the rambunctious editor of Ireland's diocesan newspaper, when to help lexicographers of the future he defined "Cahenslyism" as "a combined effort of ecclesiastics and journalists, mostly German, with the representatives of foreign powers for the purpose of pro-moting foreignism in this country and for using the Roman Catho-lic Church to that end." [27] Ireland even persuaded Senator Cush-man Davis of Minnesota to attack Cahensly's political aggression on the floor of the United States Senate.[28]

No doubt the liberals deliberately exaggerated the threat of foreign political intervention in order to get non-Catholic support for their ecclesiastical battle in Rome. The alternative, Ireland confided to O'Connell, was the "absolute subjugation of the American Church" by the German Catholics in Europe and America.[29] But the lib-erals were sure that their resistance to Cahenslyism was necessary, not just to ensure that the Germans would not rule the American Church, but — what was obviously for more important — to make it possible that a Catholic Church could exist in America at all. Only a few weeks after Gibbons had belabored "self-constituted critics" in Europe who undertook to prescribe the proper treatment of Germans in America, he was told by President Benjamin Harrison that the government was relieved to learn of the liberals' stand against foreignism.[30] Gibbons could not fail to realize that Harrison and many Americans like him could not be too often assured of the Church's patriotism. Accordingly, when the cardinal was invited to Milwaukee to bestow the pallium on Archbishop Katzer, he daringly preached a stern warning to the German nationalists in their own stronghold. Enjoining them to avoid dissensions with either Church or state, Gibbons spoke of the luminous example of Ruth, and commended her words to all immigrants: "Thy people shall be my people, and thy God my God." [31] Whatever the effect upon the Germans, the response of the secular press was all that the liberals could desire; to most papers, Gibbons' sermon proved that the leadership of the Church wholeheartedly accepted the first responsibility of American citizenship, — unqualified and undivided loyalty to the United States.

II

In the late nineteenth century, many Americans were coming to believe it the duty of liberal democracy not only to free the individual from the coercions of the state, but also to use state power to provide the social and economic environment in which meaningful freedom was possible. Liberal Catholics, who believed so firmly in the perfect separation of the political and the religious spheres, might understandably have deplored the widening responsibilities assumed by the state, bringing with them, as they inevitably would, new problems of delimitation between spheres. A "paternal government," Charles Bonaparte had once acknowledged, "must provide a legal religion." [32] But the liberals' faith in the political system and in the intentions of secular statesmen was too profound for them often to grudge the state its new activities.

Conservatives lacked any such faith. While they acknowledged the legitimacy of the American governments, they over and over insisted that a *purely secular* state like ours (call it Christian or non-Christian)" possessed only minimal powers.[33] The Jesuit Father René Holaind patiently explained that though many American rulers lived exemplary lives and taught Sunday school, they ignored

Church authority and the precepts of canon law. "We may live on excellent terms with our master," he wrote, "but we must not take him for Charlemagne. . . . The civil power can claim ampler rights when it is in union with the ecclesiastical authority, and acts under its direction," than when it has only the powers of an "autonomous corporate body" under "the grants of nature." [34]

The most bitter controversy arose over the state's constantly growing role in education. The first line of conservative Catholic resistance was the defense of family rights. Michael Mueller regarded the public school system as a disease which had already weakened, and would "finally break up and destroy the Christian family." [35] Zachariah Montgomery, a California lawyer, criticized a tract which had advocated using "the property of the State" to educate "the children of the land." Only bastards were "children of the land," he retorted. All other young people were members of families to whom the preëminent rights of control belonged. [36] Conservatives happily recurred to the older tradition of American liberalism which had led judges to declare that the "municipal law" should not disturb the parents' authority over their children "except for the strongest reasons." [37] Bishop Grace, Ireland's predecessor at St. Paul, stated flatly that "the law of majorities, the *vox populi*, has no claim against the claim of natural family rights." [38] To a non-Catholic statist, this argument for family rights seemed a disingenuous way of denying to the state a prerogative which the Church would immediately usurp. [39] But conservatives seldom pretended to vest final authority in the family. Though parents had an "inalienable and indefeasible right" to educate their children, Father James Conway argued, supervision of the elementary instruction of the Church's children "belongs exclusively to her." Catholic families suitably instructed would never deny the Church this right. [40]

A second line of conservative defense was to attack state interference in education as a violation of the rights of the parent as an individual. [41] Herbert Spencer was still the presiding social theorist, and it was symptomatic of how deeply the conservative Catholics desired safeguards for individual freedom that they were able to overlook Spencer's radical agnosticism in their fulsome praise for his antistatism. [42] No corporation attorneys were more outspoken critics of paternalism. "Too much spoon-feeding on the part of the State is weakening and degenerating," Bishop McQuaid declared.[43] Neatly merging popular *laissez faire* assumptions with his conviction that the education of Catholics must be strictly Catholic, the bishop asserted that "the Public School System is nothing else . . . than a huge conspiracy against religion, individual liberty and enterprise, and parental rights. It is a monopoly on the part of the State, usurping to itself the entire control of the teacher's business, driving out competition." We forgot American traditions, he insisted, "when the State was allowed to step in between the father and his child. We forgot them when we imported European ideas of paternal government, and began the breeding of communistic social heresies." [44] Judge Edmund Dunne, arguing before an Ohio court, admitted that he did "not object to paternalism in government, if you can get genuine, true paternalism. . . . But it is so difficult to get it . . . that the founders of our state declared that no attempt should be made to enforce it here." Since the state, "by its own deliberate act" of disavowing Christian control, has lowered itself "to the rank of policeman, it must content itself with the exercise of police power." Dunne thought educational legislation was an opening wedge toward "state absolutism." [45] Zachariah Montgomery agreed. "Free teaching draws after it free books, free clothes, free food, free time," he wrote. "All this is going very far with the communists. . . . If we admit a right . . . to take the child out of the family, they will ask next for the wife." [46]

This argument so moved Professor Henry Lyman of Chicago that he wrote Father Hecker of his conviction that only the Catholic Church stood for traditional American liberties.[47] But he had addressed his letter to the wrong Catholic. Hecker, in reply, declared in favor of a tax-supported educational system equitable to all religions. His fellow liberals explicitly approved the general legislative powers of the state. Thomas Bouquillon, professor of moral theology at the Catholic University, flatly challenged the conservative premises. "Certain abuses of the State in the exercise of its powers have filled some Catholics with dread of the State," he wrote, "and have thrown them into the opposite extreme of moral *laissez-faire,* a more irrational doctrine than that of economical *laissez-faire*." Refusing to admit that the American state was too un-Christian to exercise more than police powers, he argued that it had "the right to all legitimate temporal means it judges necessary for the attainment of the temporal common welfare." Since an educated citizenry was necessary to the general welfare, the state had a clear right to provide a public school system.[48]

This syllogism was not novel, but conservative Catholics were by no means ready to accept it. Father Holaind found authority in Chancellor Kent for the assertion that no well-ordered state set out to educate its own citizens; the *American Catholic Quarterly Review* invoked Joseph Story against the promiscuous use of the conception of "general welfare"; and Sebastian Messmer cited Jefferson's classic argument against the national bank as proof that the state could assume new powers only when they were absolutely essential.[49] Bouquillon was obviously inclining towards statism; as a European, he was, perhaps unconsciously, Bishop Chatard smugly observed, a lover of the *cultus gubernandi.*[50]

The conservatives believed that the state should limit its responsibility for an educated citizenry to providing rewards to those who acquired learning, or granting financial aid to private educational enterprises.[51] State monopoly or even control, Dunne argued, would make moral training impossible; "something must be entrusted to liberty, something to religion, something to the grace of God." [52] Or, as another conservative somewhat more lucidly argued, the American state could avoid tyrannizing over its citizens only if it left the education of most of them to the churches.[53] Because the poor would not always be able to give their children the education they needed, the state might rightfully establish pauper schools. Because some parents were "dead or notoriously vicious or cruel," the morally neutral state should be ready to act "*in loco parentis*," provided no one closer or holier was available.[54] Like the railroad attorneys of that era, who admitted the state's power to correct abuses, yet denied the constitutionality of general regulatory legislation, these Catholic conservatives saw no inconsistency in requiring the state to supplement defective educational programs at the same time officials were denied the right to establish by legislation specific criteria for sound education. "The ever-convenient, fetish-worshipped statute," John Mooney complained, always brought more evils than it relieved.[55] And Father Holaind suggested that instead of trusting in laws to compel individuals to live up to their moral responsibilities, it was better for the agents of the state to wait until the miseducation of a child had become gross and palpable, and then hail the offenders into court. The judges, the real defenders of justice in the modern state, would adjudicate on the "individual merits of the case," instead of on the basis of statute law, the mere will of a transient majority.[56]

Sharing in the adulation for the judiciary that was characteristic of conservative thought in this period, these Catholics readily grouped judges with kings and bishops, and maintained that judges possessed "more sense of religious responsibility" than other government officials.[57] It was more than the traditionally fulsome flattery of the court room when Dunne remarked that if statist "fanatics were not checked by the courts," American society was doomed.[58] Just as business lawyers had asked the Supreme Court to outlaw state legislation for violating natural law principles implicit in the Fourteenth Amendment, Dunne asked the courts to strike down the legislative aggrandizement of a compulsory school law as a violation of natural law.[59] It was the consolation of the conservatives that "our highest tribunals go behind the letter of special legislation, and, disregarding the technicalities of the statutebook, decide the most momentous cases solely on principles of equity." [60] The thesis of René Holaind's *Natural Law and Legal Practice* was that equity was necessary to remedy the "defects of the statute law." A reviewer in the *Catholic World* pointed out that such a theory practically exhorted judges to disregard statute law.[61] And Bouquillon accused Holaind of failing to understand the distinction between the legislature and the judiciary.[62]

Such rejoinders showed how unwilling the liberals were to join in any nihilistic attack on the premises or the results of the democratic process. Instead, they proposed to take an active part in hastening the passage of legislation which was worthy of America, and which no Catholic would have to look to a judge to veto.

III

The conservatives distrusted American statute law not only because the Church did not supervise the legislative process, but also because

American laws were supposed to express the will of a sovereign people. In theory, the Church declared her indifference to forms of government, so long as individual and ecclesiastical liberties were preserved. In fact, however, history had conditioned the Church to coexist with imperial and monarchical states.[63] To many Catholics the resounding political declarations of the Enlightenment seemed novel and patently unsound. One could respect the signers of the American Declaration of Independence, one Catholic wrote, only by assuming that they had endorsed, without careful consideration, a flock of vague clichés.[64] To proclaim that all power derived from the consent of the governed seemed to deny God's final sovereignty.[65] It was folly to speak of the equality of all men; it was folly compounded, therefore, to maintain that all men had an equal right to rule. In a pastoral letter of 1882, the bishops of the province of Cincinnati readily admitted that the people are "permitted a voice in the form of the government" under which they live. But just as the Church recognized a fundamental difference between clergy and laity, so should the state recognize that "some men shall rule, and some shall be ruled." Apparently the bishops, like Leo XIII, thought of democracy simply as a means by which "the government" received the consent of the masses; there was little understanding of the rights and responsibilities of citizenship in the pastoral's statement that "those who are appointed to rule have certain rights that subjects have not. Hence kings and magistrates, and bishops and priests, are appointed to rule; if to rule, then they are above those whom they rule." [66] When the pastoral, because of its emphasis on hierarchy, was attacked by non-Catholics as a blatant claim that the American political system would be sound only if the Church was given full authority over civil life, a doughty priest declared that it was too bad for American society that such a return to "medieval" society was not possible.[67]

The liberals did not share in the distrust of the democratic process which animated the Cincinnati pastoral, and its vehement defender. Democracy, they declared, was both historically Catholic and presently inevitable. Father Hecker asserted that the affirmations of the Declaration were not "glittering generalities," or the innovations of godless men; Catholic nobles and bishops had stated many of them at Runnymede.[68] Undoubtedly, some misguided theorists were convinced that the American government was founded on wholly secularist principles, but a Catholic lawyer argued that "in the preamble of at least two-thirds of the American state constitutions," there was a clear "recognition and acknowledgement of God" as the source of all authority; Father McGlynn called the Declaration "a religious profession" that men's rights were "sacred and inalienable because they are the gifts of God." [69] America, Walter Elliott boasted, was a "baptized democracy." [70]

Democracy was the form of government most conducive to all kinds of true liberty. Hecker never wearied of proclaiming that the freedom encouraged in a democracy was uniquely suitable for significant religious aspiration.[71] And while John Gilmary Shea found the assassination of President Garfield melancholy proof that the masses were bound to abuse their liberty, Bishop Stephen Ryan of Buffalo happily noted that Americans universally condemned this outrageous act of a foreigner, and, far from degenerating into anarchy, held religious services of mourning and contrition.[72] Such people were sure to use their political powers wisely. "In America," Father Jenkins wrote, "we have a State we can trust, because it is ours and the people can control it by ballot. . . . It will never hurt Christian interest to confide in a . . . state such as ours." [73] The liberals found final justification for taking a dynamic part in the political process in Leo XIII's advice to all Catholics to "make use of popular institutions, so far as can honestly be done, for the advancement of truth and righteousness." [74]

The liberals were aware that American politics were not always honest, but instead of trying to avoid contamination, they attempted to purify voting and legislative practices. Gibbons made frequent speeches on the need for reforms, and Archbishop Ireland was for a time president of the St. Paul Law and Order League, dedicated to securing a clean ballot.[75] The *Catholic World* was optimistic that the day of corrupt political leaders had nearly passed. They "will soon be ploughed under; a better class will soon appear," it prophesied.[76]

In many European countries, the formation of a Catholic party had proved very effective in bringing to the attention of voters and statesmen the relevance of Christian teaching to current social problems. With the important exception of the German-American Catholics, none of the conservatives in the United States gave many signs of favoring such an activist policy, even though they were distrustful enough of existing parties. The liberals, for their part, left no doubt that such heroic measures were neither desirable nor necessary in America. Catholics were already commonly charged with bloc voting; Bishop Doane, for example, darkly insinuated that many Catholics went to the polls like laborers going out on strike, "because a self-chosen leader orders it." [77] Even when the A.P.A. organized against the Church, Cardinal Gibbons discouraged the formation of a Catholic phalanx. And in 1900, when Bishop James McFaul of Trenton stated that the American Federation of Catholic Societies which he was organizing would be willing and able to fight back vigorously against anti-Catholic aggression, both Gibbons and Ireland withheld support.[78] A Colorado clergyman, Father Thomas Malone, asserted that such a "medieval" policy would only intensify anatagonisms. Malone's appointment to the State Board of Charities and Corrections was evidence enough that the state did not need to be coerced into heeding Catholic interests.[79] William Onahan, who had made a successful career in Chicago politics, declared roundly that the fewer "religious or national groups we have in American politics the better all around." [80]

Bad as a purely Catholic party seemed, the liberals deplored nearly as strenuously the seemingly automatic identification of most Catholics with the Democratic party. Not surprisingly, Republicans were indignant, and many felt justified in linking the Church with rum, rebellion, and every other disreputable ideal Democrats may ever have cherished.[81] Catholics, furthermore, were deprived of their rightful political influence, since the Democrats could take their support for granted, and the Republicans felt no obligation. The one-sided political alignment seemed far more likely to produce occasional violent aggressions against the Church than the continuous, peaceful influencing of public affairs that the liberals desired, and that the real popularity of the Church in America made possible.[82]

This analysis was especially appealing to the several liberal Catholic leaders who were Republicans. In their opinion, the classic example of the misuse of Catholic power was the alliance between Archbishop Corrigan and Tammany Hall.[83] In 1894, Father Thomas Ducey, one of the New York liberal priests, strongly supported the

Lexow investigations into Tammany's power; he was "canonically" admonished by Corrigan not to attend the public hearings lest non-Catholics receive the impression that the Church was taking part in politics. Ducey replied spiritedly that for twenty-five years he had protested "the efforts of Tammany Hall and its leaders to prostitute the foreign-born citizens and the Catholic name." He was convinced that had Catholic leaders "openly acted with courage in opposing the corruptions and corrupters of this great city, the Catholic Church would have glory throughout the world," instead of the shameful reputation of being an ally of evil.[84]

To obtain more enlightened Catholic activity, the liberals were sure that the clergy would have to take a public part in political life. In the past, Catholic leaders like John Hughes and Martin Spalding had refused even to vote, lest non-Catholic anatagonism be aroused; some conservatives were still abstaining in the 1890's.[85] In sharp contrast, Gibbons insisted in 1892 that his rights "as a citizen were not abdicated or abridged on becoming a Christian prelate, and the sacred character which I profess, far from lessening, rather increases, my obligations to my country." He thought that "his seclusion from popular agitation" increased his ability to discern the ethical implications of political problems, and it was his clear duty to share his understanding with the people. By timely intervention, he might forestall a "disastrous popular inundation by watching its course, and diverting it into a safe channel." Gibbons feared, however, that if a priest actually joined a political party, he would lose his reputation for dispassionate moral analysis.[86]

Archbishop Ireland, in contrast, was an intensely partisan Republican who felt a mission to lead ever more Catholics into the party. Before Gibbons left to deliver the opening prayer at the Democratic National Convention in 1912, Ireland wrote the cardinal to "pray hard for the country, not so much for the party." [87] Ireland took the whole country for his political field, but he was particularly active in New York, where he stayed at the same Fifth Avenue Hotel which Tom Platt used for his famous political "Sunday school." [88] When a Catholic member of the New York State Board of Regents died, the Democrats nominated Bishop McQuaid to replace him; the Republicans countered with Ireland's close friend, Father Sylvester Malone. McQuaid neither worked publicly for his own election, nor encouraged others to, but Ireland, seeing a chance to pay off personal scores as well as to support his party, campaigned strenuously in New York for Malone. Bishop Keane also came up from Washington to support the priest.[89]

Malone's victory, part of the Republican sweep in 1894, was hailed by a secular newspaper as clear evidence that "the American flag always wins." [90] To McQuaid, it was at least as clear that the Catholic Church had suffered severely from this exemplary working out of the liberal blueprint for Catholic political participation. After delivering from his pulpit a bitter denunciation of Ireland's meddling in other bishops' territories, he reported to Rome that Malone was an avowed enemy of the parochial schools, and that the A.P.A. had supported him. The bishop accused Ireland of accepting bribes from tainted Republicans, and characterized his conduct as "undignified, disgraceful to his episcopal office, and a scandal in the eyes of all right-minded Catholics of both parties." [91] Though McQuaid was rebuked by Rome for his public attack on Ireland, many conservatives sympathized with the bishop's conviction that open political warfare among clergymen would destroy the unity of the Church. The *American Ecclesiastical Review* argued that a priest was barred from many political activities; even to vote was permissible only if performed "without objectionable enthusiasm." [92]

Ireland refused to subside. In the February after the election, in a speech on "American Citizenship," he declared that any American who refused to vote deserved disfranchisement or even exile. Ireland gleefully reported to Gibbons that "people were wicked enough to see in those words an allusion to His Lordship of Rochester." [93] Ireland's position, as usual, won non-Catholic approval; the *Chicago Post* spoke of Ireland as "the one Metropolitan of all whose intense devotion to American institutions has been constantly conspicuous." [94]

Even more important, Ireland was winning, through his political activities, important Republican recognition of the interests of the Church. Many obstacles had to be overcome. Shortly after his election, Benjamin Harrison had antagonized Catholics by consigning the Indian Bureau which supervised the lives of many Catholic Indians to the care of notorious enemies of the Church. As early as August, 1889, Archbishop Ireland had warned Harrison that continued discrimination against Catholics would "check the drifting of their political allegiances" to the Republicans. Despite Harrison's lack of coöperation, Ireland refused to break with the party.[95] Other Catholics were less tolerant. A New York politician found the lay congress at Baltimore in November 1889 sympathetic to a free swinging attack on the Republicans and all their works.[96] And Father Joseph A. Stephan, the director of the Bureau of Catholic Indian Missions, disgusted with Ireland's conciliatory policy, launched a sustained attack on Harrison which culminated in the summer of 1892 when he mailed to over 100,000 Catholics a letter accusing the President of ineradicable hostility to the Church.[97]

The growth of the A.P.A. during Cleveland's second administration strengthened Catholic antipathy to the Republican party.[98] McKinley sidestepped all opportunities for disavowing the order, and the party convention in New York refused explicit Catholic demands that it repudiate the support of the bigots.[99] This refusal so incensed the Paulist Father Alfred Young that he ended his lifelong support of the party, and demanded to know whether Republicans would continue to sanction "this un-American religious crusade against the civil and religious rights of all Catholic citizens." [100] Ireland, however, was now in a position to make his influence felt within the party, and he reproved Young for his lack of confidence.[101] With the aid of his New York allies, he succeeded in preventing the national party convention in 1896 from adopting a resolution favoring a federal amendment which would prohibit the use of public funds for sectarian schools. His influence was so great that some A.P.A. leaders actually abandoned the Republican party in disgust.[102]

Ireland's strategy was critically tested during the 1896 campaign. Many Catholic leaders thought Bryan's free silver proposals violated the moral law. While Gibbons gave no political advice, Ireland felt no such restraint.[103] In his vigorous campaigning, he did not invoke clerical authority or the teachings of Catholic moral theology, for though Catholic voters were probably his main target, he did not wish to imply that their ideals were dissimilar from other Americans'. In an open letter to St. Paul businessmen, he preferred to rely on the traditional party accusation that the Democrats were secessionists and, that, in the lust for reform, they rivaled the Commune. He considered silver a secondary issue, but, having "convictions in this matter," he plunged into an exposition of economic theory in a manner worthy of a professor, his biographer noted with proper awe. His Republican colleagues were impressed, and ordered a quarter of a million copies for general distribution.[104]

The unprecedentedly strong Republican showing at the polls, coupled with the desertion of large numbers of Catholics from Bryan's radicalism, seemed to add up to a complete vindication of the liberals' faith in the American political system.[105] Without forming a Catholic party, without resorting to authoritarian ecclesiastical intervention, Catholics had allied with the honest, intelligent men outside the Church to checkmate a dangerous political experiment. Furthermore, having helped decide the election, they could rightly expect to have considerable influence on the new administration. Ireland, in fact, was gratified to discover that recommendations to McKinley were more favorably received than those he had made to Harrison. Joseph McKenna, a prominent Catholic, was appointed Attorney-General, and later elevated to the Supreme Court.[106] When trouble loomed with Catholic Spain, Ireland was able to play the intermediary for a time. And the administration saw to it that Catholics were on the delegation that negotiated with Rome the disposition of the Friars' Lands in the conquered Philippines.[107] Ireland also became a personal friend of Theodore Roosevelt, who, while unable to remain a consistent supporter of the Catholics more than of anyone else, was very conscious of the need to hold the sympathies of the Church.[108]

It was hardly surprising that the liberals in the winter of 1896–1897 concluded that the conservatives' distrust of American democracy had proved groundless. The future of the Church seemed to lie in supporting, not fighting that democracy. Her leaders would be wise to continue promoting in her immigrant members an unqualified loyalty to the state, in conceding wide scope to the legislative will, and in encouraging Catholics to participate fully in the definition of that will. Though technically the state would remain secular, it could well become the most perfect instrument to be found in the modern world for fostering Christian civilization.

CHAPTER VI

PERSPECTIVES

ON SOCIAL CHANGE

In the last two decades of the nineteenth century, the heady confidence of a boom America was counterpointed by an increasing recognition that pronounced social changes were in the offing. To some observers, the developing class differentiation brought the gloomy conviction that an apocalyptic struggle was imminent, in which "the dangerous classes" would be crushed (if they could be subdued at all) only by force. An English diplomat noted that Theodore Roosevelt and his friends spoke of social problems with a "sort of bitter despair . . . which is hard to describe, and not pleasant to listen to." [1] For most Americans, however, the ills of society seemed soluble; changes were inevitable, but neither a holocaust nor the complete abandonment of the traditional social and economic system seemed likely. Much would depend on how promptly and how skillfully American leaders would shape and direct the forces demanding change. Both Protestant and Catholic clergy moved in these decades towards a tentative endorsement of social reform.

The transition was particularly difficult for a Catholic priest. The clerical education of a traditional Church prepared the young man to deal with social problems as they had been known to the Church for centuries. The discipline of an authoritative Church was better designed to preserve unity by continuing traditional actions than to promote innovation. Where prelates of liberal conviction were installed, it is true, liberal priests enjoyed greater sanctuary from outside coercions than did Protestant ministers mortgaged to the approval of their middle-class congregations.[2] But since it was logical for the Church to place conservatives like Archbishop Corrigan where immigrants were most numerous, those priests who found conditions in the eastern cities an incentive to reform activities usually had to fight a running battle with tradition-minded superiors. Moreover, in most areas, unless a priest chose to conduct a one-man campaign, he had to join nondenominational reform movements, which too often in the past had been hostile to the Church. The greatest incubus to Catholic reform, however, was not organizational, but the widespread religious belief that human enterprise was presumptuous.

To the Catholic conservatives, the most proper response to social difficulties was devout passivity. All history showed that inequality and injustice were rooted in the nature of things. Condé Pallen, the St. Louis editor, believed one might as well attribute these ills to the weather as to the prevalent economic and social system.[3] Bishop Chatard declared that except before God and the law absolute equality was nonexistent; it was a "figment of the wild brain of the agitator, coquetting with the ignorance of the mass of mankind."[4] Father Thébaud argued that inequalities sometimes resulted in injustice because of men's original sin. But "the sufferings consequent upon it must be taken by man as an expiation."[5] The Church mercifully provided spiritual consolations, so great in value as to justify the hardships. Archbishop James Bayley told American Catholics in 1876 that God permits poverty as "the most efficient means of practising some of the most necessary Christian virtues, of charity and alms-giving on the part of the rich, and patience and resignation to His holy will on the part of the poor."[6]

While individuals should earnestly strive to overcome personal weaknesses, they should not regard inferior social standing as proof of moral failure or as a weakness to be overcome. Patrick McSweeny indignantly rejected the Alger ideal; "in more than ninety-nine cases in a hundred we shall have reason to rejoice if the son turns out as well as his father," he thought.[7] It was dangerous for a man to neglect the "providential" in his situation, and to "keep up a constant fight with his surroundings."[8] Catholics were reminded that "to let well enough alone is a very wise old saw."[9]

Organized efforts at reform were especially dangerous. The socialist Internationals, the state reforms of Bismarck, and the many schemes projected in America were all types of pagan "sociology" — concerted efforts to remodel society according to limited, secular perspectives. Only God, the "sole author of the social order," or His authorized representatives should attempt to modify "the social equilibrium."[10] One conservative consoled himself with the knowledge that the "Divine Individuum" would surely wreak vengeance on all other reformers.[11]

Though the liberals would never stress human impotence, they were no more able than their non-Catholic contemporaries to commit themselves wholeheartedly to social reform. Hailing the virtues of American life, they could only with difficulty stress the need for reform. Bishop Spalding rebuked the prophets of impending doom, and assured a Notre Dame graduating class that "the organs of the social body" had never been so healthy.[12] But affection for things American also made the liberals more tolerant of social reforms advocated by praiseworthy fellow countrymen. Admitting the high motives of Frances Willard, Booker Washington, and Henry George, they could not easily denounce attempts to strike down intemperance, improve the conditions of the Negroes, and solve the "social problem." They were not afraid of entrusting responsibility to the state or of coöperating with non-Catholics. "Has not Christ declared that whoever is not against us is for us?" Spalding asked; "and may we not therefore find friends in all who work for worthy ends? . . . This large sympathy . . . is Catholic, and it is also American."[13] Ireland believed that so long as the priest was prudent, he could stand "upon every platform, and mingle with every assembly, where by word or act he may serve his fellow-man . . . through the betterment and exaltation of human life."[14] In contrast, a German denounced proposals to coöperate with non-Catholics as "Free Masonry."

So long as non-Catholics pointed to the large number of Catholics in almshouses, asylums, and jails, so long as middle-class Americans shunned the Church because the faithful seemed socially unregenerate, it behooved the liberals to combat intemperance and to relieve the squalor of the depressed classes.[15] Catholic apologists might, of course, choose to rely on automatic progress and individual enterprise to remove such blots from the Church's escutcheon, but social dynamism was as logical a conclusion as complacency, and the liberals could hardly fail to notice that an increasing number of Americans were demanding concerted action.

The liberals were also influenced by developments in Europe, where, in the late 1880's, Catholic congresses finally began to declare in favor of group or even state intervention.[16] In 1891, Leo XIII issued his encyclical on the condition of the working class; Archbishop Ireland promptly claimed papal justification for social insurance and for eight-hour-day legislation.[17]

Cheerfully accepting the voluntary system of Church support, the liberals proposed to win that support by their devotion to the secular interests of the faithful. When the people understand, Ireland told the clergy, "that you have studied their problems . . . that you love works of social economy, they will go to you." [18] Cardinal Gibbons was aware that many of the people the liberals wished to serve still distrusted reform movements, but he was sure that in the future there would be an "inevitable" demand for "social amelioration." [19]

Affected by so many crosscurrents, none of the American liberal prelates ever developed the passion for reform that had gripped Bishop von Ketteler in mid-century or Cardinal Manning in their own time. Gibbons saw no serious flaws in American society. In an article prompted by Carnegie's essay on "Wealth," the cardinal managed to praise Carnegie, call on the oppressed to exercise Christian patience, and applaud the socialist enterprises of European Catholics.[20] To Gibbons, the greatest dangers to American civilization were polygamy, political corruption, and delays in executing sentences pronounced by the courts. If "social convulsions" forced him to abandon his favorite policy of "masterly inactivity," he imagined his role was to say "to the troubled waters, 'Peace, be still,' " rather than to join in the convulsion.[21] Yet, out of deference to public opinion, and from his conviction that America could absorb any number of social medicine men, he worked so skillfully to prevent Rome from condemning the American component of that incarnation of the reform spirit, the Knights of Labor, that he won the reputation as a progenitor of Catholic social reform.[22]

Archbishop Ireland accepted the bourgeois ideals of the Republican Party; "respect" for capital, he declared, "must be supreme."[23] But his great faith in enterprise led him to approve all reform efforts that did not directly jeopardize the prerogatives of property. "Speak of vested rights," he told the lay congress of Baltimore, "for that is necessary, but speak, too, of vested wrongs, and strive . . . by the enactment and enforcement of good laws to correct them."[24] His colonization projects, his campaigns for temperance legislation, his acceptance of compulsory school legislation, all demonstrated the depth of his commitment to social action.

Bishop Spalding was too free an intellect to be a day laborer in reform efforts. For the "mechanical appliances and patent remedies of reformers and empirics," he once expressed an acute distaste; "to have a grievance is to be a bore," he declared. He perceived evolutionary processes which made all human enterprises seem irrelevant, but he also hailed the discovery of techniques by which men could transform society.[25] He had the seer's ability to recognize realities that theory-ridden men denied; in testifying before a Senate labor investigation, he impatiently dismissed abstract rights, to report the actual facts of contemporary worker conditions.[26] His social understanding deepened throughout his life.[27]

The Paulists were too proud of America to demand drastic reforms in its economic or social life. But the perplexity that many Americans were experiencing was apparent in an article of Augustine Hewit's which contrasted the material progress epitomized in the Chicago Exposition and the social discontent evidenced in the Debs "revolution." Hewit approved of Cleveland's suppression of anarchy, but he did not hide his distress that such strong action was necessary. Unwilling to place all blame on the strikers, he confessed his inability to propose the desperately needed remedy.[28] And, as the leading liberal apologists, the Paulists were in the forefront in demanding legislation that would stamp out intemperance.

The Paulists opened the *Catholic World* to many priest reformers. Father John Talbot Smith of New York had no difficulty in demonstrating the fatuousness of Henry Ward Beecher's panaceas. To deny that many workers were simply underpaid, or "to say that they suffer from their own ignorance," Smith declared, "is to make a false statement and err most sinfully." [29] Morgan Sheedy of Pittsburgh knew that the real problem for many miners was not how to invest their savings most judiciously but how to secure a family wage.[30] Such critics were not halted by mere shibboleths. "Freedom of contract," the layman John J. O'Shea declared, "is a fine-sounding phrase, but it covers more infamy in ninety-nine cases out of a hundred than any other sophism of subtle man's invention." [31] To the supposedly unanswerable objection that legislation often injured innocent parties, Father Smith retorted that "in rooting out an abuse some one must suffer, and the executors of the reform must look rather to the innumerable sufferings relieved than to the few occasioned by its enforcement." [32] These writers demanded legislation to exorcise such social evils as poor recreation facilities, child labor, monopolies, slum housing, and corporation malpractices.[33]

None of the liberal priests of the 1890's committed himself to a comprehensive "new deal," and none dedicated his life to social action so completely as would Peter Dietz, John A. Ryan, and William Kerby in the next twenty-five years. Yet by the criteria of their own times they were social liberals, who by enthusiasm for some causes, tolerance for many others, helped shift the Church away from social passivity. The liberals were particularly energetic in working to develop new Catholic attitudes towards charity, the rights of workers, the obligations of property, and the remedy for intemperance.

II

By the 1890's, many social workers had become convinced that charity should not be limited to alleviating penury and suffering, but should undertake to eradicate the causes of social distress. For this greater task, charity needed "more intelligence, not more feeling and heart." Systematic organizations of workers coöperating with the state could eliminate inefficiency and prevent the fraudulent and shiftless from preying on uninformed sympathies. Many cities and states founded Charity Organization societies, and a National Conference of Charities and Corrections was established.[34]

Conservative Catholics disapproved of both the spirit and the characteristic techniques of the new program. Charity should salve, not seek to eliminate suffering. Recognizing the great spiritual benefits that came to those who were charitable, the conservatives rejoiced that the opportunity for giving alms would always exist. A Canadian editor, Jules Tardivel, declared that "a country where there are no beggars is a veritable branch of hell." [35] The new charity, conservatives suspected, humiliated recipients by treating needs as "ignominious," instead of inevitable.[36] The charity proffered by the St. Vincent de Paul societies was far better, for a "Vincentian" was not a paid, impersonal worker, but a lay missionary who brought to each sufferer spiritual advice and personal friendship as well as physical aid.[37] He did not attempt to compute an individual's need by a social calculus, nor did he invoke a "statistical Christ" in place of a Redeemer of boundless charity. He did not waste his energy on red tape and organizational setting-up exercises.[38] Conservatives were not overly concerned if inefficiency appeared; "a more precarious method of voluntary donations, which always seem to come when needed most" would produce in recipients "a firmer reliance on the providence of God." [39] Emphasizing the supernatural aspects of true charity, the conservatives concluded that charity not guided by the Church was "an anomaly . . . a blind and feeble struggling . . . dwarfed and perverted." It was wrong, therefore, for Catholics out of neighborliness, civic duty, or apologetic interest, to assist nonsectarian charity work. Catholics could do all necessary work alone, and do it in the only worthwhile way.[40]

The liberals, too, stressed the virtues of spontaneous sacrifice, and they gave unqualified praise to the work of the "Vincentians"; they recognized some of the shortcomings of the "new charity." But, like their non-Catholic contemporaries, they believed that the old charity attempted too little. Bishop Keane emphasized that Leo XIII was no "medieval theologian, preaching charity and resignation," but a modern man alive to the demands of social justice, and in favor of all lawful means of accomplishing it.[41] Father McGlynn insisted that charity "too often is taken as meaning the mere doling out of alms. . . . Charity is a noble virtue, but to make the whole world an almshouse is carrying it to the absurd. The noblest charity is to do justice." [42] In his forthright way, Spalding declared that a colonization society which removed men from impossible urban conditions was "worth a hundred St. Vincent de Paul Societies." [43]

The liberals were not convinced that poverty always produced "salutary suffering." Too often it seemed to bring out irresponsibility in the poor, and complacency in the rich. Ireland did not think that pain-and-poverty-stricken animals would regularly respond to the reasonable teachings of Christ. To the delegates at the Catholic Columbian Congress he said that the Bible was "throughout a great book of holy social work for men. The miracles of our blessed Lord were primarily exercised for the good of the body, for the temporal felicity of man." [44] Bishop Keane believed that "Christian civilization aims at a reign of universal comfort. He who said: 'Blessed and happy are the poor in spirit,' had no blessing for the destitution which breeds misery and degradation. This is a curse and blot that must be wiped away." [45]

The liberals pressed for stronger organization of charity effort. "Instinctive charity is good," Professor Thomas Dwight of Boston told the Columbian Congress, "but charity guided by reason is better." Another speaker pointed out that organization would force the miserly to contribute as never before.[46] The Catholic World happily reported that a group of ladies who named their reading circle for Frédéric Ozanam had spent some time discussing "How to Prevent Indiscriminate Charity." [47] Organization on a national scale did not come until the twentieth century when, partly as the result of the efforts of the Catholic University liberals, the National Conference of Catholic Charities was organized.[48] The New York archdiocese appointed a General Supervisor of Catholic charities in 1897, and Boston, ten years later, established a Diocesan Charitable Bureau. Much earlier, the liberals had begun to join or coöperate with non-Catholic groups. Ireland served as vice-president of the National Conference of Charities and Corrections, and assured its members that Catholics blessed the work being done.[49] At the Baltimore Home for Industry, Gibbons expressed his pleasure that Catholics and Jews were working together. "Thanks be to God," he said, "there is but one platform in charity, and I cannot fail to thank these good Hebrew women for their efforts with us." [50] Ireland thought that even the Salvation Army, despite its frank evangelism, was doing too much good to merit censure. A writer in the *Catholic World* argued that Catholics might conscientiously contribute to the Army, since almost all its money went directly to relieve physical distress.[51]

All coöperative efforts which did good work were consciously or unconsciously Catholic, Ireland declared.[52] Father Edward Mc-Sweeny wryly suggested that Christ would not have reproved the poorer priest and Levite if they had agreed to join forces with the wealthy Samaritan in charitable work. He was convinced that Protestants were anxious to render "enlightened coöperation." [53] And the Paulists rejoiced when the 1895 national convention of the St. Vincent de Paul Societies resolved to work in fellowship with all high-principled groups. "There is more hope for Christian unity in this one practical step than in tons of pamphleteering and leader-writing," the *Catholic World* wrote. Soon the "reproach of incivism" would no longer be heard against the Church.[54]

III

For many social reformers, the central problem was not what kind of aid to give to the helpless, but how to improve the condition of the working class, condemned all too frequently to "want and wretchedness," and sometimes virtually "bestialized," Bishop Spalding protested, so that a few might "keep company, eat, drink, and dawdle." [55] All Catholics who considered working-class problems called the attention of employers to their responsibilities as Christians for the workers' temporal welfare.[56] But only the most trusting believed that exhortations would solve the problem.

Anxious for action, the Catholic liberals were, nevertheless, too wedded to contemporary economic theory to advocate legislation which would diminish the areas of free economic activity. Disliking the inequities that resulted from the "iron law of wages," they almost unanimously rejected state wage-fixing. "There is no statutory method devisable," John O'Shea asserted; "we cannot go back to the days of Edward III, and lay down a scale of wages for labor." [57] The liberals at least refused to endorse the free labor contract as unqualifiedly as did conservatives like Bishops Chatard and O'Connor.[58] A living wage for the worker and his family was more important than any economic principle; admiration for the results of capitalistic enterprise did not prevent Archbishop Ireland from declaring to Catholics that

what was said to be a boon to the workingman, the open market for labor, not seldom put him in the condition of a beast of burden, or a piece of machinery, to be valued only for his power in keeping the wheels of industry in motion, and to be accorded the lowest reward that competition with fellow-laborers in a state akin to starvation made possible.

This attitude was simply "unchristian," he maintained; Bishop Keane called it a "horrible perversion of humanity." [59]

For lack of a better solution, the liberals came increasingly to hope that the countervailing power of organized labor would improve the lot of the workingman. With business abandoning pure individualism, there seemed no good reason why the workers should remain as isolated economic units.[60] Though the Second Plenary Council of Baltimore, meeting in 1866, gave approval in principle to Catholic membership in labor organizations, it was not so easy for Church leaders to sanction the unions actually in existence. James Bayley had been convinced that they intended a frontal assault on the authority of the state; "no Catholic," he said, "with any idea of the spirit of his religion will encourage them." [61] Certainly, the Knights of Labor, whose 700,000 members in 1886 made it by far the largest union in American history, exhibited all too plainly the major failings of contemporary labor organization from the conservative Catholic point of view. Its catch-all platform espoused social and economic heresies. It demanded of its members a pledge of secrecy which seemed to jeopardize the power of their confessors. Finally, though Terence Powderly was a professing Catholic, he had neither the power nor the inclination to limit the union to Catholics. "Brothers, Protestant and Catholic," he had declared in 1877, "I call upon you as you hope for eternal salvation hereafter to join hands in the amelioration of Labor, for God knows we have enemies enough arrayed against us in the ranks of Capital without our creating new ones among ourselves." [62] It was hardly surprising, therefore, that religious orders were frequently so outspokenly critical in their mission sermons that loyal Catholics felt obliged to quit the Knights.[63]

At the Third Plenary Council, while conservatives pressed for stringent penalties for membership in unions of this kind, the liberals hoped to reform their practices if not their professed principles. Under liberal urging, the Council, hoping to forestall rash attacks on suspect unions, reserved to the committee of archbishops (on which the liberals were disproportionately strong) the right to make all specific designations of societies to be shunned. In cases on which the archbishops could not agree, Rome was to decide.[64] Priests were still free to counsel individual Catholics not to belong to a union, and in certain areas the Knights continued to be pressed hard. But Gibbons, who had been enough distressed by the rapid growth of the Knights to warn them against forming a monopoly of labor, and against misusing the boycott, did not believe that the Order should be formally censured.[65] This imperfect truce between the Knights and the Church continued until the conservative Elzéar Cardinal Taschereau of Quebec obtained explicit Roman disapproval of the Knights in his province.[66] When Corrigan was asked for advice, the archbishop promptly replied that in his opinion the order was "undoubtedly forbidden" in New York as well; Catholics who persisted in their membership were automatically to be deprived of the sacraments.[67] Gibbons, however, obtained assurances from Powderly that the Order was law abiding, and that an individual Knight was required to withhold nothing from his religious director; the cardinal then called the archbishops together, and found that nine out of eleven agreed with him that Church censure was undesirable.[68]

Ireland and Keane took the council's queries to Rome, and immediately began to lobby for a favorable reply. In February, 1887, they helped draw up a memorial which Gibbons presented to the Congregation of Propaganda. A shrewd mixture of moral principle and expediency, it accurately reflected the complex liberal position towards American labor organizations.[69]

Gibbons' basic premise was that it was desirable to seek diligently for a human remedy to the problems of monopolies and starvation wages. The American people, instead of turning to invidious class legislation, watched "with perfect composure and confidence the progress of our social contest" between capital and labor. No one desired the interference of the Church; no one was afraid that the contest would lead to violence or chaos. Labor needed to be organized for this contest, and it was "the part of Christian prudence" to guide rather than to try to block this legitimate demand. The Knights intended no evil, Gibbons argued, and he repeated Powderly's assurance that anything the Church thought untoward in its resounding preamble would be eliminated. Far from sanctioning violence in labor disputes, the Order had restrained the hot-headed. It was idle to hope for purely Catholic unions in America, Gibbons declared, but he reassured Roman authorities that the Catholics in the Order were "intelligent, well-instructed and devoted children ready to give their blood, as they continually give their means" for the welfare of the Church; their associates, except for a few not-yet-Americanized immigrants, were anything but malevolent. Nowhere in his defense did Gibbons eulogize the Knights. Indeed, he noted without a trace of regret that the Order was already rapidly declining.

Awful consequences were likely if the Roman censure was maintained. Would it not be a Pyrrhic victory, Gibbons asked, to condemn a somewhat imperfect society, already on the decline, and thereby alienate Catholic workers who had been exercising what they considered "their legitimate right?" The American Church would suffer severely, and the Peter's Pence sent to Rome would probably shrink. A condemnation might also arouse the anger of those non-Catholics who belonged to the Knights, those who did not believe the Order was dangerous, and those who simply resented "Roman" interference in American problems. These last arguments were not easy for the liberals to present. Catholics were loyal, but only if not driven too far. They were generous, but they might curtail their giving if oppressed. Non-Catholics were friendly, but capable of fierce resentment.[70] Such subtleties prevented the memorial from being completely straightforward, but it still constituted an effective plea for a large tolerance.

The liberals were opposed in Rome, openly by Taschereau, more circumspectly by Corrigan and the Germans.[71] But in August, 1888, Propaganda ruled that, in the light of new evidence submitted by Gibbons, the Knights could be tolerated, provided they made a few minor changes in the preamble. Powderly finally agreed to do so, and Gibbons notified the hierarchy that the Knights were now completely free of Church censure. To the *Brooklyn Examiner*, the decision was an ignominious defeat for the "fossiliferous remnant of a past age," especially for "Sancho" Pallen, who had warned against the "tyranny of organization," and for a Catholic periodical which had advised workers simply to "Pray, Pray, Pray." [72] The *Catholic World* had long since urged Catholic workers to unite against wage slavery. "Be Knights," it said.[73]

Some conservatives speculated that the Church was abandoning the defense of the individual and of private property. The *Nation* accused Gibbons of "partaking freely of the labor beverage," and of not recognizing that the Knights were the worst kind of corporation. *Puck* ran a cartoon depicting a complacent Gibbons extending benevolent hands over a crowd of Irish toughs sallying out from a saloon to stone a neat, respectable scab.[74] Bishop John Kain of Wheeling reported ominous "mutterings" among business leaders, and asked Gibbons to allay misapprehensions by more vigorously attacking the Knights' boycotting practices.[75] These alarms were unjustified. Defending the rights of workers to join unions of their own choosing, the liberal Catholics were, with few exceptions, as critical as any conservative of the uses made of union power. Even while Gibbons was fighting the condemnation of the Knights, he warned their national convention against strikes.[76] Most of the liberals would sanction walkouts only if violence was avoided, and if scabs were allowed to take over the work. The boycott was tolerable only if it did not interfere with the rights of each man to buy what he wanted.[77]

But even to defend the right of the Knights to exist was a radical innovation for Catholics in the 1880's. In the following decade, when the liberals were reënforced by Leo's approval in *Rerum Novarum* of labor "associations," they consolidated their reputation by making no implausible demands upon existing unions. Though Joseph Schroeder clearly demonstrated that the Catholic unions Leo sanctioned were a far cry from anything to be found in the United States, Keane insisted that the American unions were tolerable.[78] And the liberals took no heed of Schroeder's reminder that the Pope desired employers and employees to belong to the same association. While strong advocates of arbitration between capital and labor, they gave no sign of believing that a return to medieval corporatism would substantially aid the cause of the working class.[79]

IV

The conservatives were steadfastly opposed to the Knights of Labor not only because it was a labor union, but because it demanded public ownership of certain industries, and even threatened the rights of private landholders. Such purposes were clearly socialistic, to be associated with the full-scale assault on individual and ecclesiastical rights which socialism had always involved. Few conservatives would admit that socialism and the Church could have anything in common.[80] "Socialism" was much less of a shibboleth for men like Bishop Spalding, who argued that since socialism was not a precise doctrine, but a stream of tendency, only the Quixotes would insist on unqualified attack.[81] Many of the liberals, recognizing much that was perceptive and more that was generous in socialist thought, believed that proposals for reform by men like Henry George should not be dealt with harshly.[82]

The *Catholic World* devoted several articles to George's theories, and only the essay by Henry Brann reflected ill-tempered hostility.[83] John T. Smith called George a "genius," especially in his refutation of Malthus' glum predictions; George certainly "deserved well of Christianity on this score." Both Brann and Smith rejected George's contention that man had an absolute right to everything he produced. Brann, characteristically, concluded that George intended to give a man absolute right to the children he produced, thus sanctioning "child-murder. . . . Here is the old despotism of pagan Roman fathers over the life and death of their children revived," he noted darkly. Smith, more generously, argued that George's principle did not provide for emergencies when starving men were properly entitled to the property of anyone.

Both Brann and Smith insisted that private property in land was justifiable, but the liberals were anxious that this right be carefully defined. The contemporary school of "naturalists" argued that private ownership was "a sheer necessity, an imperative, exclusive sole means of satisfying man's wants," and of securing respect for his rights.[84] Less absolutist, but still, in the opinion of the liberals, attributing too great a sanctity to private ownership, was the "compactist" theory, which, as advanced by the Jesuit René Holaind, traced the first distribution of land to a general desire for the better society which individual property made possible. Once society had made this choice, Holaind implied, it was virtually impotent ever to impair a title which an individual had acquired. A *Catholic World* reviewer was sharply critical. "If the sacredness of the human personality can be extended over every manageable aggregation of the means of existence, as this treatise maintains, the masses of men are going to be but as parasites upon the few. They will be looked upon and treated as vermin." Holaind was unjustified in claiming that such an extravagant hypothesis was the orthodox Catholic teaching, any more than was the "naturalist" theory. A true conception of property would recognize the right of the state to expropriate land, with fair compensation, for parks, schools, and public institutions "of every sort." Catholics, in resisting George's errors, should be careful, the *Catholic World* cautioned, not to "advocate a state of things in which the very few are granted the particularism of nearly all this world's favors, and the vast multitude of men forced to suffer the communism of all the world's miseries." [85]

The *World* considered Georgism simply "philosophical communism," and in all likelihood, there would have been no great interest in the Church had not George very early discerned a parallel between the "poverty" of America and the plight of Ireland; this quickly won him an audience among the New York Irish Catholics. The most notable cleric to espouse Georgism was Edward McGlynn, pastor of the thriving parish of St. Stephen's. A celebrated orator, McGlynn early distinguished himself as a stalwart defender of the public schools, as a critic of all governmental aid to religious groups, and as a man willing to attribute most of the Church's difficulties to the foibles of the faithful. Despite these deviations, however, McGlynn retained considerable favor with his diocesan, Cardinal McCloskey.[86]

But the enthusiasm which led McGlynn, years later, to eulogize Henry George as "a man sent of God" quickly antagonized Catholic conservatives.[87] In 1882, the prefect of the Propaganda, Cardinal Simeoni, wrote New York that he had been informed McGlynn was advocating unsound theories of property in his support of the Irish Land League. Cardinal McCloskey, after learning that the priest did not want "to cut up Manhattan Island into little bits and give each of us a bit," secured McGlynn's promise not to speak again for the deeply suspect Land League. When Simeoni protested against subsequent McGlynn speeches, McCloskey, with some asperity, defended the priest's right to sympathize with starving Irishmen. Unfortunately for McGlynn, McCloskey died in 1885, and was succeeded by the much more intransigent Corrigan.

The next year, George declared for mayor of New York. To supporters like McGlynn, his candidacy promised more than the American Revolution; to Catholic conservatives, it seemed not only a dangerous attack on a sympathetic Tammany machine, but also a formidable aggression of socialism.[88] McGlynn was happy to coöperate with the Knights of Labor in support of George, and on one occasion he shared a platform with Daniel De Leon, already an outspoken radical, and with the Reverend Heber Newton, an extremely liberal Protestant. Corrigan was outraged, and ordered McGlynn to end his political activities, but the priest refused, writing the archbishop that "I, in view of my rights and duties as a citizen, which were not surrendered when I became a priest, am determined to do what I can to support Mr. George." [89]

As the election neared, a Democratic politician wrote Thomas Preston, Corrigan's vicar-general, to ask if Father McGlynn was speaking for all the Catholic clergy. "The great majority of the Catholic Church in this city," Preston replied in an open letter, "are opposed to the candidacy of Mr. George. They think his principles unsound and unsafe, and contrary to the teachings of the Church." Preston denied that the Church would intervene in an election, but insisted that the clergy "would not wish to be misunderstood at a´ time when the best interests of society may be in danger." [90] After George's decisive defeat, Corrigan issued a pastoral which strenuously criticized socialistic land theories. McGlynn replied with a vibrant defense of Georgism, which immediately provoked censures from the archbishop and from Rome. Noisily unrepentant, he was suspended, removed from St. Stephen's, and eventually excommunicated, primarily because of his disobedience to his Archbishop.[91]

Most liberal Catholics subscribed to Corrigan's platitudes on property, and few clerics would sanction McGlynn's contumacy. But Archbishop Riordan of San Francisco wrote Keane that if prelates had to "attack somebody," they might better attack "the gigantic corporations and monopolies of the land and say a kind and tender word for the great army of the laboring classes." Father Malone wrote Leo XIII that public censure of "the best-known priest in America, the friend of the poor, the eloquent defender" of the Church, would set Catholicism back fifty years. And Gibbons acknowledged in his Knights of Labor memorial that though Corrigan's action was "just and necessary," it "fell upon a priest who was regarded as the friend of the people. . . . Sad and threatening confusion" had resulted.[92] McGlynn jeopardized much of his Catholic support by tactless remarks about the need for root-and-branch reforms in the Church.[93] Yet he steadfastly refused to renounce Catholicism, or to admit that his excommunication was valid. Many priests felt compelled to warn their people against hearing McGlynn defend his crusade for economic justice, but Gibbons never saw fit to do so.[94]

The dissension within the Church increased when Corrigan attempted to have *Progress and Poverty* placed upon the Index of Prohibited Books. Gibbons wrote Rome that such an action was imprudent. The New York mayoralty election showed clearly that Americans were unimpressed by Georgism. They would naturally resent being told not to read a book which had been widely circulated for years. Most important of all, Roman condemnation, Gibbons warned, might be misconstrued to mean papal aversion to any attempt to better the condition of the people. Many bishops, both liberal and conservative, seconded Gibbons, and suggested, as he had done, that the best solution would be an encyclical covering the whole question of property and social action.[95]

Rome's answer came in several installments. The approval of the Knights contained a special proviso that words in the Order's platform that "seem to savor of socialism and communism" should be removed.[96] George's book was not placed on the Index, but the Inquisition sent a supposedly secret letter to the American hierarchy reaffirming the principle of private property, and warning all Catholics to "beware of the false theories of Henry George." On the strength of this letter, Preston announced that *Progress and Poverty* would eventually be placed on the Index, and in the meantime was classed with other evil books which the Church had not yet deigned to consider fully.[97] Both liberals and conservatives were delighted with Leo's encyclical on the condition of the working class. Corrigan found that the first sections condemned socialism and reaffirmed the virtues of private property. Bishop Keane thought that the Pope had clearly refused to endorse "naturalist" or extreme "compactist" views on the sanctity of property, but had instead fully recognized and approved the interplay of public and private interests.[98]

As a result of liberal pressure, the Propaganda agreed, in the summer of 1892, to reopen the McGlynn case, commissioning Archbishop Ireland to interview the priest. Ireland not only sympathized with McGlynn, but saw a chance to lay Corrigan "low." "I think the McGlynn case will be reopened with a splendid chance for the poor man. This will break Corrigan's heart," he added, gloatingly.[99] McGlynn submitted a statement of his beliefs to Archbishop Satolli, the papal ablegate recently arrived in America. The priest stalwartly disavowed socialism, but he also refused to sanction full ownership rights; the state, he insisted, should retain the right to levy for "public purposes a tax that should equal the annual value of the land itself" so that the government could carry out its increasingly extensive social obligations.[100] Satolli found this statement satisfactory, and McGlynn agreed to go to Rome. There he found the Pope anxious to close the controversy. "Do you teach against private property?" the priest was asked. "I do not; I am staunch for private property," was McGlynn's reply. "I thought so," Leo said, and conferred his blessing before McGlynn could expound the speculative niceties of his position.[101]

By restoring McGlynn, the liberals succeeded in limiting the damage done to the Church by Corrigan's uncompromising insistence on a narrow orthodoxy. A layman regretfully compared Gibbons' tolerance of *Progress and Poverty* with the Corrigan-McGlynn controversy, in which "hundreds of liberal-minded men all over the country were estranged from the Church by the course of bitter denunciation and violent abuse."[102] From the tributes that poured in at McGlynn's death a few years later, the liberals could readily conclude that the priest's crusade for social justice, instead of producing scandal, heresy, or schism, had promoted goodwill among non-Catholics. Altgeld called him "a great apostle of humanity," and the Reverend William Rainsford said that McGlynn was "a saint, a crusader born ahead of his time. He and Jacob Riis knew the poor of New York, and were loved by them more than any other men in my time." The Reverend Heber Newton's words stated the liberals' case precisely; "an outsider turns to the quiet beauty and spiritual power of such a life as that of Father McGlynn and knows that if he is ever to be brought back to the Mother Church, it is through the influence of such lives." [103]

The McGlynn affair did not improve the liberals' reputation in Rome. In 1894, Leo XIII warned Keane against aligning the Church with the growing socialism in America. The liberals, however, remained serenely confident that the welfare of both Church and society was best served by a broad tolerance, and Keane replied that he hoped Rome would avoid whenever possible the condemnation of well-intentioned reform movements.[104]

V

The reform effort to which the liberals committed themselves most decisively was the campaign against the misuse of alcohol. Nineteenth-century temperance efforts were not conscious diversions from other more needed reforms. Many of the same groups struggled for temperance as had sought the betterment of the working class. Ireland and some of his allies it is true, considered temperance the prerequisite to all other social reform, but they did not remain quietistic on other proposals until temperance was achieved. And, in prosecuting temperance reform, these men were led to acknowledge so unreservedly society's share of responsibility for individual failing that few future difficulties would be regarded as requiring only individual moral enterprise.

But no reform divided Catholics more sharply. To the recent immigrant, temperance agitation seemed an impertinent attempt to curb a pleasant custom sanctioned by the Bible and eighteen hundred years of Christian practice. All the bishops in the world, Sebastian Messmer declared, could not convince a German or an Italian that a glass of beer or wine was intrinsically evil.[105] Immigrants suspected that temperance movements were the work of hypocritical Puritans and of constitutionally intemperate nationalities. Father Walburg was sure that "while an Irishman will get drunk and engage in an open street fight, and the German drink his beer in a public beergarden, the American, pretending to be a total abstainer, takes his strong drink secretly and sleeps it off on a sofa or in a club-room." [106] Catholics who insisted on "all-saving teetotalism" generally closed their eyes, Walburg suspected, to the real dangers of "irreligion." [107] Less spiritual objections came from retailers of liquor, who, in immigrant communities, were both prosperous and influential. The liberals, for their part, conspicuously failed to understand the vital part the saloon played in the social life of the immigrant. Ireland conceded that beer halls were tolerable in Europe, and that "some consideration is due to the previous conditions and social habits of immigrants." But he declared that beer halls transplanted to America invariably became intolerable saloons.[108] Morgan Sheedy considered the proposal of an Episcopalian rector to establish church-supervised drinking halls "monstrous and absurd"; nicely furnished reading clubs, he thought, were a better alternative.[109]

Catholic temperance men painted awful pictures of the physical degeneration that awaited most drinkers. They declared that most liquor was poisonously adulterated to stimulate greater thirst. And they agreed with Josiah Strong that the American climate left the human body less able to resist alcohol's deadly work.[110] Intemperance was to blame for most of the poverty in America; it also exacted a "life-tribute from industry," and robbed all too many Catholics of their rightful places in society. "If our people had saved up for the last fifty years the money that went into saloons," Ireland argued, "how different socially would they not be; how much more influence they would have." [111]

Religion also suffered. The intemperate man not only sinned gravely, but lost the instinct to seek sacramental assistance.[112] Strong though the Church was in America, it would have been stronger had not intoxication led many Catholics to disregard their religious obligations. President Thomas Walsh of Notre Dame was convinced that if whiskey drinking could be ended, the progress of the American Church would be unlimited.[113] The Church was also harmed, the liberals knew, by the impression that "Rum, Rome, the saloon and the priest," were indissolubly linked.[114] On the other hand, America would be quick to approve Catholic reform efforts.

In this spirit, Catholic groups at the Columbian Congress of Temperance met with non-Catholics in order "that they should see and recognize the work which we had done," Father Scanlan of Chicago said, "as we applauded what they accomplished. . . . It is well that we let our light shine before men." [115]

By the 1890's, the liberals believed that American opinion was beginning to change. When Thomas Conaty left his parish in Worcester, Massachusetts, he was given a generous send-off by the Protestant community. "It is well to remember," the *Catholic World* said, "that this ovation was the spontaneous expression of New England devotion to a Catholic priest [who had] won his way to New England hearts because he entered the arena of public life" to work against intemperance.[116] And Theodore Roosevelt, speaking to a Catholic convention in 1895, proclaimed that "all Americans owe a debt of gratitude to the Catholic Church for the valiant and righteous war it has waged for temperance." He singled out for especial praise "that magnificent American," John Ireland.[117] This respect for the Church's sense of social responsibility would surely lead to respect for her religious teachings, the liberals believed. Such a prospect seemed remote to most conservatives; to them, the temperance movement appeared far more likely to lead to infringements on the liberty of individual Catholics. "Temperance," the German Catholic Central Verein declared, "is a cardinal virtue and not a hygienic condition. It cannot be forced or inoculated."[118] They did not object if some Catholics needed an oath of total abstinence to keep from injuring themselves, but however many took the pledge, no moral judgment could be passed on those who used alcohol temperately. The problem of temperance was one for the individual, guided by his priest, to solve.[119]

The liberals, by contrast, came to rely less and less on the individual's resolution. Ireland was convinced of the "native comparative powerlessness of the Irish" to resist liquor. For such people, liquor, though not itself sinful, often constituted a proximate occasion for sin.[120] To reduce these occasions, the liberals turned first to the legislative power of the Church. At the Third Plenary Council, a committee which included Ireland, Keane, and Spalding secured the adoption of several temperance decrees. The Council ordered priests not to enter saloons except when necessary in the course of travel, and forbade church societies from serving alcoholic drinks. Intemperance was strenuously condemned, and total abstinence praised not only for those needing it themselves, but as a voluntary sacrifice by those wishing to set a good example.[121] The Council exhorted Catholic liquor dealers to find another occupation, or, at least, to obey all the laws against tempting the weak and the young. Though the prelates rejected Keane's plan to petition Rome to revoke the right of a Benedictine monastery near Pittsburgh to brew and market "St. Vincent's Beer," the liberals were satisfied that the Council had deprived most American Catholics of any excuse for disgracing themselves or their Church.[122]

Unfortunately, some Catholics were unwilling to forego the profit of selling liquor, and many more were unwilling to forego the pleasure of drinking it. Father Walter Elliott concluded disgustedly that European practices and rationalizations were more honored than "the positive injunctions of the American hierarchy." [123] "Since the Catholic Church in America has set its face against the saloon," Father Sheedy implored, "let us all, priests and laymen, *hear the Church*." [124]

In fact, the decrees were effective in those dioceses where the bishops enthusiastically endorsed them. In St. Paul, Irish names virtually disappeared from liquor shops as the result of Ireland's efforts. Bishop John Watterson of Columbus, Ohio, also acted decisively. Urging his clergy in March 1894 to support total abstinence, he made clear that he wanted Catholics completely out of the liquor business. He refused to approve as Catholic any society officered by a liquor dealer, or which in the future admitted liquor dealers even as members. Dealers who broke the state's regulatory laws would be denied the sacraments until they gave up their trade "altogether." [125] Indignant protests were immediately made to Archbishop Satolli, but the delegate considered the decrees a valid exercise of episcopal discretion, and suggested that its provisions were in "harmony with the laws of the Church," and, in addition, were "seasonable and necessary for the honor of the Church, especially in the State of Ohio." The thoroughly delighted liberals naturally insisted that Satolli's ruling was a command from Rome which all American Catholics should heed.[126]

Anxious to call into play "all the forces of civilized society," the liberals did not rely solely on episcopal action.[127] One auxiliary means was the temperance society. Even the conservatives could approve of the League of the Cross, founded by a Jesuit in 1883. Careful not to attack liquor itself, to think intemperance the only vice, or to call for total abstinence, it held no meetings and sedulously avoided all "hurrah." [128] In marked contrast was the Catholic Total Abstinence Union, which held its first convention in 1872, and in which Keane and Ireland were prominent from the outset. Established as a close-knit organization, with an active membership and regular meetings, it organized into state rather than diocesan units, with laymen retaining important leadership positions.[129] Conservatives criticized both the aims and the methods of the CTAU even after the Pope sent his formal approval.[130] They were especially dismayed by the union's professed willingness to coöperate with Protestants and other apostles of reform. This tolerance was most vividly demonstrated when Frances Willard, militant feminist and temperance worker, was invited to address the union in 1891.[131]

The invitation symbolized not only confidence that coöperation would redound to the benefit of the Church, but also, since Miss Willard was an advocate of prohibition, a willingness to rely on the coercive powers of the state. In 1882, the union had asserted that as a "strictly Catholic" group, it relied "wholly upon the efficacy of prayer, the influence of pastors from the pulpit, and in their private capacity . . . and not upon any compulsory means." Yet even earlier, the delegates had declared that they would "gladly hail" restrictive legislation, and, in 1884, John Ireland proposed to resolve all ambiguities by enjoining the use of every available power. "God never proposed to save men only by His sacraments," he told the CTAU convention. "God requires that we do our share." Even the saloonkeepers were in favor of "moral suasion," he contemptuously noted. Bishop Keane declared that

the Divine Law which forbids evil, and the human law which devises restraints and chastisements for the same end, are meant to go hand in hand, as they have ever done in civilized society. Moral suasion with its spiritual sanctions, and civil authority with its coercive helps, must be united in every human social system.[132]

The liberals unanimously approved of the laws requiring high license fees, Sunday closing, and no selling to minors.[133] Though many CTAU members balked at prohibition, considering it simple fanaticism, most of the Paulists and many of the liberal prelates were willing to experiment with it. "So long as saloon-keepers in defiance of law sell their wares on Sunday, or at forbidden hours, or to minors and drunkards," they argued, "so long will all good citizens have the right to . . . try what effect prohibition legislation will have." Ireland favored outright prohibition in rural areas, and helped found the Anti-Saloon League to obtain stringent legislation in the cities.[134] Most of the CTAU preferred to remain, as one liberal priest sardonically remarked, "a dignified reserve corps," which would fight for regulation but not prohibition, even of the saloon.[135]

These differences of opinion may have cost Catholic temperance advocates the opportunity of guiding the antiliquor forces towards more tenable goals than those won in 1919. But many Catholics undoubtedly profited from the liberals' campaign for temperance. And there were great apologetic benefits for the Church. Late nineteenth-century America did not demand immediate abolition of the use of alcohol, any more than it insisted upon a comprehensive re-definition of the rights of property, or of the prerogatives of the working class. It did require institutions not to reject intransigently all possibility of reform, but rather to welcome those attempts which increased human happiness without abandoning American traditions of personal liberty. The liberal Catholics succeeded in persuading many of the faithful that such an attitude was more compatible with the spiritual and temporal interests of the Church' than was the conservative program of isolation from American reform of every description.

CHAPTER VII

THE QUESTION OF THE
SCHOOLS

W hile the American people remained of two minds about reformers' plans to make special provisions for special classes of citizens, they had long agreed that universal education was desirable. In the last decades of the century, in fact, most Americans came to acknowledge that the states had the right to compel each child to obtain some schooling. A few zealots wanted the federal government to lend financial aid. Educational leagues were formed to develop ideal curricula, and the rapid growth of teachers' colleges and of school systems reflected the widespread conviction that education should not remain a haphazard process. Catholics inevitably shared in the general concern. "The education of youth is the engrossing topic of our times," Archbishop Gibbons wrote in 1883.[1] It was, without question, "the most living question of our day and for our own people," a conservative Catholic noted rather unhappily.[2]

Catholicism had a special interest in the educational question, for critics of the Church had long propagated the notion that the clergy were ineradicably hostile to the spread of knowledge.[3] Mayor Albert Ames of Minneapolis had publicly asserted that "where you find the priest, you find ignorance."[4] In 1890, the A.P.A. circulated a pastoral letter in which the American hierarchy was made to deplore "the rapid spread of educated intelligence, knowing full well that wherever the people are intelligent, the priest . . . cannot hope to live on the labor of the masses." [5] Not surprisingly, the liberals steadily insisted that the best way to end such charges was for the Church to foster every kind of educational enterprise.[6]

Conservatives suspected that anti-Catholic prejudice would not be eliminated by any amount of Church education. Furthermore, they were openly skeptical of the benefits that education, of the modern variety at least, was supposed to bring. In the history of Christianity, innocence had been more often associated with a child-like ignorance than with worldly knowledge, and René Holaind could find precedent for his belief that "ignorance, though itself an evil, often saves men from great dangers." [7] Father James Conway pointed out that society found better art critics from among illiterate Italian immigrants than among American college youth; and he argued that bespectacled German students were no better soldiers than the many members of the Irish Brigade who could neither read nor write. "We do not plead for illiteracy," he concluded, "but we are unable to perceive any great ignominy or serious inconvenience to a State in the fact that some of its colliers and ploughmen and cowboys and dairymaids are not able to read the morning paper." [8] If the general community was to achieve "the proper perfection," a few scholars were certainly necessary, but society could avoid the folly of forcing all children to prepare themselves for these responsibilities; God could be relied on to give vocations to a few able youths.[9]

To the liberals, on the other hand, the basic premise of the "American side of the school question" was that "universal suffrage demands universal education." [10] Spalding contended that "only the virtuous and enlightened can properly cherish and maintain the domestic, political, and religious institutions which consecrate and protect equal rights and liberties." [11] Essentially optimistic about human nature, the liberals believed that "from ignorance rather than from depravity have sprung the most appalling crimes, the most pervasive vices." [12] The more enthusiastic thought that educational progress could actually eliminate "ignorance" and "its train of contagious evils." [13] While newly-arrived immigrants might sometimes prove law-abiding, in spite of their parlous ignorance, even a moderate leader thought it "absurd to suppose that . . . they . . . should be under no obligation of qualifying their children to be better citizens than they themselves can in the average be." [14]

The conservatives were afraid that American education was specifically designed to unfit a man, intellectually and psychologically, for life in the station in which he had been born. "All the child is entitled to," Father Holaind stipulated, "is to receive the education necessary to live in comfort in the condition of his parents." [15] The parent, as "the owner of his child," could judge how much training should be given. [16] And he would be well advised to remember that good education was not liberation, but preparation for a wise conformity to traditional patterns.

Hecker disagreed vigorously; one of the chief virtues of education, he thought, was that it made possible the individual progress that was the basic goal of "our republic." [17] A *Catholic World* writer dismissed the idea of a "station in life" as meaningless. Education, he hoped, would inculcate "that sort of discontent which is peculiarly an American virtue, and which has inspired noble souls since the beginning to strive cheerfully and hopefully for better things." [18] Few human goals were unattainable, the liberals believed, by one who would discard the accidental dispositions of his background. Education, more than any other force except religion, would help a man find all that was "best and ennobling in life." [19]

On no point of educational theory were Catholics more sharply divided than on the desirability of providing the training more and more American women were demanding. [20] Appalled as many of the liberals were by the more brassy demands for women's rights, and anxious that the traditional womanly virtues should not be lost, they felt certain that, if society was to be reformed, women's capacities for enterprising moral action could not be neglected. [21] Christianity, they insisted had always stood for the fullest realization of women's potentialities. Spalding wanted women encouraged to become "not merely wives and mothers, but individual souls clothed with the liberty and strength of the children of God." [22] Father Hecker was convinced that women had the right to "any position whose duties and functions" they had the "intelligence or aptitude to fulfill." [23] "The day is gone," a western Catholic newspaper declared, "when you can deprive our brainy, ambitious young woman from the highest and best in education. She insists on having all the advantages of her brother, and she is right. The world 'do move.' "[24] Most liberals believed that the education typically given by the convent school was too rigid, preparing girls only for the seclusion of the nunnery or the home. For young women as for young men, education should not close the door on the opportunity for any moral career.[25]

To such arguments, conservatives sturdily replied that every Christian woman could find complete fulfillment in home life, supplemented by the diverse opportunities that the Church had traditionally offered for seemly service.[26] By seeking to emulate Mary, the American woman could avoid becoming that creature "of congresses, of committees, reforms, revolutions, contentions" that the brazen age so much admired.[27] If God required the services of a Jeanne d'Arc, conservatives were sure that He would specially notify a specific young girl to undertake the difficult role.[28] Unless given such supernatural direction, a woman should concentrate on preparing herself for the "calling for which the Creator evidently intended her: that for woman, wife, and mother." [29]

The liberals endorsed not only most of the goals but also many of the techniques of contemporary educational reform. Most parents, they believed, had neither the facilities nor the time to give their children the education they deserved.[30] In some cases, schools were needed to liberate the child from his family's warped ideals. The *Catholic World* praised kindergartens for taking little children "out of the gutters . . . close alleys and reeking slums," and placing them in "bright, clean, sunny rooms," transplanting them "from the companionship of older children already depraved, or of overworked and often drunken and brutal guardians, to the supervision of conscientious teachers." [31] The liberals emphasized that the child should not escape the tyranny of the home only to be forced to accept a "routine" or "mechanical" education. The teacher should respect the child's individuality, Gibbons argued; he should take students "as God made them," and concentrate on helping "them in bringing out the hidden powers of their soul." [32] Intellectual knowledge, too, the liberals believed, was best acquired not by memory work, but through vital participation in its discovery.[33] The liberals shared the enthusiasm of many non-Catholics for the advanced educational theories of Frederick Froebel, despite his religious radicalism. Finally, the liberals worked steadily to improve the quality of the teaching done in Catholic schools, ignoring conservative protests that the only truly important task of the teacher was the strengthening of the students' religious conviction.[34]

Every Catholic agreed that it was necessary to distinguish between "instruction" — the imparting of secular knowledge — and "education," which fostered moral and theological understanding.[35] But while the liberals did not question the greater value of "education," Bishop Spalding warned against letting a sedulous devotionalism substitute for the "love of thoroughness and excellence" necessary for sound "instruction." [36] The liberals were willing to conceive of "education" and "instruction" as separate processes, not necessarily given by the same teacher, or in the same room.[37] The conservative Michael Mueller, in contrast, argued that just "as leaven must be diffused throughout the entire mass in order to produce its effects, so religion must be thoroughly diffused throughout the child's entire education, in order to be solid and effective." [38] Sebastian Messmer insisted that "elementary school instruction is necessarily education, either good or bad; there is no medium, and the instructor, who teaches in those schools, without providing at the same time the proper education, [is offering] a necessarily defective and partial" education.[39] Only Catholic teachers would be able to keep true religious principles foremost throughout the teaching day, and one writer suggested that religious images on the walls, and religiously garbed teachers were equally necessary.[40]

Catholic leaders could not limit their consideration of education to constructing blueprints for ideal schools. In fact, these blueprints would have been far less necessary had their authors not been confronted with an existing system of schools, ubiquitous, popular, and financially very strong. To a very great degree, the root of the "school question" was the "public school question."

II

In the late nineteenth century, public schools were thriving in every state. Between 1880 and 1900, the number of students rose from one to fifteen million, and the appropriations from 80 to 210 million dollars.[41] Simultaneously, the schools were expanding their instruction. Henry Ward Beecher expressed a general determination when he said that "the common school should be so comfortable, so fat, so rich, so complete that no select school could live under its drippings." [42] The public schools had long ago lost the stigma of being mere charity schools, and now were regarded as the basic channel of American education.

Many Catholics found these schools very attractive. Hard pressed to secure enough money for their daily needs, they welcomed schools that charged no tuition fees, and which sometimes supplied free books and clothes to the children of the poor.[43] Immigrants recognized that the public schools' emphasis on English, mathematics, and American history prepared a student to make his way in American life. By associating with children of all faiths, young Catholics could lay the basis for future business advantage and social prestige.[44] Archbishop Ireland recounted all these arguments in a memorial to Propaganda in 1892, and concluded that at least 1.5 out of 2.2 million Catholics of school age were attending the public schools.[45] Some estimates were lower, but no one denied that many Catholic children were attending the public schools. The *Catholic Citizen* of Milwaukee admitted that the laity were nearly unanimously in favor of the public schools, and a Catholic member of the Boston School Board called the establishment of any church schools "a most serious mistake, if not a great misfortune, especially to those who attend them." [46]

Most of the conservatives, not surprisingly, denounced the public schools as "godless" because they gave no effective religious training.[47] Father Bayma argued that because of "the intrigues of unscrupulous men, the connivance of a rotten administration, the supineness or inattention of a distracted people, and the culpable imbecility of those whose duty it was to stand foremost," the spirit of international Free Masonry had completely captured the public schools.[48] Since all religious teaching was dropped from the Rochester schools directly after McQuaid denounced it as crypto-Protestantism, the bishop did not blame the Free Masons, but he was still able to censure his fellow citizens for "ill-considered rashness." He was not surprised that some advocates believed that the public school would "grind out the Catholicity of the children." And he spoke for all the conservatives when he declared that Catholics "loathe with supreme contempt the sectarianism of those who pretend that their particular development of sectarianism, their views . . . are so milk-and-watery (the power for good as a religious force being washed out of them) that they ought to be acceptable to all other sectarians." [49] "Let me say once and for all to Catholic parents," a conservative concluded, "the whole public school system is tainted with either Protestantism or irreligion." [50]

"Godless" education would never produce the heaven on earth some of the public school advocates had promised. Suspicious of all Protestant-Catholic association, Zachariah Montgomery argued that, far from saving the children from corruption, the public schools would mix innocents with the "crime-steeped progeny of the low and vile . . . children whose infant eyes have already grown familiar with obscene signs, lewd pictures and lecherous behavior; children to whose ears vile oaths, blasphemous language and words revolting to modesty are as ordinary habits of speech." [51] Mueller could not believe that "this wicked, detestable, irreligious system" could improve the youth; "seminaries of infidelity" were sure to be "hotbeds of immorality." He testified that "the moral character of the Public Schools in many of our cities has sunk so low, that even courtesans have disguised themselves as school-girls, in order the more surely to ply their foul vocation." [52] The products of such schools would be "educated blackguards, rotten to the core," and capable of "refined" criminality of every kind.[53] Montgomery proved statistically that crime, insanity, pauperism, and syphilis had increased proportionally to the growth of public education.[54] "Who are bursting the bonds of domestic society?" Father Conway asked. Who are the swindlers, who are the socialists and communists? Not "the much decried illiterate mass," he answered, but the "men and women who have enjoyed all the blessings of education, minus religion." [55]

Conservative Catholics proposed several alternatives to the public schools. Montgomery, claiming the support of some of the older prelates, advised the state to abandon all free schooling.[56] Some wished the state to maintain free schools for orphans and the children of irresponsible parents.[57] However, if the state was determined to collect a school fund for universal education, Catholics should be given schools they could attend in good conscience. The German government supported Catholic schools with direct grants, and England appropriated to every school a flat sum for each student brought to a given level of intellectual competence. Though either plan was satisfactory, conservatives, in drawing up an "ideal school bill," chose the English plan.[58]

The conservatives hardly expected that the hostile American society would approve of either plan, but truculent spokesmen insisted that "in season and out of season" Catholics should demand their rights. "A class that does not care enough to seek a remedy for its sufferings," Bishop McQuaid stormed, "may be left to nurse its grumblings in private, without thought or attention from their fellow-countrymen." [59] Meanwhile, Catholics would be obliged, at their own expense, to maintain schools to educate the future clergy and to give elementary training to future laymen. As early as 1850, Archbishop Hughes had announced that "the time has almost come when it will be necessary to build the school-house first, and the church afterward." A succession of Church decrees in the next fifty years reminded Catholics of the necessity of building, supporting, and attending the schools.[60]

So many decrees clearly would not have been necessary if Catholic laymen had had both the money and the desire for parochial schools. Actually, however, only the Germans, anxious to preserve their children's religious (and national) culture, supported a comprehensive system of church schools. Some of the conservatives placed especial blame on Catholics "from the green island," but Father Mueller was probably more correct in attributing difficulties to men so "liberal" they were willing to risk the religious defects of the public schools in order to get their cultural benefits.[61] Lay resistance sometimes verged on insubordination, a Catholic writer sorrowfully noted; a character in her book was made to tell the priest that he was living "in the free country of America," and in the "nineteenth century not the middle ages. His boy was educated in the public school, and if he had a dozen children he would send them where he pleased." [62]

Lay reluctance to eschew the public schools may have been increased by the tolerance many of the liberal Catholics displayed towards them. It was necessary to acknowledge, one priest noted, that the "American Public School is an excellent institution, as far as it goes." [63] Archbishop Ireland noted that it was certainly far better than the public schools of France and Italy, and "in those countries we hear of no continuous anathemas" from the clergy.[64] And the truth was, a priest pointed out, that "our public schools did not originate in hatred of Christianity, as did those in Europe; and their secularization in many cases is simply an attempt to keep peace with Catholics." [65]

Frequently invited to address national educational groups, the liberals readily congratulated non-Catholics on possessing such schools. Father Malone thought they provided the vital basis for "national intelligence," and McGlynn advised Americans to "cherish your public schools. Listen not to their enemies, no matter whence they come." [66] Archbishop Ireland made a celebrated speech to the National Education Association meeting in St. Paul in July, 1890, in which he noted some of the public school's imperfections, but hailed its virtues, and exclaimed: "Withered be the hand raised in sign of its destruction!" [67]

The liberal orators usually announced plainly that so long as the public schools remained determinedly non-sectarian, Catholics would find them unsatisfactory. And Keane defended the parochial or denominational school against the familiar charge that it would destroy national unity. Every Catholic school, he said, would teach justice and charity toward one's neighbors, and would prepare its students to coöperate in all efforts to promote the common good. "Beyond that, the homogeneousness of our people can never go. . . . We are not aiming at the communism of Sparta." [68] Father Tracy added that American unity would be safely maintained by the "ties of neighborhood, labor, recreation, business, social equality, literary association, [and] politics." [69] But though preferring parochial schools, the liberals refused to think the worst of the public school system. They would hardly agree with Mueller that for a Catholic child to emerge unscathed from a public school was an "exception to the ordinary course of Divine Providence." [70] As practical men, Gibbons and Ireland acknowledged that not for a long time to come could the Church hope to provide first-class schools for every Catholic child.[71]

For these reasons, the liberals begged the Third Plenary Council not to coerce priests and laymen into building and attending parochial schools. Bishop Fitzgerald of Little Rock thought that parents should only be advised and urged. Ireland and Spalding criticized the imposition of spiritual sanctions on uncoöperative laymen.[72]

Although during the height of the A.P.A. agitation the liberals renounced all attempts to get governmental support for the parochial schools, they had long been convinced that Catholics could justly claim such aid.[73] Their appeals for funds were not, like those of the conservatives, defiant, despairing demands. Father Tracy was confident that the non-Catholic majority would soon relieve the faithful of the necessity of supporting two sets of schools. "We are in fair and square America, Justice's providential refuge," he exclaimed, "and persecution can no more endure long in its climate, than the upas-tree can take lasting root in the prairies of Minnesota." [74] Even though the state was not yet ready to initiate a full-fledged denominational system, the liberals were sure that an acceptable beginning could and would be made. To the conservative Bishop Chatard, "any compromise means that we cannot obtain all our rights, and that we can give up something which is our due, to save the rest. This is not right on the part of the State, nor is it safe for us to accept it." [75] The *Catholic World* boldly called for a "compromise," however, and Cardinal Gibbons agreed that "a practical method of reconciling the general diffusion of elementary education with a proper regard for the sacred rights of conscience" could surely be devised by the American people "so resourceful in solving perplexing social and religious problems." [76]

III

Discussing "the amenities of the school adjustment," Father Thomas Jefferson Jenkins of Kentucky declared that the Church, like the American system of government, relegated as many decisions as possible to the lowest units of administration. "Prudent pastors" and local school boards, he was sure, could negotiate "amicable agreements," and he pointed to some thirty-two communities where compromises had been made. With more generosity than accuracy he asserted that negotiations failed only when Catholics were needlessly intransigent.[77] The most common compromise, used in Poughkeepsie, New York since 1873, allowed the priest to rent, for a nominal fee, the parochial school building during public school hours to the local school board. Only Catholic children attended the school, where they were taught the regular public school curriculum by a Catholic teacher nominated by the priest but approved and paid by the school board. Before and after regular school hours, when the building was not state property, the teacher was free to give the religious education the priest stipulated. Father Nilan of Poughkeepsie expressed "placid contentment" with the plan, as did the school committee.[78]

Not all public authorities nor all Catholics were so favorably impressed. The school board in St. Paul, Minnesota vetoed the plan lest it "romanize" the public schools. Some communities refused to allow teachers to show their Catholicism by any comment or any aspect of their dress.[79] On the other hand, Father James McTighe of Pittsburgh was unable to compel students to remain after regular school hours for catechism class.[80] And Bishop McQuaid was certain that the system would "deaden the catholicity of our school rooms." [81] No conservative regarded it as more than an unhappy expedient, to be tolerated only until the parochial school system could be made completely self-sufficient.[82]

In Faribault, Minnesota, Father James Conry agreed with the school authorities to entrust one of the parochial schools to the school board, following a formula much like that applied in Poughkeepsie. Conry's agreement, however, nowhere stipulated that after the first year the school would continue to take in only Catholic children. To conservatives, therefore, the priest seemed to have accepted blandly the possibility that the student body might become as heterogeneous in religious inclination as were the public schools. Even more ominous to the conservatives, Faribault lay in the archdiocese of St. Paul, and a plan Archbishop Corrigan might have accepted in Poughkeepsie as an exception to his general policy, Archbishop Ireland was likely to regard as the first sign of the wave of the future.[83] Thomas O'Gorman, Ireland's enthusiastic supporter, gave substance to these fears by explaining to a national audience that the archbishop's purpose was "to bring somehow under religious instruction that one million and a half children, or rather that proportion of them in his own diocese, who are now receiving their education in the public schools." [84] Conservatives could hardly be blamed for protesting that the campaign to extend the benefits of Catholic education had begun by jeopardizing the Catholic education of the fraction already receiving it.[85]

Complaints quickly went to Rome from many Germans solicitous for their extensive parochial school system, and from the archdiocese of New York, where opposition to the Faribault plan merged with the general hostility to Ireland and all his works.[86] In a very difficult position, Ireland wrote Gibbons that he was between "two enemies — one Catholic, and one Protestant. If I placate one I arouse the other. The concessions to our schools . . . are so important that I dare not fully state them, lest I bring down the wrath of the anti-Catholic bigots. If I defend the plan against Protestants, Catholic extremists are alarmed." [87] Ireland rightly suspected that the local arrangement would be doomed once it became a matter for national debate. Aroused by the Catholic clamor, the citizens of Faribault terminated the plan at the end of its first year. Though this action enabled Gibbons to dismiss all future discussion as more "speculative than practical," it did not strengthen the liberals' basic contention that America was anxious to help Catholics out of their predicament about the schools.[88]

Meanwhile, Gibbons had written Leo XIII in 1890 to deny allegations made against Ireland's address to the Education Association; and in the winter of 1892, Ireland presented a memorial defending the Faribault plan. The statements constituted an eloquent exposition of the liberals' convictions on the school question.[89] Both prelates strongly praised purely Catholic education, and neither proposed any modification of the decrees ordering Catholics to support parochial schools. But both asked toleration of compromises devised to meet Catholic problems in "frontier" areas like Minnesota. Since it was physically impossible to create overnight an adequate parochial system, Catholics should not be deprived of the benefits of arrangements like that at Faribault. Though some of the details of that plan might appear unsound, Ireland testified that "all the gentlemen with whom I dealt are personal friends of mine . . . and many things are done and permitted practically in our favor, through one kind of influence or another, that cannot be elevated into the strictness of a law." [90] Rome should capitalize on the good will of these non-Catholics, not change it into active hostility by seeming to scorn every friendly gesture towards the public school system.

In April, 1892, Rome announced that under the circumstances, Ireland's plan could be tolerated, and exhorted all bishops to labor "with harmony and unanimity, all dissensions being removed." [91] But liberals and conservatives could not agree even on the meaning of Rome's decision. Ireland interpreted *"tolerari potest"* to mean that his experiment had been "fully vindicated," and he told newspapermen he saw no reason why it could not be adopted wherever the same circumstances prevailed.[92] His suffragan, Bishop McGolrick of Duluth, said that the plan was "destined to be adopted in all the United States." [93] On the other hand, Archbishop Corrigan thought that the decision should be translated, "Faribault system condemned. Special case tolerated." And Bishop Nicholas Matz of Denver concluded that the Faribault plan, in truth little better than Free Masonry, had received the clear "disapproval of the Holy See." "May our right hand be withered," he declared, "if ever we give our approval to such a compromise." [94] The *American Catholic Quarterly Review* announced with calculated ambiguity that the "alleged" desire of a few Catholics to surrender all education to the State had been given a "stinging rebuke." [95]

Well before Rome had spoken, the school controversy had broadened. In November, 1891, Thomas Bouquillon, professor of moral theology at the Catholic University, undertook, "at the request of ecclesiastical superiors," to restate basic Catholic educational principles. In this enterprise he necessarily abandoned the familiar liberal circumstantialism in order to contend in the realm of general truths. His pamphlet, *Education: to whom does it belong?*, marshaled an impressive array of Catholic authorities to show "that in the matter of education as in all other social concerns the true doctrine of the Church was not contrary to the just desires of the American people." His major conclusion was that education belonged to neither the individual, the family, the church, nor the state "exclusively, but all combined in harmonious working." He thus more explicitly acknowledged the prerogatives of the state than any other American Catholic had yet done.[96] In a supplementary statement, Bouquillon emphasized that he had defined principles, not recommended action. He denied having in any way encouraged Catholics to send their children to public schools, except with the express consent of their bishop. He had intended his pamphlet, he said, for the edification of non-Catholics, and the guidance of religious and political authorities who were responsible for making "harmonious application" of principles to circumstances. It was a striking coincidence, however, that Bouquillon's pamphlet, published just before the archbishops met and considered the Faribault plan, explicitly defended compromises by which the state's "neutral position towards all religions may be maintained, and yet on the other hand, the demands of the various denominations as to religious instruction may be safeguarded." [97]

The liberals somewhat cautiously approved of Bouquillon's theses as useful antidotes to excessive antistatism. The *Catholic World* feared Bouquillon had put the state's claims a bit too strongly, but declared that his argument was "the true answer to the education question." [98] Conservatives, however, regarded the pamphlets as a "bugle call" to action. Jesuits in Rome and America, conservative bishops, and two German professors at the Catholic University were quick to publish scathing attacks.[99] Bouquillon, they maintained, had impaired the rights of the individual, the family, and especially the Church. He was disingenuous, they charged, in claiming to discuss theory only, as if American Catholics were not involved with "a concrete State, and schools which do a great deal of concrete damage." [100] His false principles would quickly bring practical results: politicians would conclude that the Church desired increased state activity; Catholic parents would let their children jeopardize their faith by attending public schools; priests would abandon the hard work of building a strong parochial system.[101]

The conservatives were certain that Bouquillon's pamphlet would be used to buttress the movement towards compulsory education. Nearly thirty states were to pass such legislation by 1897, in the serene conviction that it was the best "gauge of progress and civilization." [102] Ireland had "unreservedly" supported the principle in his N.E.A. address; he had endorsed the compulsory attendance features of the notorious Bennett law, which had antagonized Wisconsin German Catholics by requiring that English be used as the language of instruction in all schools recognized by the state.[103] Conservatives clearly recognized that virtually every law compelling attendance would set standards for acceptable schooling, thus making impossible fully independent parochial schools.

Father Patrick Quigley, a particularly intransigent priest in Toledo, Ohio, absolutely refused to obey the state legislature's requirement that each school report to local officials a list of the students regularly in attendance at his parochial school.[104] Calling the truant officers "robbers and thieves" he roundly declared that "we will not comply; we will fight you; we have control over our school, and we don't want you in our parish."[105] When Quigley was brought to trial, the state's lawyers seized on the declarations of both Ireland and Bouquillon as proof that "almost all the American laity and clergy of this church repudiate *in toto*" the priest's objections to state regulation. Copies of Bouquillon's pamphlet were submitted to the appeals court.[106] By upholding the law, the Ohio judiciary sealed the conservatives' conviction that the liberals were the loyal allies of an aggressive state.

In the summer of 1892, Leo XIII dispatched Francesco Satolli to America to settle, in the Pope's name, the school controversy, as well as the German-Irish dissensions with which it was intertwined.[107] In his first months in America, Satolli visualized the Church's problems very much as did the liberals. At the November 1892 meeting of the archbishops, he presented a series of theses which sanctioned virtually everything Ireland and Bouquillon had contended for. He approved the public schools, though noting some important failings. He forbade priests to deny the sacraments to parents whose children attended public schools when no "adequate" parochial school existed. "Absolutely and universally speaking," he detected no reason why children should not be "instructed" in the public schools, though he reminded priests and parents to supplement this worldly knowledge with catechism classes and other religious training.[108]

This complete vindication of the liberal program produced near mutiny among the conservative prelates.[109] Their forebodings seemed justified when, shortly after Satolli's theses were revealed to the press, one New Jersey priest broke up his struggling church school, and dispatched his pupils to the public schools; in a French Catholic school in Maine, 75 out of 100 children were withdrawn by parents who confronted the priest with the argument that he could no longer threaten to deny them the sacraments.[110] Despite fervent appeals to Rome, Leo XIII backed up his ablegate, conciliating the conservatives only to the extent of reaffirming all previous Church legislation.[111]

The liberals, with this timely aid from Rome, had won a great victory. American Catholics no longer needed to jeopardize their good relations with neighbors in proving their orthodoxy by violent attacks upon the public schools. Instead of being forced to choose between an American culture bent on giving youth the finest possible secular education, and a Church which insisted that an inadequate parochial school, or no school at all, was better than a nonsectarian one, Catholics were freed to accept profitable compromises with the state schools, even while they worked to develop, under either state or Church auspices, a perfect Catholic educational system. The applause of education enthusiasts and the explicit toleration by the Pope seemed proof positive that the American Catholics did not need to make a costly choice between religious and secular loyalties.

CHAPTER VIII

INTELLECTUAL LIFE AND
THE CHURCH

For all Christians, the turbulent intellectual life of the late nineteenth century intensified the perpetual problem of relating revealed truth and secular knowledge. For Catholics, required by their faith to accept the teaching Church's interpretation of not only the inspired Scriptures but the content of tradition as well, conflicts between dogma and "modern thought" threatened to be especially numerous. Many of the faithful, however, refused to acknowledge that any problem existed. Content with an unchanging Truth, they did not feel concerned with the novel conclusions of contemporary scholars. One conservative, recurring to an Augustinian distinction, asserted that

our evening knowledge, our science, our philosophy, may seem to have a warmer glow, . . . but it is already mingled with night, and to many of us it is barren of hope or fertility. Our morning knowledge is more austere, but it is brighter and more wholesome, . . . pregnant with the promise of the splendors of the eternal day.[1]

Because men, caught up in the search for secular knowledge, sometimes abandoned truths vital to their faith, it was prudent for the faithful to insulate themselves as far as possible from those inside or outside the Church who dabbled in new ideas. A few able clergymen would become familiar enough with current speculation to prevent its seductive errors from contaminating Church doctrine.[2] No special virtue attached to personal intellectual inquiry; "what a satisfaction it would be to a truly scientific man, and what a saving of time and trouble to the world," a conservative exclaimed, if one could obtain authoritative and infallible decisions from the Church on every question of history, philosophy, and science, instead of having to assess the opinions collected by "the able editor of our daily paper."[3]

Liberal Catholics did not think the insulation of the faithful from contemporary currents of thought was either possible or desirable. A confident rather than a grudging participation in intellectual life would be a powerful apologetic for Catholicism; it would be a fair criterion of the True Church, John Gmeiner, a liberal German priest, maintained at the Parliament of Religions, that it showed itself anxious to assimilate all that was good and true in "nature, art, science, philosophy; in human culture, civilization and progress."[4] Conversely, bigotry fed on the allegation that the Church was averse to modern intellectual progress. Archbishop Ireland declared that it would be unpardonable selfishness for Catholics to refuse to contribute to modern intellectual discussion.[5]

The liberals denied that the Church, protected from vital error by papal infallibility, could be endangered by Catholics' intellectual inquiries. And the risks an individual ran of unsettling his faith were more than offset by the benefits an active intellectual life conferred. The *Catholic World* argued that the mental vigor developed in pursuing profane knowledge was often a prerequisite to the most profound religious understanding. "The interest and excitement of investigation and the glory of discovery, as well as the innocent pride of independence, are providential incitements to that deep love of the truth which in a multitude of cases is necessary to the best results of the action of the Holy Spirit."[6] Bishop Spalding thought that diligent inquiry engendered a real superiority, since men held "vitally" only those truths which "self-activity kneads" into their "intellectual and moral constitution."[7]

The liberal attitudes put severe strains on the Church. Historians and scientists who had discarded the biblical chronology of the Creation were now arguing noisily over dozens of new timetables, robbing many of the faithful of their trusting belief in the dogmatic certainty of the Church's teaching. All too frequently scholars became involved in disputes with their ecclesiastical superiors over what problems a Catholic might properly investigate, and what conclusions might be published to the faithful. The liberal Catholic scholar could not shrug off such potential threats to Church dogma and authority; typically, he spent almost as much time justifying his intellectual pursuits as pursuing them. Of necessity, he became a "politician of the world intellectual," seeking to reconcile the claims of "liberty and intelligence with the just restraints of religion and society." [8]

II

The nineteenth century reverently designated as "science" those intellectual disciplines which compiled an unparalleled amount of factual information and assumed patterns of natural causation in order to reinterpret human and natural history. Of the new "social sciences," history enjoyed by far the greatest prestige. Each clerical student should remember, John Hogan wrote, that

he lives in an age when historical studies have assumed an importance quite unique; in which historical methods are familiar to all cultivated minds; in which historical demonstrations and conclusions have more weight than any others. . . . The controversialist, the apologist of the day, has to be, first of all, a historian. [9]

The conservative Catholics, however, frankly suspected that the "new history" was frequently more relativistic than "scientific." Hostile to its naturalism, they themselves wrote narratives which treated human events as aspects of the supernatural conflict between Christ and Satan. [10]

At the Vatican Council, Cardinal Manning, speaking for the majority of the Church, had overruled historical arguments against papal infallibility with the brusque declaration that dogma should conquer history. [11] It was in a far different spirit that Leo XIII in 1883 opened much of the Vatican Archives to research scholars, avowing his confidence that the Church had everything to gain and nothing to lose from their historical conclusions honestly arrived at and prudently stated. [12] In the next two decades, American liberals proudly echoed Leo's words. Though they attacked historians like Parkman and Bancroft for failing to appreciate Catholic motives, and for denying the possibility of miracles, they were also critical of Catholic historians who placed excessive stress on the supernatural.[13] Father John Zahm of Notre Dame argued that it was wrong for "good people" to multiply miracles to remedy their lack of understanding.[14] It was necessary, above all, the *Catholic World* believed, "to guard against cant, if we would deal seriously with serious questions."[15] The journal praised Dr. Reuben Parsons, a conservative Catholic historian, for his diligence, but could muster less "enthusiasm" for his analysis, which relied heavily on the theory of a supernaturally effective Masonic conspiracy. "Dr. Parsons has never passed as a scientific historian of the original and deep-diving sort," the *World* added. "A little more detailed and careful solution to complicated situations would be of profit."[16] Thomas O'Gorman, professor of church history at John Ireland's seminary and later at the Catholic University, was a historian whose work was more satisfactory to the liberals. Trained in Europe, and sympathetic with the rigorous practice of the great scholar of the early Church, Louis Duchesne, he wrote a volume for the *American Church History Series* which, though depending largely on the research of John Gilmary Shea, was factual and relatively dispassionate. Some conservatives complained that it displayed "a certain lack of enthusiasm," but O'Gorman was more able than the historians of the supernatural to do justice to the positive contributions of men not visibly enrolled in the legions of Christ.[17]

The liberals' conception of historical development was far closer to the age's belief in unlimited, uninterrupted progress than the gloomy view, maintained by many conservatives, that the age of Antichrist was about to begin, bringing with it unpredictable ruins and terrors.[18] The Paulist Father Augustine Hewit argued that Antichrist had already come and gone during the Dark Ages. Since that time, society had increasingly accepted Christian principles, and this acceptance, rather than a supernatural intervention, was what the biblical promise of a Kingdom of God on Earth implied. The future, in all likelihood, would proceed "in a human way, analogous to the procedure it has hitherto followed," along "lines of historical, intellectual, moral, and social development . . . toward a result which will be . . . the outcome of the past." Hewit was confident that Catholics, instead of passively acquiescing in supposedly supernatural developments, would be stirred by this "more hopeful view" to the performance of their apologetic duties.[19]

The differences between liberals and conservatives over history and historians never became as intense in America as in Europe, where the interpretation of medieval Church history had more direct implications, and where the historical study of the Bible had been carried much further.[20] In America, natural science presented a greater challenge, for its findings were of absorbing interest to a nation which had triumphed over the natural world to an unprecedented degree. Archbishop Ireland declared that the curriculum of his new seminary must follow to some extent the interests of its principal benefactor, James J. Hill, and "what he can see and value is science." [21] Father Zahm noted that scientific discussion pervaded the press, the schools, the clubs, even the railroad cars.[22]

The liberals were well aware that many scientists were espousing a natural history that detracted from God's supposed power over the world, but men like Zahm believed that only if the Church met scientific claims intelligently would it attract non-Catholics, or even hold the loyalty of many Catholics. "It is the salvation of souls which is the great interest involved in these momentous issues," Augustine Hewit argued. One of the responsibilities of the apologist had become to profess "a high and sincere esteem for . . . genuine science. Far from treating it as an enemy, he ought to salute it as a providential ally, the only one which can . . . bring back troubled or wandering souls." Hewit rejoiced that such scientists as Littré and Romanes had regained their religious faith. "May they be precursors of a crowd of similar converts! The eighteenth century was an age of infidelity and revolution. The nineteenth century has been an age of science. We may hope that the twentieth century will be an age of science, reconstruction, and faith." [23] While the errors of modern scientists should be corrected, their genuine discoveries should be gratefully added to the Catholic store of truth. Father Zahm declared that, while neither a Darwinist nor a Huxleyan, he did not wish to imply that he "found nothing good" in their work. Nor did he feel bound "to indulge in philippics against them whenever their names or theories are mentioned." [24] None of the American liberals was a scientific extremist; on the key question of human evolution, they adopted a position intermediate between Virchow's naturalism and the pious tradition.

Conservatives stubbornly defended the belief that God created man directly, constituting him a species immutably distinct from all other animals. Sociological similarities between cavemen and apes demonstrated only that man had at times dissipated most of the gifts with which he had been endowed.[25] The liberals followed Asa Gray and John Fiske in believing evolution perfectly compatible with theism. The transmutation of species, they argued, was identical with Augustine's conception of a successive creation governed by divine law. What naturalists called spontaneous generation or variation, the liberals asserted was the performance of God's will through a series of second causes which men had not yet fully understood.[26] Zahm agreed with Fiske that this view was more devout than one which confined God's creativity to the first days of the world; it enabled the "unbiased and reverent" to see "in nature the evidence of a Power which is originative, directive, immanent."[27] Liberal Catholics agreed with the age that with God thus taking an active part in the world's progress, it was easy to believe in indefinite evolution "onward and upward." Some of the liberals flatly asserted that man's body, like other physical forms, had evolved from lower animals. But even the radical Englishman, St. George Mivart, upon whom they depended for much of their biological knowledge, insisted that man's soul was immediately and directly created by God; on this question, revelation spoke too unequivocally for the liberal Catholics to sympathize with the exceedingly speculative hypotheses on the evolution of the soul.[28]

The liberal apologists won considerable applause for their judicious balancing of claims. Gladstone praised Zahm's work, and a New England Protestant paper maintained that Zahm's *Evolution and Dogma* put "the case of Christianity against agnosticism and atheism as clearly, ably, liberally and convincingly as it has yet been done."[29] But many Catholics believed that the liberals had gone much too far towards secularism, and that "the Church might need a defender against some of her defenders."[30] All but an "exceedingly small" number of Catholics, the *American Catholic Quarterly Review* reported, regarded belief in the evolution of Adam's body as "latitudinarian," and one conservative denounced Zahm as "atheist, materialist, modernist." [31] One critic wrote off the whole liberal enterprise as an unworthy bid for popularity with a skeptical age; " 'look at me, now,' " the apologist seemed to be saying. " 'I am an admirable Catholic, and yet I don't believe in Adam's apple, I don't believe in Noë's ark, I don't believe in Daniel in the lions' den; and as for the naive anthropomorphism of Genesis, it excites in me a smile no less becoming than your own.' " [32]

The gravamen of the conservatives' protest was not that the liberals had abandoned Bible literalism, but that they were untrue to the reconciliation or "concord" which the great doctors of the Church like St. Thomas had established between scientific knowledge and revelation. While the liberals welcomed the Thomistic revival, Spalding noted that Aquinas' "point of view in all that concerns natural knowledge has long since vanished from sight." [33] Zahm declared that modern Catholics, instead of attempting to shore up Thomas' concord by devising supplementary hypotheses, often more ingenious than convincing, should emulate his fearlessness in striking out in a wholly new way to deal with new facts. Were Thomas and Augustine living today, he asserted, they would not be pathetically defending past solutions, but would be "the boldest and the most comprehensive and the most liberal minds the world has ever known." [34]

Some of the liberals hoped to avoid the difficulties of "concordism" altogether by arguing that the Bible did not teach any scientific or historical truth "as such." [35] By adopting this "idealist" position, the liberals hoped to obviate the bitter and unprofitable quarrels over Biblical exegesis, leaving the apologist free to stress the moral beauty of Christ's life, the obvious wisdom of the Gospel, and the benefits Christianity brought mankind.[36] Cardinal Newman was the most famous "idealist"; in 1884, he had maintained that all scientific and historical comment in the Bible, except that bearing directly on dogmatic truth, could be regarded as *obiter dicta*, and thus subject to subsequent correction. One of Newman's disciples pointed out to readers of the *Catholic World* that the Church did not require a Catholic to believe that there were no factual errors in the Vulgate. He admitted that it would generally be difficult to distinguish between human comment and that which was so closely related to dogma as to be necessarily inspired. But only "the inexperienced" and "the young" would demand an absolutist formula for settling critical problems. In a scientific age, "the opinion safest theologically, is not always the wisest, and . . . the true road may run along the precipice," the English cleric declared.[37]

The liberals readily admitted the Church could pronounce authoritatively that certain statements in the Bible were inspired; but Hewit believed that the whole sum of such teaching up to the present could be contained "within a very moderate compass."[38] The liberals acknowledged that the Church might speak through the "universal and constant consent [of] the ordinary magisterium . . . scattered over the globe," but they considered that the advocates of a "sentimental orthodoxy" forgot what stringent criteria were required for this consent.[39] John Gmeiner denied that any such consent existed on "the great scientific questions which have been raised in recent times." "The ordinary magisterium of the Church," he declared, had never given "serious attention" to the question whether the Noachian flood had covered the whole earth. The fact of the flood and its prophetic moral had been explicitly accepted, and so could not be denied, but the physical extent and the secondary causes were subject to normal human investigation.[40]

This attitude seemed finicky to the conservatives; Bishop Chatard advised Catholics to "regard the Church as an ever-active teacher aided by the Holy Ghost . . . directing our minds to accept with the utmost docility what she says, without waiting to critically examine the manner in which she speaks, or to look for unanimity."[41] But Hewit, while admitting that it was safe for a Catholic to accept completely every doctrinal statement by every churchman, argued that it was also legitimate to withhold inner assent if one simply could not firmly believe statements made by potentially fallible authorities.[42] In all likelihood, Hewit limited the scope of this restraint to secondary matters. Without denying to the Church the ultimate interpretation of any Biblical phrase, the liberals wished to emancipate scientists and theologians from the need of maintaining continuous concord between traditional Catholic assumptions and current scholarly conclusions. They believed that most clashes between religion and science arose out of misunderstanding or arrogance.[43] Trying to describe and delimit the proper roles of scientist and theologian, they hoped to encourage a maximum of scholarly effort with a minimum of authoritative intervention. The best check against error in either realm was the corrective work of one's colleagues and successors.

The profound difference between liberal and conservative conceptions of the Catholic's obligations to Church authority was apparent in the diverse receptions accorded to *Criterions of Catholic Truth*, by the Italian Canon Salvatore di Bartolo. Bartolo accepted Newman's *obiter dicta* theory. He denied that popes in the past had often spoken infallibly, and politely requested all popes in the future to add the words *ex cathedra* in cases where they did. The universal consent of the faithful was significant only on points absolutely essential to dogma, he thought, and the common teaching of the Fathers on inessentials was often grossly in error. He maintained that historians had the right to believe that the Church had erred in canonizing certain individuals about whom new facts had later been learned, and he believed that researchers could continue to hold scientific convictions in opposition to revealed truths until further understanding was given them.[44] While not endorsing all these conclusions, the *Catholic World* was pleased that Bartolo was not "colorblind to all signals of danger except those that tell of rebellion to authority; he can see dangers in over-restrictive measures as well." His book, carefully read, would help allay non-Catholic suspicions of the Church's intolerance.[45] Cardinal Gibbons wrote that the book could not "fail to strengthen faith and to remove prejudices."[46] In sharp contrast, the *American Catholic Quarterly Review* criticized Bartolo's apparent willingness to allow perfect freedom towards all teachings not strictly *de fide*.[47] The *Ecclesiastical Review* published a series of slashing attacks by Professor Joseph Schroeder on Bartolo's "theological minimizing."[48] Just before the liberals were to publish a reply, Bartolo's work was placed on the Index, and American sympathizers lapsed into silence.[49]

The debate over the nature and extent of revealed truth continued, however, focusing increasingly on the permissibility of "higher criticism" of the Bible.[50] In 1893, Leo XIII endeavored to establish criteria for Biblical scholarship in an encyclical, *Providentissimus Deus*.[51] Encouraging further research in the interests of textual purification, he declared that "higher criticism" was "seldom of great value, except in confirmation" of conclusions the Fathers had arrived at long ago; he warned practitioners not to be so proud of their ability to reconstruct the past that they forgot the role played by the supernatural. Leo condemned the *obiter dicta* theory of inspiration, asserting that while God had allowed the use of popular language, He had permitted no substantive errors to be recorded. Catholic scholars were not free, Leo forcefully concluded, to hold convictions controverting the clear purport of the Bible. Later, in order to hasten the determination of Catholic consensus on the many points in dispute, the Pope established a Biblical Commission of scholars to hand down authoritative opinions.[52]

As usual, conservatives and liberals read the encyclical differently. The Jesuit Father James Conway was relieved that the *obiter dicta* theory, which had been "fast gaining popularity with individuals, if not with schools, in the United States," had been condemned. And he rejoiced that "minimizers" of every kind had been sharply reproved.[53] Professor Charles P. Grannan of the Catholic University, on the other hand, concluded that "true Higher Criticism" had not been censured. He regarded the encyclical as a strong encouragement to intelligent study of the Bible.[54] One of his students reported that Grannan was not accustomed to regarding the Pope's strictures on all subjects as wholly binding; "Joachim Pecci, the theologian, of course has a right to his opinions," he is supposed to have said, "but we are theologians too, and have a right to ours." [55] Father Zahm found no obstacle to scientific study in the Pope's defense of tradition and authority. In *Bible, Science, and Faith*, published the following year, Zahm happily quoted Leo's declaration that it was not the purpose of the Bible to teach science. The priest insisted that parts of the Bible, such as the story of the Creation, became more illuminating with the progressive advance of scientific knowledge. He strongly emphasized that there was, as yet, no uniform interpretation of much of the Bible. And he did not hesitate to quote liberally from Newman's essay on Bible study.[56]

But though the encyclical did not produce unanimity, it presented an unmistakable *caveat* to scientists. Hogan noted in 1898 that the split between science and theology seemed to be widening; "this means," he said, probably with some humor, "that the general principles of theology seem to lead in one direction, and the facts in another." [57] And Zahm, despite his brave words, was forced to spend more time defending not just the scientist's right to intellectual freedom, but his own right to defend the scientist's right.[58]

III

Heavily attacked by the conservatives, the liberals derived some consolation from the praise their apologetics won them from non-Catholics. Zahm released to the newspapers Gladstone's letter of appreciation, and, when *Evolution and Dogma* drew violent criticism from many Italian Catholics, Zahm asserted that "I really do not care for the approval of everyone. But I know that every eminent man of science throughout Europe is in perfect sympathy with my views." [59] But this was a scholar's consolation, and the liberal churchmen, out of loyalty to their fellow Catholics, and because their position in the Church depended ultimately upon Catholic approval, elected a more active role. By securing higher education for more of the faithful, they would promote Catholic understanding of secular discoveries, and at the same time hasten the production of a science that every Catholic could accept.

All the advanced education most priests received they got in the higher seminaries. In the 1890's, eight new seminaries were being built, and more were under consideration.[60] But while agreeing that the time had come to abandon makeshift arrangements, Catholics differed as to what changes should be made. To the conservative James Loughlin of Philadelphia, the first premise of a seminary was contempt for secular predilections. "The more decidedly the outside world tends to materialism," he declared, "all the more energetically ought the Catholic scholar to explore and defend that spirit world which is his fatherland." The only desirable reform was an intensification of theological and philosophical training.[61]

The liberals agreed that this training should be improved, but they were also anxious to have the seminaries instill an understanding of the new learning. Father Patrick Donehy, happily pointing out that Archbishop Ireland's new seminary exposed youths to modern problems, remarked that "the priest who should go forth from the seminary today with only the answers of St. Augustine or St. Thomas of Aquino to satisfy the questioning mind of our age withal, would be as unfit for his duties as would an old Roman legionary or a mailed crusader to take part in modern warfare." [62] Edward A. Pace of the Catholic University recommended that seminaries teach natural sciences in a modern rather than Thomistic way.[63] Father John T. Smith demanded an end to the shameful neglect of history. To ensure that students were not restricted by the horizons of even the most liberal curriculum, he also proposed establishing a reading room in which seminarians could find a variety of periodicals "selected solely with the view of illustrating the temper and condition of the times." [64]

But seminary training could be expanded only so far, and, in any case, its benefits would be available to only a small fraction of Catholics. As early as 1866, some American Catholics were calling for a university to emulate the work of the great non-Catholic universities in America, and the institutions just being built by European Catholics.[65] In the later decades of the century, the most eloquent and persistent advocate of a university was John Spalding. At the Third Plenary Council, he appealed for "higher education," pointing out that a seminary could never be a true "instrument of intellectual culture," with "liberal and not professional" goals.[66] A few years later, at the laying of the cornerstone of the Catholic University, he tried to silence critics of culture. "To be a Catholic," he proclaimed, "is to be drawn not only to the love of whatever is good and beautiful, but also to the love of whatever is true." The remedy for the confusions caused by a little learning was more learning. "Those who dread knowledge," he insisted, "are as far away from the life of this century as the dead whose bones crumbled to dust a thousand years ago." In a characteristically American phrase, Spalding declared that "mind is Heaven's pioneer making way for faith, hope, and love." A university, "better than anything else," symbolized "the aim and tendency of modern life." [67]

Some conservatives opposed a university as an overly ambitious project for a Church still unable to build enough parochial schools. Others, failing to understand the purpose of a graduate university, suspected that it could only prove to be an unnecessary and unfair competitor with existing Catholic colleges and seminaries.[68] This opposition was checkmated when Leo XIII endorsed the project and the nomination of the liberal John J. Keane as the first rector.[69] Keane went to Europe to attempt to get Ludwig von Pastor and

François Vigoroux, the most distinguished Catholic scholars in history and Bible study. He favored inviting William Barry, the liberal English apologist, and he strongly desired St. George Mivart to teach science, since unless this subject was ably taught, the faculty would, he feared, "count for very little in the estimation of the American public." [70] Defeated in each of these cases either by the scholar's reluctance or by the veto of conservative Catholics, Keane, nevertheless, appointed able men — O'Gorman and Thomas Shahan in history, Henri Hyvernat in Oriental studies, Bouquillon in moral theology, Grannan on the Scriptures.

In appointing Edward Pace to teach philosophy, Keane showed his preference for philosophy which was not simply worshipful Thomism; when the papal ablegate Archbishop Satolli proposed that Pace spend considerable time in Rome being "replenished" with sound scholastic doctrine, the rector politely demurred.[71] The liberals were little interested in abstract speculation of any kind. The *Catholic World* considered the "intricacies and obscurities" of theology "like the swamps on the margin of a fertile farming country; they are a refuge for untamable beasts and birds and the scene of the sportsman's exploits." [72] Dr. Thomas Bouquillon was sure that theology was "sterile and stagnant" when "cut off from the other sciences," but prospered when theory and practice were closely associated. His seminar in 1894–1895 considered the "Ethics of Workingmen's Associations, Strikes, and Arbitrations." [73] In the spring of the same year, Keane presided over a School of Applied Ethics, in which such non-Catholic experts as John G. Brooks and Carroll Wright spoke. He sent William Kerby to Louvain to prepare himself to teach sociology by the newest methods.[74]

The Catholic University's contacts with the new learning were not always happy. When Professor R. W. Shufeldt, invited to give guest lectures on biology, enlivened his scientific analyses with references to monkish superstition, and "the inquisition, the fagot, and the stake," the most liberal Catholic was necessarily annoyed.[75] The much-desired scholarly debate among the professors frequently led to such bitter personal and nationalistic antagonisms that Gibbons considered governing the University more onerous than all the other chores of his diocese.[76] The theoretical teachings and practical activities of some of the liberal professors aroused such conservative hostility that one critic eventually declared that faculty members of the University were too controversial to speak to general audiences.[77]

The Catholic University was intended to attract not just priests in search of postseminary training; but most laymen preferred to attend Catholic colleges and non-Catholic universities.[78] The liberals cheerfully did all that they could to make these recourses as profitable as possible. Ireland encouraged Notre Dame to offer genuine liberal education, not a series of professional courses.[79] Father Zahm and other instructors at Notre Dame tried to improve standards by securing graduate training for all teachers there, only to be frustrated by President Morrissey's desire to keep Notre Dame a good preparatory school. Father John Burns asked to be permitted to attend Cornell Summer School, but was denied permission, and angrily recorded in his diary "I asked him bluntly . . . if he did not admit that the more a man knows about a subject, the better he is prepared to teach it. . . . He didn't believe it. . . . How long, O Lord, how long?"[80]

The liberals refused to be alarmed for the safety of the many young men attending non-Catholic universities. No secular truth could adversely affect their Catholic faith, and since many outside the Church were simply ignorant of its claims, some priests believed that every Catholic student at Yale or Harvard would prove an effective missionary to the Gentiles.[81] The Paulists helped establish student clubs to promote this mission, and named them after Newman, who had won over such a number of Oxford intellectuals.[82] The conservative Bishop McQuaid, by contrast, seeing little value in "liberal education," and suspecting that social rather than intellectual aspiration drew most young Catholics to secular schools, worked tirelessly to discourage the practice. His veto of Keane's appearance at Cornell stemmed in part, no doubt, from a desire to avoid any seeming approval of Catholics there.[83]

The liberals also tried to bring the advantages of higher education to those for whom college was not possible. In 1889, the Columbian Reading Union was formed to coördinate the work of reading circles around the country; the Paulists assumed direction, and dedicated a section of the *Catholic World* to words of advice and reports of progress. The reading lists which they circulated included works primarily by Catholics, since one purpose was to give encouragement to deserving Catholic authors, but generous amounts of history and science by non-Catholics were also recommended.[84]

Catholic summer schools were another expedient; both liberal and conservative leaders supported the establishment of the first, which met in New London, Connecticut, in 1892. Other schools appeared at Madison, Wisconsin in 1895, and in New Orleans, Louisiana, in the winter of 1896. The first curriculum included lectures on Christian ethics, a series on Shakespeare, discussions on the philosophy of history as well as on special historical topics, and lectures by the Jesuit Father Thomas Hughes on "Christian anthropology." Offsetting archconservatives like Hughes were many of the most liberal of the Catholic University professors, as well as Zahm and Mivart. Whoever the lecturer, liberals could find satisfaction in the number of lay Catholics being exposed to contemporary intellectual problems.[85] Many conservatives regarded the summer schools as a dangerous attempt to ape the "liberal Protestantism" of Chautauqua — as no better than Catholic camp meetings, summer Sunday schools.[86] Arthur Preuss, a St. Louis editor, considered the students too frivolous for the schools to succeed. "We have no confidence in their alleged mission," he wrote, "and no hope for their future."[87] Condé Pallen thought that the schools should not busy themselves with the popular problems of secular culture, but teach such essential Catholic principles as that the Incarnation is "the Catholic explanation of things past, present and future."[88] A Catholic paper suggested that "the only kind of lectures appropriate, timely, and useful for a Catholic Summer School would be a course of plain, everyday catechetical instruction."[89]

The volleys of criticism which the liberals received after every new attempt to widen respect for the new learning were the more galling because none of these attempts elicited the mass support that developed when the liberals called for patriotism, temperance, or even a viable school compromise. In 1902, only sixteen lay students attended the Catholic University; most students at Notre Dame continued to prefer straightforward business courses; both the Reading Circles and the Summer Schools were monopolized by single young women, many of them indignant that Catholic young men were "so indifferent to their own intellectual improvement."[90] And while the rewards were scant, the risks were considerable, for, to offer a really modern education even to a few, the liberals had found it necessary to jeopardize their reputation for trusting faith by insisting on limits to the scope of Church authority.

Yet, despite such penalties, the liberals until the late 1890's remained confident of the ultimate success of their policy of rapprochement between the Church and contemporary intellectual life. The Catholic University had been established; summer schools and reading circles were going on; at least some of the seminaries had dramatically modernized their curriculum. So long as Roman authorities did not become convinced that the American enterprises were part and parcel of the "Age's" assault on the dogma of the Church, the liberal program seemed likely to prosper; and on this question more than any other, Leo XIII seemed the liberals' staunch ally. With serene confidence, the *Catholic World* declared in 1892 that "the Church in this country is becoming every day more and more the brightest jewel in the Papal crown . . . because the work of intellectual development goes hand in hand with the moral and material progress of the people." [91]

CHAPTER IX

A CHURCH OF ENERGETIC
INDIVIDUALS

T he Catholic Church is hierarchical as well as orthodox; it demands of its members organizational discipline as well as doctrinal uniformity. While the American liberals could fairly be charged with occasionally minimizing the amount of dogmatic truth binding on all Catholics, few or none of them veered into the modernist error of questioning the nature of dogma itself.[1] Conservative critics had considerable justification, however, for their protests that the liberals appeared to be abandoning the ordered harmonies of Church discipline for the individualism and frenzied activism of American secular life.

Certainly the liberals made no secret of their admiration for a culture whose "ideals of manhood are not loyalty, obedience, uniformity, but worthiness to be free." [2] The more they observed of the secular civilization which resulted when every man was encouraged to act freely in political and economic life, the more sure they became that the Church, too, would profit if each of its members acted with initiative and determination. Father Elliott insisted that America's "triumphant democracy" granted the individual so much freedom that no other government was so "peculiarly favorable" to the practice of true religion.[3] The *Catholic World* was sure that "the hierarchy of the Catholic Church in the United States share the conviction that American political institutions are in advance of those in Europe in helping a man to save his soul." [4] Elliott denounced as malicious libel an English Jesuit's allegation that political freedom unsuited men for proper deference to ecclesiastical authority. Though the early years of both church and state in America had been somewhat turbulent, experience in freedom had soon promoted highly responsible participation in both political and religious life. Turning the tables on the European "critic of the great republic," Elliott contended that the Church had no difficulty with fractious democrats, but only with those immigrants "whose Catholicity [had] been maintained by a paternal civil government," men accustomed to alternate between supine passivity and irresponsible protest. "There is a servile faith as well as a servile fear," he wrote, "a satanic independence and a bovine obedience — all equally unsuitable for both church and state in the United States." [5] Fortunately, as immigrants became more Americanized, they became better Catholics. "There may be, after all, something in the American publicist's prophecy," Father Thomas Jefferson Jenkins noted contentedly, "that, if the Church modify the state, the state here will modify the views of the Church — at least in individuals." [6]

While dubious about doctrinaire *laissez faire*, the liberals admired the opportunity American capitalism afforded the able man to exert all his energy and initiative; many of them concluded that the Church would flourish just so far as Catholics became as enterprising as their contemporaries. The layman John Reily was dissatisfied with the Catholic community of Connewago, Pennsylvania, because the people treated true faith as a substitute for "ambition and enterprise." "There is no rivalry, nor emulation, no self-dependence, no pride, no ambition," he complained, convinced as he was that piety linked with passivity would not produce a good society or a healthy Church.[7] Liberal writers pointed to conspicuous examples of Catholic prosperity in Europe as refutation of both the "shallow commentators upon progress" and those hopelessly reactionary Catholics who asserted that the bourgeois virtues of enterprise and thrift were somehow incompatible with true Catholicism.[8]

In 1890, Miss M. T. Elder formulated a liberal Catholic version of the "gospel of wealth," a vindication of economic individualism by the rewards for the individualist and by the ultimate benefits for the Church. Pointing out that the three men Christ restored to life were all men of wealth, and that a rich man had been necessary to give Christ a suitable (if temporary) burial, Miss Elder deplored the scarcity of rich American Catholics. She suspected that most Catholics were poor, not from love of holy poverty, but from aversion to holy industry. The "temptations and evils of poverty" afflicted huge numbers, while wealth constituted a proximate cause of sin for only a very few. Miss Elder, therefore, recommended that Catholics, after praying for faith, hope, and charity, should go on to ask:

O Lord! give me good sense. Give me hard, practical, everyday gumption. If I had a little of that, I shouldn't act as foolishly as I generally do; I shouldn't waste my time nor money; I shouldn't remain as now, unable to aid the Church and religion.

The ability to make "frequent and handsome donations" indicated "pretty surely," Miss Elder thought, "that a man has the right sort of zeal." [9]

Archbishop Ireland was a vigorous exponent of this rationalization of individual enterprise. He advised the Catholic Total Abstinence Union to stop considering money as evil, and to set about acquiring some. The power to do good would be immense if Catholics exerted their "will," "energy," and "ambition." [10] In an impromptu address to the Merchants' Exchange in St. Louis, Ireland attributed the great success of the Church in America to the work of "energetic, enterprising citizens." "It is energy and enterprise that win everywhere," he declared briskly; "they win in the Church, they win in the State, and they win in buisness." [11] Ireland told a French traveler that the American Church wanted the faithful to show "pluck" and "push." [12] To the Catholic Congress of 1893 he offered a theophysical postulate: "The half-hearted manner in which we evangelize the age deserves and entails failure. Steam and electricity in religion coöperating with divine grace will triumph." [13]

The liberals were openly critical of Catholics who failed to recognize what the modern Church required of its members. Hailing Leo XIII's call for Catholic action to help solve the problems of the working class, the Paulist Father Edward Brady complained that there had been "a little too much of the passive, some might be disposed to call it the contemplative spirit of religion . . . and this earnest advanced encyclical . . . is a rebuke to it. Religion must be altogether free . . . to go about the Great Father's business in whatever direction that business may lead." [14] Seven hundred years earlier, the liberals' convictions had been stated succinctly by Pope Innocent III, when he declared that "if the contemplative state is safer, the active is more fruitful; if the former is sweeter, the latter is more profitable." [15] Much as Hecker admired the religious spirit of orders like the Poor Clares who dedicated their lives wholly to prayer, he did not conceal his grave doubts about the "forms" they employed of giving it "expression." [16] He indignantly denied that the typical religious of the Middle Ages had devoted himself exclusively to contemplation. " 'Idle monks and nuns' were they?" he spluttered. "They were, as a class, men and women who ate and drank less, worked harder, and did more for intellectual progress, civilization, and social well-being than any other body of men and women . . . of history." [17] Nor could the liberals endorse those Catholics who sought purification through bodily mortification alone. Spalding warmly approved a mother superior's principle that "the work we do for others is the best mortification." [18] And Ireland stated flatly that "an honest ballot and social decorum among Catholics will do more for God's glory and the salvation of souls than midnight flagellations," or any number of penitent pilgrimages.[19]

Conservative clergymen in the nineteenth century, suspecting that work in the world was both dangerous and futile, developed an increasing number of special devotions in which Catholics might participate as the safest and most profitable way of counteracting the aggressions of a hostile age. While the liberals did not dislike all the new devotions, they carefully designated them as only "subsidiary religious aids." Most individuals, they implied, were not dramatically improved by what too often degenerated into what Ireland called the "mere frills and flounces of piety." [20] They warned the faithful against expending "their entire spiritual energy in set devotional practices and examinations and spiritual resolutions." [21] A too sedulous devotionalism, the liberals believed, was often substituted for an understanding participation in the world. Ireland rejoiced that Notre Dame did not emulate those Catholic colleges which reared their charges in "religious hothouses, nourishing them overmuch on the accidents and luxuries of religion," instead of preparing them for the battles they would later have to wage for their souls and for their Church.[22] Hecker warned Americans not to imitate the many European Catholics who, shirking resistance to secularist oppression, "evaded the accusation of criminal cowardice by an extravagant display of devotional religion." [23] And Bishop Keane warned the clergy not to let devotional societies become an end in themselves. Addressing the Priests' Eucharistic League, he declared that God was not "in the Blessed Sacrament simply to receive our homage." Nor did we priests come "simply to express our adoration, but to see what we can do among men. . . . 'What are you doing?' the Lord asks us." [24] The liberals even thought it necessary to warn Catholics against regarding the sacraments as substitutes for personal action. The Paulist Father Alexander Doyle told the Catholic Total Abstinence Union that to stop intemperance "other remedies besides those from the spiritual pharmacy of the Church are to be applied . . . , and other methods besides the ordinary ministrations of the sacraments are necessary." [25]

Hecker regretted that, at a time when Protestants were discarding the characteristic Reformation doctrines, some Catholics were still so misled by the doctrines of man's impotence that they considered the "passive" rather than the "active" virtues the most conducive to the development of "Christian manhood." [26] Father Brady elaborated on this distinction when he declared that the "faith that built up the American Church, though a simple, implicit faith, was not a passive faith. It was an active, energetic faith, a courageous faith." [27] To this kind of argument, some Catholics had retorted that since the supreme felicity of life in heaven would involve no human striving, men in the world should cultivate a spirit of passive acquiescence. Keane brushed aside this premise. In heaven a man would feel "every muscle swelling with strength . . . every fibre of his being eager for the day's work. A merely passive heaven," he dismissed as inconceivable; it would be "infinite weariness; the perfection of activity" would be a better description of eternal life. For there all the powers we have known on earth "shall be reaching forward in tireless activity; and not one of them shall be left with nothing to do." [28]

The most commendable kind of action was not performed by the disciplined soldier responding to orders from his superiors, but by the free man on his own initiative. Ireland believed that Catholics could learn a great deal from the familiar American saying "I am going to do what pleases me." [29] Hecker frequently belabored the "learned authors and distinguished controversialists" so obsessed with the risk of individual error that they defined "the essence of Catholicity" as instant, total obedience, and argued that "on becoming a Catholic one has to make an entire surrender, in religious matters, of his personal liberty and his own will." [30] "In true obedience," a *Catholic World* writer argued, "there is more of love than conformity, in patience more of love than resignation, in temperance more of love than of self-restraint." And for the true exercise of love, "individuality and independence of character" were essential.[31]

Little disposed to speculation, the liberals failed to explore either the theological or the ecclesiastical implications of their gospel of individual action. In exhorting each Catholic to practice actively the natural virtues, they sometimes seemed to imply that God was bound to bestow grace in strict proportion to man's efforts.[32] In stressing the value of action, they sometimes seemed to limit the possession of true virtue to those who possessed worldly freedom. One French critic was to complain that "Father Hecker measures out the favors of the Holy Spirit in proportion to the civil and political liberty of the Christian." [33] The liberals certainly meant no more than that God, in His ordinary providence, expected the individual to show initiative and enterprise if he wished to deserve grace. But they were frequently misunderstood.

Many of the liberals too readily accepted the age's assumption that vigorous, well intentioned individual effort would invariably result in productive harmony. Archbishop Ireland could not have imagined that he was proposing the forfeit of Church discipline in his speech to Catholics at the Columbian Congress; "let not the laymen wait for the laymen," he had thundered; "let not priest wait for priest, let not priest wait for bishop, and let not bishop wait for the Pope." [34] The archbishop, like the other liberals, believed that precisely because the structure of Church authority had been strengthened at the Vatican Council, it could never thereafter be effectively flouted. But conservatives, who believed that the Vatican Council had intensified the daily discipline of the Church, not simply provided countermeasures against future breaches, were appalled when the American liberals proceeded to counsel every Catholic, from layman to cardinal, to embark on lives of active, individual service.

II

In 1888, the *Catholic World* printed an article by a layman which declared that the American Church had suffered immeasurably from the failure to grant the laymen their proper degree of freedom. The fault stemmed in part from the traditions of the feudal era when the European Church, to strengthen clerical power against aggressive laymen, had erected chancels and protected the priests from the congregation by rood screens and strong railings. Long anachronistic, this architecture institutionalized "a certain exclusiveness of feeling, a certain distrust," even condescension towards the laity. The American Church, the writer argued, would benefit by a speedy "return to the older and more normal state of union without confusion of the clergy and the people." [35] Father Edward McSweeny agreed that the clergy needed to be recalled to "simplicity." Missionaries to equalitarian America should, he thought, "discard all titles, come in simplicity of speech and manner . . . and erect a simple democratic platform down almost to the level of the people, instead of speaking from the formal, aristocratic pulpit." [36]

Nineteenth-century ultramontanists, regarding the growing lay demand for power and responsibility as a dangerous attempt to Protestantize the Church, had sanctioned lay action only in devotions and organizations dominated and directed by the clergy. [37] Lay freedom was, if anything, more circumscribed than before. Father Elliott was appalled to find that many European immigrants had been taught to regard their priest not as "teacher, father, and friend, but boss-teacher, boss-father, boss-friend, perhaps boss-politician." [38]

Even the liberals, of course, could not sanction any laic encroachment on the powers and responsibilities vested in the clergy by the sacrament of orders, but they believed that laymen might do much both within and without the churches. The Paulist Father Alfred Young waged a long campaign to increase congregational singing. A choir, he argued, relegated the laity to a passive role, while general singing would allow each individual to praise God in his own voice and in his own spirit. [39] Writing in the *Catholic*

World, George H. Howard, a prominent Washington layman, suggested several ways in which the individual's understanding participation in the mass might be heightened. Though the officiating priest was required to use Latin, Howard saw no reason why a "lector" could not read simultaneous translations of parts of the mass; alternatively, he might lead the congregation in singing a communion hymn or reciting a psalm. He also proposed that more prayers be read in the vernacular, and that the confessions of sin be uttered in unison. By such measures, Howard thought, the services could be made to appeal "in the highest degree to the soul's intelligence, without an exercise of which there can be no worship at all." [40]

Prohibited from teaching in the Church, the laity might well teach Catholicism to outsiders, through planned missions or in casual contacts. A group of St. Paul laymen organized a Truth Society to disseminate information about the Church, as well as to answer defamatory attacks. [41] Laymen could also take more active responsibility for parish work. Priests and laymen had engaged in many unseemly wrangles over the management of Church property throughout the nineteenth century, and the liberals showed no inclination to repeat that experiment. [42] But some were willing to brave conservative censure, both in America and in Rome, by a wider use of intelligent laymen as teachers and administrators in the parochial schools. [43]

But the most dramatic vehicles for lay action were the national Catholic congresses in 1889 and 1893. As early as 1869, the *Catholic World* had called for a more inclusive gathering than the German Central Verein, but no progress was made until, twenty years later, Major Henry Brownson of Detroit, anxious to demonstrate to non-Catholics that "the laity are not priest-ridden," began a successful agitation. [44] Cardinal Gibbons at first demurred, but Ireland and other Western prelates convinced him that there was no risk of insubordination. [45] Only papers approved by an episcopal committee were read, and no general discussion of the topics covered was permitted to the hundreds of lay delegates who came to the two conventions. Even with these precautions, many of the clergy "went home thanking God that the Church escaped unharmed." [46]

To most liberals, the willing coöperation of so many able, energetic laymen was inspiring, and even the conservative John Mooney concluded that lay action was a "moral Niagara" available to the Church.[47] While Gibbons made clear in his address to the Baltimore congress that he expected the laymen to await clerical direction, Ireland challenged his hearers not to take pride in mere docile obedience. Do not, he ordered "go home and slumber, as in the past — go back to work. . . . I assure you, in the name of the bishops and the priests, that we will lead, but I shall be very glad to see you get ahead of us in something." [48] A *Catholic World* writer advised the delegates not to let their wonderful new national organization prevent them from organizing locally, or even acting as individuals when that would be profitable.[49] A few years later, a San Francisco priest summed up the liberals' expectations when he flatly declared that

it would add new life to the Church in America were the laity to take an interest in Church affairs, and to express their opinions thereon. . . . Clerical diplomacy has several centuries of mistakes to its account; free speech can hardly hope to beat the record. . . . It is far better to make a mistake in acting, than never to act at all.[50]

The liberals also attempted to increase lay freedom by limiting the extent to which parish priests could issue unconditional demands upon their people. At the Third Plenary Council, liberal prelates, while failing to secure admonitions instead of commands to attend the parochial schools, did succeed in depriving priests of the right to order the faithful not to belong to specific societies, thus making possible the toleration of the Knights of Labor.[51] But perhaps the clearest example of the liberals' concern was their running battle to prevent this legislation from being applied against secret fraternal societies.

The conservatives believed the secret societies to be the distillation, if not the active agent, of all the evils of the century, and that American societies were no less malevolent than those in Europe.[52] The liberals, on the other hand, could not believe that the American secret societies were either very important or very hostile.[53] "I have always been of the opinion," Archbishop Patrick Riordan of San Francisco declared, "that we should treat such organizations in as large a spirit as the discipline of the Church will permit us," and

Ireland argued that "as much liberty as is at all consistent with principles should be allowed Catholics" in their dealings with the fraternal orders.[54] Most of the liberals were prepared to sanction Catholic membership in those societies which dropped their offensive oaths and rituals. At the 1890 meeting of the committee of archbishops to which the question of several secret societies had been referred the liberals won a considerable victory. Only the Masons were condemned by name, and while Catholics were to be dissuaded from joining any society, the archbishops agreed that "when Catholics do belong to them, the question of leaving them or remaining in them must be decided by the conscience of each individual." When conservatives protested against such overt reliance on laymen's private judgment, the words "under the direction of his confessor" were added to the formula.[55] Even so, conservatives from the Archdiocese of Milwaukee asked Rome to establish clear criteria for forbiddable societies, and to restore to the clergy the responsibility of forthright intervention. Such measures were necessary, they contended, to establish "a uniform guide for all *in foro interno*." [56]

Rome awarded the final victory to the conservatives by officially condemning the Odd Fellows, the Knights of Pythias, and the Sons of Temperance. But so deeply did the liberals deplore the effect of this action on the liberty of Catholics and the opinion of non-Catholics that they long refused to promulgate Rome's decrees, even when directly censured for their reluctance.[57] Such costly resistance was eloquent testimony of the liberals' desire for laymen's liberty.

Instead of expanding their regulation of laymen's lives, priests should, the liberals believed, concentrate on promoting "the supreme and perfect in religion," which was not obedience to ecclesiastical superiors, but "interior union with God." [58] Isaac Hecker had been deeply impatient with his seminary superiors who frequently interrupted his spiritual communings to call him to conferences. "I used to say: Let me be, let me be! When God is heard a person feels that everything else but Him is impertinent." [59] Hecker regretted that so many Catholics failed to distinguish the two "distinct offices of the Holy Spirit"; one spoke through the authority of the Church as "the infallible interpreter and criterion of divine revelation"; the other acted in the individual soul "as the divine life-giver and sanctifier." Since the Vatican Council had answered all doubts about the locus of the first office, Catholics should now strive to experience the Holy Spirit inwardly, refusing to be content with the special devotion or sacrament which "leads to it or communicates it or guarantees its genuine presence." [60]

For this reason, Hecker deplored excessive reliance upon a spiritual director. The Holy Spirit was "the inspiration of the inner life of the regenerate man, and in that life is his Superior and Director." The Holy Spirit could never injure a man's individuality or check the "spontaneous" movements towards God "instinctive" in a good man. [61] Hecker valued true liberty of the soul so highly that he stressed the Catholic's right to change confessors and directors rather than comply with coercion of conscience. [62] Too many Europeans seemed to believe that the guileless man is not safe unless he is "provided with the greatest possible amount of guidance by the authority of God in the external order." The Paulists deplored making the "grade of one's obedience to one's director" the primary criterion of orthodoxy. [63]

Hecker, as a spiritual director, tried to be as self-effacing as possible. When he guided a community of sisters, he felt God warning him that it would be "impertinent" to interrupt; "let my spouses listen to my voice!" Hecker exhorted the timid "to break loose — give up all to God!" He refused to overwhelm a sinful man with advice or commands, thinking to himself "well, no doubt God means to save you, you poor fellow, or He wouldn't give you the grace to make this mission. . . . Just how He will do it, considering your bad habits, I can't see; but that's none of my business." [64] Hecker and his Paulists, far from wishing to "repress, to suppress, to annihilate the instincts, aspirations, and capacities God-given to human nature," believed that proper guidance would help free the individual Catholic for a more completely realized personal religious life. [65] To Ireland, the ultimate goal was action; the individual conscience must be left unintimidated, so that a man could know his duty, and not fear to do it, though he found himself alone in a strange land. [66] "Be not deceived," Elliott warned, "conformity is not the supreme virtue, and discipline is not the supreme fruit." [67]

III

The liberals were anxious that the diocesan clergy as well as the laity exercise energy and initiative. The priest should strive to be, in Gibbons' words, an "ambassador of Christ" to all society, not just a performer of rituals, and a transmittor of episcopal commands to an audience of Catholics by birthright.[68] The *Catholic World* hoped that Gibbons' exhortations would hasten the disappearance of "low views . . . , the blight of the priesthood." There was an unfortunately widespread "estimate of clerical excellence which actually concentrates everything praiseworthy in the high title of 'a safe man.' It means that priestly happiness consists in being let alone by the people and promoted by the bishop." Sanctity consisted in never being mentioned in the secular press.[69] The Paulists, in their parish church in New York, tried to demonstrate a nobler ideal; their comprehensive program provided for regular visits to the sick and needy, a plan for welcoming inquirers, a reading room, and a wide variety of young peoples' and catechism classes.[70]

If priests were to rise above "smooth mediocrity," the liberals (joined on this question by the usually intransigent McQuaid), were agreed that the American Church should abandon those traditional features of clerical training which sapped independence and initiative. Instead of sending prospective priests to a preparatory seminary, McQuaid recommended they be left under the supervision of their parents, who could guide and correct them without breaking their spirit.[71] Bishop Camillus Maes of Covington wanted them sent to regular Catholic day schools, where contact with secular life would produce more than "negative" or sheltered virtues.[72] In the higher seminaries, discipline should be lenient, lest the levite be ill fitted for "the life of self-reliance . . . young priests have to face almost immediately after leaving."[73] McQuaid believed that the young man, fortified by sacraments, prayers, teaching, and example, should be able to avoid serious dereliction "without constant watching"; the seminary should not be confused with a "reformatory." The bishop refused to ban women domestics from seminary grounds. "If in the seminary the presence of women is suggestive of evil," McQuaid declared, "it will be so after he leaves the seminary. Such a young man should avoid the priesthood or withdraw to a Trappist monastery."[74]

Before the Third Plenary Council convened, Gibbons informed Rome that the European practice of installing seminarians in clerically-supervised villas during summer vacations should not be followed in America; if a levite lost his vocation through a visit to his family and his home town, the Church was well rid of him. Despite Roman protests, the Council committed the vacationing seminarians to the watchful care of their families' parish priests.[75] In the next decade, a conservative implored these priests to exercise the greatest vigilance lest "half-healed wounds are reopened by contact with the old poison which God's providence and the kind hand of a spiritual physician had removed."[76] But Bishop Maes suggested that too close supervision would jeopardize the young men's moral independence.[77]

Conservatives sharply criticized the liberals' decision to establish the Catholic University of America so near to the public life of Washington. Archbishop Elder of Cincinnati feared that the "secular Priests and Seminarians" would be dangerously exposed to "the distractions of public affairs, — the intercourse with public men, — the gathering of unscrupulous men from all parts of the country, — the amusements — the social and convivial habits prevailing."[78] But the liberals remained confident that the benefits to be derived from the many neighboring cultural institutions far outweighed the dangers. And, in the face of conservative dismay, they encouraged the Sisters of Notre Dame of Namur to establish on property close to the university Trinity College for women.[79]

Even while seeking to develop priests of independent character, however, the liberal bishops were confronted with a number of priests whose independence verged on insubordination. In a missionary country like the United States, canon law was not yet fully applicable. Bishops were loath to designate priests as "rectors," grant them "irremovability," or create an elaborate court system to hear their appeals against episcopal censure, punishment, or transfer. On the other hand, since a priest's sense of independence was often fortified by the knowledge that every dollar of his income was presented to him directly by his own parishioners, many clergymen were inclined to fight hard for their "rights," in church courts when they were available, in civil courts as a last resort, and in the newspapers as a matter of course.[80] While the liberal bishops disliked ecclesiastical authoritarianism in principle, they generally balked at Roman proposals to strengthen the rights of priests, and they found it hard not to act vigorously when a cleric refused to coöperate with a patently desirable liberal program.[81] Even the mild Gibbons sympathized with the problems fractious priests made for his fellow bishops.

Yet contemporaries were right in believing that the liberals' eventual support of McGlynn's cause stemmed from more than a malicious delight in troubling Archbishop Corrigan. The liberals were painfully aware that strong episcopal action against a priest antagonized non-Catholics almost as much as did clerical action against a layman.[82] When McGlynn was suspended, he became a hero to Americans, who had very little sympathy with his economic views. Furthermore, the liberals could hardly fail to be influenced by the logic of their activist rhetoric, especially when the implication was spelled out by clerics like Malone, who supported the rest of their program. John Reily, although somewhat confused, as a layman, about the nature of the priesthood, used compelling terms, when, impressed by the number of clerical appeals taken to Rome against episcopal action, he insisted that "the liberty that priests are asking in all non-essentials is born of their rights as American citizens, and of the same privilege is born the love of justice and equal rights which our laws guarantee to the humblest citizen." [83] However strongly the liberal bishops resented clerical infringements of their power, they were too dedicated to the activism of all Catholics to accept with equanimity the coercion of even such an uncomfortably rebellious individual as Edward McGlynn.

IV

The liberals found little sympathy for their activist program among the traditional religious orders, whose members were frequently prevented from performing the actions suggested by conscience or individual judgment. Mother Caroline Friess found it extraordinarily difficult to persuade her German superiors to waive the "episcopal enclosure" which blocked the establishment of badly needed schools.[84] The Brothers of the Christian Schools were ordered in 1899 to stop teaching the Latin that American students needed, and which the archbishops unanimously wished to have taught; the intention of the seventeenth-century founder of the Brothers had been otherwise.[85] The Jesuits were less tradition-bound, but the American hierarchy was convinced that the order's corporate loyalty often resulted in the sacrifice of needed services as well as the frustration of individual Jesuits' instincts for usefulness.[86] Father Hecker had persuaded himself at the Vatican Council that the Jesuits, in forcing through the definition of papal infallibility, had wished to conclude the unhappy Counter-Reformation spirit, but his hope that they would turn to a less militant role was quickly blasted. Both in Europe and America, the Jesuits steadfastly opposed every aspect of the liberals' program — apologetics, political theory, schools, reforms, and secret societies.[87]

Some of the liberals were driven to conclude that the day of the regular clergy had passed. John T. Smith argued that as the world moved further towards democracy and equality, the orders would decline further.[88] A Swiss priest hailed the similarity between Hecker and a Paris priest who taught that in the present the Holy Spirit worked most effectively through the secular clergy and the laity.[89] Archbishop Ireland made no secret of his preference for working with secular priests, and his attacks on the Jesuits were particularly outspoken.[90] At the consecration of Thomas O'Gorman as bishop of Sioux Falls in April, 1896, Ireland not only asserted that the welfare of the diocese depended upon the seculars, but went out of his way to blame the Jesuits for the destruction of Catholicism in England during the penal years.[91] It was probably Ireland or one of his close associates who persuaded Senator Cushman Davis of Minnesota in his attack on Cahenslyism to refer to Leo XIII as the greatest pope since Ganganelli (Clement XIV), whose most striking action had been the dissolution of the Jesuit order.[92] Not surprisingly, Ireland acquired the reputation of "preferring the Provincial Letters of Pascal to the Institutes of St. Ignatius." [93]

The liberals, though chary in their praise of religious orders, had nothing but admiration for the Congregation of St. Paul, founded by Isaac Hecker in protest against the crippling regulations of the Redemptorists. Were the Paulists comparable to members of the religious orders? "Yes and no," Hecker believed. "Yes of their age. No of the past." One difference was that the congregation demanded no vows of its members. Committing themselves to the most strenuous pursuit of perfection and Christian service, the Paulists relied primarily on "the indwelling Holy Spirit" for guidance. Hecker admitted that a Paulist might be led into error through the exercise of this freedom, but he proudly asserted that "one of the natural signs of the true Paulist is that he would prefer to suffer from the excesses of liberty rather than from the arbitrary actions of tyranny." [94] In fact, Elliott believed, true obedience was not forfeited. Writing to a French friend, he asked: "Do I object to a Jesuit burying himself in 'methods?' Not the least. But why can't he let me try to fight without so many obediences, resulting, as they often do, in really less obedience?" [95] The ultimate justification of Paulist principles was twofold: a freer heeding of the inward guidance of the Holy Spirit, and a greater external vigor.

Because the liberal bishops so enthusiastically approved of the worldly activities the Paulists engaged in, they unreservedly approved of the congregation's remarkable energy. Ireland attributed to the Paulists the primary responsibility for the "American" spirit steadily becoming more influential in the Church. Hecker, he wrote, was a God-sent contrast to the typical nineteenth-century Catholic, "too quiet, too easily resigned to 'the will of God,' attributing to God the effects of his own timidity and indolence." At every opportunity, Hecker "rolled up his sleeves and 'pitched in' with desperate resolve." More clearly than any other American Catholic, Hecker understood that the life of confident action was the normal result of deferring to the leadings of the Holy Spirit.[96]

V

Ireland's career exemplified the active, enterprising life that the liberals expected of the episcopacy as well as of the laity and clergy. At the funeral of Bishop Stephen Ryan, Ireland declared that the prelate "who can wrap himself up in his own thought or his own spiritual interests so as not to see the broad world around him does not understand . . . the duties Christians owe to their times." In glorious contrast, Ryan had made his influence felt in every "movement of morality, temperance, Sunday observance, good government, [and] pure citizenship." [97]

Many of the liberals, however, were so anxious for the whole American Church to join in progressive enterprises that they were perfectly ready to abridge episcopal liberties on occasion. Like most nationalists, they could not recognize that organization might lessen individual liberty, so intent were they on the possible accomplishments of united action. [98] They fought hard to reserve many questions to the committee of archbishops established by the Third Plenary Council, partly, perhaps, because of the disproportionately large number of liberal metropolitans. Bishop Spalding was convinced that the committee would beneficially "gather up, harmonize, and intensify our scattered forces." This task would be even better accomplished, Spalding thought, by the national Catholic University; its faculty would educate future generations to a common understanding of the Church's real goals, and in the meantime, the prelates on the board of trustees could act as a standing council of the American Church. [99] The liberals also encouraged Gibbons to exploit to the utmost his powers as the leading spokesman, and unofficial primate, of the American Church.

Conservative bishops protested against these innovations as certain to destroy true episcopal liberty. McQuaid complained that the *"conciliabula"* of archbishops was misusing its "delegated" powers; the University was subverting the integrity of the diocesan seminaries; Gibbons was acting as if Baltimore were the American Vatican, with the Sulpicians and Paulists as the most trusted officials of the "papal *curia.*"[100] As McQuaid well knew, the only hope for the conservatives, in the short run at least, lay in Roman condemnation of the liberal projects.

The liberals, reassured by the obvious friendship of Leo XIII, did not believe that Rome would forestall their plans; but neither did they desire the American Church to be administered from the Vatican. With Hecker they believed that the definition of papal infallibility would obviate the frequent exercise of Roman authority. They endorsed Manning's contention that, in an era in which the Church was dealing directly with the people, bishops could plan the policies of the Church better than Roman bureaucrats or diplomats.[101] The liberals had begged Rome to allow American Catholics to deal as they thought best with such American problems as the public schools, the Knights of Labor, and Henry George.

All the liberals were anxious to render to Rome "what belongs to Rome," and to denounce wholeheartedly the spirit of Gallicanism; but they nevertheless looked hopefully forward to what John Reily called "a new era of control and advancement." [102] Rome should become, they thought, less a source of unchallengeable decrees, and more a forum for the democratic reconciliation of diverse spiritual concerns. One of Hecker's most frequent proposals was that the College of Cardinals, instead of being drawn primarily from the Italian Church, should represent every Catholic nation "in proportion to its importance," thus becoming "the religious senate of the world." [103] Hecker supposedly made this a deathbed request to Leo XIII. But, while Leo XIII was unquestionably more conciliatory than Pius IX towards Catholic groups or nations that deviated from the ultramontane ideal, he did not convert the College of Cardinals into a senate with proportional representation. Nor did he show any anxiety to encourage a sense of self-sufficiency in the American Church. The legislation of the Third Plenary Council was carefully reviewed by Roman authorities, and the Prefect of Propaganda made clear that the council of archbishops could never "declare ecclesiastical law." [104] Most significant of all, Leo XIII was as intent as Pius IX to establish a papal representative in Washington at the first opportune moment.

While many priests thought a delegate might protect their rights, the bishops were nearly unanimously opposed. Conservatives feared a repetition of the uproar which had greeted Archbishop Bedini in 1853. The liberals, as well as many of the conservatives, believed themselves the best authority on American conditions. Despite their articulate unenthusiasm, Leo XIII did not abandon his intentions.[105] During the Cahenslyite agitation, he asked Denis O'Connell, rector of the American College in Rome, "Why don't they want the Pope there?. . . . If I had my *Nunzio* there, all would go better." [106] In 1892, Archbishop Francesco Satolli was sent from Rome, bearing documents to the Chicago World's Fair dealing with the Columbian voyages. Although he soon informed the American archbishops that the Pope wished him to remain in America, Gibbons joined Corrigan in thanking Leo XIII for sending his representative on this "temporary mission." The next month, however, papal action established the apostolic delegation, forcing the liberals to come to terms with a new element in the American Church.[107]

At first they were eminently successful. Ireland had enjoyed great favor during his visit to Rome in the spring of 1892.[108] Convinced that a delegate would surely be sent to America soon, he characteristically decided to abandon a hopeless rearguard resistance, and be the first to welcome the mission. Not only would Ireland improve his position in Rome; the delegate might be won over in advance to the liberal cause. The Pope promised O'Connell that "Satolli will drive Corrigan to the wall," and the delegate sailed, bearing letters to Gibbons and Ireland as the two most important and presumably sympathetic, churchmen.[109] Ireland overwhelmed Satolli with hospitality; in St. Paul citizens of all faiths gave him a large dinner, thus vindicating the liberal contention that the American Church was surrounded by friends.[110] On a later visit to the city, Satolli spoke publicly of the favor Ireland enjoyed with Leo XIII:

The Holy Father sees in the administration of this diocese many and great things that give him pleasure, none that excites his displeasure. . . . He is well aware that your archbishop understands, and has at heart, the progress of the Church in the American republic, and that he promotes that progress with zeal, rectitude and prudence.[111]

This ringing endorsement, along with Satolli's liberal solutions to the school controversy, made it plausible for Thomas O'Gorman to declare that the delegate was no more a curb to true episcopal freedom than was the Pope himself. Ireland's editor, John Conway, pointing to the court set up in Washington to handle appeals of American priests, declared that Satolli's "mission here implies a kind of ecclesiastical home rule for the United States." [112]

The liberals soon altered their estimates, however, for by the time Satolli returned to Europe in 1896 he had given strong support to the conservatives' protests against religious congresses and against secret societies. The intransigent historian Reuben Parsons explained that the delegate, though misinformed by the "Faribaulters" in Rome, and handicapped by his lack of English, had finally come to understand the real condition of the American

Church; from that moment, "Faribaultism ceased to flourish in Rome." [113] He came to appreciate the German Catholics, became reconciled with Corrigan, and saw Ireland, Keane, and the Paulists for what they were. The liberals, on the other hand, preferred to believe that Satolli had been seduced from his original insight by the diabolical schemes of the conservatives, or through faults in his own character.[114]

Whatever intrigues had occurred, Satolli's alienation from the liberals was hardly surprising. Most Catholic immigrants needed a good many years before they could view American society favorably enough to be willing to approve a Church policy less intransigent than that prescribed by European ultramontanes. Furthermore, while the liberals welcomed Satolli's aid in crushing conservative opposition to a school compromise, their overriding anxiety for Catholic activism could hardly fail to place them at cross purposes with the delegate; the authority he represented they welcomed as a final check, but did not desire as a tireless omnipresence. In greeting the arrival of Satolli's successor, the *Catholic World* expressed the hope that he would dispense with the air of authority Satolli had had to use so often, and instead make his influence felt by tactful suggestion. Adding that the greatest challenge of the age was the improvement of the condition of the working class, the *World* implied that the Church should concentrate on generous activism rather than disciplinary exercises.[115] The Sulpician John Hogan hoped that the new delegate would promote all possible autonomies within the Church structure; whether he would, Hogan admitted, depended "upon many things." [116]

In advocating a strenuous, enterprising life for the laity and clergy, the liberals encountered the many ambiguities such a policy entailed in a Church whose principle of authority they themselves had no desire to subvert. Nothing was further from their minds than to promote the priesthood of all believers, the equality of priests and bishops, or an American Church in any way disaffected from Rome. Yet so resounding were their praises for liberty and action in a period when most Catholics were stressing the virtues of passive obedience that they acquired a reputation in Europe for all these heresies. And, in the late 1890's, they found that such a reputation brought sharp reprimands from Rome.

CHAPTER X

THE RESPONSE OF
EUROPEAN CATHOLICISM

During the years that the American liberals were developing a many-faceted program for Catholicizing secular culture, the larger part of the European Church remained dedicated, in the spirit of the Syllabus, to making no compromise with the demonic age. The liberal orientation of the American Church was tolerated only because of a combination of circumstances. Pope Leo XIII was far more interested than was Pius IX in winning over non-Catholics, and far more willing to permit new apologetic techniques. Anxious, furthermore, to enlist the support of secular governments for the restoration of the "Temporal Power," and for ending the *Kulturkampf*, Leo cheerfully experimented with untraditional church–state relations in France, Poland, and Germany.[1] Meanwhile, at least until 1890, the American Church had the good fortune to be relatively insignificant; its European admirers, though growing in numbers, refrained from badgering Church authorities to bring Paris and Munich into line with Baltimore and St. Paul. And the Americans themselves were, for a number of years, too humble or too circumspect to proffer the achievements of their "frontier" Church as a blueprint to help Europeans work towards the Catholicism of the future.

In the last years of the nineteenth century all these conditions changed. The American liberals, exhilarated by the dramatic extension of their nation's economic and political power, and proud of the unparalleled growth of the Church under their care, imprudently undertook to give lessons in up-to-date Catholicism to their benighted brethren abroad. They were encouraged in their impertinent charity by those European Catholics who, beleaguered by hostile secularists and ultramontanes, found in the words and deeds of Isaac Hecker and John Ireland a heaven-sent program for restoring harmony between Catholicism and culture. But in these same years, Leo XIII, disappointed in his attempts to obtain governmental support for the Temporal Power, and aghast at the pace and the boldness of intellectual innovation, was giving much more heed to the ultramontanist critiques of mediating liberal Catholicism. "Where are we now? Where are we heading?" the aged pontiff is supposed to have asked. In the early years of his rule, very few books were placed on the Index, but in the 1890's the number rose sharply.[2] With such changes taking place in America, in the Catholic countries of Europe, and especially in Rome, it would have been remarkable if the American liberals had escaped censure.

I

Throughout the nineteenth century, American businessmen and politicians had regularly proclaimed their mission to renovate Europe, but only in the last decades did they have the economic and military power to make their intentions seem ominous.[3] So expansionist had the American economy become by the 1890's that German and Austrian leaders proposed a common European alliance in "the holy cause of anti-Americanism."[4] As war with Spain neared, a diplomat reported that "on the Continent there has never been a time probably, when ill will towards the United States has been as strong as at present."[5] The easy American military victory "silenced criticism, but strengthened dislike."[6]

Unlike some unreconstructed Catholic conservatives, the American liberals did not see in each extension of national power new evidence of the militant progress of a dangerous civilization. Proud to call themselves Americans, they shared their countrymen's zeal and their pride. Hecker was delighted that America was becoming "the center of commercial and industrial activity to the whole world." [7] McGlynn thought America was "in the very vanguard of political power and progress," and Elliott found in America's "imperial civilization" "a pattern of the world." [8] God meant her to be mo.e than "a mother-land," Keane insisted. "She was meant to be a teacher, through whose lips and in whose life He was to solve the social problems of the Old World." [9] Irish-Americans swallowed hard and repeated with non-Catholic publicists that it was the special destiny of the Anglo-Saxons to dominate Western civilization.[10]

These liberal Catholics were growing ever more certain that America could teach lessons in religion as well as politics and economics. As early as 1870, Hecker had written proudly that "our course is surely fraught with the interests, hopes, and fears of the race." [11] As the Church continued to grow in America while suffering reverse after reverse in Europe, American didacticism increased. "The special significance of our American Catholic history," Bishop Spalding declared at the founding of the Catholic University, was the proof it afforded the faithful everywhere that if they would act intelligently and energetically, their Church would thrive, even though the legal privileges of the past were taken away.[12] One layman, smarting under European Catholics' long-maintained airs of superiority, found in the success of the congress at Baltimore good reason to enlarge the praise given by the London *Tablet*. "We have long been conscious of the fact," he concluded, "that 'in religion, as in other things, it' *is* — not 'seems to be' — 'the destined lot of the New World to redress the balance of the Old.' " [13]

Because of these increasingly distinct claims that the future Church would bear the imprint of American Catholicism, Europeans might well regard every innovation the liberals fostered as a dangerous challenge to their own practice. But some actions produced more immediate repercussions abroad than others. When Ireland attacked McQuaid for shirking the responsibilities of citizenship, Europeans could consider the incident an intramural clash within the Irish mission to America. They could shrug off as an expedient necessary in the peculiar American scene the toleration of the virtually unheard of "Knights of Labor." But the liberals' running fight with the older religious orders was another matter.

Even had Hecker not begged to be released from the confining policies of the Redemptorists, even had Ireland not been so outspokenly critical of the Jesuits, the liberals' clashes with the religious orders over schools, the Catholic University, and social reform would have ensured that the Jesuit periodical *Civiltà Cattolica* and the generals of the religious orders at Rome would pronounce sharp criticisms of the liberal program. When the liberals enjoined the Germans in Milwaukee to adopt the higher religious culture of the American Church, Germans in Mainz and in Rome were bound to react instantaneously. They indignantly warned other Europeans that the liberals' rapprochement with American civilization had not stirred Protestants and atheists from their aversion to the Church, but, instead, had resulted in such negligence of the immigrant Catholics that many had been lost to the faith. Father William Tappert of Covington, Kentucky told a German assembly at Cologne that the American liberals had surrendered to the extreme libertarianism and rationalism of secular America, inscribing on their banners "Union of the Church with the Age, with modern ideas, with Americanism." [14] Monsignor Joseph Schroeder told another German audience that every American attack on "foreignism" should be recognized as an assault on the universality of the Church, and ultimately on the authority of the Pope.[15] Denis O'Connell reported that such charges were readily believed by ultramontanes in Rome. "It is now the adopted rule that the German character goes more in accord with the feeling of the Propaganda." The prefect of that Congregation, O'Connell told Ireland, had declared that "the Irish in America are a bad set and the sooner the Propaganda takes hold of them the better." [16]

Convinced of the justice of their policies, the Americans did not submit humble disclaimers; instead, they aggravated the offence of building a distinctively American Catholicism by publishing invidious comparisons with the condition of the Church in European countries. The usually conservative Henry Brann responded to the Cahensly memorial by denying that America could be held responsible if some immigrants "lost" their faith. One half of all Austrian Catholics were infidels before they left home, he wrote, and Italian Catholics were "the scandal of the nineteenth century," deplorably more familiar with "the assassin's knife than with the catechism." Before European Catholics dared criticize the American Church, he advised them to care for their own needs, stop persecuting the Pope, end the Camorra and the Mafia. Brann boasted that the American Church transformed the "poor specimens of European civilization and of European Christianity" — mere "hot-house plants" — by instilling in them "ideas of American manliness, generosity, self-reliance, and independence." He confidently predicted that "the 'Americanized' children of our European Catholic immigrants, clergy and laity, may yet have a similar mission in restoring health to the decadent religious vineyards of some parts of Europe." [17]

Spokesmen more consistently liberal than Brann concentrated their criticism on European Catholics' degrading reliance on state support. "Religion reigns most worthily," Hecker loftily informed German Catholics just concluding their battle with Bismarck, "when she rules by the voluntary force of the intelligent convictions of conscience, and finds in these alone her sufficient support." [18] And the Sulpician Father John Hogan, commenting on abortive French attempts to rejuvenate their Church, declared that "what, in the judgment of most American Catholics, would effect the same results much more effectively and thoroughly is the severing, if it were possible, of the bond between Church and State, making the clergy entirely dependent on the people of France as in this country." [19]

The American "gospel" was perhaps most didactically preached when the liberals were able to speak directly to European audiences. When Gibbons took possession of his cardinal's church in Rome, he made a speech which, though avoiding reflections on European policy, was such a paean to the progress of the American Church unhampered by governmental affiliation that it necessarily constituted a challenge to his French and Italian hearers. [20]

In the spring of 1892, Leo XIII asked John Ireland, then in Rome, to do what he could to further the papal campaign to develop French Catholic loyalty to the Third Republic. The archbishop gave several lectures in Paris to French groups on the success that was sure to be theirs if they emulated American Catholics' patriotism, social welfare work, and intimate dependence on the people. [21] Though no *ralliement* to the Republic resulted, Ireland's visit was a triumph. And even to have been enlisted by the Pope was flattering to both the man and the church he represented. Denis O'Connell reflected American Catholics' pride when he reminded Ireland, in 1891, of his responsibility to "do good like Manning for the whole toiling world." Urging him not to "shrink into a simple Minnesotan," O'Connell promised that if Ireland would come abroad again, "all Europe will echo your words and you can move the entire struggling mass." [22] A New Yorker concluded from the several evidences of papal favor that Leo's "wise men come from the West," and Bishop Keane was sure that the Pope would rejoice to see the American Church "giving the tone to the future of the world." [23]

In 1894, Keane, speaking before the Third International Catholic Scientific Congress in Brussels, defended the Parliament of Religions as a suitable forum for the liberal apologetic. Catholics, he declared, did not face implacable enemies, but "brothers to be brought back to the fold"; the American Church had prospered by offering love and persuasion instead of harsh polemic. Non-Catholics at the parliament had been brought closer to the Church, as their interest and personal affection for Catholic leaders had demonstrated. Just as the United States was a symbol of the developing political unity of mankind, the parliament was a symbol of growing religious unity, which Keane held up as a "lesson" for all Christians. [24] Ireland roundly endorsed French Catholics' plan to take part in a Congress of Religions in Paris in 1900. "It will be a pity," he declared, "if, when other religions are vocal, the Catholic will keep silent and appear before the nations as dead. It is only the dying who do not love the noise of action." [25]

The large number of American clergy at the Fribourg meeting of the Catholic Scientific Congress in August, 1897, testified to the American Church's heightening participation in European Catholic affairs. [26] Even more dramatic evidence was the permission granted Denis O'Connell, now vicar of Gibbons' titular church in Rome, to speak on "Father Hecker's Americanism." More prudent than Ireland in Paris, more aware of European hostilities than Keane at Brussels, the priest nevertheless presented a manifesto to the world Church rather than a defense of certain missionary convictions. [27] Hecker's Americanism, O'Connell argued, was comprised of a theory of political authority and a view of church–state relations. The American legal system, in happy contrast with

Roman law, recognized God's ultimate sovereignty, and the immediate rule of the people, thus satisfying the demand of Christianity that both the individual and the moral law be protected. It was true that the Church had sometimes prospered under the authoritarianism and secularism of Roman law, but O'Connell expounded Hecker's contention that the Church of the future "would have to maintain its sway . . . through the use of the power of the democratic ideal, that is to say, in a sense, the American ideal." In a time when most Catholics stressed the unconditional power of the Pope, O'Connell audaciously argued that the Pope's proudest title was "the servant of the servants of God."

O'Connell did not successfully conceal the liberals' willingness to share the benefits of the American system with backward Catholic countries. This failure was especially unfortunate in the summer of 1897 when many Europeans were afraid that Hecker's Americanism would be spread not by lectures but as the by-product of American political–military expansion. Before war actually broke out, the liberal Catholics, though sympathetic with Cuban demands for self-government, did not join in the swelling belligerence towards Spain.[28] Archbishop Ireland, anxious to forestall war, undertook the responsible but thankless role of mediator between Spain, the Pope, and the McKinley administration.[29] Frustrated in attempts to preserve peace, the liberals swiftly found consolation in the praise American Catholics won by loyally participating in war with a Catholic state.[30]

The Paulists soon confirmed European suspicion of the American liberals by joining in the demand for empire. The *Catholic World* encouraged the President to keep the whole Pacific area, or "the Hawaiian group anyway." [31] Father Henry O'Keefe declared that once a nation had played its role in history, its proper place was "the tomb," and he asked Spain to be grateful to America for relieving her of the incubus of empire, thus freeing her to "construct new methods of usefulness for the future." [32] The American Church would surely benefit, the Paulists thought, for new territories would mean new outlets for her seething energy; ever new fields of enterprise were necessary if American Catholics were to avoid the torpor that characterized so many Europeans.[33] But the greatest beneficiaries of American victory would be the Filipinos;

Spanish priests, indolent because of their assured "financial welfare," would be swiftly replaced by the most "American" clergy available, and the Filipino Church would acquire a new vitality.[34] "It is no reflection upon other countries," Father O'Keefe reflected, "to believe that our methods for the propagation of Christ's gospel are quicker, healthier, and more thorough." [35]

In the fall of 1898, it was easy to believe that Americanism, both Theodore Roosevelt's and Isaac Hecker's, was destined to ever greater triumphs. The *Catholic World* rejoiced at seeing "old dame Europe going to school again to learn from the young American school-master. The events of the past few months have placed America in the forefront of the nations of the earth." [36] Ireland wrote happily to O'Connell that American influence was bound to increase. "If the pope in the future is to have any world-wide prestige, he must deal as never before with America. Tell all this in Rome." [37] 1898, an American Catholic editor declared, would "go down in history as the year when the United States first raised her voice in the world's chapter. In the same year, the Catholic Church in this country may be said to have entered into Catholic politics." [38] Genuinely anxious to extend the blessings of the American system to the whole world, these jubilant spokesmen seem to have believed for a few months that universal triumph was imminent for the liberal Catholicism which for a century had been tolerated only as an exception.

II

The liberals' optimism was fed by the appearance in Europe of enthusiastic support for the Americanist program. In England, Cardinal Manning supported Gibbons and Ireland in blocking condemnation of the Knights of Labor and Henry George.[39] Father William Barry published articles in both England and America to further "Catholic democracy" and to promote a generous spirit towards secular culture.[40] Newman regarded his life work as much like Hecker's, and Father George Tyrrell felt that he and Hecker stood together in stressing the integrity of the individual conscience.[41] English Catholics readily agreed with the American liberals on the superiority of the Anglo-Saxon virtues of responsible liberty. "It is evident," Barry wrote, "that the future of Catholicism will come to depend more and more on the English-speaking and Germanic families." [42] Robert Dell, a prominent layman, declared that the victories of the United States over Spain, and of England over the Boers, whatever the "immediate effects," ensured the eventual triumph of the highest form of Catholicism. [43] A popular novel by an English Catholic predicted that civilization would soon benefit by the election to the papacy of a Cardinal Archbishop of New York. [44]

A considerable number of French and Italian writers agreed that the modern Church should adapt itself everywhere to the Anglo-Saxon pattern. This was "the pole," the Vicomte de Vogüé maintained, towards which Leo XIII's "meditations. calculations, and hopes . . . were in preference directed." [45] Edward Demolins argued that liberty, energy, and openness to new experience made Americans the archetypes not only of secular civilization but of modern religious life. He was sure that the Church in America had greater "moral and religious energy" than in Europe. [46]

Many of the French clergy wished to emulate the American liberals' program. Some praised the campaign to save the Knights of Labor, and regarded Ireland and Gibbons as true prophets of social Catholicism. [47] Others, especially Hippolyte Gayraud and Paul Naudet, working for democracy as well as social reform, responded enthusiastically to Ireland's injunction to rally to the Republic. This group wanted the Church to copy American methods of spreading the gospel. Gayraud called for religious congresses to which Christians regardless of "their confession or profession of faith" would be invited. Naudet advocated educational reforms to fit the clergy for energetic action in the world. [48] A group of French "neo-Christians" shared the Paulists' conviction that, in an age of liberty, equality, and individuality, the Church should stress the internal direction of the Holy Spirit. [49] Some Italian churchmen, convinced that the separation of church and state was as desirable in Italy as America, recommended that the Pope abandon his claims to the "temporal power." [50] At various times in the 1890's, all these groups called themselves or were called "américanistes." [51]

Many of the Europeans who borrowed the prestige of the American Church for their analogous interests carefully stipulated that in Europe all Protestants were not as sympathetic as those in America appeared to be, that the absolute separation of Church and State was not always applicable, and that no feature of the American liberals' program should be adopted except with great caution.[52] Félix Klein, professor at the Institut Catholique in Paris, was less reserved. In 1894, he published a French translation of five of Archbishop Ireland's more buoyant addresses. American Catholicism was so pure, Klein believed, that the French Church could adopt most of its program without fear.[53] In 1897, Klein was persuaded by French friends to abridge a translation of Walter Elliott's biography of Hecker, which had appeared in America in 1891 with a glowing introduction by Archbishop Ireland.[54] In his preface Klein stated flatly that if Hecker's ideas were "fundamentally American," they were not "exclusively so." Modern life demanded "more education, more energy, more independence, more initiative. . . . Respect for custom" had become "on many points a weakness . . . and a cause of decadence." Hecker's life taught convincingly that reliance on the inner action of the Holy Spirit developed a desirably adventurous disposition. Klein was confident that by careful editing of Hecker's forthright vocabulary, and by drawing a parallel with Leo's teaching on the operation of the Holy Spirit, he had safeguarded against Europeans mistakenly detecting a latent Protestantism in Hecker's doctrines.[55] He did not hesitate, therefore, to adorn the French edition with a Swiss priest's proclamation that Hecker was "the type, not only of the American priest, but of the modern priest, of the priest the Church must have." [56]

Bold as Klein was, he accurately represented American liberal convictions.[57] But ideas and institutions when exported abroad often suffer a sea change, and in the late 1890's, the American Church acquired in Europe many friends and more enemies who only imperfectly understood what Ireland and the Paulists were working for. In March, 1898, Keane, still sure of eventual victory, nevertheless reported sadly that on a trip through Europe he had found Americanist ideas "coming into collision with misunderstandings, misrepresentations, and invective." [58]

An unfortunately prominent example was the performance of Victor Charbonnel, a French priest. Immensely enthused by the Parliament of Religions, he worked devotedly in behalf of the congress planned for Paris in 1900. When the French hierarchy vetoed Catholic participation, he indignantly left the Church. In a self-justificatory book and many articles he imputed to American liberal prelates some very disrespectful estimates of the wisdom of Cardinal Richard of Paris. In 1899 he published supposedly inside information that unless the ultramontanes were deprived of their malign influence in Rome, the Americans were bound to leave the Church.[59] Other French priests acted on their conviction that the logic of "Americanism" required them to abandon a hopelessly conservative Church.[60]

Embarrassing as the testimonials of these quondam friends proved, their misunderstanding was, in the long run, less damaging than that which led many ultraconservatives to associate Americanism with the malevolent Masonry, satanism, Protestantism, Semitism, and advanced thought of the age. Because the Masons flourished in America, a Belgian biographer of Leo XIII concluded that the order had "its true center there." [61] The French Canadian Jules Tardivel declared that America was the eldest daughter of the sect.[62] Because the liberal leaders had opposed the indiscriminate condemnation of secret societies, a Paris Catholic paper accused Cardinal Gibbons of being especially fond of the Masons.[63]

Masonry, satanism, and Americanism were linked together in the strange Diana Vaughan affair. This fictitious woman, created by Leo Taxil, a French hoaxer, had been born among the American Indians, and, in 1889, in a secret ceremony in Charleston, South Carolina, had been personally commissioned by Lucifer to war on all those who revered the Virgin Mary. After arriving in France, she was miraculously converted, and began an edifying career exposing satanists on both continents, and composing devotional works. Many European Catholics were convinced that she had not wholly renounced her unholy American origins. Taxil's revelation that he had been exploiting conservative Catholics' credulity did not, in all likelihood, destroy the stereotype he had capitalized on.[64]

One of Taxil's assistants had written a popular book proving that all Protestants were involved in the Masonic-satanist conspiracy. The ardent Ernest Renauld warned France against "the Protestant peril." Protestants were responsible for every French military defeat since the Revolution, and were heart and soul of the Anglo-Saxon aggressions of the past decade; the appalling collapse of moral and intellectual certainties was the result of Protestant sub-version.[65] To men like Renauld, the Paulists appeared as open abettors of this conspiracy of heretics, and Bishop Keane, with his defense of the Parliament of Religions, the proponent of un-conditional Catholic surrender.

The reserve of many American liberals towards the Catholic attack of Dreyfus, coupled with the open hostility in England, helped convince ultraconservatives that the Americans were pro-Semitic, just as they were pro-Masonic and pro-Protestant.[66] Despite the fact that some of the French democratic priests managed to be both anti-Semites and *américanistes*, a heresy hunter declared that it was "incontestable" that between "the Jewish spirit and the Ameri-canist spirit there is a point of contact in the principles of '89." Both groups were bent on world conquest, and both hypocritically pro-fessed a charitable broadmindedness.[67]

The final element in the "Americanist conspiracy" was the group of European Catholics whose exploits in the name of scholarly freedom and intellectual progress were distressing to even the more moderate Church leaders. Conspicuous among them were Canon di Bartolo who was condemned in 1891, and the German scholar Hermann Schell, whose demands for a virtually unqualified right to publish novel hypotheses were censured in 1899.[68] St. George Mivart, risking heresy in his writings, took it upon himself to test the ex-tent of the Church's tolerance by advancing very provocative theo-logical hypotheses.[69]

Many of the American liberals had praised Mivart's scientific work, so that, by the logic of all heresy hunters, they could be held responsible for everything Mivart ever wrote. But even more satis-factory to the ultraconservatives' purpose was an article on "Liberal Catholicism" which appeared in the *Contemporary Review* in 1897.[70] Because the anonymous author made no secret of his sense of the superiority of "English-speaking" Catholics, the American liberals stood convicted of sharing his belligerently radical ideas.[71] On the premise that the "physical and mental health of Christians of future ages" depended on intellectual freedom now, the author declared that scholars should not delay clearing away the "Augean stable of theological filth and rubbish," especially in the mooted area of Biblical criticism. For the Church to balk at this proposal would be "suicidal," since the certain result would be an "exodus" of its most valuable and intelligent members.

Certainly, a conspiracy that included the author of "Liberal Catholicism," Captain Dreyfus, Protestants more devious than Calvin, the satanic sponsors of Miss Diana Vaughan, and the ever dangerous Masons required the sternest Catholic resistance. Hostility intensified in 1898 as Americans grew more explicitly confident of their world mission. A Paris review declared that Americanism was

not only an attack of heresy; it is an *invasion of barbarism*. It is not only an adaptation of Protestantism to Catholicism; it is the assault of a new power against Christian society; . . . it is money against honor, bold brutality against delicateness . . . machinery against philosophy . . . the purchase of all, the theft of all, joyous rapine supplanting justice and the demands of duty. . . . Religious Americanism is only one of the assaults of pan-Americanism.[72]

With this objectification of the resentments of an unusually depressing decade of European Church history, the opposition which had been coalescing against "religious Americanism" was completed. Joined with the hysteria-ridden were deeply religious men who disliked the activist, self-confident, apparently worldly tone the liberals gave to Catholicism; ultramontanes indignant at the revival of a spirit they thought had finally been scotched at the Vatican Council; French monarchists who detested Ireland for his forthright endorsement of the Third Republic; Spaniards who resented American assertions that a progressive church and state could accomplish in a few years for Cuba and the Philippines what three hundred years of Spanish endeavor had failed to do; Germans anxious to win just treatment for their countrymen in America; Jesuits who treasured corporate as well as ideological antagonisms to the American hierarchy. Under direct attack from so many Catholics, the Americanists lost the privilege which, as pioneers achieving unusual success in an unusually large task, they had long enjoyed to deviate from the pattern of ultramontane Catholicism. As a result, in the decade of the 1890's the Americans received not the grateful recognition they expected but a series of official rebukes. The interplay of personalities and institutions in Rome markedly affected the phrasing and timing of the several declarations, but, taken together, the reprimands left no room for doubt that responsible authorities, including Leo XIII, had formed an unfavorable opinion of the direction toward which the American liberals seemed to be tending.[73]

III

The balance between approval and aversion began to tip against the liberals in 1893. Though Rome had just refused again to grant special privileges to the German-Americans, Denis O'Connell did not fail to recognize how strong the liberals' enemies were becoming. "Your only friends," he wrote Ireland, "are the American people; your last protection their esteem. To count on anything but opposition [in Rome] is a mistake."[74] O'Connell's estimate was too pessimistic but he was right to be gloomy. In that same year, Rome ignored liberal recommendations and condemned three American secret societies. Archbishop Riordan of San Francisco begged Gibbons to go in person to Rome "and do again what you did for the Knights of Labor." Ireland was equally confident that the cardinal's influence was potent in Rome.[75] But Gibbons was checkmated by the strenuous opposition of European and American conservatives. For the first time, Leo XIII asked him the question most disastrous to the liberals' central position: if American non-Catholics were so friendly to the Church, why expect a *Kulturkampf* if Rome proceeded as it normally would against objectionable societies?[76] No answer the liberals could give was persuasive. Though they stubbornly refused to carry out Roman instructions, believing them disastrous to the prestige of American Catholicism, they had undoubtedly suffered a major reverse. The most forthright insubordination was a far cry from those victories they had won in the past that seemed to chart the future course of the whole Catholic Church.[77]

A further setback occurred in January, 1895, when Leo issued an encyclical to the American Church. The liberals were reconciled to the Pope's main purpose, which was to strengthen the apostolic delegate's standing with American Catholics, and, since Thomas O'Gorman had been asked to prepare a first draft of the letter, most of Leo's remarks were wholly satisfactory.[78] But, while praising the growth of the American Church, and noting the absence of hostile state legislation, Leo added that it "would be very erroneous to draw the conclusion that in America is to be sought the type of the most desirable status of the Church; or that it could be universally lawful for state and church to be, as in America, dissevered and divorced." The Church had grown, not because of the favorable American environment, but because of God's especial grace. "She would bring forth more abundant fruits, if, in addition to liberty, she enjoyed the favor of the laws and the patronage of the public authority," the Pope concluded. Cardinal Gibbons was distressed that this suggestion had been added, and Ireland considered it so "unfortunate" that he canceled his contract to write an explanatory article on the encyclical for the *North American Review*, believing that Americans would never accept Leo's argument.[79]

Ireland knew that he himself had much at stake. Many European Catholics had challenged the orthodoxy of his speeches praising the American church–state system, so that he was relieved to get assurances from Cardinal Rampolla, the papal Secretary of State, that the encyclical had not been meant as a reproof to him.[80] But a disturbingly large number of Catholics were certain that the liberal group as a whole had been reprimanded. The apostolic delegate Francesco Satolli, Professor Joseph Schroeder, the *Ecclesiastical Review*, and the *Catholic Quarterly Review* all hailed the encyclical as a badly needed warning to certain Americans to stop attenuating Catholic teaching, and, above all, not to exhort Catholics in other lands to work for the separation of the church from the state.[81]

Another sign of the worsening liberal position was the forced resignation in 1895 of Denis O'Connell from the rectorship of the American College in Rome. He had offended the Germans by his adroit maneuvers against the Cahensly petitions, and he had long since ceased to represent the interests of men like Corrigan. Though Gibbons promptly appointed O'Connell vicar of his titular church in Rome, the liberals' recommendations for the rectorship were rebuffed.[82] Rome chose William O'Connell, who thus began a distinguished career in which, as an ultra-Roman, he was regularly promoted against the preferences of the American liberals.[83]

The equally involuntary resignation of Bishop Keane from the Catholic University in the fall of 1896 constituted a sharp rebuke to the liberal efforts to win back Protestants, and to work harmoniously with secular culture. The year before, Keane's and Ireland's enthusiasm for parliaments of religion had been rudely checked when the Pope advised against holding or taking part in "promiscuous conventions." [84] The liberals found themselves charged, with increasing frequency, with being neo-Pelagians because of their proclamations of "the goodness, the probity, the purity, the holiness of those who live far from the bosom of the Catholic Church." [85] Keane was also exposed to conservative attack because of the advanced views of the faculty he had recruited for the Catholic University. Shortly after Satolli returned to Rome, Keane was relieved of his post on the grounds that Leo had never intended the appointment to be permanent.[86] Keane was made a titular archbishop and offered a position of honor in Rome, but this camouflage did not prevent the press from recognizing that the Americanists had been placed on the defensive.[87] McQuaid jubilantly concluded that with Gibbons, Ireland, and Keane all rebuked, the American Church would lead a healthier life; European conservatives rejoiced at the setback to American self-confidence.[88]

Keane wanted to retire silently from public life, but the other liberals were less acquiescent. Gibbons paid an emotional tribute to the departing rector, and approved a great civic testimonial meeting. Ireland had the audacity to tell the press that the board of trustees might well reelect Keane to the rectorship; when that proved impossible, he joined in drawing up a memorial which repeatedly stressed Keane's praiseworthy associations with American Protestants. Together with Archbishop Riordan, Ireland managed to persuade Keane to go to Rome to fight for American interests. "Recent occurrences," Ireland wrote, "show us the necessity of being frank and courageous. . . . We must stop such things one way or another . . . . Nothing but stern courage on our part will avert disaster from us [for] our enemies are not timid." [89] He and Gibbons derived what comfort they could from assurances from Satolli and Rampolla that, contrary to rumor, no censures of Ireland or of the Catholic University professors were contemplated.[90] Ireland planned to visit Rome "soon after McKinley's inauguration. I will wait until I can go with all the prestige of my American influence." [91]

Though the Americanists' real popularity with non-Catholics may have helped secure Roman assent to the dismissal of the archconservative Joseph Schroeder from the Catholic University in 1897, it was of dubious value in contending with a mounting opposition which regarded secular esteem as a sign of unsoundness.[92] Ever more bitter attacks were made on the liberals. In February, 1897, an anonymous writer in the *Ecclesiastical Review* drew up a comprehensive indictment: an excessive "flaunting" of American patriotism at the expense of Catholic loyalties; an undue reliance upon scholarship as a source of truth, coupled with a disregard for doctrinal uniformity; extreme libertarianism within the Church to the detriment of sound hierarchical principles; and a muting of Catholic truths in order to attract converts from Protestantism. The individual charges were not new, but the author, apparently backed up by the editors of the *Review*, went on to declare that these errors constituted a pattern of "American religious liberalism," from which only the forthright intervention of Roman authority could save the Church.[93]

Meanwhile, European critics were publishing violent attacks on the French version of Elliott's *Life of Father Hecker*; O'Connell's address at Fribourg — a conscious attempt to direct attention away from Hecker's theories of the action of the Holy Spirit — served only to convince opponents that the Paulist was guilty of Archbishop Ireland's political heresies as well as of theological error.[94] The most notorious charges were proffered by Abbé Charles Maignen, a French priest, in a series of articles which asked whether Hecker was a saint, and answered that he was more of a radical Protestant.[95] From Hecker's scattered sayings, Maignen constructed a theology practically Quaker in its stress on inner guidance; the abbé interpreted the liberal apologetic as a neo-Kantian denial of the objective certainty of Catholic truth; and he discerned in Hecker's exhortations to activism a deep contempt for the "passive" virtues of humility and obedience. Ireland was pictured as the liberals' field marshal, ready to lead a schism from the Church if all his wishes were not immediately fulfilled.

Gibbons was only indirectly indicted, but he could not tolerate insinuations against a man most liberals agreed was the ideal American priest. Accepting a suggestion from Father Elliott, the cardinal published a letter in both America and France calling Hecker a providential gift to the American Church. He had been "a faithful child of Holy Church, every way Catholic in the fullest meaning of the term," Gibbons wrote, "and his life was adorned

with the fruits of personal piety; . . . he was inspired with a zeal
for souls of the true apostolic order . . . attracting Protestants, and
yet entirely orthodox." The cardinal rejoiced that Europe now had
the opportunity to learn more of this remarkable man.[96] The main
effect of this brave effort was to identify the liberal cause irrevocably
with the mooted biography.[97] Though it helped prevent Maignen
from securing the *imprimatur* from Cardinal Richard of Paris for a
book version of his attacks, it did not check Alberto Lepidi, the
Master of the Sacred Palace in Rome, from granting an *imprimatur*,
thus seemingly throwing behind the attack on Americanism the
authority of the Holy See itself.[98]

The liberals protested vigorously, Gibbons indignantly denying
that American patriotism had ever encouraged the slightest heresy
among the faithful, but their words were offset in Rome by contrary representations from American conservatives, including Corrigan and Sebastian Messmer, now Bishop of Green Bay.[99] Eventually, Leo XIII decided to speak authoritatively on the whole
question, and, despite frantic efforts by Keane and Ireland to dissuade
him, addressed a letter on January 22, 1899, to Cardinal Gibbons
as "an evidence of his good will." [100]

IV

His purpose, Leo XIII said, was to point out certain things "to
avoid and correct" which were thought to have been propagated in
the biography of Hecker, particularly in its translated form. Most
crucial was the conviction that the Church, in order to convert outsiders, should be ready to modify its doctrines and disciplines to
comport with the preferences of the age. The Vatican Council had
effectively denounced evolution of doctrine in any such way; and,
though the discipline of the Church varied with place and time,
it was for the supreme authority, not the individual or nation, to
decide when modifications were desirable. The Pope explicitly rejected the "strange" argument (so often advanced by Hecker) that
the definition of papal infallibility increased the scope of individual
initiative.

Several corollary errors were also to be shunned. The modern
individual needed external direction in his spiritual life as much as
did the holy men of the past. Supernatural virtues were superior to

natural virtues by the element of divine grace which alone made them possible. The invidious distinction between active and passive virtues was false; all virtues required action, and the present age could not dispense with humility, obedience, and abstinence. The binding vows of the religious orders were no impediment either to the highest personal perfection or the greatest social usefulness. Finally, all religious "discussion" with heretics was wrong, though it was permissible for an apologist to appeal to the presuppositions of the many well-intentioned American Protestants. The several errors he had mentioned, Leo said, were grouped together and defended as "Americanism" by men who were, in effect, constructing a Catholicism far removed from the faith preserved in Rome.

The Pope mentioned no names, and nowhere explicitly said that a single American avowed the condemnable opinions. He emphasized that many of the errors were undoubtedly unintentional, and that the American hierarchy would be the first to renounce them. He insisted that he had nothing but admiration for the laudable political and social qualities of the American people, which were also sometimes called "Americanism." It was easy, therefore, for Archbishop Ireland, then in Rome, for Klein in France, and for the liberals in America not only to submit to the papal teaching, but to assert that they had never entertained the erroneous beliefs.[101] In unusually strong language, Gibbons declared that the "extravagant and absurd" doctrine called "Americanism" had "nothing in common with the views, aspirations, doctrine, and conduct of Americans. I do not think that there can be found in the entire country," Gibbons wrote, "a bishop, a priest, or even a layman with a knowledge of his religion who has ever uttered such enormities." [102] The other liberals loudly agreed that such errors could only have flourished abroad. Some, noticing the temperateness of the Pope's censures, argued that Leo had discomfited the "*réfractaires* and retrogressionists," who had expected that their malevolent plot against the American Church would lead to far harsher condemnations.[103]

The liberals could not overlook, however, that the Pope's words, though measured, had condemned a doctrine called "Americanism"; had certainly not excluded the possibility that it flourished in the United States; and had, in any case, been addressed to Baltimore, not Paris, Madrid, or Munich. Only the most imaginative could contend that since Leo had probably not written the whole letter he was unaware of the implications the words seemed to carry. Unwilling to contend that Leo had been tilting at a windmill, the liberals tended to lay most blame on the Hecker biography. Father Clarence Walworth, one of the original Paulists, deftly assigned some responsibility to Elliott for not expressing Hecker's ideas more clearly, some to the "defective translations" circulated in Europe, some to the confusing introduction by Klein, and some to the European inability to understand phrases intended by their authors, primarily for American audiences.[104]

Conservatives at home and abroad, however, noisily insisted that "Americanism" was neither a "phantom heresy," nor a misinterpretation of Hecker's teaching. Corrigan, with the approval of most of his suffragans, wrote in March, 1899 to thank the Pope for his timely warning against the "multiplicity of fallacies and errors . . . under the specious title of 'Americanism.' " The archbishop made clear that the letter had been badly needed in America.[105] In June, McQuaid pointed out to his people four examples of the evil the Pope was warning against: the Parliament of Religions; liberal disobedience to the papal ban on membership in certain secret societies; Keane's speeches to non-Catholic universities; and the liberals' attitude towards the public schools.[106] The German bishops from the province of Milwaukee not only testified that the errors had been dangerously prevalent in America, but warned the Pope that the liberals' disavowals were being made with Jansenist reservations.[107]

The *Civiltà Cattolica* stated flatly that "Americanism" was in origin "purely American . . . employed at first to indicate in general the 'new idea' which was to rejuvenate the Church, and, in particular, the 'new crusade' against the uncompromising position of the Catholics of the old creed." It was no "invention of the enemies of the United States, but a sad reality" which had already damaged the American Church, and threatened Catholicism everywhere.[108] French conservatives were certain that the heresy had been overt in America, with infiltrations beginning in the French Church.[109] One Roman paper, outraged at the liberal protestations of innocence, attacked the Americans' "Satanic spirit." "Put the mask aside, O Monsignor Ireland; bow down before the Vicar of Jesus Christ and deny the blasphemous theories of the heretical sect which are embodied in you." [110]

Conservatives were certainly justified in complaining that most of the Americans remained "penitent Catholics but impenitent liberals." [111] Though the biography of Hecker was promptly withdrawn from sale, one Paulist gave an interview to the New York *Times* in which he conceded very little. Leo XIII was perhaps somewhat misinformed about American Catholics, the priest said; their loyalty to the Holy See was absolute. All of them believed that grace was above and greater than nature, though they also believed it must follow nature, and would never controvert it. Hecker's distinction between passive and active virtues was not a theological one, though it had "vernacular" importance, since Americans preferred to " 'hit out' and take action." Certainly no reputable Catholic believed that vows were "more suitable to weak than to strong minds," but the Paulist would say that weak minds needed vows more than did strong ones, and that "it simply takes a more ardent determination to live aright without the help of a vow." [112] The *Catholic World* pointed out to French clerics that the best material for a Paris exposition on the progress of the faith could be found in the American Church. "Imprudent obscurantists" could "learn a little more of this to their own profit." [113]

In the winter of 1900, John Spalding lectured on "Education and the Future of Religion" in Rome, and reaffirmed his faith in progress, liberty, and individual action. The health of the Church, he said, depended on the ability of Catholics to acknowledge authority without sinking into a "dead uniformity." There was need not for "new doctrines and new shrines," but rather for a "revivification of faith, hope, and love, fresh courage and will." Like Hecker and Keane, he called on modern Catholics to follow the example of St. Paul in meeting the pagans of Athens on their own ground; the only alternative was to settle into a "spiritual ghetto." [114] A friendly observer reported that Spalding's lectures constituted "the pure essence of Americanist ideas." [115]

Ireland made a triumphal tour through France and England the spring after the papal letter was issued, preaching his familiar themes: the special harmony between the Church and democracy; the need for activism; the social teachings of the Pope; the crusade for temperance.[116] He made no apologies for his "Americanism," for, as a practical man, he professed no admiration for "the mythological heroes of the Valhalla who pass their days in hewing down shadows." [117] President McKinley strengthened his position by commissioning him to represent America at the unveiling of a statue of Lafayette in Paris on July 4, 1900. Rome was impressed both with Ireland's prestige and with America's tolerance.[118]

The Holy See sought Ireland's good offices in the settlement of the friars' land question in the Philippines. He helped the Church by getting a friendly commission appointed, and he defended the interests of the United States by answering intemperate Catholic criticism of the commission's behavior.[119] Even before these not altogether rewarding labors had begun, he had enjoyed a friendly interview with the Pope and other high Roman officials. "They are all delighted with me . . . need my cooperation, and are resolved to have it," he wrote a friend in the summer of 1900. "The Pope told me to forget that letter on Americanism, which has no application except in a few dioceses in France!" [120]

Just as the removals of O'Connell and Keane had been sure signs of the liberals' loss of prestige, so their reappointments to important responsibilities seemed to indicate a return of their group to grace. In September, 1900, after repeated intercessions by Gibbons, Keane was appointed to the see of Dubuque, where he spent the rest of his life.[121] And in 1902, Denis O'Connell was made rector of the Catholic University. The world had turned upside down, Ireland joyfully declared. A few years earlier, O'Connell's assignment to Washington would have seemed "simply impossible. Well, he is here. *Viva l'Americanismo! Viva sempre!*" [122]

To complete the liberals' joy, Leo XIII, on whose favor so much depended, made his last message to the American hierarchy a paean of praise. Replying to congratulations on his long rule, Leo testified that his confidence in the American Church had never flagged.

A long experience compels us to acknowledge that, thanks to your efforts, we have found in your people souls endowed with all the docility of spirit and good will that could be desired. And while the vicissitudes and failings of almost all the traditionally Catholic nations inspire sadness, the state of your churches and their flourishing youth rejoice our soul.[123]

Such a halcyon summary might well seem the final proof that the reprimands of the 1890's had been only insignificant incidents in the happy growth of the American Church in the favor of God and men.[124]

The liberals had been frequently reminded, however, that Rome was still unreconciled to the Americanist program. At the very time Ireland was being assured that Americanism was only an aberration of a few French Catholics, Archbishop Keane received, along with his appointment to Dubuque, a special letter from the Pope adjuring him to heed the warnings addressed to Cardinal Gibbons; Leo apparently considered special precautions were necessary to counteract "the errors spreading" in America, and to improve the "union of souls with this infallible seat of truth." [125]

Ireland was also kept on a short string. In his speeches in England after the papal letter, he had confirmed conservative suspicions by implying that the future of the Church depended more on Roman willingness to treat English-speaking Catholics with sympathetic understanding than it did on the restoration of the "temporal power." The next year, Ireland was invited to attend a public meeting of the cardinals in Rome, where Leo asked him several pointed questions. What would he say to the American people on his return? That he was inspired with greater devotion to the Holy See than ever before. What did American Catholics think of the present situation of the Pope? They regretted his deprivations, and wished him full independence. The colloquy could hardly have been spontaneous, for Leo replied, "You have well interpreted my sentiments." [126] Ireland also promised to say more after reaching America; in the winter following, he preached a sermon in Washington, and published an article in the *North American Review* on the desirability of returning Rome to the Pope.[127] Discreet disinterest in this problem was clearly no longer a liberal prerogative.

Since 1892, Ireland had hoped to be made a cardinal, at least partly as a vindication of the policies for which he had campaigned; an impressive array of cardinals, including several liberal Italians, and American political leaders, including Theodore Roosevelt, lent strenuous if at times maladroit support.[128] But Ireland died an archbishop. Rome chose to make cardinals of American Catholics not noted for their liberalism. John Farley, elevated in 1911, had stayed aloof from the battles of the 1890's; as Corrigan's successor to the see of New York, he won respect for his personal piety and for his ability in specifically Catholic organizational work. William O'Connell, made a cardinal in the same year, had never been anything but an ardent ultramontane.[129] Meanwhile, Ireland's stock fell so low in Rome that he fully expected to be condemned by name during the "Modernist" controversy.[130] Though he did not "shrink into a simple Minnesotan," he ceased to be the familiar figure in Rome that he had been in the 1890's.[131]

The Americanist movement was too deep rooted to disappear because of the fall from favor of some of its leaders. The reproofs of the 1890's warned the American Church against moving too forcefully against the mainstream of European Catholic development; certain actions and specific formulas were effectively ruled out. But no European censure could compel the liberals to abandon their central faith that non-Catholic culture was redeemable. In the twentieth century, that faith remained strong, even though its exponents were continually reminded that both the Church and the secular society between which they sought a rapprochement were changing in ways unanticipated by Ireland and Elliott, Spalding and Father Zahm, Gibbons, and Bishop Keane.

CHAPTER XI

LIBERAL CATHOLICISM IN THE TWENTIETH CENTURY

Though the entry of the American Church into "Catholic politics" proved a not wholly happy experience, its steady growth during the twentieth century has increased its prestige. Not only has membership continued to climb, but income has also grown, to the point where one pundit guessed that more than half of Rome's normal expenses have been underwritten by American Catholics.[1] In 1919, a papal official declared that "Rome now looks to America to be the leader in all things Catholic, and to set an example to other nations."[2] Years before, Archbishop Ireland had predicted that the expansion of American political and economic power would bring greater Roman respect for those prelates in the best position to influence that power. Especially since 1940, as communism has destroyed the possibility of strong Catholic life in Poland, Hungary, and Yugoslavia, and has made great strides in organizing against the Church the nominally Catholic working classes of France and Italy, Rome has been happy to rely on the material aid of the American government for such purposes as protecting Croatian Catholics, and checking Communist election drives in Italy.[3] Though European Catholics seem as determined as ever that the honor of the papacy shall not be bestowed on any American, Francis Cardinal Spellman, the most widely-known American prelate, probably possesses far more power in Church affairs than did Gibbons two generations earlier.[4] And though no pope has undertaken to grant American Catholics representation in the College of Cardinals proportional to their numbers or financial support, for several years there have been four American cardinals instead of the one allotted from 1875 to 1911.[5]

Certain as the liberals in the 1890's were that American influence would continue to grow in the religious and political affairs of the world, their primary concern with such questions was to secure Rome's consent not to interfere unduly with their own program for Catholicizing America. American Catholics will continue to feel this concern just as long as they can believe that their country will respond to sympathetic ministrations from their Church. Contemporary America gives many reassurances. There is a steady flow of converts into the Church. Laymen and clergy have gained increasingly wide recognition in public life.[6] Early recognition of the dangers to both Church and country of secularist, imperialist communism, and the leading role Catholic clerics and laymen have played in attacking its every manifestation, real or potential, has won the Church a reputation for "soundness" that more than counterbalances the ancient shibboleth of "foreignism." In the spring and summer of 1956, Democratic politicians seriously considered nominating a Catholic for vice-president, in part at least to neutralize allegations that the party was "soft on Communism." [7] The government has not harassed the Church as in so many European countries. If the states are as far as ever from providing the still desired denominational schools, many contribute valuable auxiliary services to parochial schools.[8] A recent Supreme Court decision sustained the Catholic contention that the First Amendment does not establish such a "wall of separation" that the state cannot to some extent assist the clergy in giving religious education to public school students.[9]

The history of the "Church of the immigrants," however, has not borne out completely either liberal or conservative expectations. A statistical survey, completed in 1925, proved groundless the persistent fears of German Catholics that in the process of "Americanization" large numbers of immigrants would lose their faith.[10] The liberals, on the other hand, had optimistically believed that non-Catholic immigrants — Orangemen and Italian anticlericals for example —

would lose their prejudices once they lost their traditional European attitudes; more important, once Catholic immigrants became patriotic, English-speaking citizens, who entered professions, joined political parties, and chose residences according to individual preferences, the major obstacle to the conversion of non-Catholics would have been removed. By 1955, an observer was justified in declaring that the melting pot had virtually eliminated the identification of religions with nationalities; a generation earlier, employers had stopped warning that "No Irish [or Germans or Italians] Need Apply." [11] Yet to the discomfiture of liberal expectations, American distrust of the Church has not disappeared. The second Ku Klux Klan derived much of its strength from its rabidly anti-Catholic platform.[12] In 1927, a distinguished conservative felt called to come to the defense of the nation by challenging Al Smith to prove that Catholicism was compatible with Americanism.[13] And though anti-Catholicism was relatively dormant for the next two decades, the enthusiastic applause given Paul Blanshard's attacks after the second World War is evidence that many Americans are as hostile to the Church thirty years after large-scale immigration has been halted, as the most pessimistic Catholic conservative believed them to be in the 1890's.[14] Discouragingly, this anti-Catholicism is confined to no one class or section, but is to be found in northern industrial states like Massachusetts, where Catholics constitute a majority; in southern areas, where only a handful are to be found; among simple folk, still wary of the Whore of Babylon; and among the best educated, for whom opposition to the Church is a respectable substitute for anti-Semitism; all these "Protestants and Other Americans" have been able to "unite" against Catholicism, as on no other issue.[15]

Furthermore, by the 1950's, few could longer deny that Protestantism, instead of disappearing from the American scene as most Catholics in the 1890's expected, was, institutionally at least, certainly holding its own.[16] A dispassionate survey indicated that about as many Catholics were converting to Protestantism, as Protestants were finding the True Church.[17] Even more disheartening, a Catholic study showed that "leakage" considerably exceeded conversions in a well organized urban parish, where the Church might be expected to be strongest.[18]

Whether these unfavorable transactions between Church and

culture are attributable to Catholic failings or to non-Catholic perversity, it is not surprising that many of the faithful persist today in what Father Elliott called a "spirit of defense," and seek to preserve a prudent "Catholic separatism" from American civilization.[19] No prelate today defends this point of view as unqualifiedly as did William Cardinal O'Connell until his death in 1944. But most diocesan papers have reflected a distinctly conservative conception of the obligations of Catholicism to the world. And consistent support has been furnished by the *American Ecclesiastical Review*, under the leadership of a theologian from the Catholic University of America, Father Joseph C. Fenton. In January, 1950, he declared his surprise that, with attacks raining on the Church from every quarter, so many Catholics persisted in claiming, as did Hecker, Ireland, and Gibbons in the 1890's, that the Church had once and for all emerged from the "state of siege" of the Counter-Reformation era. A strong defensive position, Fenton argued, instead of being "essentially unnatural and disadvantageous to the Church," was a perennial necessity, for Catholicism and culture were inevitably opposed. Polemic against the errors of others was an obligation for all those who loved God. To avoid it out of sentiment for the feelings of outsiders was to trifle with the salvation of "the children of God's household." [20] Fenton was convinced that far too many American Catholics were engaging in practices verging on indifferentism, and minimizing the hard sayings of dogma out of a mistaken conception of charity towards those outside the Church.[21] He was delighted, therefore, when Pius XII issued his encyclical *Humani Generis*, warning against the manifold pitfalls in modern apologetics. The Pope's words seemed in the great tradition of Pius IX's Syllabus of Errors, and Pius X's attack on Modernism. Fenton advised his readers to receive *Humani Generis* as a criticism not only of a few misguided foreigners, but of errors prevalent in the American Church.[22]

The conservatism for which Father Fenton so clearly speaks is combated by a group of American Catholics, who, like their predecessors in the 1890's, are proud to call themselves liberals.[23] Distinctly in the minority, and lacking a leader as influential as Gibbons or as commanding as Ireland, they include such outspoken prelates as Bishop Bernard J. Sheil of Chicago, and Archbishop Robert E. Lucey of San Antonio.[24] Some of the most trenchant liberal argument is provided by the Jesuits, in marked contrast to the conservative positions they maintained in the 1890's. The Jesuit father John Courtney Murray, challenging American Catholics to become a "creative minority," has clarified some of the knottiest church–state problems.[25] *Thought*, published by Fordham University, regularly prints able analyses of the interrelationship of religion and culture. It was in this magazine in 1951 that the Jesuit Father Victor R. Yanitelli implicitly contradicted the conservative interpretation of *Humani Generis* by arguing that while Pius XII had found it necessary to correct a few French extremists, he had intentionally left a "creative liberty" for Catholic apologists.[26] The Jesuit national weekly, *America*, has maintained a generally liberal position; one of its most distinguished recent editors, Father John LaFarge, declared the paper's special obligations to the international community, war-stricken peoples, morality in the marketplace, and civil rights. "All of these issues were explosive," he has reminisced contentedly.[27]

The massive Jesuit support for the liberal cause has tended to overshadow the activities of the Paulists, founded by Father Hecker to convert America through explicit recognition of its virtues. The Congregation has continued its work, though its reputation for liberalism has been somewhat blurred by the writings of the forthright Paulist Father James M. Gillis. Lecturing on the Church to non-Catholic audiences apparently convinced him [as it nearly convinced Walter Elliott fifty years earlier] that American culture was both bigoted and decadent. He lost patience with Catholics less separatist than himself, and on one occasion declared that the "'liberal Catholic' can only with difficulty be distinguished from the non-Catholic."[28] On the other hand, John B. Sheerin, the present editor of the *Catholic World*, has maintained the periodical's charitable interest in the non-Catholic world. This interest is also conspicuous in the influential lay journal, *The Commonweal*. Among the penalties it has paid for its liberality is a circulation minute compared to that of more traditionalist Catholic journals, and the innuendoes of men like Father Gillis that its Catholicism is of a suspect variety.[29]

The latter-day liberals do not try to sustain themselves with the belief that wholehearted effort over a very few years will "make America Catholic." They are reconciled to the prospect that for a long time to come Catholics will be misunderstood, if not actually disliked, by a large share of their fellow citizens. They do not share Hecker's conviction that the well-known path from Protestant orthodoxy to natural religion continues straight on to Catholicism. Father Sheerin, commenting on the religious revival of the 1950's, concluded that the kind of faith popularized by the Reverend Norman Vincent Peale might be useful in loosening up "the hard ground of secularism." But a "long jump" still remained to reach Catholicism, and Sheerin was dubious that many would undertake it. The Paulist editor was equally dubious that the Church would eventually gain from the numbers "shocked" into a version of supernatural religion by men like Billy Graham.[30]

But neither the conviction that the conversion of America is not imminent, nor the virtual certainty that conservative Catholics will not approve of most apologetic enterprises, has prevented the liberals, like Father Elliott in the 1890's, from believing that a Catholic without a mission to outsiders is "only a half-Catholic." [31] No legitimate proselyting opportunity, they believe, should ever be passed by simply because it involves some departure from a comfortable clannishness.[32] Father George A. Tavard, a French priest stationed in New York, has passionately maintained that the reunion of Christianity requires Catholic recognition of the religious fervor intrinsic to true Protestantism; and he has reminded Americans of the heartening progress achieved by Europeans striving for Christian unity.[33] In the 1890's, Leo XIII had issued a clear warning against Catholic participation in any future ventures modeled on the Parliament of Religions. But in 1949 restrictions were loosened; subject to the approval of the local diocesan, Catholics were allowed by Rome to attend certain types of "religious congresses." [34] Since Samuel Cardinal Stritch of Chicago is considerably less venturesome than was the council of archbishops dominated by Ireland and Cardinal Gibbons, he firmly banned Catholic participation in the World Council of Churches meeting at Evanston, Illinois in the summer of 1954.[35] But Father Sheerin did not hesitate to commend the participants and their purposes, and the Jesuit Father Gustave Weigel, writing in *Thought*, expressed his hope that informal meetings between Catholics and Protestants would accomplish all that had been devoutly desired from the Council meeting.[36]

Conservatives have been deeply alarmed by the proliferation of "interfaith" groups, like the National Conference of Christians and Jews, whose goal is not the restoration of religious unity but the elimination of "prejudice." These organizations, Father Francis Connell, a Redemptorist associated with Father Fenton on the *Ecclesiastical Review*, concluded in 1940, seldom resulted in conversions to Catholicism, and all other potential benefits were incommensurate with the risk that unsuspecting Catholics might be infected with the poison of indifferentism. "Ordinarily," he declared, "the association of Catholics with non-Catholics in such organizations and meetings is a grave menace to the faith of our people." A decade later, he maintained that papal strictures in *Humani Generis* completely corroborated his warnings. Throughout the history of the National Conference, Protestants and Jews have contributed a disproportionately large share of the membership; and a recent poll disclosed that some 22 per cent of American dioceses "absolutely forbade Catholic participation." [37]

This same poll, however, showed that about 75 per cent of the dioceses encouraged Catholics to belong to such organizations. Priests and laymen now occupy prominent places in the National Conference and in the Religious Education Association. And Catholic sociologists like Professor John J. Kane of Notre Dame and Father Albert Foley of Spring Hill are outspoken in their conviction that greater Catholic participation, far from promoting indifferentism, will produce the wider understanding of the Church needed immediately for social peace, and ultimately for the spread of Catholicism.[38]

Close to the surface of these disagreements over missionary technique lies disagreement over the proper interpretation of the dogma, "no salvation outside the Church." In the 1880's and 1890's, the Paulists had successfully maintained that one who was invincibly ignorant of Catholicism might belong to the "soul" of the Church, and thus be saved. Throughout the 1940's, Father Fenton, believing as Michael Mueller did years earlier that the "lax or 'liberal'" interpretation was a screen for either indifferentism or a condemnable lack of concern for the salvation of non-Catholics, attempted to reëstablish the doctrine's stringency. He discarded the concept of the "soul" of the Church as a misleading metaphor, and argued that invincible ignorance excused a man for disobedience in remaining out of the Church, but did not excuse him for not being in. A man must also actually desire to do God's will, and exercise perfect charity. Even so, his situation would remain, Fenton was forced to conclude "distinctly unfavorable and unfortunate from the spiritual point of view." [39]

An even more intransigent priest, the Jesuit Father Leonard Feeney, along with some of his students at St. Benedict's Center in Cambridge, Massachusetts, maintained that a man's desire to belong to the Church must be explicit, if he was to be saved. When Boston College theologians disagreed, Feeney's group accused them of heresy. Archbishop Richard Cushing, far more liberal than his predecessor, William Cardinal O'Connell, backed up the college; eventually, Feeney was excommunicated, primarily for his persistent refusal to accept ecclesiastical authority. Though Father Fenton insisted on regarding the letter from the Holy Office to the Archbishop on "the Necessity of the Catholic Church" as an injunction to teach the doctrine strictly, publicly, and often, the most significant result of the controversy was the sharp reproof administered to unnecessary intransigence.[40] In February, 1956, Archbishop Cushing was honored by a Lowell, Massachusetts lodge of B'nai B'rith for "a lifetime of distinguished service to the cause of human brotherhood under God." [41] As for the doctrine itself, a priest, writing in 1953 in the influential *Homiletic and Pastoral Review*, recommended that the stark declaration of no salvation outside the Church be eliminated from the profession of faith required of Christians about to become Catholics; without elucidation, it bore an unfortunately and unnecessarily harsh ring, he thought.[42]

Contemporary liberals believe as strongly as did their forerunners that the mission to American culture requires the active participation of all Catholics; they consequently rejoice that the American laity is still renowned for its energy, although the activism they explictly praise is purged of the overweening self-confidence which at times made Archbishop Ireland resemble gospelers of wealth and success like Russell Conwell.[43] Instead of regarding devotionalism as somehow antithetical to action, they hew to a "new tradition" which, one liberal recently asserted, "attempts to bring together such strangers as religious contemplation and social consciousness." [44]

This reorientation has undoubtedly been strengthened by a series of papal warnings against "the heresy of action." [45]

In 1953 a writer prophesied in tones reminiscent of Hecker and Ireland that the Church was entering the "Era of the Catholic Layman." [46] One reason for this belief is the increasing emphasis on the "lay priesthood," to the point where Pius XII felt obliged to call attention in his encyclical *Mediator Dei* to the unique powers conferred by the sacrament of orders.[47] Meanwhile, continued lay appeals have greatly increased the likelihood that the Church will permit a wider use of English in religious services, thus answering a wish often expressed in the *Catholic World* in the 1890's.[48]

The greatest innovation in lay activism in recent years has been the development of the Christopher movement under the auspices of Father James G. Keller. Open to all Christians, it has encouraged initiative in raising to a higher spiritual level contemporary education, government, labor relations, and the arts of communication. In 1954, the Christophers were reaching ten million Americans with their exhortations.[49] But this avowedly nondenominational work, though praised by the liberals, constitutes a supplement, not a substitute, for the lay participation in the work of the Church for which the liberals have so far dreamed in vain.[50] Bishop Robert J. Dwyer in 1954 declared flatly that "a distinguishing characteristic of the vast bulk of American Catholics is an enormous absence of personal responsibility for the work of the Church"; Father Sheerin regretfully described the laity as an "apathetic, obdurate mass." [51] Lay energy, therefore, so far as it has been available for specifically Catholic action, has been necessarily channeled into clerically sponsored, clerically supervised programs for clerically defined objectives.[52]

Though anxious for individual enterprise, the liberals of the 1890's were eager to limit diocesan autonomies in order to obtain effective national action. In 1917, the Paulist Father John J. Burke was a leader in securing the establishment of a National Catholic War Council to bring about a unity he hoped would be "sensible, visible, practical, efficacious." [53] The Council was soon expanded to include the whole hierarchy, and, after the first World War, it was charged with the responsibility of promoting the Church's "welfare." [54] Dominated in the early years by liberally minded prelates, it brought such results as the "Bishops' Program" of social reconstruction, special plans to speed the "Americanizing" of Catholic immigrants, and a "standard apologetic" to guide the clergy in making compromises with public school authorities.[55] Roman fears of a new Gallicanism were augmented by protests from particularistic (and usually conservative) American prelates, so that in 1923, the "Council" was changed into a "Conference," at which episcopal attendance was purely voluntary.[56] The National Catholic Welfare Conference has proved its worth as a focus, but the American Church has continued to be plagued with local resistance to the intelligent national action Spalding and Ireland so much desired.[57]

Liberals still lament that so many Catholics remain isolated from intellectual culture, shamefully neglecting the obligations of the Church to the development of truth, secular as well as formally religious. The pioneering which Spalding, Zahm, and Keane encouraged in the 1890's had not yet developed a tradition of American Catholic scholarship when Pius X, appalled at the temerities of European Catholic researches into the history of dogma and the nature of religious assent, issued his comprehensive attack on Modernism.[58] He asked Church authorities to exercise especially close supervision over students and scholars, and later required all Catholics in responsible positions to take a detailed "anti-modernist oath." [59] Since no prominent American Catholics were notably modernist, the Church was spared the internal warfare and the humiliation that ensued in most of the countries of Europe.[60] On the other hand, American leaders, already cautious because of Leo XIII's letter to Gibbons in 1899, became so antimodernist that the infant intellectual life of the Church was retarded. The *New York Review*, in which Sulpician and Catholic University of America scholars had published incisive studies, had been surviving only with difficulty, since "the number of Catholics interested in questions which are of importance to the thinkers of the present generation — and which will be vital to all classes in the next" had proved to be very small; but it was probably for prudential, not financial reasons that Archbishop John Farley of New York closed down the journal.[61] Cardinal Gibbons was more anxious than was Rome to remove from the faculty of the Catholic University a Dutch professor who could not in conscience maintain the Mosaic authorship of the Pentateuch.[62]

The attitude of the American Church at the time was epitomized in the experience of a youthful Paulist who, perplexed by current intellectual problems, was advised by a seminary president to "preach the moral law and let dogmas alone." [63]

Since that time, there have been regular complaints from home and abroad that the American Church is intellectually "asleep." [64] Though a few universities have developed programs for graduate research far beyond what Spalding and Keane dreamed for their new university, Catholics still fall far short of contributing their share to the progress of knowledge. A distinguished Catholic historian, Msgr. John T. Ellis of the Catholic University, believes that this failure has occurred partly because in the formative years of the American Church virtually all Catholic energy and imagination were required for "brick-and-mortar" enterprises. With the Catholic population increasing in size and mobility in the twentieth century, it has been seductively easy to continue to concentrate on the financing and constructing of churches, rectories, and parochial schools. Ellis also points out that the average Catholic immigrant lacked both the educational background and the necessary financial reserves to foster intellectual interest at home or in society; the fact that in the late 1940's no member of the Catholic hierarchy was the son of a college educated parent may help explain the Church's intellectual lifelessness. Furthermore, so far as immigrants' children took their criteria of success from non-Catholic culture, those going on to higher education might well concentrate on preparation for business or law; in fact, a disproportionately large share of Catholic college students have chosen these fields.[65] For Catholics to emulate this aspect of secular culture is a "liberalism" that both Newman and Spalding would have deplored.

But equally damaging are two versions of "conservatism" which persist in the American Church. Professor Julian Pleasants of Notre Dame has complained that although most Catholics bear no "special prejudice against scientific research," an appalling percentage prefer to consider "secular knowledge . . . a sort of hobby for the human race, [having] nothing to do with the real business of existence." Beneath this appearance of disinterest, Pleasants believes, lies an unexamined fear that faith and knowledge are as antipathetic as some of the savants of previous centuries claimed them to be.[66] A variant of this attitude has been noted by the Jesuit Father Walter Ong; many in the American Church, sensing the lack of a Catholic tradition in this country, and aware that to many Europeans they seem to lack the accoutrements, both governmental and cultural, usual in "Catholic" countries, have tacitly agreed to defer the arduous, complex, and subtle tasks of Catholic intellectual life to their betters abroad.[67]

Liberals are as anxious today as was Ireland to secure for each Catholic child the best grammar school education possible. Most remain convinced that for the foreseeable future only parochial schools will give the religiously oriented training which constitutes true "education." But Professor John J. Kane of Notre Dame, perhaps heeding the common charge that a system of church schools is "divisive," advised Catholics that an unfortunate separatism might indeed be fostered unless supervisors, teachers, and parents insisted that the schools inculcate the charity and tolerance prerequisite for successful democracy.[68] Liberal leaders readily acknowledge that, despite the great efforts made, one out of two Catholic grade school children is attending a public school; most expect that the proportion will remain sizable for a long time.[69] Accordingly, they have supported local attempts to augment the secular training of the public schools through programs of "released time," a compromise Archbishop Ireland might well have approved. Joseph E. Cunneen, editor of the highly intellectual *Cross-Currents*, has warned Catholics against assuming that any kind of training in any kind of parochial school is necessarily better than anything to be obtained in a public school.[70] And Professor James M. O'Neill of Brooklyn College has published his conviction — much like that of the Paulists in the 1890's — that well-informed Catholic students, far from jeopardizing their faith by attending public schools, may well prove effective in dispelling misunderstandings about Catholicism.[71] The ultimate justification for liberal support of the public schools, however, is not the benefits that will accrue to the number of Catholics educated there. As responsible citizens, the editors of *America* declared, "we want non-Catholic American children to receive the best education they can get under state control."[72] As in the 1890's, the liberal attitude does not reduce itself to a simple "for" or "against" the public schools; it is summed up rather in the faith that Catholicism can not help but gain from the widest possible education. The liberals, therefore, are not content with the multiplication of buildings or the standardization of techniques; they will be satisfied only when all American educational enterprises, from primary school to university, adopt as the criterion of success, neither "safeness" nor novelty, but "excellence." [73]

Though the liberal leaders of the 1890's deserved the reputation they acquired of "social pioneers," they failed to establish a strong tradition of reform interest. American Catholics have been notoriously reluctant to discern a vital connection between their faith and the requirements of social justice. That is not to say either that there have not been notable exceptions, or that Catholics have been excelled by American Protestants in social consciousness. In the early years of the century, the German Catholic Central Verein established a Central Bureau for the Promotion of Social Education; its magazine, *Central-Blatt and Social Justice*, edited by Father Peter E. Dietz, crusaded for progressive legislation, and especially for justice to labor unions.[74] The National Catholic Welfare Conference from its inception sponsored such a wide variety of reforms that one of its chief figures, Monsignor John A. Ryan, could justly entitle his autobiography *Social Doctrine in Action*.[75] Over the protests of a good many Catholics, Bernard Sheil helped begin a "Christian revolution" in Chicago's treatment of its underprivileged youth.[76] And such diverse enterprises as the Young Christian Workers, the Association of Catholic Trade Unionists, the Catholic Worker movement, and a large number of Labor Schools testify to a widely felt obligation to Christianize labor-management relations by more direct action than that envisaged by the Christophers.[77] In recent years, the firm stand taken against segregation by Archbishop Robert E. Lucey of San Antonio and Archbishop Joseph F. Rummel of New Orleans has contrasted sharply with the prudence that has characterized the pronouncements of many desegregationist Southern Protestants.[78] By and large, however, these notable reformers have not succeeded in enlisting the extensive lay support that Catholic social action groups have aroused in many countries of Europe. In 1952, Bishop William Mulloy of Covington, Kentucky declared that the disposition of Catholics to give only nominal acceptance to the letter and spirit of the "social encyclicals" of Leo XIII and Pius XI "has tended to paralyze the force of the teaching Church in modern American society." [79] All too many laymen seem to accept implicitly the argument advanced by Father Edward Keller of the University of Notre Dame that the goals of these encyclicals have been pretty completely realized in contemporary capitalism.[80]

In part, this acquiescence stems from the persistence of conservative attitudes painfully familiar to Ireland and the Paulists. Some Catholics are so vividly aware of contemporary spiritual failings as to be preoccupied with the need for "saints" rather than "social crusaders." [81] Others are deeply distrustful of the non-Catholics with whom determined reformers would have to coöperate; much of the Catholic press is frequently scornful of "do-gooders" and "bleeding hearts." [82] For both these reasons state intervention is repugnant. Quite in the spirit of Condé Pallen and René Holaind, Clarence Manion, former dean of the Notre Dame Law School, defended as a fundamental American principle the conviction that "the State is a servile and secondary thing which picks up where conscience unfortunately falls down." [83]

Yet, ironically, Archbishop Ireland and his fellows are also in some measure responsible for contemporary Catholic indifference to social action. By occasionally justifying the reforms they urged as means of winning the respect of a reforming age, they helped to limit Catholics' interest in reform to periods when reformers were popular. By occasionally justifying reforms as necessities for elevating Catholic immigrants from the poorhouses into bourgeois respectability, they increased the likelihood of Catholic quiescence now that an increasing proportion of Catholics have achieved middle class status.[84] The ranks of contemporary conservatism are swelled by prosperous Catholics, who could no doubt explain away their grandparents' support for Gibbons' and Ireland's social activism as just such opportunistic commitments to reform.[85]

Furthermore, Gibbons and Ireland, by frequently referring to the separateness as well as the distinctiveness of the religious and secular spheres, stinted their responsibility of defining how the faithful should bring Catholic principles to bear on secular affairs. Very likely they assumed that where the individual, guided by conscience and the Church, could not prevail by his own efforts, non-Catholics would agree with Catholics on the clear obligations of the natural law; in democratic America, moral legislation would then be easy to obtain. Events have not borne out the crucial assumption. Non-Catholics have seldom been able to agree among themselves on the dictates of the natural law, even when they thought it a meaningful question; and when Catholics have called for joint efforts against such evils as birth control and the exhibition of obscene art, the dissidence has been conspicuous.[86]

Nor has the task of infusing Catholic principles into public life been solved — as Archbishop Ireland with his faith in the political process frequently assumed it would be — simply by the diffusion of Catholics into both major parties. Catholicism is probably less of an "issue" in the regions where this dispersion is now far along, but Catholics are right in doubting whether recognition of the just claims of conscience and religion is any more widespread. Al Smith reaffirmed the pledge of Gibbons and Ireland when he denied that his Catholicism precluded genuine loyalty to the American political tradition; but his statement, drawn up with the assistance of a liberal priest, seemed to imply that the governor's religion was wholly irrelevant — that, in effect, a Catholic's conception of the claims of conscience and the freedom of the Church would in no way differ from the belief of the most advanced secularist. Few Catholics (and probably few secularists) would accept such an implication. Yet its apparent endorsement in 1928 and after has made it easier for a man like Paul Blanshard to tax Church leaders with inconsistency or worse for encouraging Catholic laymen to defend at the polls their own rights and those of the Church. It has also probably made it easier for both Catholics and non-Catholics to fall into the opposite error of assuming that there is a Catholic position on all questions.[87] Despite liberal protests, some Catholics in the 1950's defended Senator Joseph McCarthy's activities on the assumption that they were "Catholic"; some Protestants opposed them for the same reason.[88] Clearly the mediation that liberals desire between Catholicism and American political culture has not as yet proved especially successful.

But at least as important in contemporary society as the practice of politics is the relation of the Church to the state, and in this area, the principles proclaimed by Gibbons and Ireland have retained for liberal Catholics a basic validity. Today, as in the 1890's, virtually all American Catholics accept the details of the separation of church and state, but the spirit of that acceptance varies from somber resignation that the "ideal" arrangements of the "confessional" state are unobtainable, to a glad conviction that no system could suit the Church better. American liberals have not hesitated to deplore that John Ryan, as late as 1940, wrote that should almost all Americans become Catholic, the state would be obligated to teach religious truth, and to grant only limited toleration to dissenters.[89] One correspondent asked readers of *The Commonweal* to recognize that Ryan had been so busy pioneering in social reform work that he had been unable to think through questions of Church and state with his usual thoroughness and clarity.[90] The basic liberal tradition was reaffirmed by the late Archbishop John T. McNicholas of Cincinnati; responding to nervous challenges as to what would ensue should Catholics come to predominate in America, he declared "they would not seek a union of Church and state," but "then as now, uphold the Constitution and all its Amendments." [91]

This declaration of ultimate intention has been reënforced in recent decades by an able group of philosophers and theologians, most notably Father John Courtney Murray, who, instead of arguing that the experience of the Church in America justified an "hypothesis," have contended that the "thesis" beloved by nineteenth-century conservatives was itself an hypothesis developed to meet certain historical conditions.[92] To Murray, the basic principles the Church must insist on in dealing with the state are "transtemporal;" the Church must be free to exercise her divine commission; there must be coöperation, not crippling antagonism between church and state; there must be harmony between the actions of church and state so that the individual citizen is not forced to choose between his religious and his political obligations.[93] In seeking the best realization of these principles, the Church must follow what Pius XII called "the providential path of history and circumstances," and avoid defending for all places and times applications suitable only in certain ones.[94] Murray finds in the political writings of Leo XIII a heartening restatement of the transtemporal principles, although combat with continental Liberalism led Leo to overemphasize the validity of the "confessional state" — what conservatives defended as the "thesis" — just as Boniface VIII, in battle with aggressive national monarchies, overemphasized the necessity of the rights of the "papal monarchy." [95] Father Murray of course accepts Leo XIII's warning against considering the American system as "ideal," but he considers ambiguous the Pope's remark, so disturbing to Gibbons and Ireland, that the Church would prosper more in America if in "union" with the state. "It is hard to believe," Murray notes, "that the Pope was trying to play the role of the seer of history." [96]

Indeed, Father Murray is as firmly convinced as were the liberal prelates of the 1890's that the American system is providential for American circumstances. Like other Catholics, he assumes that the state is not a "totalitarian democracy," but rather is committed to the supremacy of natural law, or "public philosophy." [97] And he insists that the First Amendment not be interpreted as a secular dogma of wholly negative implication. Rightly construed, it provides "articles of peace," "true law" based on intelligent understanding of the problems of religious pluralism. Catholics owe these "articles" more than a grudging adherence; the necessity of social peace is a "divine and Christian imperative," Murray reminds them.[98]

To many Catholics in Europe and America, vibrant defense of a system they wish only to tolerate is a dangerous liberalism. Spanish Catholics remain as convinced as they were in the 1890's that the American system is pitifully inadequate to the needs of the Church.[99] And in 1953, Alfredo Cardinal Ottaviani of the Holy Office argued with considerable force that the "confessional" state was the only modern polity which met Leo XIII's strict requirements. Not surprisingly, Father Fenton defended Cardinal Ottaviani's contention.[100] But the Jesuit editors of *America* have strongly demurred, and *The Commonweal*, while admitting the orthodoxy of the thesis or "textbook" view, declared that to attempt to force church–state relations back into that confining pattern would be "tragically unwise." [101]

In 1950, an American conservative charged that Murray, in bestowing Catholic approval on the American system, overlooked the obligation of the state to worship God as He ordained.[102] Murray's response was to distinguish between the state as a popularly created agency, which has no more religious obligation than the flag, and the state as a description of the aggregate of the people, each of whom is of course obligated to worship God.[103] The state, in the first sense, is "lay," though not "laic," and is rightly concerned with religious unity only so far as that may prove necessary to civic unity. It would err if it attempted to produce this unity for the sake of the Church; once it has granted her freedom, "government has no essential duties in the area of religious life."[104] And today in America, the "Church is free to form the consciences of her members; and they are free to conform the life of the City to the demands of their consciences," Murray has written.[105] Thus Murray reaffirms, as he clarifies, the perception of Ireland and Gibbons that the advent of American democracy obviated many of the problems that existed when a king could declare that he himself was the state.

As a natural consequence of his vindication of the American system, Murray can find little justification for those who, like Father René Holaind in 1892, declare that the American state can rightly exercise only limited powers, not those that would be the prerogative of a "Charlemagne." He has forthrightly declared that the "modern 'welfare-state,'" of which America is perhaps the purest type, "simply by serving human welfare, would serve the Church better than Justinian or Charlemagne ever did."[106] Because "of its aspirations towards an order of personal and associational freedom, political equality, civic friendship, social justice, and cultural advancement, it offers to the Church the kind of coöperation which she presently needs, and it merits in turn her coöperation in the realization of its own aspirations."[107]

So far as this reassertion and refinement of the liberal tradition wins acceptance as common Catholic belief among American Protestants, it promises to remove some of the most thorny grounds of church–state contention, reorienting discussion to the question confronting all religious leaders: how to secure "the freedom of the human person, Christian and citizen, to live at peace in Christ and in society, that he may thus move straight to God."[108] So far as it wins widespread acceptance among American Catholics, it promises to reduce their inhibiting sense of apartness from both American secular and European Catholic traditions. For Murray has reëmphasized Hecker's familiar contention that the American system stems not from the Jacobin principles of the French Revolution, but from medieval constitutionalism and English political practice. Catholics who have emigrated from Cork or Munich or Naples need feel no alienation from "the Americans," need not abstain from working "toward the purification of the liberal tradition (which is their own tradition) and of the democratic state in which it finds expression. . . . This form of state is presently man's best, and possibly last, hope of human freedom." [109] Creative participation in American political culture need not be apologetically explained to European Catholics as only a tactical expedient. The American Church has had a distinctive history, which has meant, Murray declares, "a new kind of spiritual existence, not tasted on the Continent." [110] She enjoys here "as good a hope of freedom" to pursue her every goal "as she has ever had." [111]

Father Walter Ong, though manifestly sympathetic with aspirations to promote profitable interaction with American culture, has warned contemporary Catholics against regarding the deeds and words of Hecker, Ireland, and Gibbons as "sources." [112] Certainly their formulations of Catholic principles were idiomatic to the 1890's, and some details of their strategies have become outmoded, as American history has unfolded in ways they did not predict. But modern Catholics can not easily deny that the liberals of the late nineteenth century were among the first to see the real meaning of the experience of the American Church, and to realize the great possibilities that lay open to Catholics if they would approach culture with confidence and charity, or, as Archbishop Ireland might well have put it, liberally.

NOTES

NOTES

Abbreviations
used in the notes

ACQR   American Catholic Quarterly Review
AER   American Ecclesiastical Review
CHR   Catholic Historical Review
COM   The Commonweal
CUB   Catholic University Bulletin
CW   Catholic World
DAB   Dictionary of American Biography
HRS   Historical Records and Studies
LD   Literary Digest
NAR   North American Review
RACHS   Records of the American Catholic Historical Society
RR   Review of Reviews (United States)
TS   Theological Studies

Chapter I

Catholicism and Culture in Nineteenth-Century Europe

1. The ambitions of a "church" as contrasted with those of a sect are lucidly defined in H. R. Niebuhr, "Sects," *Encyclopedia of the Social Sciences*, 13 (New York, 1937), 624–631; see also his *Christ and Culture* (New York, 1951). For analysis of diverse Catholic attitudes, see Emmanuel Cardinal Suhard, *Growth or Decline? The Church Today*, trans. J. A. Corbett (South Bend, Ind., 1948), 8–12.

2. Quoted in J. H. Newman, *The Idea of a University* (London, 1893), 235. Two eulogistic studies of Neri are M. L. M., "The Loveliness of Sanctity," *CW*, 49 (August 1889), 608–636 and (September, 1889), 779–792.

3. J. R. Strayer and D. C. Munro, *The Middle Ages: 395–1500* (New York, 1942), 404–405.

4. R. R. Palmer, *Catholics and Unbelievers in Eighteenth-Century France* (Princeton, 1939).

5. Wilfrid Ward, *William George Ward and the Catholic Revival* (London, 1893), 40–41, and A. J. Thébaud, "The Church and the State, the Two 'Cities' in the Present Age," *ACQR*, 2 (July 1877), 430–431.

6. For the French conviction of anti-Catholic conspiracy, see R. F. Byrnes, *Antisemitism in Modern France* (New Brunswick, N. J., 1950), 120ff. See also chapter 10 of this essay.

7. *The Philosophy of History*, trans. J. B. Robertson, 2 vols. (London, 1835), 2:300.

8. Felix Dupanloup, *A Study of Freemasonry*, English trans. (London, 1875), 89. Dupanloup's concern is impressive for he was far from credulous on most intellectual and political matters; see later, pp. 13–22, and Emile Faguet, *Mgr. Dupanloup, Bishop of Orleans*, trans. Lady Herbert, 2 vols. (London, 1885).

9. Reuben Parsons, *Studies in Church History* (New York, 1897–1900), 5: 247, 261–262, 480–496, 518. Thébaud, "Freemasonry," *ACQR*, 6 (October 1881), 582–583.

10. Jean Gaume, *La Situation: douleurs, dangers, devoirs, consolations des catholiques dans les temps actuels*, second edition (Paris, 1860), 10; for a similar remark of Gaume's, see Wilfrid Ward, *The Life of John Henry Cardinal Newman* (London, 1912), 1:463.

11. Quoted in Gaume, *La Révolution* (Paris, 1856), 1:2; for a similar opinion, see F. Méjécaze, *Frédéric Ozanam et l'église catholique* (Lyon, 1934), 4. On de Maistre, see H. J. Laski, *Authority in the Modern State* (New Haven, 1919), chapter 1.

12. Donoso Cortes, quoted in Gaume, *Situation*, 99.

13. G. A. Beck, ed., *The English Catholics, 1850–1950* (London, 1950), 476–477.

14. *Les Catholiques libéraux* (Paris, 1864), 250.

15. R. F. Clarke, "The Training of a Jesuit," *Nineteenth Century*, 40 (August 1896), 212–213.

16. Ward, *Newman*, 2:127.

17. C. F. Montalembert, *De l'avenir politique de l'Angleterre*, fifth edition (Paris, 1857), 217.

18. Méjécaze, *Ozanam*, 57–58; see also Ozanam, "Des devoirs littéraires des chrétiens," in *Mélanges* (Paris, 1859), 1:129–147. See also Carlo Curci, *Le Dissentiment moderne entre l'église et l'Italie*, French trans. (Paris, 1878), 46.

19. *Les Catholiques libéraux*, 245–246.

20. For a good summary of this cast of thought, see E. L. Woodward, "The Catholic Church in the Nineteenth Century," in *Three Studies in European Conservatism* (London, 1929), 231–344; see also Ward, *Ward and the Catholic Revival*, 82–129.

21. *Du pape*, second edition (Paris, 1821), 2:218; see also Edouard Lecanuet, *Montalembert* (Paris, 1899–1902), 3:68.

22. *Du pape*, 1:16, 196.

23. Ward, *Newman*, 2:224.

24. *Ibid.*, 2:79–83.

25. Ward, *Ward and the Catholic Revival*, 14.

26. Ward, *Newman*, 2:312; see also Maisie Ward, *The Wilfrid Wards and the Transition* (London, 1934), 2:41.

27. Curci, *Dissentiment*, 152–165.

28. E. S. Purcell, *Life of Cardinal Manning* (London, 1895), 2:138; J. T. Ellis, *The Life of James Cardinal Gibbons, Archbishop of Baltimore, 1834–1921* (Milwaukee, 1952), 1:170–171.

29. Purcell, *Manning*, 2:301; Montalembert, *De l'avenir*, 214–216; David Mathew, *Catholicism in England, 1535–1935* (London, 1936), 138n.

30. Ward, *Newman*, 1:366; Fergal McGrath, *Newman's University, Idea and Reality* (Dublin, 1951), 95n.

31. Wilfrid Ward, *The Life and Times of Cardinal Wiseman* (London, 1897), 2:418; Fredrik Nielsen, *The History of the Papacy in the Nineteenth Century*, trans. A. J. Mason (London, 1906), 2:89; H. Leclercq, "Prosper Louis Pascal Guéranger," *Catholic Encyclopedia* (New York, 1910), 7:58–59.

32. *The Genius of Christianity*, trans. C. I. White (Baltimore, n.d.).

33. *Du pape*, 1:209.

34. Ward, *Wiseman*, 1:372; Bernard Ward, *The Sequel to Catholic Emancipation* (London, 1915), 1:82–121.

35. Ward, *Ward and the Catholic Revival*, 119ff.; see also K. S. Latourette, *The Great Century, A.D. 1800 — A.D. 1914; Europe and the United States of America*, volume 4 of *A History of the Expansion of Christianity* (London, 1941), 27.

36. Ward, *Newman*, 1:463.

37. Ward, *Sequel*, 2:21.

38. Cuthbert Butler, *The Life and Times of Bishop Ullathorne, 1806–1889* (London, 1926), 1:154–157; see also Beck, ed., *English Catholics*, 260.

39. Butler, *Ullathorne*, 1:183; Beck, ed., *English Catholics*, 253; J. G. Snead-Cox, *The Life of Cardinal Vaughan* (London, 1910), 1:260.

40. Charles Seignobos, *A Political History of Europe since 1814*, trans. S. M. Macvane (New York, 1899), 698; *Sacrorum Conciliorum Nova et Amplissima Collectio*, Louis Petit and J. B. Martin, eds., 53 (Arnhem, Holland, 1927), 482–487. (This edition will hereafter be referred to as *Nova Collectio*.)

41. J. H. Newman, *A Letter to the Rev. E. B. Pusey, D.D. on his recent Eirenicon* (London, 1866), 121.

42. *Du pape*, 1:xxxvii.

43. Latourette, *Great Century*, 32; C. J. H. Hayes, *A Generation of Materialism* (New York, 1941), 133.

44. *Situation*, 111.

45. Paul Thureau-Dangin, *The English Catholic Revival in the Nineteenth Century*, trans. Wilfred Wilberforce, revised edition (New York, n.d.), 2:386–396.

46. Waldemar Gurian, "Louis Veuillot," *CHR*, 36 (January 1951), 389.

47. Byrnes, *Antisemitism*, 194–196, describes the growth of this popular religious journalism; see also Hayes, *Generation of Materialism*, 179–180.

For Veuillot's activities, see the third volume of Lecanuet, *Montalembert;* Parsons, *Studies,* 6:427–444; and Philip Spencer, *Politics of Belief in Nineteenth-Century France* (New York, n.d.), 201–253.

48. R. F. Byrnes, "The Christian Democrats in Modern France," in E. M. Earle, ed., *Modern France* (Princeton, 1951), 160. On Lamennais, see Laski, *Authority in the Modern State,* chapter 3; Waldemar Gurian, "Lamennais," *Review of Politics,* 9 (April 1947), 205–229; F. Brunetière, "Lamennais," *Revue des deux mondes,* 115 (February 11, 1893), 674–685; William Gibson, *The Abbé de Lamennais and the Liberal Catholic Movement in France* (London, 1896).

49. On von Ketteler, see F. F. Nitti, *Catholic Socialism,* trans. Mary Mackintosh (London, 1895), 100–129; Ward, *Newman,* 2:469–472.

50. Méjécaze, *Ozanam,* 51.

51. LaGrange, *Dupanloup,* 1:481.

52. *L'Eglise libre dans l'état libre* (Paris, 1863), 173–174.

53. Montalembert, *Des intérêts catholiques au dix-neuvième siècle* (Paris, 1852), 192; Dupanloup cited in Montalembert, *L'Eglise,* 70; Ozanam in Méjécaze, *Ozanam,* 40, 138–139, and in J. B. Duroselle, *Les Debuts du catholicisme social en France, 1822–1890* (Paris, 1951), 166.

54. Montalembert, *L'Eglise,* 159; von Ketteler, *Liberté, autorité, église: Considerations sur les grands problèmes de notre époque,* trans. Abbé Belet (Paris, 1862), 8–10; Antonio Rosmini-Serbati, *Of the Five Wounds of the Holy Church,* trans. H. P. Liddon (London 1883), 90–99.

55. *L'Eglise,* 169–170.

56. Lecanuet, *Montalembert,* 3:141.

57. Méjécaze, *Ozanam,* 146.

58. *Lettre de Mgr. l'Evêque d'Orléans au clergé et aux fidèles de son diocèse avant son départ pour Rome* (Paris, 1869), 16.

59. E. Barbier, *Histoire du catholicisme libéral et social* (Bordeaux, 1924), 1:13.

60. *Des intérêts,* 68.

61. Pages 131n, 300–303, 349.

62. *L'Eglise,* 107–109.

63. *Des intérêts,* 68–69.

64. *L'Eglise,* 180–184.

65. Lecanuet, *Montalembert,* 2:471.

66. *L'Eglise,* 66. Dupanloup was even more "anti-social;" Duroselle, *Debuts,* 702.

67. *Ibid.,* 173–175; D. T. McColgan, *A Century of Charity* (Milwaukee, 1951), 26–52.

68. Kathleen O'Meara, *Frédéric Ozanam,* third American edition (New York, 1883), 237.

69. Henry Somerville, *Studies in the Catholic Social Movement* (London, 1933), 40–41; Max Turmann, *Le Développement du catholicisme social* (Paris, 1909), second edition, 4–6.

70. Méjécaze, *Ozanam*, 117; Lecanuet, *Montalembert*, 2:131–139; Barbier, *Catholicisme libéral*, 1:30.

71. Newman's *An Essay on the Development of Christian Doctrine*, C. F. Harrold, ed. (New York, 1949) is a sharp contrast with the work Ward wrote just before becoming a Catholic, demanding a Church which gave infallible truth which never changed; see Ward, *Ward and the Catholic Revival*, 12.

72. *Idea of a University*, 177–203. The other liberals were also anxious for university training for Catholics, though they usually conceived it as a place for advanced research, rather than as a center of liberal education. The guiding ideal in both cases was to promote a rapprochement between Catholicism and the mind of the age. Lecanuet, Montalembert, 2:458–460.

73. Gaume, *Paganism in Education*, trans. Robert Hill (London, 1852); for an English parallel, see Henry Formby, *The Growing Unbelief of the Educated Classes* (New York, 1880). For Dupanloup's indignant response, see Faguet, *Dupanloup*, 43.

74. Nielsen, *Papacy*, 145–182; Woodward, *European Conservatism*, 292–293.

75. Rosmini-Serbati, *Five Wounds*, xxx–xxxv; Seignobos, *Political History*, 698.

76. Ward, *Ward and the Catholic Revival*, 159–161.

77. Pertinent extracts are in Raymond Stearns, *The Pageant of Europe* (New York, 1947), 526–528.

78. Seignobos, *Political History*, 703n.

79. Dupanloup, *La Convention du 15 septembre et l'encyclique du 8 décembre* (Paris, 1865), 49–70; the bishop employed the familiar liberal technique of prefacing his criticism of conservative Catholics with an assault on such an acknowledged enemy of the Church as Cavour. Newman's interpretation used Gladstone's criticisms in a similar way; *A Letter addressed to his Grace, the Duke of Norfolk on occasion of Mr. Gladstone's recent Expostulation.* (London, 1875), 105.

80. *Des intérêts*, 93.

81. Cited in J. N. Figgis and R. V. Lawrence, eds., *Selections from the Correspondence of the First Lord Acton* (London, 1917), 1:38.

82. J. E. D. Acton, "The Vatican Council," in *The History of Freedom and Other Essays*, J. N. Figgis and R. V. Lawrence, eds. (London, 1909), 492–515; Woodward, *European Conservatism*, 325–344; Nielsen, *Papacy*, 2:290–375; Cuthbert Butler, *The Vatican Council, The Story Told from Inside in Bishop Ullathorne's Letters*, 2 vols. (London, 1930).

83. Butler, *Vatican Council*, 1:120ff.

84. Besides *Nova Collectio* (see footnote 40), I have used for the chronology of the Council the seventh volume of *Acta et Decreta Sacrorum Conciliorum Recentiorum: Collectio Lacensis* (Freiburg, 1890).

85. *Nova Collectio*, 51 (1925), 71–77.

86. Nielsen, *Papacy*, 2:430–440.

87. J. R. Moody, "American Catholicism's Influence on Europe," *HRS*, 38 (1952), 5–21.

88. A good example is Claudio Jannet, *Les Etats-Unis contemporains* (Paris, 1876), part 1.

89. Gregory XVI specifically denounced the Christian Alliance; R. A. Billington, *The Protestant Crusade*, 1800–1860 (New York, 1938), 264. As late as the 1880's, Catholics were protesting that Protestant missionaries in France and Italy were "helping with main and might the anti-Christian work of demolition done by the Secret Societies, [and] by the Radical Revolutionists;" Bernard O'Reilly, "The Propaganda Question and Our Duty," *ACQR*, 9 (April 1884), 288.

90. Charles de T'Serclaes, *Le Pape Léon XIII* (Paris, 1894), 2:282; Louis Pechenard, ed., *Un Siècle. Mouvement du monde, 1800–1900* (Paris, 1899), 802; Pius' remark is quoted in S. B. Hedges, "Father Hecker and the Establishing of the Poor Clares in the United States," *CW*, 61 (June 1895), 381–382.

91. Jannet, *Etats-Unis*, 483; Henri Delassus, *L'Américanisme et la conjuration antichrétienne* (Lille, 1899), 1–2.

92. Weninger, *Protestantism and Infidelity* (8th ed., New York, 1865), pp. 191–192; Francis Kenrick's opinion is noted in a speech by his brother, Peter R. Kenrick, *Concio Habenda et Non Habita*, printed and translated in R. T. Clancy, "American Prelates in the Vatican Council," *HRS*, 28 (1937), 107–108.

93. J. L. Spalding, *The Life of the Most Reverend M. J. Spalding, Archbishop of Baltimore* (New York, 1873), 383.

94. Lamennais, *Affaires de Rome* (Paris, 1837), 50–51; J. H. Nichols, *Democracy and the Churches* (Philadelphia, 1951), 59; Henry Cardinal Manning, "Preface," to O'Meara, *Ozanam*, xv; Anatole Leroy-Beaulieu, *Les Catholiques libéraux* (Paris, 1885), 83–84; W. T. Stead, *The Americanization of the World* (New York, 1901), 263; John McCarthy, "American Influence on the Democratic Movement in Europe," *ACQR*, 5 (October 1880), 648–651.

95. Nichols, *Democracy*, 87–91; J. J. Meng, "A Century of American Catholicism as seen through French eyes," *CHR*, 27 (April 1941), 43–45.

96. Butler, *Vatican Council*, 1:120.

97. John Cardinal Farley, *The Life of John Cardinal McCloskey* (New York, 1918), 383.

98. Clancy, "American Prelates," *HRS*, 28 (1937), 41 and Appendix 1.

99. Two clear statements of the American opposition are P. R. Kenrick, and J. B. Purcell, *Lettre à Mgr. l'Evêque d'Orléans*, in Dupanloup, *Réponse . . . à Mgr. Spalding* (Naples, 1870), 23–28; and Kenrick's speech, reported in full in *Nova Collectio*, 52 (1926), 453–481, and in Clancy, "American Prelates," *HRS*, 28 (1937), 93–131.

100. Response by Rev. Vincent Holden, C.S.P. to a question at the annual meeting of the Catholic Historical Society, Chicago, December, 1953.

101. *Collectio Lacensis*, 7:947.

102. Ferdinand Brunetière, "Le Catholicisme aux Etats-Unis," *Revue des deux mondes*, 150 (November 1, 1898), 153–157.

103. Walter Elliott, *The Life of Father Hecker* (New York, 1891), 362–370.

104. Barbier, *Catholicisme libéral*, 3:259–260.

Chapter II

Liberals and Conservatives in the American Church

1. Gerald Shaughnessy, *Has the Immigrant Kept the Faith?* (New York, 1925), 161–178.

2. F. J. Warne, *The Immigrant Invasion* (New York, 1913), 77; A. B. Faust, *The German Element in the United States* (New York, 1927), 2:581; C. J. Barry, *The Catholic Church and German Americans* (Washington, 1953), 7–8. M. J. McDonald's *History of the Irish in Wisconsin in the Nineteenth Century* (Washington, 1954) appeared too late for me to use its very valuable information.

3. Theodore Roemer, *The Catholic Church in the United States* (St. Louis, 1950) provides a survey by decades of the Church's growth.

4. John Rothensteiner, *History of the Archdiocese of St. Louis* (St. Louis, 1928), 1:806. The national origins of the American hierarchy are given in an appendix to J. B. Code, *Dictionary of the American Hierarchy* (New York, 1940).

5. A revealing case study is Oscar Handlin, *Boston's Immigrants, 1790–1865* (Cambridge, 1941); the psychological impact is explored more fully in his *The Uprooted* (Boston, 1951). See also Billington, *Protestant Crusade*, 291–314.

6. Handlin, *Boston's Immigrants*, 182, 195, 213; S. G. Messmer, ed., *Works of John England* (Cleveland, 1908), 4:317–318.

7. B. L. Pierce, *A History of Chicago* (New York, 1937–1940), 2:26n.; Handlin, *Boston's Immigrants*, 67; a personal experience is reported in Thomas Sugrue, *A Catholic Speaks His Mind on America's Religious Conflict* (New York, 1951), 39.

8. *The Autobiography of William Allen White* (New York, 1946), 6, 31. Compare the conclusion of Will Herberg, "The 'Triple Melting Pot,'" *Commentary*, 20 (August 1955), 101–108.

9. M. G. Kelly, *Catholic Immigrant Colonies in the United States, 1815–1860* (New York, 1939); J. E. Roohan, "American Catholics and the Social Question, 1865–1900," (Unpublished Ph.D. dissertation, Department of History, Yale University, 1952), 207–210. See H. J. Browne, "Archbishop Hughes and Western Colonization," *CHR*, 36 (October 1950), 257–285.

10. Billington, *Protestant Crusade*; Handlin, *Boston's Immigrants*, 184–215; H. J. Nolan, *The Most Reverend Francis Patrick Kenrick, Third Bishop*

of Philadelphia, 1830–1851 (Washington, 1948), 288–342; Peter Guilday, "Gaetano Bedini," *HRS*, 18 (1928), 7–73.

11. E. J. Hickey, *The Society for the Propagation of the Faith* (Washington, 1922), 81–93; Theodore Roemer, *The Ludwig-missionsverein and the Church in the United States (1838–1918)* (Washington, 1933), 23–25; Roemer, *Ten Decades of Alms* (St. Louis, 1942), 186–187. The Redemptorist is quoted in P. M. Abbelen, *Venerable Mother M. Caroline Friess*, authorized trans. (St. Louis, 1893), 91.

12. J. T. Ellis, "Some Student Letters of John Lancaster Spalding," *CHR*, 29 (January 1944), 536.

13. Roemer, *Ludwig-missionsverein*, 148; Barry, *German Americans*, 37.

14. R. H. Lord, J. E. Sexton, and E. T. Harrington, *History of the Archdiocese of Boston* (Boston, 1945), 2:624–627; J. H. Moynihan, *The Life of Archbishop John Ireland* (New York, 1953), 11–12; John O'Grady, *Catholic Charities in the United States* (Washington, 1930), 235.

15. Moynihan, *Ireland*, 10.

16. J. G. Shea, "The Anti-Catholic Issue in the Late Election," *ACQR*, 6 (January, 1881), 37, 45; J. T. Reily, *Passing Events in the Life of Cardinal Gibbons* (Martinsburg, West Virginia), 1:48; M. C. Klinkhamer, "The Blaine Amendment of 1875," *CHR*, 42 (April, 1956), 15–49.

17. Parsons, *Studies*, 6:437; Barry, *German Americans*, 36; P. Bayma, "The Liberalistic view of the Public School Question," *ACQR*, 2 (April 1877), 246.

18. Weninger, *Protestantism and Infidelity*, 191–192.

19. The Polish became a serious problem in the next decade, producing a schismatic movement under "Bishop" Anthony Kozlowski. "The Excommunication of Father Kozlowski," *LD*, 17 (24 September 1898), 381; A Close Observer, "Recent Schismatical Movements among Catholics of the United States," *AER*, 21 (July 1899), 1–13. The Italians presented an even greater problem, not because of schismatical tendencies, but from indifference to Catholicism; they did not present a united front, nor did they struggle with the Irish and the Germans for Church leadership. See also H. J. Browne, "The 'Italian Problem' in the Catholic Church of the United States," *HRS*, 35 (1946), 46–72.

20. Barry, *German Americans*, 24, 29n, 42, 96, 131n.

21. *The Question of Nationality* (St. Louis, 1889), 43–45, 51, 61–62.

22. R. J. Purcell, "Michael Augustine Corrigan," *DAB*, 4 (1930), 450–452; J. T. Smith, *The Catholic Church in New York* (New York, 1905), 2:414–429. The best picture of Corrigan is in F. J. Zwierlein, *Letters of Archbishop Corrigan to Bishop McQuaid, and Allied Documents* (Rochester, 1946), and Zwierlein, *The Life and Letters of Bishop McQuaid* (Rome, 1925), vols. 2, 3.

23. Zwierlein, *McQuaid*; R. J. Purcell, "Bernard McQuaid," *DAB*, 12 (1933), 163–164.

24. R. J. Purcell, "Thomas Scott Preston," *DAB*, 15 (1935), 215; Preston, "American Catholicity," *ACQR*, 16 (April 1891), 396–408.

25. R. J. Purcell, "Richard Gilmour," *DAB*, 7 (1931), 313–314; Purcell, "Francis Silas Chatard," *DAB*, 4 (1930), 39–40; R. C. McGrane, "William Henry Elder," *DAB*, 6 (1931), 69; Purcell, "Patrick John Ryan," *DAB*, 15 (1935), 263–265.

26. A. J. Thébaud, *Forty Years in the United States of America*, volume 3 of *Three Quarters of a Century (1807–1882)* (New York, 1904).

27. C. B. Pallen, *What is Liberalism?*, "Englished and Adapted from the Spanish of Dr. Don Felix Sarda y Salvany" (St. Louis, 1899), 31. See also his *The Catholic Church and Socialism* (St. Louis, 1890). There is a biographical sketch in *CW*, 65 (September 1897), 853–854. For Preuss' point-of-view, see his *A Study in American Freemasonry* (St. Louis, 1908), and *The Fundamental Fallacy of Socialism* (St. Louis, 1909).

28. Pallen, *Liberalism*, 14, 174.

29. For an American liberal Catholic definition of "liberalism" as "large-mindedness and large-heartedness," see S. L. Malone, *Memorial of the Golden Jubilee of the Reverend Sylvester Malone* (Brooklyn, 1895), 123, 97–98.

30. T. T. McAvoy, "The Formation of the Catholic Minority," *Review of Politics*, 9 (April 1947), 205–229; for the English parallel, see Butler, *Ullathorne;* Purcell, *Manning;* and Ward, *Wiseman.*

31. Katherine Burton, *In No Strange Land* (New York, 1942); "Very Reverend Augustine F. Hewit, D.D.," *CW*, 65 (August 1897), i–xvi before 577; Hewit, *Memoir of the Life of the Rev. Francis A. Baker*, 7th ed. (New York, 1889); M. H. Yeager, *The Life of James Roosevelt Bayley, 1814–1877* (Washington, 1947).

32. A. M. Schlesinger, Jr., *Orestes A. Brownson* (Boston, 1939); Theodore Maynard, *Orestes Brownson, Yankee, Radical, Catholic* (New York, 1943). A good example of his double criticism is *The American Republic* (New York, 1866); see T. I. Cook and A. B. Leavelle, "Orestes A. Brownson's *The American Republic*," *Review of Politics* 4 (January 1942), 77–90 and 4 (April 1942), 173–193.

33. I have depended heavily in this analysis upon the lectures of Professor Oscar Handlin in his course "The Immigrant in American History," Harvard University, 1950–1951. See also his *The Uprooted.*

34. W. L. Warner and Leo Srole, *The Social Systems of American Ethnic Groups* (New Haven, 1945), p. 30 claim that immigrants arriving younger than eighteen were usually able to make the break successfully.

35. Handlin, *Boston's Immigrants*, 216–219; Reily, *Passing Events*, 2:84; B. J. McQuaid, "Religious Teaching in Schools," *Forum*, 8 (December 1889), 387. However, A. P. Stauffer, "Anti-Catholicism in American Politics, 1865–1900" (Unpublished Ph.D. dissertation, Department of History, Harvard University, 1933), 89, questions if anti-Irish feeling was significantly lessened by the wide Irish participation in the war.

36. Moynihan, *Ireland*, 8.

37. Malone, *Memorial*, 64; J. J. Keane, "The Reunion of Christendom," *ACQR*, 13 (April 1889), 309; Edward McGlynn, "The Bugbear of Vaticanism," *ACQR*, 1 (January 1876), 77; "The American Congress of Churches," *CW*, 42 (December 1885), 415; Walter Elliott, "The Experiences of a Missionary," *CW*, 58 (November 1893), 277; P. J. O'Callaghan, "The Puritan Catholicized," *CW*, 65 (April 1897), 113–114.

38. "The Higher and Lower Education of the American Priesthood," *ACQR*, 15 (January 1890), 105.

39. "The American Congress of Churches," *CW*, 42 (December 1885), 415; I. T. Hecker, "The Things that Make for Unity," *CW*, 47, (April 1888), 105.

40. Review of Rev. W. Gleeson, *The Trials of the Church*, 2 vols. (New York, 1880), *CW*, 33 (May 1881), 282.

41. For general surveys, see Gustavus Myers, *History of Bigotry in the United States* (New York, 1943) and Reuben Maury, *The Wars of the Godly* (New York, 1928). A detailed study is Stauffer, "Anti-Catholicism." For a list of aggressions as they appeared to an indignant Catholic, see James McFaul, "Catholics and American Citizenship," *NAR*, 171 (September 1900), 330.

42. "The Anti-Catholic Issue," *ACQR*, 6 (January 1881), 48.

43. "An American Viceroy from the Vatican," *Forum*, 15 (May 1893), 269–270. Compare J. H. Vincent, "The Pope in Washington," *Forum*, 15 (May 1893), 261–267.

44. W. K. Hermes, "Non-Catholic Regard for Archbishop Ireland," *RACHS*, 59 (September 1948); A. M. Schlesinger, "A Critical Period in American Religion, 1875–1900," *Proceedings of the Massachusetts Historical Society*, 64 (June 1932), 528, notes that the two bestsellers in 1888 were on the theme of religious toleration.

45. Munger, *Horace Bushnell, Preacher and Theologian* (Boston, 1899), 37–40; H. H. Wyman, "Professor Briggs' Doctrine of the Middle State," *CW*, 51 (April 1890), 118.

46. *The Failure of Protestantism in New York and its Causes*, 2nd ed. (New York, 1896), 87–88.

47. Philip Schaff, *Church and State in the United States* (New York, 1888), 83; "Are Catholics and Protestants Drawing Together?" *LD*, 15 (23 October 1897), 768; Washington Gladden, "The Outlook for Christianity," *NAR*, 172 (June 1901), 924.

48. Dorchester, *Christianity in the United States*, revised ed. (New York, 1895), 680; Bacon, *A History of American Christianity* (New York, 1897), 419.

49. Newman Smyth, *Passing Protestantism and Coming Catholicism* (New York, 1908); B. O. Flower, "Present Day Tendencies and Signs of the Times," *Arena*, 7 (1893), 507–512; compare Schaff, *Church and State*, 83, who desired each sect to retain some distinguishing peculiarities.

50. The *Catholic Standard and Times* of Philadelphia, cited in *LD*, 12 (14 March 1896), 590; E. D. Mead, *The Roman Catholic Church and the Public Schools* (Boston, 1890), 14–15.

51. Flower, "Present Day Tendencies," *Arena*, 7 (1893), 509.

52. Dorchester, *Christianity*, 694–695; Lyman Abbott, "The Growth of Religious Tolerance in the United States," *Forum*, 23 (August 1897), 624.

53. Walter Elliott, "The Evangelical Conference at Washington," *CW*, 47 (August 1888), 647; *The World's Catholic Columbian Congresses* (Chicago, 1893), 1:14–15.

54. Malone, *Memorial*, 67.

55. Dixon, *Failure*, 16–19.

56. Dixon, *Failure*, 16–19; Theodore Abel, *Protestant Home Missions to Catholic Immigrants* (New York, 1933), 104; H. F. May, *Protestant Churches in Industrial America* (New York, 1949); Pierce, *Chicago*, 1:233, 2:355; G. D. Wolff, "Catholicism and Protestantism in relation to our Future as a People," *ACQR*, 4 (January 1879), 159–163.

57. J. B. Harrison, *Certain Dangerous Tendencies in American Life* (Boston, 1880), 34; W. H. Lyon, *A Study of the Christian Sects* (Boston, 1891), 60; W. L. Sullivan, *The Priest, a Tale of Modernism in New England*, 2nd ed. (Boston, 1914), 4–5; Augustin McNally, *The Catholic Centenary* (New York, 1908); Henry Bargy, *La Religion dans la société aux Etats-Unis* (Paris, 1902), 180–181; Alfred de Meaux, *L'Eglise catholique et la liberté aux Etats-Unis* (Paris, 1893), 63; J. H. Vincent, "The Pope in Washington," *Forum*, 15 (May 1893), 266–267.

58. Dixon, *Failure*, 88; W. C. Doane, "The Roman Catholic Church and the School Fund," *NAR*, 158 (January 1894), 34; Mead, *Roman Catholic Church*, 30–31.

59. J. G. Pyle, *The Life of James J. Hill* (New York, 1917), 1:64–65.

60. "Editorial Notes," *CW*, 65 (September 1897), 851; Smith, *Catholic Church in New York*, 2:566; Stephen Bell, *Rebel, Priest, and Prophet. A Biography of Edward McGlynn* (New York, 1937), 59.

61. For Hanna's remark, see A. I. Abell, "The Reception of Leo XIII's Labor Encyclical in America, 1891–1919," *Review of Politics*, 7 (October 1945), 479; H. F. Pringle, *The Life and Times of William Howard Taft* (New York, 1939), 2:834. One Protestant professed that he had converted to Catholicism primarily out of gratitude for "the Church's contribution to political conservatism." "The Story of a Conversion," *CW*, 45 (July 1887), 563.

62. Lord, *et al.*, *Boston*, 3:68; "Shall We Adopt a Sixteenth Amendment?" *RR*, 5 (March 1892), 160–162; the quotation is from Félix Klein, *La Séparation aux Etats-Unis* (Paris, 1908), 33.

63. T. A. Bailey, *A Diplomatic History of the American People* (New York, 1940), 408n.

64. W. W. Astor, "America and the Vatican," *NAR*, 141 (October 1885),

346–350; Bernard O'Reilly, "The Propaganda Question and Our Duty," *ACQR*, 9 (April 1884), 285–303.

65. J. M. King, *Facing the Twentieth Century* (New York, 1899), 263; P. C. Phillips, "Thomas Henry Carter," *DAB*, 3 (1929), 544–545; on Joseph Harrity, the Democratic chairman, see *Catholic Times* of Philadelphia, December 3, 1892, 4.

66. H. L. McBain, "Edward Douglass White," *DAB*, 20 (1936), 96–98; F. S. Philbrick, "Joseph McKenna," *DAB*, 12 (1933), 87–88; R. J. Purcell, "Justice Joseph McKenna," *RACHS*, 56 (September 1945), 177–222. Catholics were also being elected to local office; William R. Grace was chosen Mayor of New York in 1880, and Hugh O'Brien, Mayor of Boston in 1884. Lord *et al.*, *Boston*, 3:86–87.

67. A good example of mingled protest and pleasure is J. L. Spalding, *Religion and Art, and other essays* (Chicago, 1905), 63.

68. The best source is Ellis, *Gibbons*; A. S. Will, *Life of Cardinal Gibbons*, 2 vols. (New York, 1922) and Reily, *Passing Events* are valuable for personal records of the cardinal. See also de Meaux, *Eglise catholique*, 396–399 and J. J. Walsh, *Our American Cardinals*, (New York, 1926), 71–88.

69. Ellis, *Gibbons*, 1:48.

70. *Ibid.*, 2:589–592.

71. See "The Catholic Democracy of America," *Edinburgh Review*, 171 (April 1890), 505; Reily, *Passing Events* 1:i–ii, 2:820; de Meaux, *Eglise catholique*, 144n.

72. The best source is Moynihan, *Ireland*; R. J. Purcell, "John Ireland," *DAB*, 9 (1932), 494–497, and Claude d'Hablonville, *Grandes figures de l'église contemporaine* (Paris, 1925), 229–265.

73. Quick to adopt the daring methods of his age, he speculated so widely in Western lands that in the 1890's he had to borrow nearly a half-million dollars to remain solvent. Moynihan, *Ireland*, 380.

74. Ellis, *Gibbons*, 1:405.

75. D'Hablonville, *Grandes figures*, 236–237; Ireland, *The Church and Modern Society, Lectures and Addresses* (New York, 1903–1904), 2:32–33.

76. Moynihan, *Ireland*, 345–361.

77. *Ibid.*, 20–32; J. C. Murphy, *An Analysis of the Attitude of American Catholics toward the Immigrant and the Negro, 1825–1925* (Washington, 1940), 21–30; M. S. Pahorezki, *The Social and Political Activities of William J. Onahan* (Washington, 1942), 88, 105; Onahan, "The Catholic Movement in Western Colonization — Colonization in Nebraska," *ACQR*, 6 (July 1881), 434–445.

78. See Chapter 6.

79. King, *Facing*, 214; de Meaux, *Eglise catholique*, 145–146.

80. Quoted in P. F. Quigley, ed., *Compulsory Education. The State of Ohio versus the Rev. Patrick Francis Quigley, D.D.* (New York, 1894), 547.

81. Moynihan, *Ireland*, 35.

82. Zwierlein, *Corrigan*, 135.

83. Barry, *German Americans*, 230n.; P. H. Ahern, *The Catholic University of America, 1887–1896* (Washington, 1948), 185n.

84. R. J. Purcell, "John Lancaster Spalding," *DAB*, 17 (1935), 422–423; T. T. McAvoy, "Bishop John Spalding and the Catholic Minority (1877–1908)," *Review of Politics*, 12 (January 1950), 3–19; Félix Klein, *In the Land of the Strenuous Life*, author's trans. (Chicago, 1905), 153–160; M. F. Egan, *Recollections of a Happy Life* (New York, 1924), 170–184.

85. Ellis, "Some Student Letters of John Lancaster Spalding," *CHR*, 29 (January 1944), 510–539; Spalding, *Essays and Reviews* (New York, 1877).

86. (New York, 1880).

87. Representative works are *Education and the Higher Life* (Chicago, 1890); *Means and Ends of Education* (Chicago, 1895); *Opportunity and Other Essays and Addresses* (Chicago, 1900); *Religion, Agnosticism, and Education* (Chicago, 1902); *Religion and Art, and other essays* (Chicago, 1905).

88. Merle Curti, *The Social Ideas of American Educators* (New York, 1935), 348–373; Franz de Hovre, *Catholicism in Education*, E. B. Jordan, trans. (New York, 1934), chapter 2.

89. Review of J. L. Spalding, *Things of the Mind*, *ACQR*, 20 (April 1895), 431.

90. C. G. Herbermann, *The Sulpicians in the United States* (New York, 1916); J. F. Fenlon, "Sulpicians in the United States," *Catholic Encyclopedia*, 14 (1912), 329–332; Klein, *In the Land*, 305–308; A. R. Vidler, *The Modernist Movement in the Roman Church* (Cambridge, England, 1934), 228; Albert Houtin, *Histoire du modernisme catholique* (Paris, 1913), 61; J. T. Smith, *The Training of a Priest: an Essay on Clerical Education* (New York, 1908), 5.

91. Ellis, *Gibbons*, 2:472–475.

92. Herbermann, *Sulpicians*, 312–337; Klein, *In the Land*, 305; J. E. Sexton and A. J. Riley, *History of St. John's Seminary, Brighton* (Boston, 1945), 63–65; Albert Houtin, *L'Américanisme* (Paris, 1904), 81.

93. Zwierlein, *McQuaid*, 3:152.

94. "The Congregation of Saint Paul," *AER*, 17 (September 1897), 269–282; Ruth Everett, "The Paulist Fathers and their Work," *Arena*, 21 (April 1899), 407–420; J. M. Gillis, *The Paulists* (New York, 1932); R. W. Adams, "Isaac Thomas Hecker,"*DAB*, 8 (1932), 495; Walter Elliott, *The Life of Father Hecker* (New York, 1891); V. F. Holden, *The Early Years of Isaac Thomas Hecker, 1819–1844* (Washington, 1939).

95. "Rev. Alfred Young, C.S.P.," *CW*, 71 (May 1900), 257–264; Richard Cartwright, "Walter Hackett Elliott," *DAB*, 6 (1931), 99–100.

96. "The Congregation of St. Paul," *AER*, 17 (September 1897), 281.

97. G. N. Shuster, "Louis Aloisius Lambert," *DAB*, 10 (1933), 557–558.

98. J. A. Ryan, "Edward McGlynn," *DAB*, 12 (1933), 53–54; Bell, *McGlynn;* S. L. Malone, ed., *Dr. Edward McGlynn* (New York, 1918); see chapter 6.

99. R. J. Purcell, "Sylvester Malone," *DAB*, 12 (1933), 226–227; Malone, *Malone.*

100. On Keane, one of the outstanding liberals of the era, see W. J. Kerby, "John Joseph Keane," *DAB*, 10 (1933), 267–268 and Ahern, *Catholic University;* Malone, *Malone,* 84–85.

101. Malone, *Malone,* 97–98. For use of a similar image, see *Catholic Times* of Philadelphia, December 10, 1892, 4.

102. The reasons for lay inactivity are examined in chapter 9. On O'Reilly, see Arthur Mann, *Yankee Reformers in the Urban Age* (Cambridge, 1954), 24–51; Pahorezki, *Onahan;* on Spaunhorst, see M. L. Brophy, *The Social Thought of the German Roman Catholic Central Verein* (Washington, 1941), 40.

103. A. I. Abell, "Preparing for Social Action: 1880–1920," in L. R. Ward, ed., *The American Apostolate: American Catholics in the Twentieth Century* (Westminster, Maryland, 1952), 20–28.

104. "The Transformation of New England," *Forum*, 15 (March 1893), 110; King, *Facing,* 214–215.

105. Quoted in Ahern, *Catholic University,* 168–173.

106. Eduardo Soderini, *The Pontificate of Leo XIII*, B. B. Carter, trans. (London, 1934), 91–113; Seignobos, *Political History,* 710; Hayes, *Generation,* 142.

107. Soderini, *Pontificate,* 69–77.

108. Parsons, *Studies,* 5:139–140, 6:39–43, 287–290, 317; E. M. de Vogüé, "Pope Leo XIII," *Forum*, 22 (January 1897), 520; John McCarthy, "The Papacy and the European Powers, 1870–1882," *ACQR*, 7 (April 1882), 311–330; H. A. Brann, "Leo XIII and the Septennate," *ACQR*, 12 (April 1887), 220–232; "Why the Pope Honored Bismarck," *LD*, 12 (February 22, 1896), 504; "The Policy of the Pope," *Contemporary Review*, 62 (October 1892), 459.

109. Latourette, *Great Century,* 165.

110. Representative encyclicals are in Joseph Husslein, ed., *Social Wellsprings, Fourteen Epochal Documents of Pope Leo XIII* (Milwaukee, 1940). See a series of articles by J. C. Murray, "The Church and Totalitarian Democracy," *TS*, 13 (December 1952), 525–563; "Leo XIII on Church and State: the General Structure of the Controversy," *TS*, 14 (March 1953), 1–30; "Leo XIII; Government and the Order of Culture," *TS*, 15 (March 1954), 1–33; and "On the Structure of the Church-State Problem," in Waldemar Gurian and M. A. Fitzsimons, eds., *The Catholic Church in World Affairs* (Notre Dame, 1954),11–32.

111. Husslein, ed., *Social Wellsprings,* 167–204.

112. Soderini, *Pontificate,* 201–203.

113. Bacon, *History,* 411; "Are Catholics and Protestants Drawing Together?" *LD*, 15 (October 23, 1897), 768.

114. J. C. Murray, "Leo XIII on Church and State," *TS*, 14 (March 1953), 2; Washington Gladden, "The Outlook for Christianity," *NAR*, 172 (June

1901), 924; "A Protestant Tribute to Pope Leo," *LD*, 16 (January 22, 1898), 111.

115. "The Sacerdotal Jubilee of His Holiness Pope Leo XIII," *ACQR*, 13 (January 1888), 50.

116. Dixon, *Failure*, 89; "A Protestant Tribute to Pope Leo," *LD*, 16 (January 22, 1898), 110; "The Pope, Leo XIII," *RR*, 3 (June 1891), 465–473.

117. Quoted in Quigley, ed., *Compulsory Education*, 548.

118. Moynihan, *Ireland*, 287; Smith, *Catholic Church in New York*, 2:386.

119. J. A. Corcoran, "The Recent Encyclical Letter of Pope Leo XIII," *ACQR*, 4 (October 1879), 720–724; J. P. Tardivel, *Mélanges* (Quebec, 1903), 2:25–29. Tardivel was a French Canadian editor, aligned with the American conservatives; see his *La Situation religieuse aux Etats-Unis* (Lille, 1900).

120. Egan, *Recollections*, 128. On McMaster, an editor proud to be called the American Veuillot, see M. C. Minahan, "James A. McMaster: A Pioneer Catholic Journalist," *RACHS*, 47 (June 1936), 87–131.

121. *Church and Modern Society*, 1:125; Reily, *Passing Events*, 2:916–917.

122. *The Church and the Age* (New York, 1887), 189.

123. (Baltimore, 1888). For its Roman reception, see I. T. Hecker, "The Mission of Leo XIII," *CW*, 48 (October 1888), 1–2, and J. T. Ellis, *The Formative Years of the Catholic University of America* (Washington, 1946), 343n.

124. On the attitude of Gregory XVI, see Weninger, *Protestantism*, 267; on Pius IX, see J. J. O'Shea, *The Two Kenricks* (Philadelphia, 1904), 171, and Mueller, *Public School Education*, 245; for a more representative attitude of Pius IX's, see S. B. Hedges, "Father Hecker," *CW*, 61 (June 1895), 381–382.

125. Parsons, *Studies*, 6:213n.; "The Pope, Leo XIII," *RR*, 3 (June 1891), 473.

126. J. J. Meng, "Cahenslyism: the Second Chapter," *CHR*, 32 (October 1946), 322n., 323n. For Gibbons' belief in an alliance with Leo, see Reily, *Passing Events*, 2:815.

127. "The Mission of Leo XIII," *CW*, 48 (October 1888), 12.

128. See chapter 10.

129. P. E. Hogan, *Thomas J. Conaty, Second Rector of the Catholic University of America, 1896–1903* (Washington, 1949), 41; *CW*, 64 (February 1897), opposite 573; Ireland, *Church and Modern Society*, 1:126.

Chapter III

The Church and American Protestantism

1. *Nova Collectio*, 51 (1925), 71–77.

2. F. M. Crawford, *Casa Braccio* (New York, 1895), 1:22 writes of the conviction of an Italian peasant that Protestants "were under the most especial protection of the devil, who fattened them in this world that they might burn the better in the next." L. H. Bugg, The People of Our Parish, (Boston, 1900); Sugrue, *A Catholic*, 47; Albert Houtin, *Une Vie de prêtre, 1867–1912* (Paris, 1926), 161–162.

3. Elliott, *Hecker*, 147–173; I. T. Hecker, "Dr. Brownson and Bishop Fitzpatrick," *CW*, 45 (April 1887), 1–7; Hecker, "Dr. Brownson's Road to the Church," *CW*, 46 (October 1887), 3.

4. Smith, *Catholic Church in New York*, 1:300.

5. B. J. McQuaid, "The Decay of Protestantism," *NAR*, 136 (February 1883), 151; J. F. Loughlin, "Rome a True Ally of the Republic," *Forum*, 15 (May 1893), 282; Mueller, *Public School Education*, 8.

6. *Three-Quarters of a Century*, 3:182.

7. "American Catholicity," *ACQR*, 16 (April 1891), 407; Reily, *Passing Events*, 2:226: Pallen, *Liberalism*, 13–14.

8. *What the Catholic Church Most Needs in the United States*, 40–46; T. A. Becker, "Vocations to the Priesthood," *ACQR*, 5 (January 1880), 29; Spalding, *Mission*, 37–38; T. J. Jenkins, *Foreign Societies and American Schools* (Buffalo, 1894), 55.

9. Hewit, *Baker*, 129; Spalding, *Opportunity*, 107; Corrigan, *What the Catholic Church Needs*, 43; Klein, *In the Land*, 25; James Gibbons, *The Ambassador of Christ* (Baltimore, 1896), vi.

10. Malone, *Memorial*, 122; Moynihan, *Ireland*, 48; *Columbian Congress*, 1:34.

11. "Missionary Experiences," *CW*, 61 (May 1895), 246; Gibbons, *Ambassador*, vi; *Catholic Standard and Times* of Philadelphia, December 28, 1895, 3; see Schlesinger, *Proceedings of the Massachusetts Historical Society*, 64 (June, 1932), 546. For examples of initial Catholic bitterness, see Lucian Johnston, "Americanism vs. Ultramontanism," *CW*, 59 (September 1894), 731–743; Alfred Young, "The Coming Contest — with a Retrospect," *CW*, 58 (January 1894), 457–472. Compare John Higham, *Strangers in the Land* (New Brunswick, 1955), 81–87.

12. James Gibbons, *Our Christian Heritage* (Baltimore, 1889), 4.

13. *Columbia Congress*, 1:40; *Catholic Times* of Philadelphia, December 31, 1892, 3; "The Plea for Positivism," *CW*, 30 (January 1880), 439.

14. "Introduction," Lewis Lambert, *The Tactics of Infidels* (Buffalo, 1887), xxv.

15. *Ambassador*, viii.

16. Alfred Young, quoted in Michael Mueller, *The Catholic Dogma* (New York, 1888), 98; Elliott, "The Human Environments of the Catholic Faith," *CW*, 43 (July 1886), 470; Joan Bland, *Hibernian Crusade: the Story of the Catholic Total Abstinence Union of America* (Washington, 1951), 132.

17. Quoted in J. A. Ryan and M. F. X. Millar, *The State and the Church* (New York, 1922), 293; Ireland, *Church and Modern Society*, 1:81; Fran-

cesco Satolli, *Loyalty to Church and State* (Baltimore, 1895), 56; Smith, *Training of a Priest*, 136; P. J. O'Callaghan, "The Puritan Catholicized," *CW*, 65 (April 1897), 113–114.

18. Review of J. F. Morse, *Benjamin Franklin* (Boston, n.d.), *CW*, 50 (March 1890), 844.

19. "Editorial Notes," *CW*, 67 (April 1898), 134.

20. *Opportunity*, 108.

21. "Our Converts," *ACQR*, 18 (July 1893), 542.

22. Malone, McGlynn, 105. McGlynn was suspended at the time he made this and other remarks even closer to ecclesiastical liberalism; a strong liberal like Bishop Edward Fitzgerald of Little Rock protested to Gibbons that McGlynn had gone much too far. Ellis, *Gibbons*, 1:560n.

23. *Clerical Studies* 2nd ed. (Boston, n.d.), 87–88; for Archbishop Ryan's praise of Phillips Brooks, see *Catholic Times* of Philadelphia, January 28, 1893, 5.

24. "The Closing Scene," *CW*, 55 (June 1892), 336–337.

25. "God is Love," *CW*, 47 (August, 1888), 705–706.

26. Review of E. C. Lesserteur, *Saint Thomas et la prédestination*, (Paris, n.d.), *CW*, 48 (March 1889), 856–857; A. F. Hewit, "Review of Father Tanquerey's Special Dogmatic Theology," *CW*, 60 (February 1895), 612–613; J. H. Barrows, ed., *The World's Parliament of Religions* (Chicago, 1893), 1:463–465.

27. *Nova Collectio*, 51:541–542.

28. Maynard, *Brownson*, 167–169; Preston, "American Catholicity," *ACQR*, 16 (April 1891), 399.

29. Reily, *Passing Events*, 2:310.

30. Alfred Young, "A Plea for Erring Brethren," *CW*, 50 (December 1889), 352.

31. Page xii. It is difficult to determine how far Mueller's views were typical of conservative thinking. He was published by Benziger Brothers, the leading Catholic house, and he won the approval of many Catholic authorities, according to Walter Elliott, "A Plea for Honest Protestants," *CW*, 48 (December 1888), 351. On the other hand, Young reported that his counter-statement had received "almost universal approbation." "A Plea for Erring Brethren," *CW*, 50 (December 1889), 355.

32. *Passing Events*, 1:394, 2:310–311; McGlynn, "The Bugbear of Vaticanism," *ACQR*, 1 (January 1876), 78; R. H. Clarke, "Our Converts," *ACQR*, 18 (July 1893), 539; Mead, *Catholic Church*, 72.

33. J. J. Keane, "Father Hecker," *CW*, 49 (April 1889), 4; "History of a Conversion," *CW*, 45 (August 1887), 710; John La Farge, *The Manner is Ordinary* (New York, 1954), 25.

34. Mueller, *Catholic Dogma*, 174; Hewit, "How I Became a Catholic," *CW*, 46 (October 1887), 35; J. P. Ryan, "Out of the Church there is no Salvation," *CW*, 48 (January 1889), 517; Hewit, "Review of Tanquerey's Theology," *CW*, 60 (February 1895), 616; John Conway, *Rational Religion* (Milwaukee, 1890), pp. 87–96.

35. The epithets are Brownson's, quoted in Mueller, *Catholic Dogma*, 201.

36. "A Plea for Honest Protestants," *CW*, 48 (December 1888), 356; M. F. Egan, "A Catholic on the School Question," *NAR*, 152 (May 1891), 638.

37. Ryan, "Out of the Church there is no Salvation," *CW*, 48 (December 1888), 512.

38. Hewit, "How I Became a Catholic," *CW*, 46 (October 1887), 36–37.

39. *Catholic Dogma*, 158–170, 249.

40. *Ibid.*, 44, 64, 80, 101–107, 124.

41. Elliott, "A Plea for Honest Protestants," *CW*, 48 (December 1886), 353–355.

42. Quoted in Mueller, *Catholic Dogma*, 187.

43. *Ibid.*, p. 63.

44. "A Plea for Erring Brethren," *CW*, 50 (December 1889), 358.

45. "Editorial Notes," *CW*, 70 (December 1900), 716; *LD*, 15 (December 11, 1897), 980.

46. *Ambassador*, 347; *LD*, 16 (April 2, 1898), 411. The Archdiocese of Baltimore apparently began keeping records of conversions before others did, and Gibbons' figure seems to be an extrapolation from these reports. For Ireland's confidence, see *Church and Modern Society*, 2:716. Richard Clarke estimated the total number of converts or children of converts as 700,000; "Our Converts," *ACQR*, 18 (July 1893), 542.

47. "Christian Unity *vs.* Unity of Christians," *CW*, 44 (November 1886), 185–188.

48. Spalding, *Mission*, 60–61; de Meaux, *L'Eglise catholique*, 41–42; Patrick Cronin, *Memorial of the Life and Labors of Rt. Rev. Stephen Vincent Ryan* (Buffalo, 1896), 86; Hewit, "Pure *vs.* Diluted Catholicism," *ACQR*, 20 (July 1895), 478; Hewit, "A Crisis in Congregational Theology," *CW*, 36 (November 1882), 290; Alfred Young, "A Plea for Erring Brethren," *CW*, 50 (December 1889), 357. For the rationale of this individualistic spirit, see chapter 9.

49. J. F. Loughlin, "Rome a True Ally of the Republic," *Forum*, 15 (May 1893), 282; T. S. Preston, "American Catholicity," *ACQR*, 16 (April 1891), 399, 407; "*Aquinas Resuscitatus*," *ACQR*, 16 (October 1891), 678; Parsons, *Studies*, 5:603.

50. "Bostonian Ignorance of Catholic Doctrine," *ACQR*, 14 (January 1889), 94–102.

51. *Three-Quarters of a Century*, 3:186.

52. "The Conversion of the American People," *CW*, 55 (September 1892), 884–887; *Columbian Congress*, 1:161–162; Tardivel, *Situation*, 236.

53. "*Aquinas Resuscitatus*," *ACQR*, 16 (October 1891), 673–690.

54. C. A. Walworth, *Reminiscences of Edgar P. Wadhams, First Bishop of Ogdensburg* (New York, 1893), 121.

55. Walter Elliott, "Half-Converts," *CW*, 63 (July 1896), 431.

56. Converts' narratives of the history of their religious development began to appear in the *Catholic World* in 1887. Representative examples are: 45

(July 1887), 522–524; 45 (August 1887), 708–710; 46 (October 1887), 134–136; 46 (December 1887), 420–423; 46 (February 1888), 708–712; 47 (April 1888), 128–132; 48 (October 1888), 130–134. See also Hewit, *Baker*, 144; Gibbons, *Faith*, xv.

57. Young, "A Plea for Erring Brethren," *CW*, 50 (December 1889), 351, 366.

58. J. J. Keane, "The Reunion of Christendom," *ACQR*, 13 (April 1888), 310–311.

59. Review of Wilfrid Ward, *William George Ward and the Catholic Revival*, (London, 1893), *CW*, 57 (July 1893), 584.

60. "The Human Environments of the Catholic Faith," *CW*, 43 (July 1886), 468. See also William Stang, "The 'Ever' and 'Never' of Preaching," *AER*, 14 (March 1896), 218.

61. H. A. Adams, "Pillars of Salt," *CW*, 64 (October 1896), 13.

62. A. M. Clark, "What Are We Doing for Non-Catholics," *CW*, 57 (June 1893), 347n.; J. J. Keane, "The Reunion of Christendom," *ACQR*, 13 (April 1886), 318.

63. *Proceedings of the Catholic Congress, held at Baltimore, Md., November 11th and 12th, 1889* (Detroit, 1889), 29.

64. *Church and Modern Society*, 1:88–89.

65. *Ibid.*, 1:353; Reily, *Passing Events*, 2:915.

66. *Means and Ends*, 186. Charges and countercharges on this theme are explored in chapters 9 and 10.

67. *Columbian Congress*, 1:58; Elliott, "Human Environments," *CW*, 43 (July 1886), 486. Compare Barry, *German Americans*, 11.

68. "Why Not?" *CW*, 62 (February 1896), 621–626.

69. "Baptized Democracy," *CW*, 43 (September 1886), 729; Elliott, "The True Man of the Times," *CW*, 44 (December 1886), 296; Hewit, "Pure *vs.* Diluted Catholicism," *ACQR*, 20 (July 1895), 483; Mueller, *Catholic Dogma*, 280.

70. *Columbian Congress*, 1:58; Elliott, "Human Environments," *CW*, 43 (July 1886), 467–469.

71. Elliott, *Hecker*, 356; "The Intellectual Outlook of the Age," *CW*, 31 (May 1880), 151.

72. J. J. Keane, "The Reunion of Christendom," *ACQR*, 13 (April 1888), 309; Elliott, "Half-Converts," *CW*, 63 (July 1896), 434; for examples of the argument the liberals disliked, see "Shall there be another Parliament of Religions," *LD*, 15 (25 December 1897), 1039, and S. M. Brandi, "Why Am I a Catholic?" *NAR*, 143 (August 1886), 119–132. The *Catholic World*, reviewing a reprint of Brandi's article, protested that it should have been entitled, "Why I Am Not a Protestant." 45 (May 1887), 284.

73. "Dr. Brownson's Road to the Church," *CW*, 46 (October 1887), 6; Maynard, *Brownson*, 167.

74. Houtin, *Modernisme*, 27–46.

75. Hecker admired the common sense philosophy of McCosh because of

his resistance to subjectivism. "Dr. Brownson's Road to the Church," *CW*, 46 (October 1887), 10. The liberals' enthusiasm for Newman was marred by their belief that his teachings verged on subjectivism; Hewit, "Cardinal Newman," *CW*, 51 (April 1890), 717–718; H. E. O'Keefe, "Another Aspect of Newman," *CW*, 71 (April 1900), 81–83.

76. "Dr. Brownson and Catholicity," *CW*, 46 (November 1887), 225.

77. "Half-Converts," *CW*, 63 (July 1896), 434.

78. "The Congregation of Saint Paul," *AER*, 17 (September 1897), 281; Elliott, "The Convention of the Apostolate of the Press," *CW*, 54 (December 1891), 381–389.

79. A. P. Doyle, "The Future of Catholicity in America," *CW*, 64 (November 1896), 211; "Editorial Notes," *CW*, 68 (February 1899), 712; Smith, *Catholic Church in New York*, 2:440–441; *Catholic Standard and Times* of Philadelphia, September 26, 1896, 4.

80. Klein, *In the Land*, 274–275.

81. Elliott et al., "The Experiences of a Missionary," *CW*, 58 (November 1893), 264–277; 58 (December 1893), 389–402; 59 (April 1894), 107–119; "Missionary Experiences on the Cleveland Plan," *CW*, 60 (December 1894), 409–414; J. M. Cleary, "The Public-Hall Apostolate," *CW*, 61 (August 1895), 577–587. See Elliott, *Non-Catholic Missions* (New York, 1895) summarized in *Catholic Standard and Times* of Philadelphia, December 14, 1895, 4.

82. "Street Preaching," *CW*, 46 (January 1888), 504.

83. "A Plea for Erring Brethren," *CW*, 50 (December 1889), 360; Bland, *Hibernian Crusade*, 212; Thomas O'Gorman, *A History of the Roman Catholic Church in the United States* (New York, 1895), 399.

84. See clippings from Boston papers bound with J. J. Keane, "Revealed Religion," 1890, Harvard University Archives.

85. M. A. Ray, *American Opinion of Roman Catholicism in the Eighteenth Century* (New York, 1936), 128.

86. "Not spoken" is written across this portion of the typescript.

87. Jenkins, "The Amenities of the School Adjustment," *CW*, 54 (January, 1892), 584; *AER*, 17 (July 1897), 65.

88. Ahern, *Catholic University*, 63–68; Zwierlein, *McQuaid*, 3:396.

89. Hogan, *Conaty*, 108–109.

90. Barrows, ed., *Parliament of Religions*, 1:18.

91. Moynihan, *Ireland*, 39–44; Reily, *Passing Events*, 2:842, 858; Houtin, *Américanisme*, 114–115.

92. This attitude is more fully explored in chapter 9.

93. *Neely's History of the Parliament of Religions and Religious Congresses at the World's Columbian Exposition* (Chicago, 1894), 905–913.

94. According to Barrows' account, only Bishop Keane varied from this rule. Reading a paper written by Charles Donnelly of Boston, dealing with charity work, he felt it desirable to add several points in order to emphasize the area of agreement with an address made earlier by Francis Peabody. Barrows, ed., *Parliament of Religions*, 2:1024–1036.

95. A French critic alleged that the only Lord's Prayer used was the Protestant version, thus implying indifferentism to the liberal Catholic participants. Charles Maignen, *Le Père Hecker, est-il un saint?* (Rome, 1898), 220–221; compare Ellis, *Gibbons,* 2:13–22.

96. Barrows, ed., *Parliament of Religions,* 1:127–128.

97. Zwierlein, *McQuaid,* 3:453.

98. The quotation is from an attack by Bishop John Fitzpatrick on the appearance of Father Mathew, the famous temperance advocate, with Protestant clergy and state officials; Lord *et al., Boston,* 2:645.

99. Barrows, ed., *Parliament of Religions,* 1:94.

100. *Ibid.,* 1:487; the paper was read by Keane, and was entitled "The Needs of Humanity Supplied by the Catholic Religion," an apologetic theme highly favored by the liberals and eminently orthodox as Gibbons used it. A non-Catholic journal, however, construed the Cardinal to be saying that he was "more drawn to the Catholic Church by her system of organized benevolence than by her unity of faith, her sublime morals, or world-wide catholicity, or apostolical succession." Quoted and rebutted in Ellis, *Gibbons,* 2:21.

101. Barrows, ed., *Parliament of Religions,* 2:1266.

102. *Ibid.,* 2:1573.

103. "Editorial Notes," *CW,* 58 (October 1893), 142.

104. Victor Charbonnel, *Congrès universel des religions en 1900* (Paris, 1897), 171–172.

105. Barry, *German Americans,* 221n.

106. *Columbian Congress,* 1:75.

107. "The Diocesan Clergy and Missions to Non-Catholics," *AER,* 11 (September 1894), 233.

108. "The Church and Temperance," *CW,* 51 (September 1890), 823; Moynihan, *Ireland,* 19; Corrigan, *What the Church Needs,* 41.

109. Retranslated from Tardivel, *Situation,* 239–240.

110. Barry, *German Americans,* 243.

Chapter IV

Catholicism and a Non-Catholic State

1. The classic statement is Leo XIII's encyclical *Immortale Dei,* reprinted in Husslein, *Social Wellsprings,* 63–90.

2. S. B. A. Harper, "The Relations of the Church and the Constitution of the United States," *ACQR,* 2 (October 1877), 700.

3. "The Church and the State. The Two 'Cities' in the Present Age," *ACQR,* 2 (July 1877), 430–431, Pallen, *Liberalism,* 37–38.

4. Quoted in Delassus, *Américanisme,* 341–342.

5. J. T. Ellis, "Church and State: an American Catholic Tradition," *Harpers,* 207 (November 1953), 63–67.

6. *Opportunity*, 88–89; Gibbons, *Faith of Our Fathers*, 247; T. H. Malone, "Catholic Citizens and Constitutional Rights," *NAR*, 171 (October 1900), 599; Francis Howard, "The Church and Social Reform," *CW*, 63 (June 1896), 290–291.

7. "The Lesson of 'The White City,'" *CW*, 60 (October 1894), 77.

8. Quoted in Cronin, *Ryan*, 55.

9. E. B. Brady, "Church and State," *CW*, 54 (December 1891), 391; Lucian Johnston, "Americanism vs. Ultramontanism," *CW*, 59 (September 1894), 736; Gibbons, *Faith of Our Fathers*, 246; Ellis, *Gibbons*, 2:343n.

10. *Religious Mission*, 28–29.

11. "Church, State, and School," *CW*, 50 (January 1890), 531.

12. Malone, *McGlynn*, 92.

13. Pages 61, 99; M. J. H., "Church and State," *ACQR*, 21 (January 1896), 104–105.

14. Cronin, *Ryan*, 53; Reily, *Passing Events*, 2:213; Ireland, *Church and Modern Society*, 1:82; Tracy, "Church, State, and School," *CW*, 50 (January 1890), 531.

15. Protestant fears are reported in F. R. Coudert, "The American Protective Association," *Forum*, 17 (July 1894), 520–523, and in Lucian Johnston, "Americanism," *CW*, 59 (September 1894), 740. Keane's apologia is in "The Encyclical *Sapientiae Christianae*," *ACQR*, 15 (April 1890), 301–311; see also Keane, "A Chat about the Catholic University," *CW*, 48 (November 1888), 224.

16. "Church and State," *CW*, 54 (December 1891), 396.

17. "Freedom of Worship in Practice," *CW*, 41 (June 1885), 371.

18. Reily, *Passing Events*, 2:219. Gibbons' attitude contrasted sharply with that of conservatives like Shea who argued that Baltimore was justified in making such a regulation only if the concession was absolutely necessary for an English charter. "The Catholic Democracy of America," *Edinburgh Review*, 171 (April 1890), 476–481.

19. *Columbian Congress*, 1:31.

20. *Faith of Our Fathers*, 248; Reily, *Passing Events*, 1:384, 2:219; R. H. Clarke, "Freedom of Worship in Practice," *CW*, 41 (July 1885), 479–493.

21. Review of John Rickaby, *Moral Philosophy* (New York, 1888), *CW*, 49 (April 1889), 138.

22. See chapter 6.

23. "The Troubles of a Catholic Democracy," *Contemporary Review*, 76 (July 1899), 81.

24. "Converts — Their Influence and Work in this Country," *ACQR*, 8 (July 1883), 513; "The Mission of Leo XIII," *CW*, 48 (October 1886), 10.

25. Malone, *McGlynn*, 80; Clarke, "George Washington," *ACQR*, 21 (April 1896), 250–269; Clarke, "George Washington in his Relations with Catholics," *ACQR*, 21 (July 1896), 636–656.

26. Cronin, *Ryan*, 56–57; M. F. Egan, ed., *Onward and Upward: a yearbook . . . of discourses of Archbishop Keane* (Baltimore, 1902), 254.

27. J. B. Bishop, *Charles Joseph Bonaparte, His Life and Services* (New York, 1922), 87; Review of J. G. Shea, *Life and Times of John Carroll* (New York, 1888), *CW*, 48 (January 1889), 568; M. J. H. "Church and State," *ACQR*, 21 (January 1896), 101; Jenkins, *Foreign Societies*, 113.

28. Reily, *Passing Events*; Review of John Fiske, *The Critical Period of American History* (Boston, 1889), *CW*, 49 (May 1889), 280; Satolli, *Loyalty*, 218; see C. H. Metzger, "Some Catholic Tories in the American Revolution," *CHR*, 25 (October 1949), 276–300, and (January 1950), 408–427.

29. *Situation*, 135: Pallen, *Liberalism*, 37–38.

30. Review of Shea, *Carroll*, *CW*, 48 (January 1889), 568

31. The question is extensively discussed in Félix Klein, *La Séparation aux Etats-Unis* (Paris, 1908), and by a non-Catholic lawyer, I. A. Cornelison, *The Relation of Religion to Civil Government in the United States of America* (New York, 1895). See also Auguste Carlier, *La République américaine* (Paris, 1890), especially 3:505ff.

32. C. H. Robinson, "Religion in American Law," *CW*, 37 (May 1883), 155.

33. R. F. McNamara, "Trusteeism in the Atlantic States, 1785–1863," *CHR*, 30 (July 1944), 135–154. Ireland is quoted in Klein, *La Séparation*, 94.

34. *Ibid.*, 33–36; for diverse interpretations of the justification of this aid, see Cornelison, *Relation*, 292–329, C. L. Brace, *The Dangerous Classes of New York* (New York, 1872), 378, and John Farley, "Why Church Property Should Not be Taxed," *Forum*, 17 (June 1894), 434–442.

35. "Shall We Adopt a Sixteenth Amendment." *RR*, 5 (March 1892), 160–162.

36. Farley, "Church Property," *Forum*, 17 (June, 1894), 434–442.

37. Lucien Vigneron, *De Montréal à Washington* (Paris, 1887), 193; Gibbons, "The Necessity of Religion for Society," *ACQR*, 9 (October 1884), 681.

38. Robinson, "Religion in American Law," *CW*, 37 (May 1883), 149.

39. *Church and the Age*, 113.

40. Gibbons, "Necessity of Religion," *ACQR*, 9 (October 1884), 681, 690–693; Brother Azarias, "Church and State," *ACQR*, 16 (January 1891), 39; Reily, *Passing Events*, 2:29–30; Malone, *Memorial*, 35; Satolli, *Loyalty*, 59; Cornelison, *Relation*, 164; A. P. Stokes, *Church and State in the United States* (New York, 1950), 3:571.

41. Reily, *Passing Events*, 2:29.

42. Brady, "Church and State," *CW*, 54 (December 1891), 391–392.

43. Ireland's translation of Satolli's conclusion to a speech to the Columbian Congress; Satolli, *Loyalty*, 150.

44. Zwierlein, *McQuaid*, 1:211.

45. *Facing the Twentieth Century*, 183, 215.

46. Robinson, "Religion in American Law," *CW*, 37 (May 1883), 149.

47. "Leo XIII and the Safeguards of Republics," *AER*, 8 (January 1893), 1–14.

48. Satolli, *Loyalty*, 92–93.

49. Jacques Maritain, *The Things That Are Not Caesar's*, J. F. Scanlan, trans. (New York, 1931), 193–194.

50. *Ibid.*, xv; J. C. Murray, "Contemporary Orientations of Catholic Thought on Church and State in the Light of History," *TS*, 10 (June 1949), 218–219.

51. May, *Protestant Churches*, 43.

52. "The Roman Catholic Church and the School Fund," *NAR*, 158 (January 1894), 37.

53. "Compulsory Education," *AER*, 6 (April 1892), 294.

54. King, *Facing the Twentieth Century*, 247; Stauffer, "Anti-Catholicism," 40–55, 219; see the Henry George incident, chapter 6.

55. "Real Danger from the Roman Catholic Church," *LD*, 12 (December 21, 1895), 231; J. T. Smith, "Fair Play for Catholic Christians," *RR*, 11 (June 1895), 696–697.

56. "The Catholic Church," *NAR*, 158 (January 1894), 39.

57. Myers, *History of Bigotry*, 221–222.

58. Stokes, *Church and State*, 3:392–393.

59. K. F. Conway and M. W. Cameron, *Charles Francis Donnelly: A Memoir* (New York, 1909); Hewit, "Catholic and American Ethics," *CW*, 50 (March 1890), 804–807.

60. "A New Definition of Papal Authority," *LD*, 20 (January 13, 1900), 54–55.

61. "The Church and the Republic," *NAR*, 189 (March 1909), 320–336; Gibbons, *Faith of Our Fathers*, 123; Hewit, "The Temporal Sovereignty of the Pope," *CW*, 52 (December 1890), 340; for Ireland, see excerpt in B. L. Masse, ed., *The Catholic Mind through Fifty Years* (New York, 1952), 147.

62. "Leo XIII and the Safeguards of Republics," *AER*, 8 (January 1893), 4.

63. *Church and Modern Society*, 1:214.

64. Spalding, *Lectures*, 114–116; Reily, *Passing Events*, 2:814; O'Gorman, *Catholic Church*, 273; Keane, "Loyalty to Rome and Country," *ACQR*, 15 (July 1890), 509–522; J. V. Tracy, "Church, State, and School," *CW*, 50 (January 1890), 530; E. B. Brady, "Church and State," *CW*, 54 (December 1891), 393.

65. *Letter of Bellamy Storer to the President and Members of his Cabinet* (Cincinnati, 1906), 9.

66. Review of Reuben Parsons, *Studies in Church History*, vol. 4, *CW*, 66 (February 1898), 702; Tracy, "Church, State, and School," *CW*, 50 (January 1890), 533; Brady, "Church and State," *CW*, 54 (December 1891), 394; Spalding, *Lectures*, 116.

67. Maritain, *The Things That Are Not Caesar's*, 124.

68. Ireland, *Church and Modern Society*, 1:vii, 2:201.

69. "The Church and Modern Society," *CW*, 65 (May 1897), 216–217.

70. *Nova Collectio*, 51:545.

71. Benedetto Croce, *A History of Italy, 1871–1915*, trans. C. M. Ady (Oxford, 1929), 32–33, 176–177.

72. Husslein, *Social Wellsprings*, 71.

73. Croce, *Italy*, 176–177; J. A. R. Marriott, *The Makers of Modern Italy* (Oxford, 1931), 141; Parsons, *Studies*, 6:404; "The Roman Question — Does It Concern Us?" *AER*, 1 (November and December 1889), 442–443; W. J. D. Croke, "The Situation in Rome," *ACQR*, 22 (April 1897), 355–364.

74. S. M. Brandi, "When Is the Pope Infallible?" *NAR*, 155 (November 1892), 655–656; Brandi, "The Policy of Leo XIII," *Contemporary Review*, 63 (May 1893), 663–681; *Catholic Standard and Times* of Philadelphia, December 28, 1895, 4; see the protests of Curci, *Dissentiment*, 98.

75. M. O. Kolbeck, *American Opinion on the Kulturkampf* (Washington, 1942), 29.

76. Rothensteiner, *St. Louis*, 2:316; Ellis, *Formative Years*, 329n.

77. George Zurcher, *The Apple of Discord; or Temporal Power in the Catholic Church* (Buffalo, 1905), 32.

78. "The Roman Question," *AER*, 1 (November and December 1889), 444; see also Smith, *Catholic Church in New York*, 2:385.

79. For an early example, see Ellis, *Gibbons*, 2:345n.

80. "Theological Minimizing and its Latest Defender," *AER*, 4 (February 1891), 122–126; Schroeder, "American Catholics and the Temporal Power," *ACQR*, 17 (January 1892), 72–97.

81. S. M. Brandi, "When Is the Pope Infallible?" *NAR*, 155 (November 1892), 655–656; "The Pope and the Bible," *Contemporary Review*, 63 (April 1893), 458; Charles Coupé, "The Temporal Power," *ACQR*, 26 (October 1901), 797–798.

82. Francis Chatard, "The Temporal Power of the Pope," *CW*, 50 (November 1889), 213–217; O'Connor, "The Roman Question," *ACQR*, 11 (April 1886), 201; Brann, "Sacerdotal Jubilee of Leo XIII," *ACQR*, 13 (January 1888), 48; Preston, "American Catholicity," *ACQR*, 16 (April 1891), 405.

83. Hecker, "The Liberty and Independence of the Pope," *CW*, 35 (April 1882), 1–10; Hecker, "Leo XIII," *CW*, 46 (December 1887), 297–298; Hecker, *The Church and the Age*, 143; Keane, *Providential Mission*, 31–32.

84. "State Socialism," *CW*, 46 (February 1888), 692–693; Reily, *Passing Events*, 1:306.

85. A footnote by Augustine Hewit to J. J. O'Shea, "Old Rome and Young Italy," *CW*, 62 (October 1895), 113.

86. Beck, ed., *The English Catholics*, 260; Purcell, *Manning*, 2:612ff.; E. M. de Vogüé, "Pope Leo XIII," *Forum*, 22 (January 1897), 518; W. J. D. Croke, "The Situation in Rome," *ACQR*, 22 (April 1897), 356–357.

87. Ellis, *Formative Years*, 334n.

88. Ellis, *Gibbons*, 2:336–341; Reily, *Passing Events*, 1:311–313; Eduardo Soderini, *Leo XIII, Italy and France*, trans. B. B. Carter (London, 1935), 84.

89. *Proceedings of the Catholic Congress*, 18–25; Brophy, *Social Thought*, 28–32; Schroeder, "The Catholic German Congress at Pittsburgh," *CW*, 52 (November 1890), 270; M. P. Villamil, "The First Catholic Congress of Spain," *CW*, 50 (October 1889), 31–38 and (November 1889), 218–227.

90. Pahorezki, *Onahan*, 112n; Ellis, *Gibbons*, 2:342-343; *Proceedings of the Catholic Congress*, 4.

91. Pahorezki, *Onahan*, 125.

92. Ellis, *Gibbons*, 2:344.

93. "Our Recent American Catholic Congress, and its Significance," *ACQR*, 15 (January 1890), 158-159.

94. "The Temporal Sovereignty of the Pope," *CW*, 52 (December 1890), 340-346; "American Catholics and the Roman Question," *CW*, 55 (June 1892), 425-436.

95. J. J. O'Shea, "Old Rome and Young Italy," *CW*, 62 (October 1895), 113.

Chapter V

The Expectations of American Democracy

1. On Elliott, see chapter 3; on the other events, see later in this chapter. Moynihan, *Ireland*, 63; Barry, *German Americans*, 102, 150n., 305-306; Reily, *Passing Events*, 1:371-372; Bargy, *La Réligion*; D. F. Reilly, *The School Controversy (1891-1893)* (Washington, 1943), 256; Elliott, "Our Centenary: A Glance into the Future," *CW*, 50 (November 1889), 246.

2. Barry, *German Americans*, 102; A. M. Schlesinger, *The Rise of the City, 1878-1898* (New York, 1933), 410; Handlin, *The Uprooted*.

3. "Irish Agitation in America," *Forum*, 4 (December 1887), 400-401.

4. An exception was Spalding, who expressed his cultural pluralist position most clearly in his introduction to Abbelen, *Friess*, 16.

5. "The Church and Modern Society," *CW*, 65 (May 1897), 218; L. R. Hubbard, "Nationality and Religion," *CW*, 50 (December 1889), 396-400; see Charles Bonaparte's discussion of the operation of the "gastric juices" in *Catholic Standard and Times*, December 28, 1895, 3; Higham, *Strangers in the Land*, 118.

6. *Church and Modern Society*, 1:91, 206-207; Barry, *German Americans*, 119.

7. Reily, *Passing Events*, 2:916; Smith, *Training*, 264; Klein, *In the Land*, 35; Ireland, *Church and Modern Society*, 2:226. Compare Rothensteiner, *St. Louis*, 2:573; Barry, *German Americans*, 173.

8. *Ibid.*, 102, 296.

9. Ellis, *Gibbons*, 1:364n.; Moynihan, *Ireland*, 62-63. McQuaid thought the liberal leaders secretly in favor of everything Irish; Zwierlein, *McQuaid*, 2:462.

10. The best source is Barry, *German Americans*. J. J. Meng has written two able articles, "Cahenslyism: the First Stage, 1883-1891," *CHR*, 31 (January 1946), 389-413, and "Cahenslyism: the Second Chapter," *CHR*, 32 (October 1946), 302-340. Ellis, Gibbons, 1:331-388, places the struggle in the

context of difficulties with other nationalities. Moynihan, *Ireland*, 54–78, is uncritically hostile to the Germans.

11. Zwierlein, *McQuaid*, 3:41; Barry, *German Americans*, 212–213; Rothensteiner, *St. Louis*, 2:573.

12. *Question of Nationality*, 36–37.

13. Barry, *German Americans*, 78.

14. Roemer, *Ludwig-missionsverein*, 95; Barry, *German Americans*, 24, 42, 96, 131n.; Schroeder, "The Catholic German Congress at Pittsburgh," *CW*, 52 (November 1890), 268.

15. J. T. Smith, *Training*, 350; Barry, *German Americans*, 78.

16. *Ibid.*, 151n.

17. Rothensteiner, *St. Louis*, 2:225.

18. Brophy, *Social Thought*, 8ff.; Barry, *German Americans*, 27n.

19. Schroeder, "The Catholic German Congress," *CW*, 52 (November 1890), 266; Barry, *German Americans*, 98.

20. *Ibid.*, 113–114; Tardivel, *Situation*, 222–223.

21. Barry, *German Americans*, 124.

22. *Ibid.*, 170n.

23. *Ibid.*, 214n. for liberal Catholic criticism of the same meeting, see *Catholic Standard and Times* of Philadelphia, December 3, 1892, 5.

24. H. A. Brann, "Mr. Cahensly and the Church in the United States," *CW*, 54 (January 1892), 568–581.

25. Barry, *German Americans*, 140; Rothensteiner, *St. Louis*, 2:574.

26. Barry, *German Americans*, 139.

27. " 'Cahenslyism' *versus* Americanism," *RR*, 6 (August, 1892), 47; Moynihan, *Ireland*, 72.

28. *Ibid.*, 202–203.

29. Barry, *German Americans*, 142.

30. Ellis, *Gibbons*, 1:371–374.

31. *Ibid.*, 376–378; compare Barry, *German Americans*, 169n.

32. *Catholic Standard and Times* of Philadelphia, December 28, 1895, 1–3.

33. James Conway, *The State Last: A Study of Dr. Bouquillon's Pamphlet*, 2nd revised edition (New York, 1892), 103; Quigley, ed., *Compulsory Education*, 192.

34. *The Parent First: An Answer to Dr. Bouquillon's query, 'Education: to whom does it belong?'* (New York, 1891), 5–6, 18; Conway, *State Last*, 20; Quigley, ed., *Compulsory Education*, 185. The Jesuits opposed intervention by every state in the world; Nitti, *Catholic Socialism*, 325.

35. *Public School Education*, 182.

36. *Poison Drops*, 46.

37. Quigley, ed., *Compulsory Education*, 135; C. H. Robinson, "Religion in American Law," *CW*, 37 (May, 1883), 156.

38. Montgomery, *Poison Drops*, 89; Conway, *State Last*, 7.

39. E. D. Mead, *Catholic Church*, 63–66.

40. *State Last*, 14, 78.

41. For example, Mueller, *Public School Education*, 182.

42. Quigley, ed., *Compulsory Education*, 253–254, 342; "State Control and Relative Rights in the School," *AER*, 6 (April 1892), 301.

43. "Religious Teaching in Schools," *Forum*, 8 (December 1889), 390; Zwierlein, *McQuaid*, 2:137; Review of E. F. Dunne, *Compulsory Education* (St. Louis, 1891), *ACQR*, 17 (January 1892), 220.

44. *The Public School Question* (Boston, 1876), 28; "Religion in Schools," *NAR*, 132 (April 1881), 342–344; Zwierlein, *McQuaid*, 2:136.

45. Quigley, ed., *Compulsory Education*, 208, 185.

46. *Poison Drops*, 46; Quigley, ed., *Compulsory Education*, 211.

47. Hecker, "What Does the Public-School Question Mean?" *CW*, 34 (October 1881), 84.

48. *Education: to whom does it belong?* (Baltimore, 1891), 12; Reilly, *School Controversy*, 119n. Earlier versions of the logic are found in "The American Side of the School Question," *CW*, 30 (January 1880), 515–519, and in "The State and Religious Education," *CW*, 45 (September 1887), 849–851.

49. Holaind, *Parent First*, 11; J. G. Shea, "Federal Schemes to Aid Common Schools in the Southern States," *ACQR*, 13 (April 1888), 355; Messmer, "Compulsory Education," *AER*, 6 (April 1892), 284; Quigley, ed., *Compulsory Education*, 208, 423, 527–529; Conway, "The Rights and Duties of Family and State in Regard to Education," *ACQR*, 9 (January 1884), 125.

50. "Dr. Bouquillon on the School Question," *AER*, 6 (February 1892), 99; H. J. Heuser, Review of *Education . . . A Rejoinder to the Civiltà Cattolica* (Baltimore, 1892), *AER*, 6 (March 1892), 238; James Corcoran, "Pius IX and his Pontificate," *ACQR*, 3 (April 1878), 347.

51. Mueller, *Public School Education*, 151; Conway, *State Last*, 20, 66; Holaind, *Parent First*, 18–19; Quigley, ed., *Compulsory Education*, 81.

52. Quigley, ed., *Compulsory Education*, 81.

53. S. B. A. Harper, "The Relations of the Church and the Constitution of the United States," *ACQR*, 2 (October 1877), 61; Holaind, *Parent First*, 19.

54. P. Bayma, "The Liberalistic View of the Public School Question," *ACQR*, 2 (April 1877), 248; J. G. Shea, "The Proposed American Catholic University," *ACQR*, 10 (April 1885), 322; Review of Dunne, *Compulsory Education*, *ACQR*, 17 (January 1892), 220; Messmer, "The Right of Instruction," *AER*, 6 (February 1892), 114; H. J. Heuser, "State Control and Relative Rights in the School," *AER*, 6 (April 1892), 302; Montgomery, *Poison Drops*, 74; Holaind, *Parent First*, 18; Mueller, *Public School Education*, 151; Conway, *State Last*, 64; Quigley, ed., *Compulsory Education*, 407.

55. "Our Recent American Catholic Congress," *ACQR*, 15 (January 1890), 164.

56. Holaind, *Parent First*, 20; Quigley, ed., *Compulsory Education*, 407, 414; Messmer, "The Right of Instruction," AER, 6 (February 1892), 114.

57. "The Cincinnati Pastoral and its Critics," *ACQR*, 7 (April 1882), 372; M.J.H., "Church and State," *ACQR*, 21 (January 1897), 102. For conservative

Catholic dissent, see Robinson, "Religion in American Law," *CW*, 37 (May 1883), 158. For contemporary thought, see R. G. McCloskey, *American Conservatism in the Age of Enterprise* (Cambridge, 1951), and B. R. Twiss, *Lawyers and the Constitution* (Princeton, 1942).

58. Quigley, ed., *Compulsory Education*, 326.

59. *Ibid.*, 35, 70–74.

60. M. J. H., "Church and State," *ACQR*, 21 (January 1897), 102.

61. *CW*, 69 (July 1899), 566.

62. *Education: to whom does it belong? A rejoinder to critics* (Baltimore, 1892), 39.

63. Most political theory was couched in these terms; see, for example, Holaind, *Parent First*, 20.

64. S. B. A. Harper, "Church and the Constitution," *ACQR*, 2 (October 1877), 700.

65. See the Catholic protest against this attitude in W. S. Kress, *Questions of Socialists and Their Answers* (Cleveland, 1905).

66. "The Cincinnati Pastoral and its Critics," *ACQR*, 7 (April 1882), 371–4.

67. J. F. Callaghan, "The Cincinnati Pastoral and Its Critics," *CW*, 35 (August 1882), 639–659.

68. *Church and the Age*, 68, 82–83; Walter Elliott, "The Revolutionary Dogma," *CW*, 50 (October 1889), 134.

69. H. J. Desmond, *The Church and the Law* (Chicago, 1898), 11–12; Malone, *McGlynn*, 80.

70. "Baptized Democracy," *CW*, 43 (September 1886), 721.

71. *Church and the Age*, 68–69; Elliott, *Hecker*, 293; Ellis, *Formative Years*, 357; Hecker, "The Mission of Leo XIII," *CW*, 48 (October 1888), 4–5; Keane, "The Yorktown Centennial Celebration," *CW*, 34 (November 1881), 281. See chapter 9 for the liberals' conception of the highest religious life.

72. Shea, "The Lesson of President Garfield's Assassination," *ACQR*, 6 (October 1881), 683–690; Cronin, *Ryan*, 60.

73. *Foreign Societies*, 97; Reily, *Passing Events*, 2:11; Jenkins, "American Christian State Schools," *CW*, 52 (February 1891), 652–653.

74. In *Immortale Dei*, quoted in Husslein, *Social Wellsprings*, 88.

75. Gibbons, "Patriotism and Politics," *NAR*, 154 (April 1892), 385–390; Stokes, *Church and State*, 2:362; "An Army Without Leaders," *CW*, 45 (July 1887), 567. Spalding took a much more pessimistic view of the possibility of reforming political life; "The Basis of Popular Government," *NAR*, 139 (September 1884), 203; "Is Our Social Life Threatened?" *Forum*, 5 (March 1888), 25–26.

76. "An Army Without Leaders," *CW*, 45 (July 1887), 567.

77. "The Roman Catholic Church and the School Fund," *NAR*, 158 (January 1894), 35–38; Josiah Strong, *Our Country* (New York, 1885), 142; L. W. Reilly, "The Weak Points of the Catholic Press," *AER*, 10 (February 1894), 117–125.

78. McFaul, "Catholics and American Citizenship," *NAR*, 171 (September 1900), 320–332; Ellis, *Gibbons*, 2:375–378; Moynihan, *Ireland*, 285–286.

79. Malone, "Catholic Citizens and Constitutional Rights," *NAR*, 171 (October 1900), 594–599.

80. Pahorezki, *Onahan*, 173–190.

81. L. W. Reilly, "The Weak Points of the Catholic Press," *AER*, 10 (February 1894), 117–125; J. T. Smith, "Partisan Politics in the Catholic Press," *AER*, 10 (May 1894), 343–349; F. R. Coudert, "The American Protective Association," *Forum*, 17 (July 1894), 520–523; Reily, *Passing Events*, 1:xiv–xv.

82. Reily, *Passing Events*, 1:148.

83. Bell, McGlynn, 161.

84. Reily, *Passing Events*, 1:148; King, *Facing the Twentieth Century*, 433. For Paulist desire not to be associated with bossism, see Walton Bean, *Boss Ruef's San Francisco* (Berkeley, California, 1952), 289–290.

85. Spalding, *Martin Spalding*, 188–189; de Meaux, *Eglise catholique*, 147; Zwierlein, *McQuaid*, 3:204.

86. "Patriotism and Politics," *NAR*, 154 (April 1892), 385; "The Preacher and His Province," *NAR*, 160 (May 1895), 522; *Ambassador of Christ*, 523.

87. Ellis, *Gibbons*, 2:526.

88. Matthew Josephson, *The President-Makers* (New York, 1940), 94.

89. Malone, *Memorial*, 53; Zwierlein, *McQuaid*, 3:204–205: Moynihan, *Ireland*, 262.

90. Malone, *Memorial*, 72.

91. Zwierlein, *McQuaid*, 3:208, 216–225.

92. *Quirinus*, "The Catholic Clergy in Politics," *AER*, 12 (January 1895), 44–50, and (March 1895), 218–226.

93. Ellis, *Gibbons*, 2:30.

94. Moynihan, *Ireland*, 263.

95. *Ibid.*, 282.

96. Reily, *Passing Events*, 1:xiii.

97. H. J. Sievers, "The Catholic Indian School Issue and the Presidential Election of 1892," *CHR*, 38 (June 1952), 129–155; Stauffer, "Anti-Catholicism," 311–314; Storer, *Letter*, 21; F. E. Gibson, *The Attitudes of the New York Irish toward State and National Affairs, 1848–1892* (New York, 1951), 310–315.

98. Desmond, *The A.P.A. Movement*, (Washington, 1912), 65.

99. *Ibid.*, 32–33

100. "The Coming Contest—Have the Catholics a Political Enemy," *CW*, 58 (February 1894), 706–708.

101. Moynihan, *Ireland*, 285.

102. Desmond, *A.P.A.*, 82–90; King, *Facing the Twentieth Century*, 265–266; Stauffer, "Anti-Catholicism," 411–412; H. F. Gosnell, *Boss Platt and His New York Machine* (Chicago, 1924), 67; "McKinley and the A.P.A.,"

LD, 13 (May 2, 1896), 8–9; "The APA and McKinley," *LD*, 13 (May 30, 1896), 130–131.

103. "Politics in the Pulpit," *LD*, 13 (August 22, 1896), 518–519 declares that Gibbons' favor of McKinley was well-known. Ellis, *Gibbons*, 2:522–523, denies that the Cardinal's political views were known to anyone. Storer, *Letter*, 22.

104. Moynihan, *Ireland*, 261; "Archbishop Ireland Opposes the Chicago Platform," *LD*, 13 (October 1896), 806–807.

105. Most of the Catholic press, however, supported Bryan; A. I. Abell, "The Catholic Church and the American Social Question," in Gurian and Fitzsimons, eds., *Catholic Church and World Affairs*, 383.

106. R. J. Purcell, "Justice Joseph McKenna," *RACHS*, 56 (September 1945), 177–222.

107. See chapter 10.

108. M. L. Storer, *In Memoriam Bellamy Storer* (privately printed, 1923).

Chapter VI

Perspectives on Social Change

1. Matthew Josephson, *The President-Makers*, 22; Josephson, *The Politicos, 1865–1896* (New York, 1938), 387; Daniel Aaron, *Men of Good Hope* (New York, 1951), 100. This spirit is diffused through contemporary studies like Josiah Strong, *Our Country* (New York, 1885); J. G. Brooks, *The Social Unrest* (New York, 1904), and J. B. Harrison, *Certain Dangerous Tendencies in American Life* (Boston, 1880). For Catholic recognition, see Satolli, *Loyalty*, 111, and Morgan Sheedy, *Social Problems* (Chicago, 1896), 69.

2. J. A. Ryan, *Social Doctrine in Action* (New York, 1941), 114.

3. *The Catholic Church and Socialism* (St. Louis, 1890).

4. "Catholic Societies," *ACQR*, 4 (April 1879), 218

5. "Socialism at the Present Day," *ACQR*, 5 (June 1880), 61; G. D. Wolff, "Socialistic Communism in the United States," *ACQR*, 3 (July 1878), 552–558; James O'Connor, "Socialism," *ACQR*, 8 (April 1883), 233–234.

6. Quoted in an able summary of this attitude in J. E. Roohan, "American Catholics and the Social Question, " unpublished Ph.D dissertation, Department of History, Yale University, 1952. See also Mann, *Yankee Reformers*, chapter 2; *Columbian Congress*, 1:49; Pallen, *Catholic Church and Socialism*, 47.

7. "Heartless, Headless, and Godless," *CW*, 46 (January 1888), 437.

8. Wolff, "Socialistic Communism," *ACQR*, 3 (July 1878), 533–536.

9. P. F. de Gournay, "Cause and Cure," *CW*, 43 (April 1886), 9–10.

10. Thébaud, "Socialism, considered in its Origins and First Manifestations," *ACQR*, 4 (July 1879), 432–437; Thébaud, "Socialism at the Present Day," *ACQR*, 5 (June 1880), 60–66; Review of Claudio Jannet, *Le Socialisme d'état et la reforme sociale*, *ACQR*, 14 (July 1889), 560–562.

11. Willibald Hackner, "Disturbances of the Social Equilibrium," *CW*, 46 (November 1887), 221.

12. *Means and Ends of Education*, 96; "Are We in Danger of Revolution?" *Forum*, 1 (July 1886), 405–415; "Is Our Social Life Threatened?" *Forum*, 5 (March 1888), 16–26.

13. Spalding, *Education and the Higher Life*, 184–185.

14. *Church and Modern Society*, 1:xx–xxi; 2:274. Edward McSweeny, "Social Problems," *CW*, 44 (February 1887), 586–587; T. J. Jenkins, "The Priest in his Relations to Church and Society," *AER*, 11 (October 1894), 289; Malone, *Memorial*, 64, 211; O'Gorman, *Catholic Church*, 399; A. I. Abell, "Origins of Catholic Social Reform in the United States: Ideological Aspects," *Review of Politics*, 11 (July 1949), 302. On attitudes toward state action, see chapter 5.

15. Some contemporary Catholics regard this as the dominant motive of the liberal reformers, underestimating, in my opinion, the genuine desire to bring about, by human action, a better earthly life. See Abell, *ibid*, 307, and Roohan, "American Catholics and the Social Question."

16. Max Turmann, *Le Développement du catholicisme social, depuis l'encyclique "Rerum Novarum,"* 2nd ed. (Paris, 1909), 95–100.

17. Moynihan, *Ireland*, 225–226; on other receptions to the encyclical, see later.

18. *Church and Modern Science*, 1:94, 2:245; d'Hablonville, *Grandes figures*, 253–255; " 'The Poor You Have Always With You,' " *CW*, 47 (July 1888), 567.

19. Quoted in Zwierlein, *McQuaid*, 2:451; Edward McSweeny, "State Socialism," *CW*, 46 (February 1888), 690–694.

20. "Wealth and its Obligations," *NAR*, 152 (April 1891), 385–394; *Our Christian Heritage*, 486ff; "Some Defects in our Political and Social Institutions," *NAR*, 145 (October 1887), 345–354.

21. *Ambassador of Christ*, x; H. J. Browne, *The Catholic Church and the Knights of Labor* (Washington, 1949), 314–315.

22. Compare the conclusions of Roohan that the actions of Gibbons and Ireland "belied their reputations as social liberals;" American Catholics and the Social Question." See also Browne, *Knights of Labor*, 356, and Abell, "Origins of Catholic Social Reform," *Review of Politics*, 11 (July 1949), 294–309.

23. *Church and Modern Society*, 2:357.

24. Moynihan, *Ireland*, 36.

25. *Religion and Art*, 175; *Opportunity*, 219–222; *Socialism and Labor*, 30, 32, 97, 173–174, 180–182.

26. Senate Document 3259, 58th Congress, 2nd Session, 33–40.

27. Roohan, "American Catholics and the Social Question," 412; A. G. Schroll, *The Social Thought of John Lancaster Spalding* (Washington, 1944).

28. "The Lesson of 'The White City,' " *CW*, 59 (September 1894), 770–779, and 60 (October, 1894), 73–82.

29. "The Children at Work," *CW*, 43 (August 1886), 619–625; "The Eight-Hour Law," *CW*, 44 (December 1886), 397–406; "Kitchens and Wages," *CW*, 44 (March 1887), 780; "The Homes of the Poor," *CW*, 45 (July 1887), 509–517.

30. *Social Problems*, 48–54; "The Encyclical and American Iron-Workers and Coal-Miners," *CW*, 53 (September 1891), 858–861. For a biographical sketch of Sheedy, see *CW*, 65 (May 1897), 280–281.

31. "The White-Slave Trade," *CW*, 59 (June 1894), 418; "The Evolution of a Great City," *CW*, 63 (August 1896), 694; George McDermot, "The Ann Arbor Strike and the Law of Hiring," *CW*, 58 (February 1894), 670–684.

32. "The Children at Work," *CW*, 43 (August 1886), 624.

33. A. I. Abell, "The Reception of Leo XIII's Labor Encyclical in America, 1891–1919," *Review of Politics*, 7 (October 1945), 471; Edward Priestley, "The Wage-Earner and his Recreation," *CW*, 47 (July 1888), 513; C. A. Oliver, "Moral Theology and Monopolies," *CW*, 48 (March 1889), 727.

34. J. S. Lowell, "The True Aim of Charity Organization Societies," *Forum*, 21 (June 1896), 494; Robert Woods, ed., *The City Wilderness* (Boston, 1898), 248–251.

35. *Mélanges*, 1:146.

36. Review of S. H. Gurten, *A Handbook of Charity Organization* (Buffalo, 1882), *ACQR*, 7 (April 1882), 380; H. M. Beadle, "Charity as it Was and Is," *CW*, 69 (April 1889), 81–87.

37. O'Grady, *Catholic Charities*, 111, 238–239; A. de G., "The Sociological Aspect of Christian Charity," *ACQR*, 9 (April 1884), 358–365; M. A. Selby, "A Word About Non-Sectarian Charities," *AER*, 7 (December 1892), 438; Gibbons, "Wealth and its Obligations," *NAR*, 152 (April 1891), 392.

38. The phrase is John Boyle O'Reilly's, quoted in Handlin, *Boston's Immigrants*, 165; Pahorezki, *Onahan*, 207; *Proceedings of the National Conference of the Society of St. Vincent de Paul* (Boston, 1911).

39. P. A. Baart, "How Shall We Support Our Orphans?" *CW*, 44 (February 1887), 649.

40. M. A. Selby, "Non-Sectarian Charities," *AER*, 7 (December 1892), 438–439.

41. "The Encyclical 'Rerum Novarum,'" *ACQR*, 16 (July 1891), 598–599; John Conway, "America's Workmen," *CW*, 56 (January 1893), 496.

42. Malone, *McGlynn*, 95; Bell, *McGlynn*, 103; Joseph McSorley, "The Christian Idea of Justice and Equality," *CUB*, 4 (January 1898), 113–114.

43. *Education and the Higher Life*, 77–78, 179; *Religious Mission*, 211; Moynihan, *Ireland*, 36.

44. *Church and Modern Society*, 1:xi–xii; P. F. McSweeny, "The Church and the Classes," *CW*, 47 (July 1888), 480; *Columbian Congress*, 1:74.

45. Egan, ed., *Onward and Upward*, 217.

46. *Columbian Congress*, 1:129–130.

47. "The Columbian Reading Union," *CW*, 49 (August 1889), 701.

48. O'Grady, *Catholic Charities*, 265–266; Lord *et al.*, Boston, 3:532–533, 533n.

49. Moynihan, *Ireland*, 224; Ireland, *Church and Modern Society*, 1:345.

50. Reily, *Passing Events*, 2:230.

51. Ireland, *Church and Modern Society*, 1:94n–95n; Gilbert Simmons, "The Salvation Army and its Latest Project," *CW*, 52 (February 1891), 643–644. For conservative-liberal dissension in England over the Salvation Army, see Snead-Cox, *Vaughan*, 1:478–482. For French opinion, see Maignen, *Hecker*, 230–231.

52. *Columbian Congress*, 1:19, 75.

53. "Social Problems," *CW*, 44 (February 1887), 587. For a biographical sketch of McSweeny, a professor at Emmitsburg and a friend of McGlynn, see *CW*, 64 (January 1897), 561–562.

54. "Editorial Notes," *CW*, 62 (October 1895), 136.

55. *Socialism and Labor*, 15–16; *Religion and Art*, 77; *Things of the Mind*, 74.

56. See John Conway's reminder to Carnegie, "America's Workmen," *CW*, 56 (January 1893), 492–493.

57. "The White-Slave Trade," *CW*, 59 (June 1894), 423; J. T. Smith, "Workmen should not only act, but think," *CW*, 47 (September 1888), 843; Edward McSweeny, "Lacordaire on Property," *CW*, 45 (June 1887), 346; *Columbian Congress*, 1:52–55; Spalding, "Is Our Social Life Threatened?" *Forum*, 5 (March 1888), 23–24. For extremely tentative proposals for wage-fixing, see Edward Priestley, "The Wage-Earner and his Recreation," *CW*, 47 (July 1886), 512–513, and George McDermot, "The Ann Arbor Strike and the Law of Hiring," *CW*, 58 (February 1894), 670ff.

58. Chatard, "Catholic Societies," 4 (April 1879), 220; James O'Connor, "Capital and Labor," *ACQR*, 8 (July 1883), 485–488. For examples of liberal perplexity, see Sheedy, *Social Problems*, 48–49, and J. J. Keane, "'Rerum Novarum,'" *ACQR*, 16 (July 1891), 605–606.

59. *Ibid.*, 599–600; Ireland, *Church and Modern Society*, 1:411, 2:352–353.

60. Gibbons, *Our Christian Heritage*, 411; Leclerc, *Choses*, 256.

61. *Concilii Plenarii Baltimorensis II. . . Acta et Decreta* (Baltimore, 1868), 263; for Bayley's remark, see A. I. Abell, "Preparing for Social Action: 1880–1920," in L. R. Ward, ed., *The American Apostolate*, 12.

62. Browne, *Knights of Labor*, 44.

63. *Ibid.*, 56–59.

64. *Ibid.*, 100–114; Fergus MacDonald, *The Catholic Church and the Secret Societies in the United States* (New York, 1946), 117–119.

65. Browne, *Knights of Labor*, 155–156.

66. Ellis, *Gibbons*, 1:492.

67. Browne, *Knights of Labor*, 179.

68. Ellis, *Gibbons*, 1:502–503.

69. For the text, see Browne, *Knights of Labor*, 365–378; for a summary, see Ellis, *Gibbons*, 507–510.

70. Ireland had the same problems when appealing for toleration of the Faribault school system; see chapter 7.

71. For German-American opposition, see Barry, *German Americans*, 105.

72. Browne, *Knights of Labor*, 245.

73. "Intemperance an Enemy to Labor," *CW*, 45 (May 1887), 230.

74. Browne, *Knights of Labor*, 275.

75. Roohan, "American Catholics and the Social Question," 121.

76. Ellis, *Gibbons*, 1:520.

77. Roohan, "American Catholics and the Social Question," 400–430; Browne, *Knights of Labor*, 114, 155–156, 165–167, 274n; Spalding, *Socialism and Labor*, 169; Pahorezki, *Onahan*, 171; Ireland, *Church and Modern Society*, 1:205n, 2:328–329; Keane, "'Rerum Novarum,'" *ACQR*, 16 (July 1891), 608.

78. *Ibid.*, 595–609; Review of *Discours du comte Albert de Mun* (Paris, n.d.), *CW*, 47 (August 1888), 714; Sheedy, "The Encyclical and American Iron-Workers," *CW*, 53 (September 1891), 859–860; Joseph Schroeder, "Leo XIII and the Encyclical 'Longinqua,'" *ACQR*, 20 (April 1895), 386–387.

79. *Ibid.*, 384; Spalding, *Religion and Art*, 227–234; Spalding, *Socialism and Labor*, 59.

80. Walburg, *Question of Nationality*, 36; Browne, *Knights of Labor*, 202–203; A. I. Abell, "The Reception of Leo XIII's Labor Encyclical," *Review of Politics*, 7 (October 1945), 468; T. S. Preston, "Socialism and the Catholic Church," *Forum*, 5 (April 1888), 216–220.

81. *Socialism and Labor*, 6; *Religion and Art*, 179–181; Barrows, ed., *Parliament of Religions*, 2:1036; Sheedy, *Social Problems*, 88; Gibbons, "Wealth and its Obligations," *NAR*, 152 (April 1891), 394; "Catholics and Socialism in Europe," *CW*, 52 (November 1890), 273.

82. Spalding, *Religion and Art*, 186; *Socialism and Labor*, 21; Gibbons, *Ambassador of Christ*, 263; C. M. O'Keefe, "Florey Estrada and his Land Theory," *CW*, 45 (April 1887), 72.

83. *Ibid.*, 63–72; Review of George, *The Irish Land Question* (Newark, 1881), *CW*, 33 (May 1881), 286–287; H. A. Brann, "Henry George and his Land Theories," *CW*, 44 (March 1887), 810–828; J. T. Smith, "Where Henry George Stumbled," *CW*, 45 (April 1887), 116–123; Edward McSweeney, "Lacordaire on Property," *CW*, 45 (June 1887), 338–347; J. A. Cain, "The Common and Particular Ownership of Property," *CW*, 45 (July 1887), 433–443; Cain, "Individualism and Exclusive Ownership," *ACQR*, 13 (January 1888), 82–95.

84. J. de Concilio, "The Right of Individual Ownership—Does It Spring from the Natural or the Human Law?" *ACQR*, 13 (April 1888), 270–303.

85. Review of R. I. Holaind, *Ownership and Natural Right* (Baltimore, 1887), *CW*, 46 (December 1887), 429–430; "The State and the Land," *CW*,

46 (October 1887), 102; Joseph McSorley, "The Christian Idea of Justice and Equality," *CUB*, 4 (January 1898), 101–106.

86. Full-length studies are Bell, *McGlynn*, and Malone, *McGlynn*: see also Ellis, *Gibbons*, 1:549ff and Smith, *Catholic Church in New York*, 1:287–291, 2:542–544. By far the best recent study is Roohan, "American Catholics and the Social Question," 332–383.

87. Quoted in Arthur Preuss, ed., *The Fundamental Fallacy of Socialism*, 2nd rev. ed. (St. Louis, 1909), 113.

88. L. F. Post and F. C. Leubuscher, *The George-Hewitt Campaign* (New York, n.d.), 131, 152; Reily, *Passing Events*, 1:184.

89. Bell, *McGlynn*, 34.

90. Post and Leubuscher, *George-Hewitt Campaign*, 132–133.

91. *Ibid.*, 134–139; Zwierlein, *McQuaid*, 3:8–10; Browne, *Knights of Labor*, 233–234; Ellis, *Gibbons*, 1:550–553.

92. Browne, *Knights of Labor*, 225; Malone, *Memorial*, 161; Bell, *McGlynn*, 51, 65–66; Roohan, "American Catholics and the Social Question," 338. Ellis, *Gibbons*, 1:553–594, acquits the Cardinal of anything but the most correct attitude towards what was, technically, Corrigan's problem.

93. "The New Know-Nothingism and the Old," *NAR*, 145 (August 1887), 192–205; even after he was restored, he was noisily critical: "The Vatican and the United States," *Forum*, 16 (September 1893), 11–21; see also "Career of Dr. Edward McGlynn," *LD*, 20 (January 20, 1900), 86–87.

94. Smith, *Catholic Church in New York*, 2:546; Reily, *Passing Events*, 1:385–386.

95. Roohan, "American Catholics and the Social Question," 355–363; Browne, *Knights of Labor*, 319–320; Zwierlein, *McQuaid*, 3:66; Zwierlein, *Corrigan*, 115; J. T. Ellis, "Cardinal Gibbons and Philadelphia," *RACHS*, 58 (March 1947), 95.

96. Browne, *Knights of Labor*, 324.

97. Zwierlein, *Corrigan*, 126; Browne, *Knights of Labor*, 337; Preston, "Socialism and the Catholic Church," *Forum*, 5 (April 1888), 225.

98. Henry George Jr. *The Life of Henry George* (New York, 1900), 565, 565n.; Abell, "The Reception of Leo XIII's Labor Encyclical," *Review of Politics*, 7 (October 1945), 476–477; Keane, " 'Rerum Novarum,' " *ACQR*, 16 (July 1891), 596–598; Sheedy, *Social Problems*, 28, 73–74; Browne, *Knights of Labor*, 349.

99. Reilly, *School Controversy*, 114; Zwierlein, *Corrigan*, 135.

100. McGlynn's statement is in Bell, *McGlynn*, 226–231; for various analyses, see George, *George*, 562; Ellis, *Gibbons*, 1:590; and Preuss, *Fundamental Fallacy*, 113–137.

101. Roohan, "American Catholics and the Social Question," 380–383; for an alternative phraseology, see McGlynn, "The Vatican and the United States," *Forum*, 16 (September 1893), 16.

102. Reily, *Passing Events*, 1:385–386; compare Sugrue, *An American Catholic*, 44.

103. Malone, *McGlynn*, 116–121; Rainsford, *Story*, 369.

104. Browne, *Knights of Labor*, 358; Corrigan told the Paulists that Rome had detected "liberalizing tendencies" in the *Catholic World's* treatment of property rights; Ellis, *Gibbons*, 2:12.

105. "A Catholic Temperance League," *AER*, 11 (December 1894), 416.

106. *Question of Nationality*, 43; Ahern, *Catholic University*, 140–141; Abell, "Origins of Catholic Social Reform," *Review of Politics*, 11 (July 1949), 302.

107. *Ibid.*

108. Ireland, "The Catholic Church and the Saloon," *NAR*, 159 (October 1894), 498–505.

109. Rainsford, *Story*, 338; Sheedy, "Suggestions for the Coming Total-Abstinence Convention," *CW*, 55 (July 1892), 569.

110. J. A. Mooney, "Our Drinks and Our Drunkards," *CW*, 47 (June 1888), 346–354; Mooney, "The Beer-Drinkers' 'Trust,'" *CW*, 47 (July 1888), 482–494; Strong, *Our Country*, 381.

111. Bland, *Hibernian Crusade*, 225.

112. See the several works of George Zurcher, *Monks*, 48–49; *Hand-cuffs for Alcoholism* (Buffalo Plains, New York, 1890), 129; *The Apple of Discord*, 141–143.

113. Hope, *Notre Dame*, 231; J. C. Gibbs, *History of the Catholic Total Abstinence Union of America* (Philadelphia, 1907), 65.

114. Stauffer, "Anti-Catholicism," 170; Bland, *Hibernian Crusade*, 199.

115. Bland, *Hibernian Crusade*, 177; J. M. Cleary, "The Public-Hall Apostolate," *CW*, 61 (August 1895), 199.

116. "Editorial Notes," *CW*, 64 (February 1897), 707.

117. Gibbs, *CTAU*, 119; Bland, *Hibernian Crusade*, 199.

118. Brophy, *Social Thought*, 69.

119. Bland, *Hibernian Crusade*, 37.

120. Gibbs, *CTAU*, 64; Bland, *Hibernian Crusade*, 106–107.

121. *Ibid.*, 121–128; Zurcher, *Monks*, 35–37; Abell, "Origins of Catholic Social Reform," *Review of Politics*, 11 (July 1949), 303–304.

122. "The Catholic National Council," *CW*, 40 (February 1885), 710.

123. "The Church and Temperance," *CW*, 51 (September 1890), 821.

124. "Suggestions for the Coming Total-Abstinence Convention," *CW*, 55 (July 1892), 568.

125. J. J. Rooney, "Bishop Watterson," *CW*, 69 (June 1899), 407–410; the text of his message is in Satolli, *Loyalty*, 115–117; Bland, *Hibernian Crusade*, 184.

126. Satolli, *Loyalty*, 118–121; Ireland, *Church and Modern Society*, 1:313; Ireland, "The Catholic Church and the Saloon," *NAR*, 159 (October 1894), 498–505.

127. Thomas McMillan, "A Medieval Study of the Temperance Question," *CW*, 41 (September 1885), 722.

128. M. P. Dowling, "The American League of the Cross," *AER*, 12 (March 1895), 200–209.

129. Bland, *Hibernian Crusade*, 80–85; Gibbs, *CTAU*, 66, 141.

130. Bland, *Hibernian Crusade*, 126.

131. For the coöperative spirit of the CTAU, see O'Gorman, *History of the Catholic Church*, 399; Gibbs, *CTAU*, 118; Bland, *Hibernian Crusade*, 118, 177, 189–191. On the Willard incident, see *ibid.*, 166–167, and J. M. Cleary, "The Public-Hall Apostolate," *CW*, 61 (August 1895), 581.

132. Gibbs, *CTAU*, 67; Bland, *Hibernian Crusade*, 65, 117–118, 154.

133. *Ibid.*, 268–270; Ireland, *Church and Modern Society*, 1:297–301; Bell, *McGlynn*, 261; Walworth, *Walworth*, 273; J. T. Smith, "Workmen should not only act but think," *CW*, 47 (September 1888), 843.

134. Bland, *Hibernian Crusade*, 116, 155, 269; Gibbs *CTAU*, 73.

135. Joseph Tracy, "Prohibition and Catholics," *CW*, 51 (August 1890), 669–674.

Chapter VII

The Question of the Schools

1. Reily, *Passing Events*, 2:1.

2. Review of E. F. Dunne, *Compulsory Education* (St. Louis, 1891), *ACQR*, 17 (January 1892), 220; J. G. Shea, "Federal Schemes to Aid Common Schools," *ACQR*, 13 (April 1888), 345–359.

3. Stauffer concludes that only charges of condoning intemperance and political corruption rivaled this in the armory of anti-Catholicism; "Anti-Catholicism in American Politics," 217–222.

4. *Ibid.*, 167; Brace, *Dangerous Classes*, 436.

5. Stauffer, "Anti-Catholicism," 226; Pierce, *Chicago*, 2:380; M. C. Byrne, "What is the Catholic School Policy?" *NAR*, 140 (June 1885), 521–528.

6. Hecker, *Church and the Age*, 87–88.

7. *Parent First*, 20; Quigley, ed., *Compulsory Education*, 346; *Columbian Congress*, 3:17; S. G. Messmer, "Compulsory Education," *AER*, 6 (April 1892), 284.

8. "The Rights and Duties of Family and State," *ACQR*, 9 (January 1884), 121–125.

9. P. F. McSweeny, " 'Heartless, Headless, and Godless,' " *CW*, 46 (January 1888), 437; Quigley, ed., *Compulsory Education*, 424–425; McQuaid, "Religious Teaching in Schools," *Forum*, 8 (December 1889), 387.

10. "The American Side of the School Question," *CW*, 30 (January 1880), 516.

11. *Religion and Art*, 71; Malone, *McGlynn*, 84–86; E. M. White, "Frederick Froebel's Kindergarten," *CW*, 56 (January 1893), 511.

12. Spalding, *Education and the Higher Life*, 180.

13. F. M. Edselas, "An Educational Bureau and Journal," *CW*, 56 (Febru-

ary 1893), 652; see the educationists' boasts in James Conway, "Rights and Duties," *ACQR*, 9 (January 1884), 118.

14. H. J. Heuser, "Compulsory Education in the United States," *AER*, 3 (December 1890), 430.

15. *Parent First*, 20; G. D. Wolff, "Socialistic Communism in the United States," *ACQR*, 3 (July 1878), 533.

16. Francis Chatard, "Are Catholics Right?" *ACQR*, 15 (July 1890), 568; Quigley, ed., *Compulsory Education*, 527.

17. "Catholics and Protestants Agreeing on the School Question," *CW*, 32 (February 1881), 712.

18. B. N. Taylor, "Educated Above Their Station?" *CW*, 53 (May 1891), 172–175.

19. J. A. Burns, "Catholic Secondary Schools," *ACQR*, 26 (July 1901), 495; Morgan Sheedy, "The School Question in the Pennsylvania Legislature," *CW*, 53 (July 1891), 488; "The Forces at Work," *CW*, 46 (January 1888), 564.

20. The ferment is evident in T. W. Higginson, *Common Sense About Women* (Boston, 1881); Thérèse Blanc, *The Condition of Women in the United States*, trans. A. L. Alger (Boston, 1895); C. V. de Varigny, *The Women of the United States*, trans. *Arabella Ward* (New York, 1895).

21. For some of the more unusual demands, see Gibbons, *Christian Heritage*, 354–364; Barrows, ed., *Parliament of Religions*, 1:viii, 506–507, 752–758; 2:1149–1150; Gibbs, *CTAU*, 85, Hogan, *Conaty*, 95–100; J. J. O'Shea, "The White-Slave Trade," *CW*, 59 (June 1894), 418–424; "The Evolution of a Great City," *CW*, 63 (August 1896), 694. For liberal affirmations, see Spalding, "Has Christianity Benefitted Woman?" *NAR*, 140 (May 1885), 410; *Means and Ends of Education*, 104; Egan, ed., *Onward and Upward*, 131–150; Edward McSweeny, "*Das Ewige Weiblich*," *CW*, 49 (June 1889), 326–333.

22. *Religion and Art*, 22.

23. *Church and the Age*, 117–118; Ireland, *Church and Modern Society*, 2:300; F. M. Edselas, "An Educational Bureau," *CW*, 56 (February 1893), 652.

24. Hogan, *Conaty*, 99.

25. Katherine Tynan, "The Higher Education for Catholic Girls," *CW*, 51 (August 1890), 620; F. M. Edselas, "Institute for Women's Professions," *CW*, 57 (June 1893), 376–377; F. C. Farinholt, M. A. Spelissy, and K. F. Mullaney, "The Public Rights of Women," *CW*, 59 (June 1894), 301–312; Spalding, *Opportunity*, 59; Spalding, "Introduction," to Abbelen, *Friess*, 16; for Gibbons' more qualified support, see Reily, *Passing Events*, 2:211–212.

26. "The Woman Question Among Catholics," *CW*, 57 (August 1893), 669–671.

27. E. C. Donnelly, "The Home is Women's Sphere," *CW*, 57 (August 1893), 680.

28. Isabel O'Reilly, "The Maid of Orleans and the New Womanhood," *ACQR*, 19 (July 1894), 597.

29. Mueller, *Public School Education*, 127; *Columbian Congress*, 1:110–

111; Bugg, *People of Our Parish*, 79–91, 101–115, 157; J. P. MacCorrie, "'The War of the Sexes,'" *CW*, 63 (August 1896), 616–617.

30. Barrows, ed., *Parliament of Religions*, 1:762; Smith, *Catholic Church in New York*, 2:483; Reilly, *School Controversy*, 98; "The State and Religious Education," *CW*, 45 (September 1887), 512.

31. E. M. White, "Frederick Froebel's Christian Kindergarten," *CW*, 56 (January 1893), 512.

32. "The Teacher's Duty to the Pupil," *NAR*, 163 (July 1896), 59. In this, Gibbons was following the principles of the admired Bishop Dupanloup; de Hovre, *Catholicism in Education*, 208–209.

33. Review of B. J. Spalding, *History of the Church of God*, (New York, 1884), *CW*, 39 (September 1884), 854–855; J. Thomas, "What is the Good of the Kindergarten," *CW*, 48 (October 1888), 16–17; E. W. White, "Froebel's Kindergarten," *CW*, 56 (January 1893), 509; see J. J. Chapman, *Causes and Consequences* (New York, 1898); Brace, *Dangerous Classes*, 182.

34. F. P. Cassidy, "Catholic Education in the Third Plenary Council of Baltimore," *CHR*, 34 (January 1949), 418, 430; A. D. Small, "The Common Schools and Citizenship," *CW*, 48 (January 1889), 562; Spalding, "Normal Schools for Catholics,' *CW*, 51 (April 1890), 88–97; F. M. Edselas, "An Educational Bureau," *CW*, 56 (February 1893), 650; Spalding, "The Catholic Educational Exhibit in the Columbian Exposition," *CW*, 55 (July 1892), 580–587; J. A. Burns, "Catholic Secondary Schools," *ACQR*, 26 (July 1901), 487; Hogan, *Conaty*, 66–86; Burns, *The Growth and Development of the Catholic School System in the United States* (New York, 1912), 215; Burns and B. J. Kohlbrenner, *A History of Catholic Education in the United States* (New York, 1937), 223.

35. Gibbons, *Christian Heritage*, 464; Spalding, *Religion and Art*, 103–104; Walter Elliott, "A Practical View of the School Question," *CW*, 35 (April 1882), 53–54.

36. "The Catholic Educational Exhibit," *CW*, 55 (July 1892), 585.

37. Bell, *McGlynn*, 121; Spalding, *Means and Ends*, 179–180; see later, pages 140–141, for liberal approval of "plans" which envisioned the separation of the two processes.

38. *Public School Education*, 27.

39. "The Right of Instruction," *AER*, 6 (February 1892), 105; Quigley, ed., *Compulsory Education*, 369, 428.

40. Bugg, *People of Our Parish*, 175ff.

41. *World Almanac, 1951* (New York, 1951), 580.

42. McQuaid, *Public School Question*, 27.

43. F. M. Edselas, "An Educational Bureau," *CW*, 56 (February 1893), 652.

44. Lord *et al.*, *Boston*, 3:81; Bugg, *People of Our Parish*, 170ff.; Mead, *Roman Catholic Church*, 28n.; C. B. Pallen, *The Education of Boys* (New York, 1916), iv.

45. Reilly, *School Controversy*, 256–266; G. D. Wolff, "Our Parochial School System — The Progress It has Made and is Making," *ACQR*, 17

(October 1892), 870; J. A. Burns, "Catholic Secondary Schools," *ACQR*, 26 (July 1901), 492; Mueller, *Public School Education*, 338.

46. King, *Facing the Twentieth Century*, 345; Mead, *Roman Catholic Church*, 8, 289; F. R. Coudert, "The American Protective Association," *Forum*, 17 (July 1894), 518.

47. McQuaid, "Religion in Schools," *NAR*, 132 (April 1881), 341; T. S. Preston, "What the Roman Catholics Want," *Forum*, 1 (April 1886), 167; Richard Gilmour, "What Shall the Public Schools Teach?" *Forum*, 5 (June 1888), 457; J. G. Shea, "The Lesson of President Garfield's Assassination," *ACQR*, 6 (October 1881), 690; Malone, *Memorial*, 72; Montgomery, *Poison Drops*, 77.

48. "The Liberalistic View of the Public School Question," *ACQR*, 2 (January 1877), 14.

49. McKelvey, *Rochester*, 152; McQuaid, "Religion in Schools," *NAR*, 132 (April 1891), 332; McQuaid, "Religious Teaching in Schools," *Forum*, 8 (December 1889), 385; McQuaid, *Public School Question*, 44.

50. M. A. "Convention of the National Education Association in Toronto," *CW*, 53 (September 1891), 863; Pallen, *Education*, 50.

51. "Contemplated Educational Alliance Between Church and State," *AER*, 7 (November 1892), 349.

52. *Public School Education*, 108, 139–140, 346.

53. Stauffer, "Anti-Catholicism in American Politics," 180; Reily, *Passing Events*, 2:5; Walburg, *Question of Nationality*, 44; J. G. Shea, "The Rapid Increase of the Dangerous Classes in the United States," *ACQR*, 4 (April 1879), 245n.

54. *Poison Drops*, 12n., 18, 24–25, 77; Quigley, ed., *Compulsory Education*, 347: Richard Gilmour, "What Shall the Public Schools Teach?" *Forum*, 5 (June 1888), 457.

55. "The Rights and Duties of Family and State," *ACQR*, 9 (January 1884), 118; Mueller, *Public School Education*, 133; Lamott, *Cincinnati*, 276.

56. *Poison Drops*, 89; Reilly, *School Controversy*, 33n.

57. See chapter 5.

58. McQuaid, "Religious Teaching in Schools," *Forum*, 8 (December 1889), 386; H. L. Richards, "An Ideal School Bill," *AER*, 7 (July 1892), 1–6.

59. McQuaid, *Public School Question*, 55; Mueller, *Public School Education*, 351; T. S. Preston, "American Catholicity," *ACQR*, 16 (April 1891), 403–404; Preston, "What the Roman Catholics Want," *Forum*, 1 (April 1886), 171; F. S. Chatard, "Dr. Bouquillon on the School Question," *AER*, 6 (February 1892), 102.

60. *Columbian Congress*, 1:120; Spalding, *Martin Spalding*, 154; Barry, *German Americans*, 37; Minahan, "McMaster," *RACHS*, 47 (June 1936), 95; Zwierlein, *McQuaid*, 1:304–308, 2:97–99; Lord *et al.*, *Boston*, 3:79; for church legislation see F. P. Cassidy, "Catholic Education," *CHR*, 34 (October 1948), 257–293, and *ibid.* (January 1949), 433–434.

61. Barry, *German Americans*, 36–37; Brophy, *Social Thought*, 61; Wal-

burg, *Question of Nationality*, 26; Rothensteiner, *St. Louis*, 2:110; McKelvey, *Rochester*, 39, 150; Lord *et al.*, *Boston*, 3:80; Woods, ed., *City Wilderness*, 214; Mueller, *Public School Education*, 338.
62. Bugg, *People of Our Parish*, 175.
63. William Stang, "The 'Ever' and 'Never' of Preaching," *AER*, 14 (March 1896), 221.
64. Reilly, *School Controversy*, 240.
65. H. A. Brann, "Mr. Cahensly and the Church in the United States," *CW*, 54 (January 1892), 577. As noted earlier, Brann was deeply conservative, except when he joined in the pan-Irish attack on the Germans.
66. Malone, *Memorial*, 72; Malone, *McGlynn*, 84; Satolli, *Loyalty*, 75–77; Reilly, *School Controversy*, 46; Spalding, *Means and Ends*, 143–148.
67. Moynihan, *Ireland*, 79–82; Reily, *Passing Events*, 1:368–370.
68. "Should Americans Educate their Children in Denominational Schools?" *CW*, 49 (September 1889), 816; compare Malone, *McGlynn*, 84.
69. "Church, State and School," *CW*, 50 (January 1890), 538.
70. *Public School Education*, 354. Compare Gibbons, *Ambassador*, 325; Cassidy, "Catholic Education," *CHR*, 34 (October 1948), 303.
71. Reilly, *School Controversy*, 221; Ireland, *Church and Modern Society*, 1:248; Moynihan, *Ireland*, 85.
72. Cassidy, "Catholic Education," *CHR*, 34 (October 1948), 304–305, and (January 1949), 416.
73. Morgan Sheedy, "The Educational Grievances of Catholics," *CW*, 49 (May 1889), 246–251; Sheedy, "The School Question in the Pennsylvania Legislature," *CW*, 53 (July 1891), 495.
74. "Is the Catholic School System Perfect?" *CW*, 51 (July 1890), 432.
75. "Dr. Bouquillon on the School Question," *AER*, 6 (February 1892), 103.
76. Moynihan, *Ireland*, 9–10; Reilly, *School Controversy*, 240. P. F. McSweeny, "Is there 'No Reason for a Compromise?'" *CW*, 47 (September 1888), 798; H. H. Wyman, "Patriotism and the Catholic Schools," *CW*, 52 (February 1891), 685–686; Reily, *Passing Events*, 2:812; Gibbons, *Ambassador*, 324.
77. *Foreign Societies*, 69–71, 107; "American Christian State Schools," *CW*, 52 (February 1891), 651–653; "The Amenities of the School Adjustment," *CW*, 54 (January 1892), 582–589.
78. Stauffer, "Anti-Catholicism," 282; Ireland, *Church and Modern Society*, 1:230n–231n; Jenkins, *Foreign Societies*, 105; P. F. McSweeny, "Christian Public Schools," *CW*, 44 (March 1887), 796–797.
79. Stauffer, "Anti-Catholicism," 237, 280, 386.
80. *Ibid.*, 280n.
81. "Religious Teaching in Schools," *Forum*, 8 (December 1889), 385; Reily, *Passing Events*, 2:879–891.
82. J. F. Loughlin, "The School Controversy in the United States," *AER*, 6 (February 1892), 122.

83. Reily, *Passing Events*, 2:927; Tardivel, *Situation*, 172.
84. *RR*, 5 (July 1892), 729.
85. Moynihan, *Ireland*, 100.
86. Ellis, "Gibbons and Philadelphia," *RACHS*, 58 (March 1947), 99; Montgomery, "Contemplated Educational Alliance Between Church and State," *AER*, 7 (November 1892), 341–354; Lord *et al.*, *Boston*, 3:177; Ellis, Gibbons, 1:660–661; Parsons, *Studies*, 6:321.
87. Reilly, *School Controversy*, 86.
88. *Ibid.*, 220–221.
89. Ellis, *Gibbons*, 1:680; Moynihan, *Ireland*, 91–93; Reilly, *School Controversy*, 237–241; Zwierlein, *McQuaid*, 3:169–170; Reily, *Passing Events*, 2:927–929.
90. Reilly, *School Controversy*, 87.
91. *Ibid.*, 164.
92. *Ibid.*, 195.
93. Tardivel, *Situation*, 177.
94. *Ibid.*, 275; Ellis, *Gibbons*, 1:684.
95. Review of James Conway, *The State Last*, *ACQR*, 17 (April 1892), 432.
96. *Education*, 31; Reilly, *School Controversy*, 106.
97. *Education*, 31; Bouquillon, *Education: to whom does it belong? A rejoinder to critics* (Baltimore, 1892), 4, 34.
98. "Dr. Bouquillon and the School Question," *CW*, 54 (February 1892), 735–737.
99. For criticism in the *Civiltà*, see Quigley, ed., *Compulsory Education*, 422–425.
100. Holaind, *The Parent First*, 17.
101. Conway, *The State Last*, 57, 74, 97, 167; S. G. Messmer, "The Right of Instruction," *AER*, 6 (February 1892), 104; J. F. Loughlin, "The School Controversy in the United States," *AER*, 6 (February 1892), 122; H. J. Heuser, review of Bouquillon, *Education: to whom does it belong; a rejoinder to the Civiltà Cattolica* (Baltimore, 1892), *AER*, 6 (March 1892), 238.
102. Quigley, ed., *Compulsory Education*, 488; Brace, *Dangerous Classes*, 351–352.
103. Ireland, *Church and Modern Society*, 1:219; Reily, *Passing Events*, 1:369; Spalding, "Catholicism and APAism," *NAR*, 159 (September 1894), 286; Elliott, "The School Grievance and its Remedy," *CW*, 36 (February 1883), 717. On the Bennett law which required all schools to make English the language of instruction, see W. F. Vilas, "The 'Bennett Law' in Wisconsin," *Forum*, 12 (October 1891), 196–207; McDonald, *Irish in Wisconsin*; Joseph Schroeder, "The Catholic German Congress at Pittsburgh," *CW*, 52 (November 1890), 268–269; E. A. Higgins, "The American State and the Private School," *CW*, 53 (July 1891), 521–527.
104. The priest's earlier difficulties with his bishop are noted in Ellis,

Gibbons, 2:331–335; the school issue is the substance of Quigley, ed., *Compulsory Education*.

105. *Ibid.*, 476.
106. *Ibid.*, 492, 546–548.
107. For the background of Leo's action, see chapter 9.
108. The theses are in Satolli, *Loyalty*, 27–39, Reilly, *School Controversy*, 271–276, and the *Catholic Times* of Philadelphia, December 10, 1892, 2. See also Zwierlein, *McQuaid*, 3:182–186; Ellis, *Gibbons*, 1:694–695.
109. Ellis, *Gibbons*, 1:695–696.
110. *Ibid.*, 696–698; Reilly, *School Controversy*, 218–222.
111. P. J. Ryan, "The Pope's Letter to the American Bishops on the School Question," *ACQR* (July 1893), 642–643.

Chapter VIII

Intellectual Life and the Church

1. B. B., "Scientific Freedom," *CW*, 47 (May 1888), 231.
2. *Ibid.*, 225; Montgomery, *Poison Drops*, 75, 83; Thébaud, "Superior Instruction in Our Colleges," *ACQR*, 7 (October 1882), 698–699; "Intellectual Liberty and Contemporary Catholicism," *Contempory Review*, 66 (August 1894), 280–304; Review of Franz Hettinger, *Revealed Religion* (London, n.d.), *ACQR*, 20 (July 1895), 662–663.
3. B. B., "Scientific Freedom," *CW*, 47 (May 1888), 230.
4. Barrows, ed., *Parliament of Religions*, 2:1266; Edward Pace, "St. Thomas and Modern Thought," *CUB*, 2 (April 1896), 197; "Catholicism *vs.* Science, Liberty, Truthfulness," *CUB*, 2 (July 1896), 356–387.
5. Houtin, *Américanisme*, 193.
6. In a footnote sharply differing from the article by B. B., "Scientific Freedom," *CW*, 47 (May 1888), 229n.
7. *Opportunity*, 75.
8. This was a characterization of Wilfrid Ward, an English liberal Catholic and friend of the Americanists; Maisie Ward, *The Wilfrid Wards*, 1:336.
9. *Clerical Studies*, 374–376; Thomas Shahan, "The Study of Church History," *CUB*, 4 (October 1898), 442.
10. See chapter 1; a good example would be Parsons, *Studies*.
11. Acton, "The Vatican Council," in *The History of Freedom*, 515.
12. J. A. Zahm, "Leo XIII and Science," *CUB*, 2 (January 1896), 35; J. P. Cadden, *The Historiography of the American Catholic Church: 1785–1943* (Washington, 1944), 35–36.
13. Reily, *Passing Events*, 2:12.
14. *Bible, Science, and Faith* (Baltimore, 1894), 133.
15. "A New Book on Freemasonry," *CW*, 32 (February 1881), 615; H. P. McElrone, "Joseph de Maistre," *CW*, 33 (May 1881), 221.

16. Review of Reuben Parsons, *Studies in Church History*, vol. 5 (New York, n.d.), *CW*, 68 (February 1899), 707–708.

17. Review of O'Gorman, *History*, *ACQR*, 21 (January 1896), 220–221; Barry, *German Americans*, 165; Cadden, *Historiography*, 93–94.

18. Thomas Hughes, *Principles of Anthropology and Biology*, 2nd ed. (New York, 1890), 14–20; S. B. A. Harper, "The Relations of the Church and the Constitution," *ACQR*, 2 (October 1877), 701; Review of M. J. Griffith, *The Mystery Solved; or, the Prophetic History of the Church* (New York, 1882), *CW*, 36 (January 1883), 570–571; Roemer, *Ludwig-missionsverein*, 95; Reily, *Passing Events*, 2:311.

19. "The Coming Kingdom of Christ," *ACQR*, 19 (April 1894), 225–243; Review of Griffith, *The Mystery Solved*, *CW*, 36 (January 1883), 571; J. T. Smith, "Let Us Study the Land and Labor Question," *CW*, 47 (April 1888), 56.

20. For the European conflict, see Houtin, *Une Vie de prêtre, 1867–1912* (Paris, 1926). Houtin was in correspondence with a few Sulpicians in America who were vitally interested, especially in Bible history; *ibid.*, 242.

21. Hogan, *Conaty*, 45n.; Moynihan, *Ireland*, 293; Ellis, *Gibbons*, 1:432; see also G. J. Garraghan, *The Jesuits of the Middle United States* (New York, 1938), 3:471.

22. *Scientific Theory and Catholic Doctrine* (Chicago, 1896), 16–17.

23. "Scriptural Questions," *CW*, 44 (January 1887), 447–451; William Barry, "The Key of the Position," *CW*, 47 (May 1888), 180.

24. *Scientific Theory*, 8–9; Spalding, *Thoughts and Theories of Life and Education* (Chicago, 1897), 203; Edward Pace, "St. Thomas and Modern Thought," *CUB*, 2 (April 1896), 197.

25. Hughes, *Principles*, 14–20, 45, 126–127; Barrows, ed., *Parliament of Religions*, 2:450–456; Review of Herbert Spencer, *The Principles of Sociology*, *ACQR*, 2 (July 1877). Notice the assent by some liberals; Gibbons, *Our Christian Heritage*, 283–317; Edward McSweeny, "The Logic of Evolution," *ACQR*, 4 (July 1879), 551–561.

26. A. M. Kirsch, "Professor Huxley on Evolution," *ACQR*, 2 (October 1877), 660–664; Zahm, *Evolution and Dogma*, 139, 339; Zahm, *The Catholic Church and Modern Science* (Notre Dame, Indiana, 1886), 27–28; John Gmeiner, *Modern Scientific Views and Christian Doctrines Compared* (Milwaukee, 1884), 169; see also the review of Gmeiner's book, *CW*, 40 (December 1884), 428; Joseph Pohle, "Darwinism and Theism," *AER*, 7 (September 1892), 170–176; *Catholic Times* of Philadelphia, December 10, 1892, 4; compare H. A. Brann's attack on Fiske in " 'Dude' Metaphysics," *CW*, 42 (February 1886), 635–641.

27. Zahm, *Evolution and Dogma*, 376–390, 436; William Barry, "The Key of the Position," *CW*, 47 (May 1898), 180–181.

28. Hewit, "Scriptural Questions," *CW*, 44 (February 1887), 665–666; Zahm, *Catholic Church and Modern Science*, 28–29; Gmeiner, *Modern Scientific Views*, 182–183; A.M. Kirsch, "Professor Huxley on Evolution,"

ACQR, 2 (October 1877), 663; Malone, *McGlynn*, 22. Joseph Selinger, "The Evolution Theory Applied to Man in the Light of the Vatican Council," *AER*, 10 (June 1894), 439–448; Barry, *German Americans*, 191n.

29. "Gladstone on Evolution and the Gospel," *LD*, 13 (June 25, 1896), 403; see also the enthusiastic reviews of Gmeiner's *Modern Scientific Views* in his *Emmanuel, the Savior of the World* (Milwaukee, 1888), 121–122.

30. J. A. White, *The Founding of Cliff Haven. The Early Years of the Catholic Summer School of America* (New York, 1950), 74.

31. Review of J. A. Zahm, *Evolution and Dogma* (Chicago, 1896), *ACQR*, 21 (July 1896), 665–666; "Can a Good Catholic be an Evolutionist?" *LD*, 13 (July 18, 1896), 370–371.

32. B. B., "Scientific Freedom," *CW*, 47 (May 1888), 226.

33. Spalding, *Education and the Higher Life*, 196; Hewit, "The Stonyhurst Philosophical Series," *CW*, 52 (March 1891), 822; Review of William Lockhart, ed., *Life of Antonio Rosmini-Serbati* (London, 1886), *CW*, 44 (March 1887), 857–858. For the liberals' estimate of "concordism," see Hewit, "Scriptural Questions," *CW*, 44 (January 1887), 449; Review of John Smyth, *Genesis and Science* (New York, 1898), *CUB*, 4 (October 1898), 501–503.

34. *Bible, Science, and Faith*, 170; Gmeiner, *Medieval and Modern Cosmology* (Milwaukee, 1891), iii; Edward Pace, "St. Thomas and Modern Thought," *CUB*, 2 (April 1896), 195; "The Intellectual Outlook of the Age," *CW*, 31 (May 1880), 149; Hecker, "Leo XIII," *CW*, 46 (December 1887), 296.

35. Hewit, "Scriptural Questions," *CW*, 44 (January 1887), 449; B. B., "Scientific Freedom," *CW*, 47 (May 1888), 225–226; B. B., *"In Necessariis Unitas, in Dubiis Libertas, in Omnibus Caritas,"* *ACQR*, 17 (January 1892), 32–46.

36. J. B. Hogan, *Clerical Studies*, 89.

37. H. I. D. Ryder, "Scripture, Inspiration, and Modern Biblical Criticism," *CW*, 56 (March 1893), 742–754, and "Rival Theories of Scriptural Interpretation," *CW*, 57 (May 1893), 206–218; see also Clarence Walworth, "The Nature and Extent of Inspiration," *CW*, 40 (October 1884), 1–13; Review of Basil Manly, *The Bible Doctrine of Inspiration* (New York, n.d.), *CW*, 47 (September 1888), 859.

38. "The Divine Authority of the Church," *CW*, 42 (November 1885), 161, 165.

39. This formulation of Pius IX is quoted in Gmeiner, "The Liberty of Catholics in Scientific Matters," *CW*, 48 (November 1888), 146.

40. *Ibid.*, 149; Hewit, "Scriptural Questions," *CW*, 44 (January 1887), 447, and (March 1887), 742; Hewit, "The Divine Authority of the Church," *CW*, 42 (November 1885), 165; Zahm, *Bible, Science, and Faith*, 144; for extensive discussion of Catholic views on the Flood, see *Catholic Standard and Times* of Philadelphia, December 28, 1895, 4.

41. "Human Certitude and Divine Faith," *CW*, 55 (April 1892), 87; S. M. Brandi, "The Touch-Stone of Catholicity," *AER*, 6 (February 1892), 89–97.

42. "Human Authority in the Church," *CW*, 42 (December 1885), 324–339.

43. G. M. Searle, "Evolution and Darwinism," *CW*, 56 (November 1892), 223–231; on Searle, a Paulist and a distinguished astronomer, see Klein, *In the Land*, 362.

44. "Criterions of Catholic Truth," *CW*, 52 (October 1890), 115–123.

45. *Ibid.*

46. Barry, *German Americans*, 194; Review of di Bartolo, *Les Critères théologiques* (Paris, 1889), *ACQR*, 16 (January 1891), 216.

47. Review of di Bartolo, *Les Critères théologiques*, *ACQR*, 16 (January 1891), 216–218.

48. "Theological Minimizing and its Latest Defender," *AER*, 4 (February 1891), 115–132; 4 (March 1891), 161–178; 4 (April 1891), 286–305; 5 (July 1891), 51–65.

49. *AER*, 5 (July 1891), 50. A later conservative attack is B. B., *"In Necessariis Unitas,"* *ACQR*, 17 (January 1892), 32–46.

50. An anonymous British author claimed that a sizable number of American Catholics were vitally involved in "The Papal Encyclical on the Bible," *Contemporary Review*, 65 (April 1894), 576–608.

51. The text is in *ACQR*, 19 (April 1894), 388–411; a balanced interpretation is in Maisie Ward, *The Wilfrid Wards*, 1:309–313.

52. John Corbett, "The Biblical Commission," *Catholic Encyclopedia*, 2 (New York, 1907), 557–558.

53. "The Pope and the Scriptures," *ACQR*, 19 (April 1894), 425; a more moderate Jesuit critique is A. J. Maas, "A Negative View of the Encyclical *Providentissimus Deus*," *ACQR*, 20 (January 1895), 162–175.

54. "Higher Criticism and the Bible," *ACQR*, 19 (July 1894), 581; Grannan, "A Program of Biblical Studies," *CUB*, 1 (January 1895), 35–52.

55. W. L. Sullivan, *Under Orders, the Autobiography of William Laurence Sullivan* (New York, 1944), 61; it perhaps should be noted that Sullivan had left the Church before he published this recollection.

56. Pages 9–10, 34, 40–42, 84–87.

57. *Clerical Studies*, 476.

58. See, for example, *Evolution and Dogma*, 389.

59. "Gladstone on Evolution and the Gospel," *LD*, 13 (July 25, 1896), 403; "Dr. Zahm's Retraction," *LD*, 19 (August 12, 1899), 200.

60. A. J. Scanlan, "The Great Seminaries," *Catholic Builders of the Nation*, C. E. McGuire ed. (Boston, 1923), 5:172–195.

61. "The Higher and Lower Education of the American Priesthood," *ACQR*, 15 (January 1890), 108.

62. "The New Seminary of St. Paul," *CUB*, 1 (April 1895), 222.

63. "Our Theological Seminaries," *CUB*, 1 (July 1895), 390–395; "The College Training of the Clergy," *CUB*, 4 (July 1898), 390–396; Gmeiner, *Medieval and Modern Cosmology*, ii, 12–13; Donehy, "The New Seminary of St. Paul," *CUB*, 1 (April 1895), 224.

64. *Training of a Priest*, 143, 266–275; in many of the new seminaries, historians of "scientific" disposition were installed; Herbermann, *Sulpicians*, 320–326; Moynihan, *Ireland*, 244–245.

65. Farley, *McCloskey*, 268.

66. *Means and Ends of Education*, 209–212.

67. *Education and the Higher Life*, 184, 193, 199; Ellis, *Formative Years*, 282; Reily, *Passing Events*, 1:292.

68. J. F. Loughlin, "The Higher and Lower Education of the American Priesthood," *ACQR*, 15 (January 1890), 109–119; "*Aquinas Resuscitatus*," *ACQR*, 16 (October 1891), 673–690; Ahern, *Catholic University*, 32; Zwierlein, *McQuaid*, 3:440–441; for the mixed attitude of the Jesuits, see Ellis, *Formative Years*, 103–107, 361; Ellis, *Gibbons*, 1:398–407.

69. Ahern, *Catholic University*, 89.

70. *Ibid.*, 17; Ellis, *Formative Years*, 348–349, 350n.

71. Ahern, *Catholic University*, 8; Moynihan, *Ireland*, 305.

72. "Criterions of Catholic Truth," *CW*, 52 (October 1890), 123; Review of Engelbert Gey, *Dissertationes Quaedam Philosophicae* (Quincy, Illinois, 1888), *CW*, 49 (May 1889), 277.

73. Bouquillon, "Theology in Universities," *CUB*, 1 (January 1895), 30; "University Chronicle," *ibid.*, 90.

74. "University Chronicle," *CUB*, 1 (April 1895), 263–346; White, *Cliff Haven*, 68.

75. Review of R. W. Shufeldt, *Lectures on Biology* (Chicago, n.d.), *CW*, 60 (November 1894), 282.

76. Egan, *Recollections*, 189.

77. Ahern, *Catholic University*, 71, 158; Barry, *German Americans*, 191n.

78. Austin O'Malley, "Catholic Collegiate Education in the United States," *CW*, 67 (June 1898), 289–304; "Editorial Notes," *CW*, 67 (July 1898), 563; Zwierlein, *McQuaid*, 3:402–404.

79. *Church and Modern Society*, 1:241.

80. Hope, *Notre Dame*, 166–181, 257, 262, 343–345; Garraghan, *Jesuits*, 2:124; Smith, *Azarias*, 117.

81. O'Malley, "Catholic Collegiate Education," *CW*, 67 (June 1898), 299; Zwierlein, *McQuaid*, 3:396.

82. Beck, ed., *English Catholics*, 312–313.

83. Zwierlein, *McQuaid*, 3:396.

84. Malcolm MacLellan, *The Catholic Church and Adult Education* (Washington, 1935), 8–34; Smith, *Catholic Church in New York*, 2:441; *Columbian Congress*, 1:107; "The Columbian Reading Union," *CW*, 52 (October 1890), 147–149; *CW*, 55 (September 1892), 923–927. See also columns of advice in *Catholic Standard and Times*, December 14, 1895, *et seq.*

85. White, *Cliff Haven*; *Columbian Congress*, 1:108; Hogan, *Conaty*, 19–20; "The Columbian Reading Union," *CW*, 55 (August 1892), 775–781; J. F. Mullaney, "University Extension of Catholic Summer School," *ACQR*, 18 (January 1893), 172.

86. White, *Cliff Haven*, 88; J. Mc. M., "The Clergy and the Summer School," *AER*, 16 (April 1897), 421.

87. White, *Cliff Haven*, 91.

88. Pallen, "The Catholic Idea of Popular Summer Schools," *AER*, 15 (July 1896), 69.

89. White, *Cliff Haven*, 89.

90. Hogan, *Conaty*, 137; Hope, *Notre Dame*, 181; MacLellan, *Adult Education*, 23–24; "The Columbian Reading Union," *CW*, 55 (September 1892), 924.

91. "The Columbian Reading Union," *CW*, 55 (August 1892), 775.

Chapter IX

A Church of Energetic Individuals

1. See Hewit's reservations about Newman's concept of "development"; "Cardinal Newman," *CW*, 51 (September 1890), 723; for allegations of American "modernism," see chapter 11.

2. Moynihan, *Ireland*, 18.

3. "Baptized Democracy," *CW*, 43 (September 1886), 724; "The Forces at Work," *CW*, 46 (January 1888), 564; Elliott, "A Critic of the Great Republic," *CW*, 40 (November 1884), 244; Hecker, "The Mission of Leo XIII," *CW*, 48 (October 1888), 2.

4. "Catholic National Council," *CW*, 40 (February, 1885), 714; Gibbons, *Ambassador*, ix.

5. "A Critic of the Great Republic," *CW*, 40 (November 1884), 247–249.

6. "The Amenities of the School Adjustments," *CW*, 54 (January 1892), 588.

7. *Passing Events*, 2:307.

8. "Religion and Thrift," *CW*, 45 (August 1887), 712–713; "Forces at Work," *CW*, 46 (January 1888), 563–565; Thomas Bouquillon, "Catholicity and Civilization," *CUB*, 4 (October 1898), 467–480.

9. " 'Put Money in Thy Purse,' " *CW*, 50 (February 1890), 618–628; see also her remarks in *Columbian Congress*, 1:179–193.

10. Bland, *Hibernian Crusade*, 225–227.

11. O'Shea, *The Two Kenricks*, 388–391.

12. Leclerc, *Choses d'Amérique*, 249.

13. *Church and Modern Society*, 1:129.

14. "The Pope and the Proletariat," *CW*, 53 (August 1891), 639.

15. Strayer and Munro, *The Middle Ages*, 298.

16. Katherine Burton, *Celestial Homespun, the Life of Isaac Thomas Hecker* (London, 1943), 370–375; S. B. Hedges, "Father Hecker and the Establishing of the Poor Clares in the United States," *CW*, 61 (June 1895), 383–386.

17. *Church and the Age*, 175; Barrows, ed., *Parliament of Religions*, 2:1036.

18. Abbelen, *Friess*, 17.

19. Reily, *Passing Events*, 1:373; Elliott, *Hecker*, 293.

20. See chapter 1. For parallel developments in America, see Lord *et al.*, Boston, 3:224ff., 383; Smith, *Catholic Church in New York*, 1:315–317.

21. Elliott, *Hecker*, 327; Ireland, *Church and Modern Society*, 2:243; Hecker, "Leo XIII," *CW*, 46 (December 1887), 294.

22. *Church and Modern Society*, 1:254; 2:243–245, 325; A. A. McGinley, "A New Field for the Convent Graduate in the Social Settlement," *CW*, 71 (June 1900), 400–401; William Barry, "A Study of Modern Religion," *CW*, 49 (September 1889), 719.

23. A paraphrase in Elliott, *Hecker*, 327.

24. A paraphrase in "University Chronicle," *CUB*, 2 (January 1896), 104; J. V. Tracy, "The Eucharistic Movement," *AER*, 16 (February 1897), 155–164; compare William Cluse, "The Nature and Aim of the Priests' Eucharistic League," *AER*, 11 (November 1894), 321–328.

25. Bland, *Hibernian Crusade*, 186.

26. *Church and the Age*, 16.

27. "Catholic Progress, Old and New," *CW*, 50 (January 1890), 431.

28. Egan, ed., *Onward and Upward*, 369–370; Review of Elié Méric, *The Blessed Will Know Each Other in Heaven* (London, n.d.), *CW*, 47 (April 1888), 142.

29. Moynihan, *Ireland*, 247.

30. *Church and the Age*, 194–198; Elliott, "The True Man of the Times," *CW*, 44 (December 1886), 294; Spalding, *Things of the Mind*, 70.

31. Review of H. R. Buckler, *The Perfection of Man by Charity* (London, n.d.), *CW*, 52 (October 1890), 144–146; Barrows, ed., *Parliament of Religions*, 1:465; Egan, ed., *Onward and Upward*, 327–329.

32. *Ibid.*, 321; Cronin, *Ryan*, 87; *Columbian Congress*, 1:57; Ireland, *Church and Modern Society*, 1:72; Ireland, "The Catholic Church and the Saloon," *NAR*, 159 (October 1894), 503; Elliott, "The Church and Temperance," *CW*, 51 (September 1890), 813.

33. Delattre, *Un Catholicisme américain*, 118; Tardivel, *Situation*, 112–113.

34. *Columbian Congress*, 1:175; "Some of our Present Weapons against Socialism in America," *CW*, 31 (September 1880), 728–729.

35. A Layman, "The Laity," *CW*, 47 (April 1888), 15–16.

36. "The Priest and the Public," *CW*, 47 (September 1888), 743–751; Reily, *Passing Events*, 1:399–406; Edward McGlynn, "The New Know-Nothingism and the Old," *NAR*, 145 (August 1887), 198; McGlynn, "The Vatican and the United States," *Forum*, 16 (September 1893), 11–15.

37. Georges Weill, *Histoire de l'idée laïque en France au dix-neuvième siècle* (Paris, 1929).

38. "The True Man of the Times," *CW*, 44 (December 1886), 295.

39. "Shall the People Sing?" *CW*, 45 (July 1887), 444–453; "Will Congregational Singing Profit Faith and Morals?" *CW*, 49 (May 1889), 159–172; H. T. Henry, "*Cantate Domino*," *AER*, 7 (July 1892), 19–29; Henry, "*Quomodo Cantabimus?*" *AER*, 7 (August 1892), 120–133; Gibbons, *Ambassador*, 349–367.

40. G. H. Howard, "The English Language in Catholic Public Worship," *CW*, 51 (April 1890), 31–40; A Western Priest, [Letter], *CW*, 51 (September 1890), 837–838 pointed out that German Catholics had long practiced congregational singing, and enjoyed prayers in the vernacular. Godfrey Diekmann, "The Primary Apostolate," in L. R. Ward, ed., *American Apostolate*, 29–46.

41. W. F. Markoe, "The Catholic Truth Society," *CW*, 52 (January 1891), 491–496; M. L. M., "The Loveliness of Sanctity," *CW*, 49 (August 1889), 618–636, and 49 (September 1889), 779–782.

42. R. F. McNamara, "Trusteeism in the Atlantic States, 1785–1863," *CHR*, 30 (July 1944), 135–154. See the much more bold article by William Barry, "The Troubles of a Catholic Democracy," *Contemporary Review*, 76 (July 1899), 79–80.

43. J. V. Tracy, "Is the Catholic School System Perfect?" *CW*, 51 (July 1890), 430–431; Corrigan, *What the Catholic Church Most Needs*, 6; F. P. Cassidy, "Catholic Education," *CHR*, 34 (October 1948), 296, and 34 (January 1949), 417.

44. *Proceedings of the Catholic Congress*, 18–25.

45. Ellis, *Gibbons*, 1:413–418.

46. Smith, *Azarias*, 258.

47. "Our Recent American Catholic Congress," *ACQR*, 15 (January 1890), 155ff.

48. Reily, *Passing Events*, 1:130.

49. Albert Reynaud, "Organize the Laymen," *CW*, 50 (December 1889), 287–289; E. B. Brady, "Catholic Progress, Old and New," *CW*, 50 (January 1890), 433–435.

50. Quoted in Zurcher, *Apple of Discord*, 490–491. See B. C. Cronin, *Father Yorke and the Labor Movement in San Francisco 1900–1910* (Washington, 1943) for the career of this outspoken priest.

51. See chapters 6 and 7.

52. For suspicion of European secret societies, see Thébaud, "Freemasonry," *ACQR*, 6 (October 1881), 577–608; J. A. Mooney, "The School Question in Belgium," *ACQR*, 10 (July 1885), 532–560; A. de G., "The Impending Conflict in French Politics," *ACQR*, 9 (January 1884), 92–104; M. P. Villamil, "Religion in Spain," *CW*, 49 (July 1889), 494–502; F. S. Chatard, "Pius VI and the French Directory," *CW*, 64 (October 1896), 1–12.

For the indictment of American societies, see most of the above references, and Charles Coppens, "The Laws of the Church with regard to Secret Societies," *ACQR*, 5 (April 1880), 239–252; Thomas Hughes, "Freemasonry in the United States," *AER*, 8 (April 1893), 250–266; Arthur Preuss, *A Study in American Freemasonry* (St. Louis, 1905); Peter Rosen, *The Catholic Church and Secret Societies* (Milwaukee, 1902).

53. Reily, *Passing Events*, 1:140–141.

54. Macdonald, *Catholic Church and the Secret Societies*, 138, 158.

55. *Ibid.*, 163–170.

56. *Ibid.*, 181; F. X. Katzer, "Societies Forbidden in the Church," *AER*, 6 (April 1892), 241–247; F. Janssens, "Are the Knights of Pythias a Forbidden Society for Catholics," *AER*, 6 (June 1892), 450–455.

57. See chapter 10.

58. Elliott, "A Critic of the Great Republic," *CW*, 40 (November 1884), 250; "Our Centenary: A Glance into the Future," *CW*, 50 (November 1889), 239–243.

59. S. M. D., "The Sisters of Mercy in New York," *CW*, 50 (December 1889), 390–391; H. E., "The Late Father Hecker," *CW*, 49 (May 1889), 245; Hecker, "The Guidance of the Holy Spirit," *CW*, 45 (August 1887), 710.

60. Elliott, *Hecker*, 308–309; Elliott, "The Human Environments of the Catholic Faith," *CW*, 43 (July 1886), 467.

61. Hecker, *Church and the Age*, 142–143; Elliott, "Our Centenary," *CW*, 50 (November 1889), 248; Review of H. R. Buckler, *The Perfection of Man* (London, n.d.), *CW*, 52 (October 1890), 146; Elliott, "The Longing for God and its Fulfillment," *CW*, 55 (June 1892), 347.

62. Klein, *Américanisme*, 369n.

63. H. E., "The Late Father Hecker," *CW*, 49 (May 1889), 243–244; M. D. Petre, "Lawful Liberty and Reasonable Service," *ACQR*, 24 (July 1899), 100–101.

64. S. M. D., "The Sisters of Mercy in New York," *CW*, 50 (December 1889), 390–391; H. E., "The Late Father Hecker," *CW*, 49 (May 1889), 245; Review of R. F. Clarke, *The Existence of God* (New York, 1887), *CW*, 45 (August 1887), 717; *Columbian Congress*, 1:57.

65. Elliott, *Hecker*, 308–321.

66. D'Hablonville, *Grandes figures*, 233; Moynihan, *Ireland*, 248.

67. "A Critic of the Great Republic," *CW*, 40 (November 1884), 250; "Our Centenary: A Glance into the Future," *CW*, 50 (November 1889), 239–243.

68. *Ambassador of Christ, passim.*

69. "The Ambassador of Christ," *CW*, 64 (March 1897), 826.

70. Smith, *Catholic Church in New York*, 2:438.

71. "Introduction," to J. T. Smith, *Training of a Priest*, xxv–xxvi.

72. "Preparatory Seminaries for Clerical Students," *AER*, 14 (April, 1896), 312–321; compare Henry Brinkmeyer, "The Rt. Rev. Bishop of Covington's Views on Preparatory Seminary Training in the United States," *AER*, 14 (June 1896), 531–537; "Vocations to the Priesthood and Our Seminaries," *AER*, 3 (August 1890), 169–195.

73. Maes, "The Theological Seminary," *AER*, 14 (May 1896), 435.

74. "Introduction," to Smith, *Training of a Priest*, xxiii, xxvii; Zwierlein, *McQuaid*, 3:443–445.

75. F. P. Cassidy, "Catholic Education," *CHR*, 34 (October 1948), 267–288.

76. "Ecclesiastical Students in Vacation," *AER*, 7 (July 1892), 52.

77. "The Theological Seminary," *AER*, 14 (May 1896), 439–446.

78. Ellis, *Formative Years*, 135.

79. Hogan, *Conaty*, 96–98.

80. Smith, *Catholic Church in New York*, 2:432; R. L. Burtsell, *The Canonical Status of Priests in the United States* (n.p., n.d.); Zwierlein, *Corrigan*, 117–121; Zwierlein, *McQuaid*, 2:36–37, 173–192.

81. *Ibid.*, 2:313–315; Barry, *German Americans*, 111–116.

82. Stauffer, "Anti-Catholicism," 205, 398.

83. *Passing Events*, 2:829; Bell, *McGlynn*, 85.

84. Abbelen, *Friess*, 106–109.

85. Ellis, *Gibbons*, 2:373–375; Smith, *Catholic Church in New York*, 2:490, 507.

86. Farley, *McCloskey*, 247–248; Snead-Cox, *Vaughan*, 1:270–343; Purcell, *Manning*, 2:509; Peter Guilday, *A History of the Councils of Baltimore* (New York, 1932), 234.

87. For a comprehensive indictment of Jesuit illiberalism in Europe, see Maud Petre, *Life of George Tyrrell*, volume 2 of *Autobiography and Life of George Tyrrell* (London, 1912), 2:463–465.

88. *Training of a Priest*, 9.

89. Abbé Dufresne, "Personal Recollections of Father Hecker," *CW*, 67 (June 1898), 340.

90. Bland, *Hibernian Crusade*, 271; Reily, *Passing Events*, 1:373.

91. Moynihan, *Ireland*, 113–114.

92. Barry, *German Americans*, 203n.

93. Egan, *Recollections*, 202.

94. Elliott, *Hecker*, 293–294.

95. Moynihan, *Ireland*, 120.

96. "Introduction" to Elliott, *Hecker*.

97. Cronin, *Ryan*, 87.

98. Many desired a regular series of plenary councils; Hogan, *Clerical Studies*, 328; Leclerc, *Choses d'Amérique*, 258.

99. *Means and Ends of Education*, 223–224.

100. Zwierlein, *McQuaid*, 2:462–466; 3:152–153.

101. *Ibid.*, 2:457; Reily, *Passing Events*, 1:146.

102. *Passing Events*, 1:300.

103. Elliott, *Hecker*, 390; Hecker, *Church and the Age*, 114, 140; Hecker, "The Mission of Leo XIII," *CW*, 48 (October 1888), 10; R. de Cesare, "The Next Conclave," *NAR*, 173 (November 1901), 599.

104. Zwierlein, *McQuaid*, 3:178.

105. For the opinion of many priests, see *Catholic Times* of Philadelphia, January 14, 1893, 4. The best account of the debate is Ellis, *Gibbons*, 1:595–652.

106. J. J. Meng, "Cahenslyism: the Second Chapter," *CHR*, 32 (October 1946), 332n.

107. Reilly, *School Controversy*, 214–216; Moynihan, *Ireland*, 298–299; Zwierlein, *Corrigan*, 136–138; Ellis, *Gibbons*, 1:630–631; *Catholic Times* of Philadelphia, December 9–23, 1892.

108. See chapter 10.

109. Moynihan, *Ireland*, 96–299; Lord *et al.*, *Boston*, 3:180; Barry, *German*

Americans, 318–319; for a biographical sketch of Satolli, see *Catholic Times* of Philadelphia, December 31, 1892, 2.

110. Cronin, *Ryan*, 65; Smith, *Catholic Church in New York*, 2:518–519.

111. Satolli, *Loyalty*, 133.

112. *History of the Catholic Church*, 472; *LD*, 11 (October 19, 1895), 738; *Catholic Times* of Philadelphia, December 31, 1892, 2.

113. Parsons, *Studies*, 6:334n.

114. *Voces Catholicae*, "Is a Catholic University Possible?" *Contemporary Review*, 75 (May 1899), 639; St. George Mivart, "Some Recent Catholic Apologists," *Fortnightly Review*, 73 (January 1900), 37n.; J. St. Clair Etheridge, "The Genesis of 'Americanism,'" *NAR*, 170 (May 1900), 688.

115. "The New Apostolic Delegate," *CW*, 64 (October 1896), 1–3.

116. *Clerical Studies*, 329.

Chapter X

The Response of European Catholicism

1. See Chapter II.

2. Maisie Ward, *The Wilfrid Wards*, 2:42, 310.

3. W. T. Stead, *The Americanization of the World* (New York, 1901), 180–181; J. W. Pratt, *Expansionists of 1898* (New York, 1951), 238–240; F. H. Giddings, *Democracy and Empire* (New York, 1900), 273; A. T. Mahan, *The Interest of America in Sea Power* (Boston, 1898), 49, 66, 165, 255; J. W. Burgess, *Political Science and Comparative Constitutional Law* (Boston, 1902), 1:38, 44–45.

4. Stead, *Americanization*, 168–173; Pratt, *Expansionists*, 259; "All Americans *vs.* All Europe," *LD*, 15 (December 11, 1897), 964–965.

5. Orestes Ferrara, *The Last Spanish War: Revelations in "Diplomacy"* trans. W. E. Shea (New York, 1937), 97.

6. David Kinley, "European Feeling toward the United States," *Forum*, 32 (October 1901), 217; "Will America Swallow Europe?" *LD*, 20 (January 27, 1900), 126; Delassus, *Américanisme*, 1; R. A. Heindel, *The American Impact on Great Britain, 1898–1914* (Philadelphia, 1940), 167ff.

7. "To Our Readers," *CW*, 30 (February 1880), prefatory to 721; John MacCarthy, "A Dish of Diplomacy," *CW*, 32 (October 1880), 57; C. M. O'Keefe, "The Late War Between Chile and Peru," *CW*, 34 (January 1882), 484.

8. Malone, *McGlynn*, 81; "Editorial Notes," *CW*, 57 (June 1895), 438; Elliott, "The Diocesan Clergy and Missions to Non-Catholics," *AER*, 11 (September 1894), 229; Elliott, "The Human Environments of the Catholic Faith," *CW*, 43 (July 1886), 469.

9. "The Yorktown Centennial Celebration," *CW*, 34 (November 1881), 279; Spalding, *Education and the Higher Life*, 119, 177.

10. Hecker, *Church and the Age*, 42–58; Elliott, *Hecker*, 399; Hecker, "The Mission of Leo XIII," *CW*, 48 (October 1888), 6–12; Spalding, *Means and Ends*, 96–97; *Socialism and Labor*, 19; Schroll, *Social Thought*, 221n.; Elliott, "Experiences of a Missionary," *CW*, 59 (August 1894), 638; Elliott, "Missionary Experiences," *CW*, 61 (May 1895), 246; Zahm, "Leo XIII and the Social Question," *NAR*, 161 (August 1895), 214.

For Irish reluctance to expound Anglo-Saxonism, see Farrell, "Archbishop Ireland and Manifest Destiny," *CHR*, 33 (October 1947), 295; H. P. McElrone, "Kelt and Teuton," *CW*, 34 (November 1881), 212–220; J. T. Smith, "The Truth about the French-Canadians," *CW*, 49 (July 1889), 444; M. L. M. "The Columbian Reading Union," *CW*, 69 (May 1899), 288.

11. Elliott, *Hecker*, 370.

12. *Education and the Higher Life*, 179; Ireland, *Church and Modern Society*, 1:64; Reily, *Passing Events*, 1:119–120; 2:915.

13. Mooney, "Our Recent American Catholic Congress," *ACQR*, 15 (January 1890), 152; note that Mooney was in most respects a conservative. Ireland, *Church and Modern Society*, 1:192; Spalding, *Martin Spalding*, 321.

14. Barry, *German Americans*, 221n., 222n.

15. *Ibid.*, 210; Walburg, *Question of Nationality*, 18.

16. Barry, *German Americans*, 219.

17. "Mr. Cahensly and the Church in the United States," *CW*, 54 (January 1892), 574–581.

18. "The German Problem," *CW*, 34 (December 1881), 289–297.

19. "Church and State in France," *ACQR*, 17 (April 1892), 333–355; Hogan, "Priests and People in France," *ACQR*, 24 (January 1899), 123–236; Samuel Byrne, "Church and State in France," *CW*, 50 (October 1889), 8–19; *Catholic Times* of Philadelphia, December 10, 1892, 4.

20. Ellis, *Gibbons*, 1:308–309; Hecker's analysis was even less restrained; "Cardinal Gibbons and American Institutions," *CW*, 45 (June 1887), 330–337.

21. Moynihan, *Ireland*, 137–145; see the French edition of his speeches, *L'Eglise et le siècle, conférences et discours*, 9th ed. (Paris, 1902); Turmann, *Développement du catholicisme social*, 61; Hoog, *Histoire de catholicisme social*, 119.

22. Barry, *German Americans*, 197.

23. *CW*, 65 (September 1897), 857; Keane, *Providential Mission*, 24–25; Reily, *Passing Events*, 2:916.

24. The text is in Victor Charbonnel, *Congrès universel des religions en 1900* (Paris, 1897), 110–118.

25. Moynihan, *Ireland*, 25.

26. E. A. Pace, "The Fribourg Congress," *CW*, 66 (November 1897), 262.

27. *L'Américanisme d'après le père Hecker. Ce qu'il est et ce qu'il n'est pas* (Paris, 1897). The address is summarized in Moynihan, *Ireland*, 108–109.

28. H. L. DeZayas, "The Causes of the Present War in Cuba," *CW*, 62 (March 1896), 807–816; compare Thomas Hughes, "Catholic Spain — Its Politics and Liberalism," *ACQR*, 22 (July 1897), 493–517.

29. J. T. Farrell, "Archbishop Ireland and Manifest Destiny," *CHR*, 33 (October 1947), 269–301.

30. "Loyalty of American Catholics," *LD*, 16 (May 28, 1898), 650–651.

31. "Editorial Notes," *CW*, 67 (June 1898), 426.

32. "A Word on the Church and the New Possessions," *CW*, 68 (December 1898), 319–322; "Editorial Notes," *CW*, 68 (January 1889), 571.

33. *Ibid.*; A. P. Doyle, "Religious Problem of the Philippines," *CW*, 68 (October 1898), 124; O'Keefe, "A Word on the Church and the New Possessions," *CW*, 68 (December 1898), 321.

34. A. P. Doyle, "Religious Problem of the Philippines," *CW*, 68 (October, 1898), 124; Ireland's public comments are in "The Roman Catholic Church in our New Possessions," *LD*, 17 (September 17, 1898), 348; similar liberal comment, with an indignant conservative attack, is in B. J. Clinch, "The Truth about the Church in the Philippines," *CW*, 69 (June 1899), 289–303.

35. O'Keefe, "A Word on the Church and the New Possessions," *CW*, 68 (December 1898), 319.

36. "Editorial Notes," *CW*, 68 (December 1898), 421.

37. Farrell, "Archbishop Ireland," *CHR*, 33 (October 1947), 292.

38. *LD*, 18 (February 11, 1899), 167.

39. See chapter 6.

40. See for example his series, "A Study of Modern Religion," *CW*, 49 (September 1889), 711–719; 50 (October 1889), 72–80; and 50 (November 1889), 187–195; also his "The Troubles of a Catholic Democracy," *Contemporary Review*, 76 (July 1899), 70–86.

41. M. P. Smith, "Isaac Thomas Hecker," *Catholic Encyclopedia* (New York, 1910), 7:186–187; Petre, *Tyrrell*, 2:73–78, 474–476.

42. "Catholic and Democratic Ideals," *CW*, 51 (May 1890), 143–152; "The Treasures of the Church," *ACQR*, 20 (January 1895), 176–193.

43. "A Liberal Catholic View of the Case of Dr. Mivart," *Nineteenth Century*, 47 (April 1900), 684.

44. M. F. Egan, "A Chat about New Books," *CW*, 44 (January 1887), 555–556.

45. "Pope Leo XIII," *Forum*, 22 (January 1897), 513.

46. *Anglo-Saxon Superiority*, trans. L. B. Lavigne (London, 1899), 93; "Catholicism in the United States," *LD*, 11 (October 12, 1895), 709–710; Moynihan, *Ireland*, 274; Charbonnel, *Congrès*, 587–588; for Italian attitudes, see *RR*, 3 (May 1891), 419.

47. R. F. Byrnes, "The Christian Democrats in Modern France," in E. M. Earle, ed., *Modern France*, (Princeton, 1951), 160ff.; Klein, *Américanisme*, 52–53; Houtin, *Américanisme*, 71; Moynihan, *Ireland*, 226.

48. Byrnes, *Antisemitism*, 206–210, 220; Byrnes, "Christian Democrats," in Earle, ed., *Modern France*, 162–163; Klein, *Américanisme*, 50–53; Houtin, *Crise du clergé*, 115, 126.

49. "The Neo-Christian Movement in France," *RR*, 5 (February 1892), 74–75; Klein, *Nouvelles tendances en religion et en littérature* (Paris, 1893).

50. King and Okey, *Italy Today*, 51–52; Klein, *Américanisme*, 57; Delassus, *Américanisme*, 303–304; Hogan, *Conaty*, 159.

51. There were also "Americanists" in Germany, such as Professors Hermann Schell and F. X. Kraus; "'Americanism' in Europe," *LD*, 18 (April 8, 1899), 404; Klein, *Américanisme*, 57; Barry, *German Americans*, 231; Houtin, *Histoire du modernisme catholique* (Paris, 1913), 58.

52. As examples, see three generally sympathetic articles in the *Revue des deux mondes*: André Chevrillon, "Les Etats-Unis et la vie américaine," 110 (April 1, 1892), 568; Duc de Broglie, "L'Eglise et la France moderne," 141 (May 15, 1897), 303–305; Ferdinand Brunetière, "Le Catholicisme aux Etats-Unis," 150 (November 1, 1898), 167–171.

53. *L'Eglise et le siècle*, 6–8.

54. (New York, 1891).

55. Klein, *Américanisme*, 15–28.

56. Maignen, *Hecker*, 6; Houtin, *Américanisme*, 227.

57. Klein, *Américanisme*, 152–154.

58. "America as seen from Abroad," *CW*, 66 (March 1898), 721–730.

59. Charbonnel, *Congrès*, 587; Charbonnel, "Americanism *versus* Roman Catholicism," *Outlook*, 61 (March 11, 1899), 584–590; for criticism of Charbonnel's reliability, see Ellis, *Gibbons*, 2:72.

60. Delassus, *Américanisme*, 273–274, 423–425.

61. T'Serclaes, *Léon XIII*, 2:255n.

62. *Situation*, 130.

63. Ellis, *Gibbons*, 2:41; Delassus, *Américanisme*, 342–343.

64. H. C. Lea, "An Anti-Masonic Mystification," *Lippincott's Monthly Magazine*, 66 (December 1900), 950–955; for a typically credulous account, see Georges de Bessonies, *La Question Miss Diana Vaughan au Congrès de Trente* (Paris, 1896); "A Crusade against Freemasonry," *LD*, 13 (October 31, 1896), 857–858; "Leo Taxil and his 'Greatest Joke of all Times,'" *ibid.*, 15 (June 5, 1897), 176.

65. Ernest Renauld, *Le Péril protestant*, 11th ed. (Paris, 1899), 17, 27–45, 381ff.; Julien Fontaine, *Infiltrations kantiennes et protestantes et le clergé français* (Paris, 1902), 341; Delassus, *Américanisme*, 44, 97–98, 273–274, 423–425; "Growing Hostility to Protestantism in France," *LD*, 15 (August 14, 1897), 471; "Startling Demands of the Spanish Catholics," *LD*, 19 (October 28, 1899), 534; "An Anti-Protestant Crusade in France," *LD*, 20 (May 12, 1900), 581–582; William Gibson, "An Outburst of Activity in the Roman Congregations," *Nineteenth Century*, 45 (May 1899), 787.

66. "Cardinal Vaughan, the Catholic Church, and the Dreyfus Affair," *LD*, 19 (October 21, 1899), 499–500. Gibbons was outspokenly opposed to anti-Semitism; Will, *Gibbons*, 2:797; so was the *Catholic Times* of Philadelphia, 14 December 1895, 4; the *Catholic World* printed some anti-Semitic articles, but its general tone was pronouncedly tolerationist: Review of the *Catholic Home Almanac* for 1886, *CW*, 42 (December 1885), 424; B. "Jewish Preponderance," *CW*, 52 (November 1890), 200–207; "The Old World Seen from

the New," *CW*, 53 (April 1891), 124; "The Columbian Reading Union," *CW*, 66 (March 1898), 860–861; "Editorial Notes," *CW*, 68 (January 1899), 571.

67. Delassus, *Américanisme*, 81; Valerian Grubayedoff, "M. Drumont, Who Rings the Tocsin," *RR*, 17 (March 1898), 311–315; Byrnes, *Antisemitism*, *passim*.

68. On Bartolo, see chapter 8; on Schell, see J. A. Bain, *The New Reformation; Recent Evangelical Movements in the Roman Catholic Church* (Edinburgh, 1906), 16–20.

69. R. F. Clarke, "Dr. Mivart on the Continuity of Catholicism," *Nineteenth Century*, 47 (February 1900), 244–259; Mivart, "Scripture and Roman Catholicism," *ibid.*, (March 1900), 425–442; R. E. Dell, "A Liberal Catholic View of the Case of Dr. Mivart," *ibid.*, (April 1900), 669–684. Mivart had differed seriously with the Church for a number of years.

70. *Romanus*, "Liberal Catholicism," *Contemporary Review*, 72 (December 1897), 854–866.

71. Maignen, *Hecker*, 295–296.

72. Edouard Lecanuet, *La Vie de l'église sous Léon XIII* (Paris, 1930), 577–578.

73. T. T. McAvoy's forthcoming book will presumably discuss the European negotiations in detail. Already available are the accounts in Houtin, *Américanisme*; Klein, *Américanisme*; Ellis, *Gibbons*, 2:1–80; T. T. McAvoy, "Americanism and Frontier Catholicism," *Review of Politics*, 5 (July 1943), 275–301; V. C. Holden, "A Myth in '*L'Américanisme*,'" *CHR*, 31 (July 1945), 133–153; accounts by contemporaries are referred to in later footnotes.

74. Barry, *German Americans*, 219, 143, 149, 175.

75. Ellis, *Gibbons*, 1:461–485.

76. *Ibid.*, 1:473–474.

77. Macdonald, *Secret Societies*, 189–208; Zwierlein, *McQuaid*, 2:472–474; Tardivel, *Situation*, 27n, 28n; Moynihan, *Ireland*, 214–220.

78. The text of the encyclical *Longinqua Oceani* is in *CUB*, 1 (April 1895), 231–247.

79. Ellis, *Gibbons*, 2:30.

80. Moynihan, *Ireland*, 329–334.

81. "The Mind of the Apostolic Delegate," *AER*, 13 (July 1895) 101–107; Schroeder, "Leo XIII and the Encyclical '*Longinqua*,'" *ACQR*, 20 (April 1895), 381; M. J. H., "Church and State," *ACQR*, 21 (January 1896), 98–124; compare A. F. Hewit, "Encyclical of Leo XIII to the Bishops of the United States," *CW*, 60 (March 1895), 721–726.

82. Ellis, *Gibbons*, 2:31–34.

83. Lord *et al.*, *Boston*, 3:461–478.

84. Moynihan, *Ireland*, 43–44; "Pope Leo XIII on Religious Congresses," *LD*, 12 (November 9, 1895), 50.

85. *Ibid.* See the stringent comments of the *Civiltà* reported in *LD*, 12 (February 22, 1896), 20.

86. Ahern, *Catholic University*, 168–177.

87. "The Resignation of Bishop Keane," *LD*, 13 (October 24, 1896), 821; "Meaning of Bishop Keane's Removal," *LD*, 13 (October 31, 1896), 851–853. Compare *Catholic Standard and Times* of Philadelphia, September and October 1896.
88. Zwierlein, *McQuaid*, 3:242; Klein, *Américanisme*, 129–130.
89. Ellis, *Gibbons*, 2:40; Zwierlein, *McQuaid*, 3:240; Ahern, *Catholic University*, 176–177; Hogan, *Conaty*, 148.
90. *Catholic Standard and Times* of Philadelphia, November 28, 1896, 4; December 12, 1896, 2.
91. Ellis, *Gibbons*, 2:43.
92. Hogan, *Conaty*, 150–177; "A Conflict in the Catholic University," *LD*, 15 (November 13, 1897), 859–860.
93. Ho Tharseus, "The Chapter 'De Fide Catholica' in the Third Plenary Council of Baltimore," *AER*, 16 (February 1897), 147–154; for similar convictions, see Barry, *German Americans*, 189n.
94. Klein, *Américanisme*, 100–103.
95. Published in book form as *Le Père Hecker, est-il un saint?* (Rome and Paris, 1898).
96. Ellis, *Gibbons*, 2:56.
97. Klein, *Américanisme*, 204–210.
98. *Ibid.*, 245–263.
99. Hogan, *Conaty*, 163.
100. The text of "*Testem Benevolentiae*" is in Klein, *Américanisme*, 363–374.
101. Klein, *Américanisme*, 375–398.
102. Ellis, *Gibbons*, 2:71.
103. "More about 'Américanisme,'" *LD*, 18 (March 18, 1899), 314–315; "The Papal Letter and the *Outlook*," *CW*, 69 (April 1899), 8; J. St. Clair Etheridge, "The Genesis of 'Americanism,'" *NAR*, 170 (May 1900), 690; Lecanuet, *Vie de l'église*, 544–602; Barbier, *Catholicisme libéral*, 3:277–284.
104. Walworth, *Walworth*, 155; for the persistence of this interpretation, see F. X. Curran, *Major Trends in American Church History* (New York, 1946), 139.
105. Zwierlein, *Corrigan*, 199; Klein, *Américanisme*, 392–393.
106. Zwierlein, *McQuaid*, 3:453–459.
107. Rothensteiner, *St. Louis*, 2:564; Klein, *Américanisme*, 391; Houtin, *Américanisme*, 360; Moynihan, *Ireland*, 241–242.
108. Parsons, *Studies*, 6:342n–343n.
109. P. L. Pechenard, "The End of 'Americanism' in France," *NAR*, 170 (March 1899), 425–428; Barbier, *Catholicisme libéral*, 3:242.
110. "European Comment on 'Americanism,'" *LD*, 18 (April 29, 1899), 496.
111. See Spencer, *Politics of Belief*, chapter 1.
112. "The Pope on Americanism," *LD*, 18 (March 11, 1899), 287–288.
113. Review of Louis Picard, *Christianity and Agnosticism* (London, n.d.),

CW, 69 (April 1899), 124–125; "Editorial Notes," *CW*, 69 (April 1889), 128.

114. *Religion, Agnosticism, and Education,* 147–192.
115. Barbier, *Catholicisme libéral,* 3:308.
116. Moynihan, *Ireland,* 145–151.
117. J. St. Clair Etheridge, "The Genesis of 'Americanism,'" *NAR*, 170 (May 1900), 693; Moynihan, *Ireland,* 397–398, attributes this article to Ireland, though Ellis, *Gibbons,* 2:75n, questions this.
118. Moynihan, *Ireland,* 151–157; Ellis, *Gibbons,* 2:76, 76n; Klein, *Américanisme,* 438.
119. Moynihan, *Ireland,* 177–210.
120. M. L. Storer, *In Memoriam Bellamy Storer,* privately printed (1923), 46.
121. Ellis, *Gibbons,* 2:78.
122. Moynihan, *Ireland,* 305; Hogan, *Conaty,* 172.
123. Lecanuet, *Vie de l'église,* 601–602.
124. Hogan, *Conaty,* 172, states this flatly; Ellis, *Gibbons,* 2:80, by closing his chapter with this quotation, leaves that implication.
125. Moynihan, *Ireland,* 132.
126. *Ibid.,* 308.
127. "The Pope's Civil Princedom," *NAR*, 172 (March 1901), 337–351.
128. *Ibid.,* 345–361.
129. Walsh, *Our Cardinals,* 121–221; P. J. Hayes, "John Cardinal Farley," *HRS*, 6 (1913), 5–68.
130. Maisie Ward, *The Wilfrid Wards,* 2:273.
131. Moynihan, *Ireland,* 358.

Chapter XI

Liberal Catholicism in the Twentieth Century

1. William Teeling, *Pope Pius XI and World Affairs* (New York, 1937), 133, 158–160.
2. "The National Catholic Welfare Council," *CW*, 109 (July 1919), 436.
3. For examples, see *New York Times,* March 6–22, 1948, and April 14, 1948.
4. François Mauriac, "Why No American can be Elected Pope," *Look,* 19 (March 8, 1955), 32–33; compare G. Bocca, "Who will be the next pope?" *Look,* 20 (May 15, 1956), 116–121.
5. Walsh, *Our Cardinals.*
6. Samuel Lubell, *The Future of American Politics* (New York, 1952), 78–79; but see also 220–226.
7. F. Knebel, "Can a Catholic become Vice-President?" *Look,* 20 (June 12, 1956), 33–35; J. J. Kane, "Catholic President?" *COM*, 63 (February 17, 1956), 511–513.

8. *Everson* v. *Board of Education of the Township of Ewing, New Jersey*, 330 U.S., 17–18 (1946).

9. *Zorach* v. *Clauson*, 342 U.S., 306 (1952). For Catholic criticism of the McCollum case, see Wilfrid Parsons, *The First Freedom: Considerations on Church and State in the United States* (New York, 1948). For Catholic criticism of the grounds of the Zorach decision, see W. R. Frasca, "Confusion in the Supreme Court," *Thought*, 28 (Winter 1953–1954), 547–570.

10. Shaughnessy, *Has the Immigrant Kept the Faith?*

11. See two articles in *Commentary* by Will Herberg: "The Triple Melting-Pot," 20 (August 1955), 101–108, and "America's New Religiousness," 20 (September 1955), 243.

12. J. M. Mecklin, *The Ku Klux Klan* (New York, 1924).

13. C. C. Marshall, *The Roman Catholic Church in the Modern World* is the fuller form of his indictment; for Catholic comment, see Michael Williams, *The Shadow of the Pope* (New York, 1932). For an analysis of the campaign, see E. A. Moore, *A Catholic Runs for President* (New York, 1956).

14. Blanshard's best known books are *American Freedom and Catholic Power* (Boston, 1949), and *Communism, Democracy, and Catholic Power* (Boston, 1951). Other books in the same vein are C. H. Moehlman, *The Wall of Separation between Church and State* (Boston, 1951), and H. R. Rafton, *The Roman Catholic Church and Democracy* (Boston, 1951). An interesting study was made by G. C. Zahn of the attitudes implicit in 4000 letters Blanshard received; "'Catholic Separatism' and Anti-Catholic Tensions," *America*, 96 (October 27, 1956), 94–98. For a comprehensive rejoinder by a liberal Catholic, see J. M. O'Neill, *Catholicism and American Freedom* (New York, 1952).

15. J. J. Kane, *Catholic-Protestant Conflicts in America* (Chicago, 1955); Kane, "Protestant-Catholic Tensions," *American Sociological Review*, 16 (October 1951), 663–672; Will Herberg, "Sectarian Conflict over Church and State," *Commentary*, 14 (November 1952), 450–462; J. B. Sheerin, "Protestant-Catholic Cold War," *CW*, 182 (December 1955), 161–165.

16. "Growth of U.S. Churches," *Time*, 57 (April 2, 1951), 81.

17. A Gallup poll, reported in "Conversion poll ends in a dead heat," *Christian Century*, 72 (April 6, 1955), 411.

18. G. J. Schnepp, *Leakage from a Catholic Parish* (Washington, 1942); for a somewhat more optimistic view, see L. R. Ward, "The Church in America," in Ward, ed., *American Apostolate*, 8–10.

19. J. J. Kane, "Catholic Separatism," *COM*, 58 (June 26, 1953), 293–296; John Fearon, "Tribal Feelings in Catholic Evaluations," *Homiletic and Pastoral Review*, 54 (January 1954), 306–309.

20. J. C. Fenton, "The Direction of Catholic Polemic," *AER*, 122 (January 1950), 48–55; "Catholic Polemic and Doctrinal Accuracy," *AER*, 132 (February 1955), 107–117.

21. "The Church and God's Promises," *AER*, 123 (October 1950), 295–

308; F. J. Connell, "If the Trumpet Give an Uncertain Sound," *AER*, 118 (January 1948), 23–30.

22. Fenton, "The Lesson of *Humani Generis*," *AER*, 123 (November 1950), 359–378; Connell, "Theological Content of *Humani Generis*," *ibid.*, 321–330.

23. W. P. Clancy, "The Liberal Catholic," *COM*, 56 (July 11, 1952), 335–337.

24. For testimony to the extent of conservative opposition, see John Cogley, "*Anathema Sit*," *COM*, 58 (June 12, 1953), 248.

25. "Catholics in America — A Creative Minority?" *Catholic Mind*, 53 (October 1955), 590–597.

26. "Catholic Climate Abroad," *Thought*, 26 (Spring 1951), 128.

27. John LaFarge, *The Manner is Ordinary* (New York, 1954), 302.

28. Gillis, *This Our Day* (New York, 1933), 98–103; *On Almost Everything* (New York, 1955), 145–147; John Cogley, "*Anathema Sit*," *COM*, 59 (February 26, 1954), 516; *COM*, 59 (March 19, 1954), 601; "Father Gillis on *America*," *America*, 87 (May 24, 1952), 219–220; "Father Gillis replies," *America*, 87 (June 7, 1952), 280.

29. John Cogley, "*Anathema Sit*," *COM*, 59 (February 26, 1954), 516.

30. "The Catholic Minority is Growing," *CW*, 181 (July 1955), 242.

31. The phrase was used by the visiting Bishop J. J. Blomjous, "The Lay Apostolate," *Catholic Mind*, 53 (April 1955), 193–198; *America*, 84 (February 10, 1951), 572; John LaFarge, "Catholic Impact: 1949–1950," *America*, 82 (January 7, 1950), 410–412; "Let's Build the Spiritual Front," *America*, 83 (August 19, 1950), 508–509.

32. See the demands that the Newman clubs at secular universities not foster Catholic separatism; J. G. Kerwin, "Newman Clubs — New Tasks and Opportunities," *America*, 83 (September 9, 1950), 583–588; compare J. S. Duryea, "Newman Clubs," *Catholic Mind*, 53 (April 1955), 210–212; R. J. Walsh, "Interreligious Student Work," *Religious Education*, 51 (November–December 1956), 425–428.

33. *The Catholic Approach to Protestantism* (New York, 1955); "Peace Among Christians," *Integrity*, 7 (July 1953), 33–37.

34. "Cooperation with non-Catholics," *America*, 82 (March 11, 1950), 658.

35. "The Gulf," *Christian Century*, 71 (July 21, 1954), 869–871.

36. Sheerin, "Catholics and Evanston," *CW*, 180 (October 1954), 4; Weigel, "Ecumenicism and the Catholic," *Thought*, 30 (Spring 1955), 5–17.

37. On the general spirit of the National Council, see E. R. Clinchy, *All in the Name of God* (New York, 1934), especially 140–141; Connell, "Catholics and 'Interfaith' Groups," *AER*, 105 (November 1941), which I consulted in offprint form in the library of Crozer Theological Seminary; Connell, "The National Conference of Christians and Jews," *AER*, 121 (October 1949), 341–342; "Theological Content of *Humani Generis*," *AER*, 123 (November 1950), 321–330; for the poll, see A. S. Foley, "Catholic Participation in Intergroup Activities," *McAuley Lectures*, 1955, 131. I am in-

debted for this reference to Miss Charlotte Epstein of the Philadelphia office of the National Conference of Christians and Jews.

38. Foley, "Catholic Participation," *McAuley Lectures, 1955*, 132, 146; Kane, *Catholic-Protestant Conflicts*, 208–210.

39. *"Extra Ecclesiam Nulla Salus,"* AER, 110 (April 1944), 300–306; "The Theological Proof for the Necessity of the Catholic Church," *AER*, 118 (March 1948), 214–228, and *ibid.* (April 1948), 290–305.

40. C. G. Clark, *The Loyolas and the Cabots* (Boston, 1950); J. C. Fenton, "The Holy Office Letter on the Necessity of the Catholic Church," *AER*, 127 (December 1952), 450–461.

41. *New York Times*, February 15, 1956.

42. E. S. Schwegler, "Sacerdotal Squawks," 53 (August 1953), 993–994.

43. For contemporary Catholic embarrassment with Ireland's self-confidence, see Bland, *Hibernian Crusade*, 227, and J. T. Farrell, "Archbishop Ireland and Manifest Destiny," *CHR*, 33 (October 1947), 269–301.

44. Ed Willock, "Catholic Radicalism," *COM*, 58 (October 2, 1953), 630; Dorothy Dohen, "An Inquiry on Confession and Spiritual Direction," *Integrity*, 9 (October 1954), 24.

45. Pius XII's criticism is referred to in Sugrue, *An American Catholic*, 29; for the earlier criticism by Pius X of the activism of "americanism," see his *"Pascendi dominici gregis,"* ACQR, 32 (October 1907), 705–730.

46. W. R. Fleege, "The Coming Era of the Catholic Layman," *Homiletic and Pastoral Review*, 54 (November 1953), 134–139.

47. P. F. Palmer, "Lay Priesthood: Towards a Terminology," *TS*, 10 (June 1949), 235–250.

48. W. J. Whalen, "A Layman Looks at Latin," *CW*, 179 (September 1954), 449–455.

49. J. G. Keller, *You Can Change the World!* (New York, 1948), 363–374; *Three Minutes a Day* (Garden City, N.Y., 1949), x–xii; *Stop, Look, and Live* (Garden City, N.Y., 1954), xii.

50. See this attitude in W. J. Ong, "American Catholicism and America," *Thought*, 27 (Winter 1952–1953), 421–451.

51. R. J. Dwyer, "The American Laity," *COM*, 60 (August 27, 1954), 506; D. V. Sheehan, "It's easier to carp than to cooperate," *America*, 82 (March 18, 1950), 691–693; J. B. Sheerin, "The Catholic Minority is Growing," *CW*, 181 (July 1955), 245; compare J. F. Reilly, "Meet Mr. Lay Teacher," *CW*, 179 (September 1954), 456–459.

52. L. R. Ward, "The Church in America," in Ward, ed., *American Apostolate*, 1–5.

53. Michael Williams, *American Catholics in the War* (New York, 1921), 113.

54. *Ibid.*, 144–146; *National Catholic Welfare Conference* (Washington, 1947), 6.

55. *Social Reconstruction* (Washington, 1919); volumes 1–2 of the *National Catholic Welfare Council Bulletin* (1919–1921); Austin Dowling,

"The National Catholic Welfare Conference," *Ecclesiastical Review*, 79 (October 1928), 337–354.

56. The decree is in Michael Williams, "The Possibilities of National Catholic Cooperation," in *Catholic Builders*, 2:297–299; Teeling, *Pope Pius XI*, 160–163.

57. T. T. McAvoy, "The Catholic Church in the United States," in Gurian and Fitzsimons, eds., *Catholic Church in World Affairs*, 358–376.

58. "*Pascendi dominici gregis*," ACQR, 32 (October 1907), 705–730.

59. Loisy, *My Duel*, 311.

60. "Modernism in the Church in America," *AER*, 38 (January 1908), 1–10; Anthony Viéban, "Who are the Modernists of the Encyclical?" *AER*, 38 (May 1908), 489–508; for very free allegations against Spalding and a number of Sulpician and Catholic University of America professors, see Houtin's books, *Crise du clergé*, 269–271; *Vie de prêtre*, 242, 242n; and *Histoire du modernisme catholique*, 113–114, 240–242.

61. *New York Review*, 3 (May–June 1908), front inside cover; Ellis, *Gibbons*, 2:170.

62. *Ibid*, 2:171–182.

63. Sullivan, *Under Orders*, 111.

64. Vidler, *Modernist Movement*, 213; Sugrue, *An American Catholic*, 54; G. N. Shuster, *The Catholic Spirit in America* (New York, 1928), 170; Maynard, *American Catholicism*, 585; L. R. Ward, "The Church in America," in Ward, ed., *American Apostolate*, 1–5.

65. J. T. Ellis, "American Catholics and the Intellectual Elite," *Thought*, 30 (Autumn 1955), 351–388.

66. "Catholics and Science," COM, 58 (August 28, 1953), 509–514; W. M. Cashin, "Catholics and Science Doctorates," *America*, 82 (December 21, 1949), 388; Milton Lomask, "Feature 'X,'" *America*, 84 (March 3, 1951), 642–644; W. C. Bier, "The Catholic Psychologist's Contribution to Group Understanding," *McAuley Lectures, 1955*, 109.

67. "American Catholicism and America," *Thought*, 27 (Winter 1952–1953), 521–541.

68. "Catholic Separatism," COM, 58 (June 26, 1953), 293–296; COM, 58 (August 21, 1953), 490; Dorothy Dohen, "Are Catholic Schools Divisive?" *Integrity*, 7 (May 1953), 1–5.

69. "Catholics and our Public Schools," *America*, 84 (March 31, 1951), 743; 85 (August 18, 1951), 472; 87 (May 3, 1952), 124.

70. "Catholics and Education," COM, 58 (August 7, 1953), 437–441, and (August 14, 1953), 461–464.

71. *The Catholic and Secular Education* (New York, 1956), reviewed in *Newsweek*, 47 (June 4, 1956), 88.

72. "Catholics and our Public Schools," *America*, 84 (March 31, 1951), 743; J. C. Murray, "Catholics in America," *Catholic Mind*, 53 (October 1955), 592.

73. L. R. Ward, *Blueprint for a Catholic University* (St. Louis, 1949);

Ward, "Is there a Christian Learning?" *COM*, 58 (September 25, 1953), 607; "Hustler for Quality," *Time*, 67 (May 1956), 77.

74. A. I. Abell, "The Reception of Leo XIII's Labor Encyclical," *Review of Politics*, 7 (October 1945), 486.

75. W. F. Montavon, "The National Catholic Welfare Conference," in Ward, ed., *American Apostolate*, 241–277; Ryan, *Social Doctrine in Action, A Personal History* (New York, 1941).

76. R. E. Burns, "CYO and the Christian Revolution," in Ward, ed., *American Apostolate*, 204–216.

77. Jim Cunningham, "Specialized Catholic Action," and Ed Marciniak, "Catholics and Labor-Management Relations," in Ward, ed., *American Apostolate*, 47–65, 66–81; Ed Willock, "Catholic Radicalism," *COM*, 58 (October 2, 1953), 630–633; A. I. Abell, "The Catholic Church and the American Social Question," in Gurian and Fitzsimons, eds., *Catholic Church in World Affairs*, 377–399.

78. V. J. O'Connell, "The Church in the South," in Ward, ed., *American Apostolate*, 109–119; "Ban on Segregation," *COM*, 60 (April 30, 1954), 85.

79. "Soft Spot in American Catholicism," *America*, 87 (September 2, 1952), 530.

80. E. A. Keller, *Christianity and American Capitalism* (Chicago, 1954); J. P. Fitzpatrick, "The Encyclicals and the United States," *Thought* (Autumn, 1954), 391–402; *America*, 83 (August 26, 1950), 522.

81. E. A. Marciniak, "Catholics and Social Reform," *COM*, 58 (September 11, 1953), 459.

82. James O'Gara, "Catholics and Isolationism," *COM*, 59 (November 13, 1953), 137.

83. *The Key to Peace* (Chicago, 1950), 77.

84. For evidence that Catholics are still predominantly in lower income strata, see Kane, *Catholic-Protestant Conflicts*, 79; compare Murray's conclusion that "we are established as an economic middle class," in his "Catholicism in America," *Catholic Mind*, 53 (October 1955), 591.

85. Richard Hofstadter, "The Pseudo-Conservative Revolt," *American Scholar*, 24 (Winter 1954–1955), 9–27.

86. Reinhold Niebuhr, "A Protestant Looks at Catholics," *COM*, 58 (May 8, 1953), 118–119.

87. "Catholics and McCarthy," *COM*, 61 (December 10, 1954), 276–277; John Cogley, "Two Images of One Man," *COM*, 62 (June 3, 1955), 233.

88. W. R. Bechtel, "Protestants and Catholics," *New Republic*, 128 (July 27, 1953), 11–12; V. P. de Santis, "A Catholic View of McCarthy," *New Republic*, 130 (June 7, 1954), 22.

89. J. A. Ryan and M. F. X. Millar, *The State and the Church* (New York, 1922); and Ryan and F. J. Boland, *Catholic Principles of Politics* (New York, 1943).

90. *COM*, 58 (June 12, 1953), 250; Francis Dowling, "American Catholi-

cism and the Socio-Economic Evolution in U.S.A.," in J. N. Moody, ed., *Church and Society* (New York, 1953), 878.

91. Quoted in John Cogley, "Catholics and American Democracy," *COM*, 58 (June 5, 1953), 224; J. T. Ellis, "Church and State: an American Catholic Tradition," *Harper's*, 207 (November 1953), 63–67.

92. Murray has published his work in a series of articles, most of which will be cited later. A good summary is V. R. Yanitelli, "A Church-State Anthology, the work of Father Murray," *Thought*, 27 (Spring 1952), 6–42. For a Protestant summary, see G. H. Williams, "Issues between Catholics and Protestants at Mid-Century," *Religion in Life*, 23 (November 1954), 176–181.

93. "The Problem of 'The Religion of the State,' " *AER*, 124 (May 1951), 327–352.

94. "Contemporary Orientations of Catholic Thought on Church and State in the Light of History," *TS*, 10 (June 1949), 229.

95. "On the Structure of the Church-State Problem," in Gurian and Fitzsimons, eds., *Catholic Church in World Politics*, 19–25; "St. Robert Bellarmine on the Indirect Power," *TS*, 9 (December 1948), 491–535.

96. "The Church and Totalitarian Democracy," *TS*, 13 (December 1952), 551n–552n.

97. "Catholics in America," *Catholic Mind*, 53 (October 1955), 594.

98. "The Problem of Pluralism in America," *Thought*, 29 (Summer 1954), 190–193; "Contemporary Orientations," *TS*, 10 (June 1949), 220; see also two unsigned articles in *America*: "Religious Liberty in Spain," 87 (April 5, 1952), 1, and (May 24, 1952), 218.

99. *Ibid.*

100. "Toleration and the Church-State Controversy," *AER*, 130 (May 1954), 330–343; "Catholic Polemic and Doctrinal Accuracy," *AER*, 132 (February 1955), 107–117.

101. "The Church-State Problem," *COM*, 58 (August 7, 1953), 431–432; see also Murray, "Current Theology on Religious Freedom," *TS*, 10 (September 1949), 426–432.

102. G. W. Shea, "Catholic Doctrine and 'The Religion of the State,' " *AER*, 123 (September 1950), 161–174; compare Gustave Weigel, "The Church and the Democratic State," *Thought*, 27 (Summer 1952), 165–175.

103. "The Problem of 'The Religion of the State,' " *AER*, 124 (May 1951), 330n–332n; "Contemporary Orientations," *TS*, 10 (June 1949), 233.

104. "Leo XIII: Two Concepts of Government," *TS*, 14 (December 1953), 560–567.

105. "Contemporary Orientations," *TS*, 10 (June 1949), 225; "Church-State Problem," in Gurian and Fitzsimons, eds., *Catholic Church in World Affairs*, 28.

106. Quoted in J. W. Evans and L. R. Ward, eds., *The Social and Political Philosophy of Jacques Maritain* (New York, 1955), 284n.

107. "The Problem of 'The Religion of the State,'" *AER*, 129 (May 1951), 327ff.

108. Murray, "Freedom of Religion," *TS*, 6 (June 1945), 238.

109. Same as note 107.

110. "Leo XIII: Separation of Church and State," *TS*, 14 (June 1953), 179.

111. Same as note 107.

112. "American Catholicism and America," *Thought*, 27 (Winter 1952–1953), 541.

BIBLIOGRAPHY

PRIMARY SOURCES FOR CHAPTERS I–X

UNPUBLISHED MATERIAL

Keane, J. J. "Revealed Religion." Unpublished Dudleian lecture. October 23, 1890, Harvard University Archives.

BOOKS

Abbelen, P. M. *Venerable Mother M. Caroline Friess.* Authorized translation. St. Louis, 1893.

Abbot, F. E. *The Public School Question.* Boston, 1876.

Acton, J. E. *The History of Freedom and Other Essays.* Edited by J. N. Figgis and R. V. Laurence. London, 1909.

Bacon, L. W. *A History of American Christianity.* New York, 1897.

Balmes, J. L. *Protestantism and Catholicity compared in their Effects on the Civilization of Europe.* Translated by C. J. Hanford. 2nd ed. Baltimore, 1851.

Bargy, Henry. *La Religion dans la société aux Etats-Unis.* Paris, 1902.

Barry, W. F. *Memories and Opinions.* London, 1926.

Berthelet, Giovanni. *Si le pape doit être italien.* Rome, 1894.

de Bessonies, G. *La Question Miss Diana Vaughan au Congrès de Trente.* Paris, 1896.

Blanc, Thérèse. *The Condition of Woman in the United States.* Translated by A. L. Alger. Boston, 1895.

—— *Choses et gens d'Amérique.* Paris, 1898.

Bouquillon, Thomas. *Education: to whom does it belong?* Baltimore, 1891.

—— *Education: to whom does it belong? A rejoinder to critics.* Baltimore, 1892.

Brace, C. L. *The Dangerous Classes of New York.* New York, 1872.

Brooks, J. G. *The Social Unrest.* New York, 1904.

Bugg, L. H. *The People of our Parish.* Boston, 1900.

Burgess, J. W. *Political Science and Comparative Constitutional Law.* 2 vols. Boston, 1902.

Burtsell, R. L. *The Canonical Status of Priests in the United States.* n. p., n. d.

Butler, Charles. *Historical Memoirs of the English, Irish, and Scottish Catholics since the Reformation.* 3rd ed. revised. 4 vols. London, 1822.

Carlier, Auguste. *La République américaine.* 4 vols. Paris, 1890.

Cathrein, Victor. *The Champions of Agrarian Socialism. A Refutation of Emile de Laveleye and Henry George.* Buffalo, 1889.

—— *Socialism Exposed and Refuted.* Translated by James Conway. 2nd ed. New York, 1902.

Chapman, J. J. *Causes and Consequences.* New York, 1898.

Charbonnel, Victor. *Congrès universel des religions en 1900.* Paris, 1897.

Chateaubriand, François. *The Genius of Christianity.* Translated by C. I. White. Baltimore, n. d.

Conway, J. J. *The Fundamental Principles of Christian Ethics.* Chicago, 1896.

—— *The State Last: A Study of Dr. Bouquillon's pamphlet, "Education: to whom does it belong?" with a Supplement Reviewing Dr. Bouquillon's "Rejoinder to Critics."* 2nd revised ed. New York, 1892.

Cornelison, I. A. *The Relation of Religion to Civil Government in the United States of America. A State without a Church but not without a Religion.* New York, 1895.

Corrigan, Patrick. *What the Catholic Church Most Needs in the United States.* New York, 1884.

Curci, C. M. *Le Dissentiment moderne entre l'église et l'Italie.* French translation. Paris, 1878.

De Garmo, Charles. *Herbart and the Herbartians.* New York, 1895.

Delassus, Henri. *L'Américanisme et la conjuration anti-chrétienne.* Lille, 1899.

Demolins, Edward. *Anglo-Saxon Superiority.* Translated by L. B. Lavigne. London, 1899.

Desmond, H. J. *The Church and the Law, with special reference to Ecclesiastical Law in the United States.* Chicago, 1898.

Dixon, Thomas. *The Failure of Protestantism in New York and its Causes.* 2nd ed. New York, 1896.

von Doellinger, I., and Heuber, J. (Janus, *pseud.*). *The Pope and the Council.* Authorized translation. Boston, 1870.

Dorchester, Daniel. *Christianity in the United States.* Revised edition. New York, 1895.

Dugard, Marie. *La Société américaine.* Paris, 1896.

Dupanloup, Felix. *Avertissement adressé par Mgr. l'Evêque d'Orléans à M. Louis Veuillot, rédacteur en chef du journal L'Univers.* Paris, 1869.

—— *La Convention du 15 septembre et l'encyclique du 8 décembre.* Paris, 1865.

—— *Femmes savantes et femmes studieuses.* Paris, 1867.

—— *Lettre de Mgr. l'Evêque d'Orléans au clergé de son diocèse relativement à la définition de l'infaillibilité au prochain concile.* Paris, 1869.

—— *Lettre de Mgr. l'Evêque d'Orléans au clergé et aux fidèles de son diocèse avant son départ pour Rome.* Paris, 1869.

—— *Réponse à Mgr. Spalding.* Naples, 1870.

—— *A Study of Freemasonry.* English translation. London, 1875.

Egan, M. F., ed. *Onward and Upward: a yearbook . . . of discourses of Archbishop Keane.* Baltimore, 1902.

—— *Recollections of a Happy Life.* New York, 1924.

Egremont, Charles. *L'Année de l'église 1898.* Paris, n. d.

Elliott, Walter. *The Life of Father Hecker.* New York, 1891.

Fessler, Joseph. *La vraie et la fausse infaillibilité des papes.* Translated by Emmanuel Cosquin. Paris, 1873.

Figgis, J. N. and R. V. Lawrence, eds. *Selections from the Correspondence of the First Lord Acton.* London, 1917.

Fogazzaro, Antonio. *The Saint.* Translated by M. A. Pritchard. New York, 1906.

Fontaine, Julien. *Infiltrations kantiennes et protestantes et le clergé français.* Paris, 1902.

Fox, J. J. *Religion and Morality.* New York, 1899.

Friedrich, Johann. (Quirinus, *pseud.*). *Letters from Rome on the Council.* Authorized translation. New York, 1870.

Gaume, Jean, *Paganism in Education.* Translated by Robert Hill. London, 1852.

——— *La Révolution. Recherches historiques sur l'origine et la propagation du mal depuis la Renaissance jusqu'à nos jours.* Vol. 1. Paris, 1856.

——— *La situation: douleurs, dangers, devoirs, consolations des catholiques dans les temps actuels.* 2nd ed. Paris, 1860.

George, Henry. *The Condition of Labour.* 2nd ed. London, 1892.

——— *The Irish Land Question.* New York, 1881.

——— *Progress and Poverty.* Modern Library edition. New York, n. d.

Gibbons, James. *The Ambassador of Christ.* Baltimore, 1891.

——— *The Faith of our Fathers.* 88th ed. Baltimore, n. d.

——— *Our Christian Heritage.* Baltimore, 1889.

——— *A Retrospect of Fifty Years.* 2 vols. Baltimore, 1916.

Gladstone, W. E. *The Vatican Decrees in their Bearing on Civil Allegiance.* London, 1874.

——— *Vaticanism. An Answer to Reproofs and Replies.* London, 1875.

Gmeiner, John. *Emmanuel, the Savior of the World.* Milwaukee, 1888.

——— *Medieval and Modern Cosmology.* Milwaukee, 1891.

——— *Modern Scientific Views and Christian Doctrines Compared.* Milwaukee, 1884.

Gompers, Samuel. *Seventy Years of Life and Labor.* 2 vols. New York, 1925.

Hamilton, Henry. *See* Spalding, J. L.

Harrison, J. B. *Certain Dangerous Tendencies in American Life, and other papers.* Boston, 1880.

Hecker, I. T. *Aspirations of Nature.* New York, 1857.

——— *The Church and the Age.* New York, 1887.

——— *Questions of the Soul.* New York, 1855.

Hergenroether, Joseph. *Anti-Janus: An Historico-Theological Criticism of the Work entitled "The Pope and the Council," by Janus.* Translated by J. B. Robertson. Dublin, 1870.

Hewit, A. F. *Memoir of the Life of the Reverend Francis A. Baker.* 7th ed. New York, 1889.

———— *Problems of the Age, with Studies in Saint Augustine on Kindred Topics.* New York, 1868.

———— *The Teaching of St. John the Apostle to the Churches of Asia and the World.* New York, 1895.

Higginson, T. W. *Common Sense about Women.* Boston, 1881.

Hogan, J. B. *Clerical Studies.* 2nd ed. Boston, n. d.

Holaind, R. J. *The Parent First: An Answer to Dr. Bouquillon's Query, "Education: to whom does it belong?"* New York, 1891.

Houtin, Albert. *L'Américanisme.* Paris, 1904.

Keane, J. J. *The Providential Mission of Leo XIII.* Baltimore, 1888.

———— *See also* Egan, M. F.

von Ketteler, Wilhelm. *Liberté, autorité, église: considérations sur les grands problèmes de notre époque.* Translated by Abbé Belet. Paris, 1862.

King, J. M. *Facing the Twentieth Century.* New York, 1899.

Klein, Felix. *America of To-morrow.* Translated by E. H. Wilkins. Chicago, 1911.

———— *L'Américanisme.* Paris, 1949.

———— *In the Land of the Strenuous Life.* Chicago, 1905.

———— *Nouvelles Tendances en religion et en littérature.* Paris, 1893.

———— *La Séparation aux Etats-Unis.* Paris, 1908.

Kress, W. S. *Questions of Socialists and Their Answers.* Cleveland, 1905.

La Chesnais, P. G. *L'Eglise et les états: trois examples de séparation.* Paris, 1904.

La Follette, R. M. *Autobiography.* Madison, Wisconsin, 1913.

Lambert, L. A. *Ingersoll's Christmas Sermon.* Akron, Ohio, 1898.

———— *Private Judgment.* Milwaukee, 1916.

———— *Tactics of Infidels.* Buffalo, 1887.

de Lamennais, H. F. *Les Affaires de Rome.* Paris, 1837.

———— *Paroles d'un croyant.* 7th ed. Paris, 1834.

Lawrence, R. V. *See* Figgis, J. N.

Leclerc, Max. *Choses d'Amérique.* Paris, 1895.

Loisy, Alfred. *My Duel with the Vatican, the autobiography of a Catholic Modernist.* Translated by R. W. Boynton. New York, 1924.

Lyon, W. H. *A Study of the Christian Sects.* Boston, 1891.

McQuaid, B. J. *The Public School Question.* Boston, 1876.

Mahan, A. T. *The Interest of America in Sea Power, Present and Future.* Boston, 1898.

Maignen, Charles. *Le Père Hecker, est-il un saint?* Rome and Paris, 1898.

———— *La vraie Situation du catholicisme aux Etats-Unis et M. Ferdinand Brunetière.* Paris, 1899.

de Maistre, Joseph. *Du pape.* 2nd ed. 2 vols. Paris, 1821.

Manning, H. E. *The True Story of the Vatican Council.* London, 1877.

———— *The Vatican Decrees in their Bearing on Civil Allegiance.* London, 1875.

Manzoni, Alessandro. *The Betrothed.* Translated by Archibald Colquhoun. London, 1951.
Mead, E. D. *The Roman Catholic Church and the Public Schools.* Boston, 1890.
de Meaux, Alfred. *L'Eglise catholique et la liberté aux Etats-Unis.* Paris, 1893.
de Montalembert, C. F. *De l'avenir politique de l'Angleterre.* 5th ed. Paris, 1857.
—— *L'Eglise libre dans l'état libre.* Paris, 1863.
—— *Les Intérêts catholiques au dix-neuvième siècle.* Paris, 1852.
—— *The Monks of the West, from St. Benedict to St. Bernard.* Authorized translation. Vol. 1. Edinburgh, 1861.
Montgomery, Zachariah. *Poison Drops in the Federal Senate. The School Question from a Parental and Non-Sectarian Standpoint.* Washington, 1896.
Morel, Jules. *Les Catholiques libéraux.* Paris, 1864.
Morton, F. T. *The Roman Catholic Church and its Relations to the Federal Government.* Boston, 1909.
Mozans, H. J. *See* Zahm, J. A.
Mueller, Michael. *The Catholic Dogma.* New York, 1888.
—— *Public School Education.* New ed. New York, 1873.
Newman, J. H. *An Essay on the Development of Christian Doctrine.* Edited by C. F. Harrold. New York, 1949.
—— *The Idea of a University, defined and illustrated.* London, 1893.
—— *A Letter addressed to his Grace, the Duke of Norfolk on occasion of Mr. Gladstone's recent Expostulation.* London, 1875.
—— *A Letter to the Reverend E. B. Pusey, D.D. on his recent Eirenicon.* London, 1866.
O'Connell, D. J. *L'Américanisme d'après le père Hecker. Ce qu'il est et ce qu'il n'est pas.* Paris, 1897.
O'Gorman, Thomas. *A History of the Roman Catholic Church in the United States.* New York, 1895.
Ozanam, A. F. *Mélanges.* 2 vols. Paris, 1899.
Pallen, C. B. *The Catholic Church and Socialism. A Solution of the Social Problem.* St. Louis, 1890.
—— *The Education of Boys.* New York, 1916.
—— *What is Liberalism?* "Englished and Adapted from the Spanish of Dr. Don Felix Sarda y Salvany." St. Louis, 1899.
Parkhurst, C. M. *Our Fight with Tammany.* New York, 1895.
Parsons, Reuben. *Studies in Church History.* Vols. 4–6. New York, 1897–1900.
Pechenard, Louis, ed. *Un Siècle. Mouvement du monde 1800–1900.* Paris, 1899.
The Programme of Modernism. Translated by George Tyrrell. New York, 1908.

Preuss, Arthur. *The Fundamental Fallacy of Socialism.* 2nd revised edition. St. Louis, 1909.

———— *A Study in American Freemasonry.* St. Louis, 1905.

Quigley, P. F., ed. *Compulsory Education. The State of Ohio versus the Reverend Patrick Francis Quigley, D. D.* New York, 1894.

———— *Points in Canon Law.* Cleveland, 1878.

Quirinus. *See* Friedrich, Johann.

Rosen, Peter. *The Catholic Church and Secret Societies.* Milwaukee, 1902.

Rosmini-Serbati, Antonio. *Of the Five Wounds of the Holy Church.* Translated by H. P. Liddon. London, 1883.

Salmond, C. A. *Exposition and Defence of Prince Bismark's Anti-Ultramontane Policy.* Edinburgh, 1876.

Satolli, Francesco. *Loyalty to Church and State.* Baltimore, 1895.

Schaff, Philip. *Church and State in the United States.* New York, 1888.

von Schlegel, Friedrich. *The Philosophy of History.* Translated by J. B. Robertson. 2 vols. London, 1835.

von Schulte, J. F. *Le Pouvoir des papes depuis la proclamation du dogme de l'infaillibilité.* Translated by Etienne Patrie. Paris, 1879.

Shea, J. G. *History of the Catholic Church in the United States.* 4 vols. New York, 1890–1892.

Sheedy, M. M. *Christian Unity.* New York, 1895.

———— *Social Problems.* Chicago, 1896.

Smith, J. T. *Brother Azarias, the life story of an American monk.* New York, 1897.

———— *The Training of a Priest: an Essay on Clerical Education, with a Reply to Critics.* New York. 1908.

Smyth, Newman. *Passing Protestantism and Coming Catholicism.* New York, 1908.

Soderini, Eduardo. *Socialism and Catholicism.* Translated by Richard Jenery-Shea. London, 1896.

Spalding, J. L. (Henry Hamilton, *pseud.*) *America, and other poems.* New York, 1885.

———— *Aphorisms and Reflections.* Chicago, 1901.

———— *Education and the Higher Life.* Chicago, 1890.

———— *Essays and Reviews.* New York, 1877.

———— *Glimpses of Truth.* Chicago, 1903.

———— *God and the Soul.* New York, 1901.

———— *A Kentucky Pioneer.* Champaign, Illinois, 1932.

———— *Lectures and Discourses.* New York, 1882.

———— *The Life of the Most Reverend M. J. Spalding, Archbishop of Baltimore.* New York, 1873.

———— *Means and Ends of Education.* Chicago, 1895.

———— *Opportunity and Other Essays and Addresses.* Chicago, 1900.

———— *The Poet's Praise.* New York, 1887.

———— *Religion, Agnosticism, and Education.* Chicago, 1902.

—— *Religion and Art, and other essays*. Chicago, 1905.

—— *The Religious Mission of the Irish People and Catholic Colonization*. New York, 1880.

—— *Socialism and Labor, and other arguments, social, political, and patriotic*. Chicago, 1902.

—— *Songs Chiefly from the German*. Chicago, 1896.

—— *Things of the Mind*. 5th ed. Chicago, 1903.

—— *Thoughts and Theories of Life and Education*. Chicago, 1897.

Spalding, M. J. *Miscellanea . . . on Historical, Theological, and Miscellaneous Subjects*. 2nd ed. Louisville, Kentucky, 1855.

—— *Lectures on the Evidences of Catholicity*. Baltimore, 1870.

Stead, W. T. *The Americanization of the World*. New York, 1901.

—— *The Pope and the New Era, being Letters from the Vatican in 1889*. London, 1890.

Storer, Bellamy. *Letter of Bellamy Storer to the President and Members of his Cabinet*. Cincinnati, 1906.

Strong, Josiah. *Our Country: its possible future and its present crisis*. New York, 1885.

Sullivan, W. L. *Letters to His Holiness, Pius X, by a Modernist*. 2nd ed. Chicago, 1911.

—— *The Priest, a tale of modernism in New England*. 2nd ed. Boston, 1914.

—— *Under Orders, the autobiography of. . . .* New York, 1944.

Tardivel, J. P. *Mélanges: un recueil d'études religieuses, sociales, politiques, et littéraires*. 3 vols. Quebec, 1887–1903.

—— *La Situation religieuse aux Etats-Unis*. Lille and Paris, 1900.

Thébaud, A. J. *Forty Years in the United States of America*. Vol. 3 of *Three Quarters of a Century* (1807–1882). *A Retrospect*. New York, 1904.

de T'Serclaes, Charles. *Le Pape Léon XIII*. 2 vols. Paris, 1894.

Tyrrell, George. *Autobiography and Life of George Tyrrell*. Vol. I. New York, 1912.

de Varigny, C. V. *The Women of the United States*. Translated by Arabella Ward. New York, 1895.

Vigneron, Lucien. *De Montréal à Washington*. Paris, 1887.

Walburg, A. H. *The Question of Nationality in its relations to the Catholic Church in the United States*. St. Louis, 1889.

Walworth, C. A. *Reminiscences of Edgar P. Wadhams, First Bishop of Ogdensburg*. New York, 1893.

Weninger, F. X. *Protestantism and Infidelity. An Appeal to candid Americans*. 8th ed. New York, 1865.

Woods, Robert, ed. *Americans in Process*. Boston, 1903.

—— *The City Wilderness*. Boston, 1898.

Zahm, J. A. *Bible, Science, and Faith*. Baltimore, 1894.

—— *The Catholic Church and Modern Science*. Notre Dame, Indiana, 1886.

———— *Evolution and Dogma.* Chicago, 1896.
———— *Scientific Theory and Catholic Doctrine.* Chicago, 1896.
———— (H. J. Mozans, *pseud.*) *Woman in Science.* New York, 1913.
Zurcher, George. *The Apple of Discord; or Temporal Power in the Catholic Church.* Buffalo, 1905.
———— *Handcuffs for Alcoholism.* Buffalo Plains, New York, 1890.
———— *Monks and their Decline.* Buffalo, 1898.

COLLECTIONS

Acta et Decreta Sacrorum Conciliorum Recentiorum. Collectio Lacensis. Vol. 7. Freiburg, 1890.
Barrows, J. H., ed., *The World's Parliament of Religions.* 2 vols. Chicago, 1893.
Collectio Lacensis. See *Acta et Decreta.*
Concilii Plenarii Baltimorensis II . . . Acta et Decreta. Baltimore, 1868.
Neely's History of the Parliament of Religions and Religious Congresses at the World's Columbian Exposition. Chicago, 1894.
Nova Collectio. See *Sacrorum Conciliorum.*
Proceedings of the Catholic Congress. Baltimore, Maryland, November 11th and 12th, 1889. Detroit, 1889.
Sacrorum Conciliorum, Nova et Amplissima Collectio. Edited by Louis Petit and J. B. Martin. Vols. 49–53. Arnhem, Holland, 1923–1927.
The World's Columbian Catholic Congresses, with an epitome of Church Progress. 3 vols.-in-one. Chicago, 1893.

PERIODICALS

American Catholic Quarterly Review
American Ecclesiastical Review (briefly, *Ecclesiastical Review*)
Arena
Atlantic
Catholic Times (after December, 1895, *Catholic Standard and Times*) of Philadelphia
Catholic University Bulletin
Catholic World
Contemporary Review
Edinburgh Review
Forum
International Journal of Ethics
Literary Digest
Nineteenth Century
North American Review
Quarterly Review
Review of Reviews (United States)
Revue des deux mondes

SECONDARY SOURCES

(Many of the items in this section are also, in varying degree, primary sources for Chapter XI.)

UNPUBLISHED MATERIAL

Roohan, J. E. "American Catholics and the Social Question." Unpublished Ph.D. dissertation. Department of History, Yale University, 1952.

Stauffer, A. P. "Anti-Catholicism in American Politics, 1865–1900." Unpublished Ph.D. dissertation. Department of History, Harvard University, 1933.

BOOKS

Aaron, Daniel. *Men of Good Hope: A Story of American Progressives.* New York, 1951.

Abel, Theodore. *Protestant Home Missions to Catholic Immigrants.* New York, 1933.

Abell, A. I. *The Urban Impact on American Protestantism, 1865–1900.* Cambridge, 1943.

Ahern, P. H. *The Catholic University of America, 1887–1896. The Rectorship of John J. Keane.* Washington, 1948.

Bain, J. A. *The New Reformation: Recent Evangelical Movements in the Roman Catholic Church.* Edinburgh, 1906.

Barbier, E. *Histoire du catholicisme libéral et social.* 8 volumes. Bordeaux, 1924.

Barry, C. J. *The Catholic Church and German Americans.* Washington, 1953.

Baumgartner, A. W. *Catholic Journalism; a Study of its Development in the United States, 1789–1930.* New York, 1931.

Bean, Walton. *Boss Ruef's San Francisco.* Berkeley, 1952.

Beck, G. A., ed. *The English Catholics, 1850–1950.* London, 1950.

de la Bedoyère, Michael. *The Life of Baron von Huegel.* London, 1951.

Beiser, J. R. *The Vatican Council and the American Secular Newspapers, 1869–1870.* Washington, 1941.

Bell, Stephen. *Rebel, Priest and Prophet. A Biography of Edward McGlynn.* New York, 1937.

Billington, R. A. *The Protestant Crusade, 1800–1860. A Study of the Origins of American Nativism.* New York, 1938.

Bishop, J. B. *Charles Joseph Bonaparte, His Life and Services.* New York, 1922.

Bland, Joan. *Hibernian Crusade; The Story of the Catholic Total Abstinence Union of America.* Washington, 1951.

Blanshard, Paul. *American Freedom and Catholic Power.* Boston, 1949.

———— *Communism, Democracy, and Catholic Power.* Boston, 1951.

Blum, J. M. *Joe Tumulty and the Wilson Era.* Boston, 1951.

Boland, F. J. *See* Ryan, J. A.

Bonet-Maury, Gaston. *Le Congrès des religions à Chicago en 1893.* Paris, 1895.
Bowers, C. G. *Beveridge and the Progressive Era.* New York, 1932.
Bowers, S. J. *See* Lord, Eliot.
Brann, H. A. *History of the American College of the Roman Catholic Church of the United States, Rome, Italy.* New York, 1910.
Brophy, M. L. *The Social Thought of the German Roman Catholic Central Verein.* Washington, 1941.
Browⁿ, I. V. *Lyman Abbott, Christian Evolutionist.* Cambridge, 1953.
Browne, H. J. *The Catholic Church and the Knights of Labor.* Washington, 1949.
Burns, J. A. *Catholic Education, A Study of Conditions.* New York, 1917.
—— *The Growth and Development of the Catholic School System in the United States.* New York, 1912.
—— and Kohlbrenner, B. J. *A History of Catholic Education in the United States.* New York, 1937.
Burton, Katherine. *Celestial Homespun, The Life of Isaac Thomas Hecker.* London, 1943.
—— *In No Strange Land.* New York, 1942.
Butler, Cuthbert. *The Life and Times of Bishop Ullathorne, 1806–1889.* 2 vols. London, 1926.
—— *The Vatican Council: the story told from inside in Bishop Ullathorne's letters.* 2 vols. London, 1930.
Bury, J. B. *History of the Papacy in the Nineteenth Century (1864–1878).* Edited by R. H. Murray. London, 1930.
Byrnes, R. F. *Antisemitism in Modern France.* New Brunswick, New Jersey, 1950.
Cadden, J. P. *The Historiography of the American Catholic Church: 1785–1943.* Washington, 1944.
Callahan, Adalbert. *Medieval Francis in Modern America.* New York, 1936.
Cameron, M. W. *See* Conway, K. E.
Ciesluk, J. E. *National Parishes in the United States.* Washington, 1947.
Clark. C. G. *The Loyolas and the Cabots.* Boston, 1950.
Clinchy, E. R. *All in the Name of God.* New York, 1934.
Conway, K. E. and Cameron, M. W. *Charles Francis Donnelly, a Memoir.* New York, 1909.
Coughlin, C. E. *Father Coughlin's Radio Discourses, 1931–1932.* Royal Oak, Michigan, 1932.
Croce, Benedetto. *A History of Italy, 1871–1915.* Translated by C. M. Ady. Oxford, 1929.
Crowley, J. J. *Romanism, A Menace to the Nation.* 2nd ed. Cincinnati, 1912.
Curti, M. E. *The Growth of American Thought.* New York, 1943.
—— *The Social Ideas of American Educators.* New York, 1935.
Desmond, H. J. *The A. P. A. Movement.* Washington, 1912.
Destler, C. M. *American Radicalism, 1865–1901.* New London, Connecticut, 1946.

Duroselle, J. B. *Les Débuts du catholicisme social en France, 1822–1890.* Paris, 1951.

Earle, E. M., ed. *Modern France. Problems of the Third and Fourth Republics.* Princeton, 1951.

Egan, M. F. and Kennedy, J. B. *Knights of Columbus in Peace and War.* 2 vols. New Haven, 1920.

Ellis, J. T. *The Formative Years of the Catholic University of America.* Washington, 1946.

—— *The Life of James Cardinal Gibbons, Archbishop of Baltimore, 1834–1921.* 2 vols. Milwaukee, 1952.

Evans, J. W. and Ward, L. R., eds. *The Social and Political Philosophy of Jacques Maritain.* New York, 1955.

Faguet, Emile. *Mgr. Dupanloup.* Paris, 1914.

Farley, John. *The Life of John Cardinal McCloskey.* New York, 1918.

Ferrara, Orestes. *The Last Spanish War. Revelations in "Diplomacy."* Translated by W. E. Shea. New York, 1937.

Fitzsimons, M. A. *See* Gurian, Waldemar.

Foerster, R. F. *The Italian Emigration of our Times.* Cambridge, Mass., 1919.

Gabriel, R. H. *The Course of American Democratic Thought.* New York, 1940.

Garraghan, G. J. *The Jesuits of the Middle United States.* vol. 3. New York, 1938.

Garrison, W. E. *Catholicism and the American Mind.* Chicago, 1928.

Gasquet, F. A. *Lord Acton and His Circle.* New York, 1906.

George, Henry, Jr. *The Life of Henry George.* New York, 1900.

Gibbs, J. C. *History of the Catholic Total Abstinence Union of America.* Philadelphia, 1907.

Gibson, F. E. *The Attitudes of the New York Irish toward State and National Affairs, 1848–1892.* New York, 1951.

Gillard, J. T. *Colored Catholics in the United States.* Baltimore, 1941.

Gillis, J. M. *On Almost Everything.* New York, 1955.

—— *The Paulists.* New York, 1932.

—— *This Our Day.* New York, 1933.

Goldman, E. F. *Rendezvous with Destiny.* New York, 1952.

Gosnell, H. F. *Boss Platt and his New York Machine.* Chicago, 1924.

Graham, Aelred. *Catholicism and the World Today.* New York, 1952.

Guilday, Peter. *A History of the Councils of Baltimore.* New York, 1932.

Gurian, Waldemar, and Fitzsimons, M. A., eds. *The Catholic Church in World Affairs.* Notre Dame, Indiana, 1954.

Guyot, Yves. *Le Pape et l'Irlande.* Paris, 1888.

d'Hablonville, Claude. *Grandes figures de l'église contemporaine.* Paris, 1925.

Hall, P. F. *Immigration and its Effects upon the United States.* New York, 1906.

Handlin, Oscar. *Boston's Immigrants, 1790–1865.* Cambridge, Mass., 1941.
―――― *The Uprooted.* Boston, 1951.
Harrington, E. T. *See* Lord, R. H.
Heindel, R. A. *The American Impact on Great Britain, 1894–1914.* Philadelphia, 1940.
Henthorne, M. E. *The Career of the Right Reverend John Lancaster Spalding, Bishop of Peoria, as President of the Irish Catholic Colonization Association of the United States, 1879–1892.* Urbana, Illinois, 1932.
Herbermann, C. G. *The Sulpicians in the United States.* New York, 1916.
Hibben, Paxton. *Henry Ward Beecher: An American Portrait.* New York, 1927.
Hickey, E. J. *The Society for the Propagation of the Faith. Its Foundation, Organization and Success (1882–1922).* Washington, 1922.
Higham, John. *Strangers in the Land.* New Brunswick, New Jersey, 1955.
Hofstadter, Richard. *Social Darwinism in American Thought, 1860–1915.* Philadelphia, 1945.
Hogan, P. E. *Thomas J. Conaty, Second Rector of the Catholic University of America, 1896–1903.* Washington, 1949.
Holden, V. F. *The Early Years of Isaac Thomas Hecker, 1819–1844.* Washington, 1939.
Hoog, Georges. *Histoire du catholicisme social en France, 1891–1931.* Paris, 1946.
Hope, A. J. *Notre Dame. One Hundred Years.* Notre Dame, Indiana, 1943.
Hopkins, C. H. *History of the Y.M.C.A. in North America.* New York, 1951.
―――― *The Rise of the Social Gospel in American Protestantism, 1865–1915,* New Haven, 1940.
Houtin, Albert. *Histoire du modernisme catholique.* Paris, 1913.
de Hovre, Franz. *Catholicism in Education.* Translated by E. B. Jordan. New York, 1934.
Hughes, H. L. *The Catholic Revival in Italy, 1815–1915.* London, 1935.
Husslein, Joseph. *See* Ryan, J. A.
Johnson, P. L. *Centennial Essays for the Milwaukee Archdiocese, 1843–1943.* Milwaukee, 1943.
Josephson, Matthew. *The Politicos, 1865–1896.* New York, 1938.
―――― *The President Makers: the culture of politics and leadership in an age of enlightenment, 1896–1919.* New York, 1940.
―――― *The Robber Barons: the great American capitalists, 1861–1901.* New York, 1934.
Kane, J. J. *Catholic-Protestant Conflicts in America.* Chicago, 1955.
Keller, E. A. *Christianity and American Capitalism.* Chicago, 1954.
Keller, J. G. *Stop, Look, and Live.* Garden City, New York, 1954.
―――― *Three Minutes a Day.* Garden City, New York, 1949.
―――― *You Can Change the World!* New York, 1948.
Kennedy, J. B. *See* Egan, M. F.
Kerby, W. J. *Prophets of the Better Hope.* New York, 1922.

King, Bolton and Okey, Thomas. *Italy Today*. London, 1901.

Klinkhamer, M. C. *Edward Douglas White, Chief Justice of the United States*. Washington, 1943.

Kohlbrenner, B. J. *See* Burns, J. A.

Kolbeck, M. O. *American Opinion on the Kulturkampf*. Washington, 1942.

LaFarge, John. *The Manner is Ordinary*. New York, 1954.

Lagrange, François. *Life of Mgr. Dupanloup, Bishop of Orléans*. Translated by Lady Herbert. 2 vols. London, 1885.

Lamott, J. H. *History of the Archdiocese of Cincinnati, 1821–1921*. Cincinnati, 1921.

Laski, H. J. *Authority in the Modern State*. New Haven, 1919.

Latourette, K. S. *The Great Century A. D. 1800 A. D. 1914: Europe and the United States of America*. Vol. 4 of *A History of the Expansion of Christianity*. London, 1941.

Lecanuet, Edouard. *Montalembert*. 3 vols. Paris, 1899–1902.

—— *La Vie de l'église sous Léon XIII*. Paris, 1930.

Leflon, Jean. *La Crise révolutionnaire, 1789–1846*. Paris, 1949.

Leroy-Beaulieu, Anatole. *Les Catholiques libéraux*. Paris, 1885.

Leubuscher, F. C. *See* Post, L. F.

Lord, Eliot, Trenor, J. J., and Bowers, S. J. *The Italian in America*. New York, 1905.

Lord, R. H., Sexton, J. E., and Harrington, E. T., *History of the Archdiocese of Boston*. 3 vols. Boston, 1945.

Lubell, Samuel, *The Future of American Politics*. New York, 1952.

MacCaffrey, James. *History of the Catholic Church in the Nineteenth Century*. 2 vols. Dublin, 1910.

McCloskey, R. G. *American Conservatism in the Age of Enterprise*. Cambridge, 1951.

McColgan, D. T. *A Century of Charity: the first one hundred years of the Society of St. Vincent de Paul in the United States*, Vol. 1. Milwaukee, 1951.

Macdonald, Fergus. *The Catholic Church and the Secret Societies in the United States*. New York, 1946.

McEntee, G. P. *The Social Catholic Movement in Great Britain*. New York, 1927.

McGrath, Fergal. *Newman's University, Idea and Reality*. Dublin, 1951.

McGrath, J. F. *History of the Ancient Order of Hibernians*. Cleveland, 1898.

McKelvey, Blake. *Rochester the Flower City: 1855–1900*. Cambridge, Mass., 1949.

MacLellan, Malcolm. *The Catholic Church and Adult Education*. Washington, 1935.

McMurry, D. LeC. *Coxey's Army*. Boston, 1929.

McNally, Augustin. *The Catholic Centenary*. New York, 1908.

McQuade, V. A. *The American Catholic Attitude on Child Labor since 1891*. Washington, 1938.

Malone, S. L., ed. *Dr. Edward McGlynn.* New York, 1918.
—— *Memorial of the Golden Jubilee of the Reverend Sylvester Malone.* Brooklyn, 1895.
Mangano, Antonio. *Sons of Italy.* New York, 1919.
Manhattan, Avro. *The Catholic Church against the Twentieth Century.* 2nd British ed. London, 1952.
Manion, Clarence. *The Key to Peace.* Chicago, 1950.
Mann, Arthur. *Yankee Reformers in the Urban Age.* Cambridge, Mass., 1954.
Maritain, Jacques. *The Things That Are Not Caesar's.* Translated by J. F. Scanlan. New York, 1931.
Marriott, J. A. *The Makers of Modern Italy.* Oxford, 1931.
Marshall, C. C. *The Roman Catholic Church in the Modern State.* New York, 1928.
Mathew, David. *Catholicism in England, 1535–1935.* London, 1936.
Maury, Reuben. *The Wars of the Godly.* New York, 1928.
May, H. F. *Protestant Churches and Industrial America.* New York, 1949.
Maynard, Theodore. *Orestes Brownson, Yankee, Radical, Catholic.* New York, 1943.
—— *The Story of American Catholicism.* New York, 1941.
Mecklin, J. M. *The Ku Klux Klan.* New York, 1924.
Méjécaze, F. *Frédéric Ozanam et l'église catholique.* Lyon, 1934.
Millar, M. F. *See* Ryan, J. A.
Moehlman, C. H. *The Wall of Separation between Church and State.* Boston, 1951.
Moody, J. N., ed. *Church and Society.* New York, 1953.
Moynihan, J. H. *The Life of Archbishop John Ireland.* New York, 1953.
Murphy, J. C. *An Analysis of the Attitudes of American Catholics toward the Immigrant and the Negro, 1825–1925.* Washington, 1940.
Myers, Gustavus. *History of Bigotry in the United States.* New York, 1943.
—— *History of the Great American Fortunes.* Vol. 3. Chicago, 1910.
—— *The History of Tammany Hall.* New York, 1901.
National Catholic Welfare Conference. Washington, 1947.
Nichols, J. H. *Democracy and the Churches.* Philadelphia, 1951.
Niebuhr, H. R. *Christ and Culture.* New York, 1951.
Nielsen, Fredrik. *The History of the Papacy in the Nineteenth Century.* Translated by A. J. Mason. 2 vols. London, 1906.
Nitti, F. F. *Catholic Socialism.* Translated by Mary Mackintosh, London, 1895.
O'Grady, John. *Catholic Charities in the United States.* Washington, 1930.
Okey, Thomas. *See* King, Bolton.
O'Meara, Kathleen. *Frederick Ozanam.* 3rd American ed. New York, 1883.
O'Neill, J. M. *Catholicism and American Freedom.* New York, 1952.
O'Shea, J. J. *The Two Kenricks.* Philadelphia, 1904.

Pahorezki, M. S. *The Social and Political Activities of William J. Onahan.* Washington, 1942.

Palmer, R. R. *Catholics and Unbelievers in Eighteenth-Century France.* Princeton, 1939.

Parsons, Wilfrid. *The First Freedom: Considerations on Church and State in the United States.* New York, 1948.

Pearson, C. S. *The Politico-Social Ideas of Hugues Félicité Robert de Lamennais, 1830–1854.* New York, n. d.

Petre, M. D. *Life of George Tyrrell.* Vol. 2 of *Autobiography and Life of George Tyrrell.* 2 vols. London, 1912.

Pierce, B. L. *A History of Chicago.* 2 vols. New York, 1937–1940.

Piolet, J. B. *Les Missions catholiques françaises au dix-neuvième siecle.* 6 vols. Paris, 1900.

Post, L. F. and Leubuscher, F. C. *The George-Hewittt Campaign.* New York, n. d.

Pratt, J. W. *Expansionists of 1898.* New York, 1951.

Pringle, H. F. *The Life and Times of William Howard Taft.* 2 vols. New York, 1939.

———— *Theodore Roosevelt.* New York, 1931.

Purcell, E. S. *Life of Cardinal Manning.* 2 vols. London, 1895.

Pyle, J. G. *The Life of James J. Hill.* 2 vols. New York, 1917.

Rafton, H. R. *The Roman Catholic Church and Democracy.* Boston, 1951.

Ray, M. A. *American Opinion of Roman Catholicism in the Eighteenth Century.* New York, 1936.

Reilly, D. F. *The School Controversy (1891–1893).* Washington, 1943.

Riley, A. J. *See* Sexton, J. E.

Roemer, Theodore. *The Catholic Church in the United States.* St. Louis, 1950.

———— *The Ludwig-missionsverein and the Church in the United States (1838–1918).* Washington, 1933.

———— *Ten Decades of Alms.* St. Louis, 1942.

Rollet, Henri. *L'Action social des catholiques en France, 1871–1901.* Paris, 1947.

Rose, P. M. *The Italians in America.* New York, 1922.

Rothensteiner, John. *History of the Archdiocese of St. Louis.* 2 vols. St. Louis, 1928.

de Ruggiero, Guido. *The History of European Liberalism.* Translated by R. G. Collingwood. London, 1927.

Ryan, J. A. and Boland, F. J. *Catholic Principles of Politics.* New York, 1943.

———— and Husslein, Joseph. *The Church and Labor,* New York, 1920.

———— *Social Doctrine in Action, A Personal History.* New York, 1941.

———— and Millar, M. F. *The State and the Church.* New York, 1922.

Sartorio, E. C. *Social and Religious Life of Italians in America.* Boston, 1918.

Schepp, G. J. *Leakage from a Catholic Parish.* Washington, 1942.

Schieber, C. E. *The Transformation of American Sentiment toward Germany, 1870–1914.* Boston, 1923.
Schlesinger, A. M. *The Rise of the City, 1878–1898.* New York, 1933.
Schlesinger, A. M. Jr. *Orestes A. Brownson.* Boston, 1939.
Schroll, A. G. *The Social Thought of John Lancaster Spalding.* Washington, 1944.
Schuster, G. N. *The Catholic Spirit in America.* New York, 1928.
Seignobos, Charles. *A Political History of Europe since 1814.* Translated by S. M. Macvane. New York, 1899.
Seldes, George. *The Catholic Crisis.* New York, 1939.
Sexton, J. E. *See* Lord, R. H.
——— and Riley, A. J. *History of St. John's Seminary, Brighton.* Boston, 1945.
Sharp, Dores. *Walter Rauschenbusch.* New York, 1942.
Shaughnessy, Gerald. *Has the Immigrant Kept the Faith?* New York, 1925.
Smith, J. T. *The Catholic Church in New York.* 2 vols. New York, 1905.
Snead-Cox, J. G. *The Life of Cardinal Vaughan.* 2 vols. London, 1910.
Social Reconstruction. A General Review of the Problems and Survey of the Remedies. New York, 1919.
Soderini, Eduardo. *Leo XIII, Italy and France.* Translated by B. B. Carter. London, 1935.
——— *Léon XIII, l'Irlande et l'Angleterre.* Rome, 1883.
——— *The Pontificate of Leo XIII.* Translated by B. B. Carter. London, 1934.
Somerville, Henry. *Studies in the Catholic Social Movement.* London, 1933.
Spencer, Philip. *Politics of Belief in Nineteenth-Century France.* New York, n. d.
Stebbing, George. *The Position and Prospects of the Catholic Church in English-Speaking Lands.* Edinburgh, 1930.
Steiner, Edward. *On the Trail of the Immigrant.* New York, 1906.
Stephenson, G. W. *A History of American Immigration.* Boston, 1926.
Stephenson, N. W. *Nelson W. Aldrich.* New York, 1930.
Stokes, A. P. *Church and State in the United States.* 3 vols. New York, 1950.
Storer, M. L. *In Memoriam Bellamy Storer.* Privately printed, 1923.
Strachey, Lytton. *Eminent Victorians.* Garden City, New York, n. d.
Strayer, J. R. and Munro, D. C. *The Middle Ages: 395–1500.* New York, 1942.
Sugrue, Thomas. *A Catholic Speaks His Mind on America's Religious Conflict.* New York, 1951.
Suhard, Emmanuel. *Growth or Decline? The Church Today.* Translated by J. A. Corbett. South Bend, Indiana, 1948.
Teeling, William. *Pope Pius XI and World Affairs.* New York, 1937.
Thompson, David. *Democracy in France.* London, 1946.
Thureau-Dangin, Paul. *The English Catholic Revival in the Nineteenth Century.* Revised ed. Translated by Wilfred Wilberforce. 2 vols. New York, n. d.
Thurston, Herbert. *No Popery. Chapters on Anti-Papal Prejudice.* New York, 1930.

Torrielli, A. J. *Italian Opinion on America, as revealed by Italian Travellers, 1850–1900*. Cambridge, Mass., 1941.

Trenor, J. J. *See* Lord, Eliot.

Turmann, Max. *Le Développement du catholicisme social, depuis l'encyclique "Rerum Novarum."* 2nd ed. Paris, 1909.

Twiss, B. R. *Lawyers and the Constitution*. Princeton, 1942.

Vidler, A. R. *The Modernist Movement in the Roman Catholic Church, Its Origins and Outcome*. Cambridge, England, 1934.

Walsh, J. J. *Our American Cardinals*. New York, 1926.

Walworth, E. J. *Life Sketches of Father Walworth*. Albany, 1907.

Ward, Bernard. *The Sequel to Catholic Emancipation (1830–1850)*. 2 vols. London, 1915.

Ward, L. B. *Father Charles E. Coughlin*. Detroit, 1933.

Ward, L. R., ed. *The American Apostolate: American Catholics in the Twentieth Century*. Westminster, Maryland, 1952.

—— *Blueprint for a Catholic University*. St. Louis, 1949.

—— *See also* Evans, J. W.

Ward, Maisie. *The Wilfrid Wards and the Transition*. 2 vols. London, 1934.

Ward, Wilfrid. *The Life of John Henry Cardinal Newman*. 2 vols. London, 1912.

—— *The Life and Times of Cardinal Wiseman*. 2 vols. New York, n. d.

—— *William George Ward and the Catholic Revival*. London, 1893.

Weill, Georges. *Histoire de l'idée laïque en France au dix-neuvième siecle*. Paris, 1929.

Weinberg, A. K. *Manifest Destiny: a Study of Nationalist Experience in American History*. Baltimore, 1935.

White, J. A. *The Founding of Cliff Haven. The early years of the Catholic Summer School of America*. Edited by J. J. Meng. New York, 1950.

Whyte, Frederic. *The Life of W. T. Stead*. 2 vols. London, 1925.

Wiley, S. W. *History of Y.M.C.A. — Church Relations in the United States*. New York, 1949.

Will, A. S. *Life of Cardinal Gibbons*. 2 vols. New York, 1922.

Williams, D. D. *The Andover Liberals, a Study in American Theology*. New York, 1941.

Williams, Michael. *American Catholics in the War*. New York, 1921.

—— *The Shadow of the Pope*. New York, 1932.

Woodward, E. L. *Three Studies in European Conservatism*. London, 1929.

The World's Parliament of Religions and the Religious Parliament Extension. Chicago, 1896.

Zollman, Carl. *American Civil Church Law*. New York, 1917.

Zwierlein, F. J. *Letters of Archbishop Corrigan to Bishop McQuaid and Allied Documents*. Rochester, New York, 1946.

—— *The Life and Letters of Bishop McQuaid, prefaced with the History of Catholic Rochester before his Episcopate*. 3 vols. Rome and Louvain, 1925.

PERIODICALS (in addition to those listed on page 302)
America
American Scholar
American Sociological Review
Catholic Historical Review
Catholic Mind
Christian Century
Commentary
Commonweal
Harpers
Historical Records and Studies
Homiletic and Pastoral Review
Integrity
Look
McAuley Lectures
National Catholic Welfare Council Bulletin (later *National Catholic Welfare Conference Bulletin*)
New Republic
New York Review
New York Times
Proceedings of the Massachusetts Historical Society
Records of the American Catholic Historical Society
Religion in Life
Religious Education
Review of Politics
Theological Studies
Thought
Time

COLLECTIONS AND MISCELLANEOUS

Catholic Builders of the Nation. Edited by C. E. McGuire. 5 vols. Boston, 1923.
Catholic Encyclopedia. Edited by C. G. Herbermann *et al.* 15 vols. New York, 1907–1912.
The Catholic Mind Through Fifty Years. Edited by B. L. Masse. New York, 1952.
Dictionary of American Biography. Edited by Allen Johnson *et al.* 20 vols. New York, 1928–1936.
Dictionary of the American Hierarchy. Edited by J. B. Code. New York, 1940.
Encyclopedia of the Social Sciences. Edited by E. R. A. Seligman. 15 vols. New York, 1931–1935.
Papal Pronouncements on the Political Order. Edited by F. J. Powers. Westminster, Maryland, 1952.
Social Wellsprings, Fourteen Epochal Documents of Pope Leo XIII. Edited by Joseph Husslein. Milwaukee, 1940.

INDEX

INDEX